The 50 Worst
Terrorist Attacks

The 50 Worst
Terrorist Attacks

EDWARD F. MICKOLUS
AND SUSAN L. SIMMONS

Praeger Security International

PRAEGER

AN IMPRINT OF ABC-CLIO, LLC
Santa Barbara, California • Denver, Colorado • Oxford, England

Library of Congress Cataloging-in-Publication Data

Mickolus, Edward F.
    The 50 worst terrorist attacks / Edward F. Mickolus and Susan L. Simmons.
      pages cm
    Includes indexes.
    ISBN 978-1-4408-2827-0 (hardback) — ISBN 978-1-4408-2828-7 (ebook)
1. Terrorism—History.   I. Simmons, Susan L.   II. Title.   III. Title: Fifty worst terrorist attacks.
    HV6431.M487   2014
    363.32509—dc23   2014004392

ISBN: 978-1-4408-2827-0
EISBN: 978-1-4408-2828-7

18   17   16   15   14   1   2   3   4   5

This book is also available on the World Wide Web as an eBook.
Visit www.abc-clio.com for details.

Praeger
An Imprint of ABC-CLIO, LLC

ABC-CLIO, LLC
130 Cremona Drive, P.O. Box 1911
Santa Barbara, California 93116-1911

This book is printed on acid-free paper ∞

Manufactured in the United States of America

To our parents

Contents

Preface

Unfortunately, when considering international terrorism, any list of the *worst* is a "living document," requiring continuous adjustment as new incidents occur. When this book was in final editing in late September 2013, three significant attacks needed to be reflected upon and evaluated for the *50 Worst* list.

On Sunday, September 22, 2013, a bombing at a Protestant church in Peshawar, Pakistan, killed at least 85 people and wounded 141, numbers comparable to other attacks included in the list. The day before saw a wave of bombings in Iraq that led to 96 deaths and an al-Shabaab attack on the Westgate Mall in Nairobi, Kenya, that killed at least 62 people and injured 175 people, including many foreigners. Although the bombings entailed more deaths, the Kenya attack is a more important milestone in the maturation of international terrorism. Al-Shabaab demonstrated that although it was riven with factionalism, it was able to assemble a multinational strike team that could engage in a sophisticated operation outside its primary sanctuary, involving multiple attack points and a more nuanced style of attack. Not limiting itself to a straightforward multiple-death bombing, al-Shabaab used the Westgate attack to seize international headlines for several days, likely establishing its credentials as a group worthy of its new al Qaeda affiliation and attractive to wannabe jihadis as capable of daring exploits.

Sadly, the use of terrorism by an individual or group to attempt to achieve political ends continues to gain traction. Whether or not terrorism is an effective coercive tactic in the short term continues to be debated. As a long-term strategy, terrorism can only achieve a Pyrrhic victory so the stated motives of anyone choosing to perpetrate an act of terrorism must be questioned. Destroying lives is the ultimate price and takes resolute malevolence—not virtue or justice.

What we need are nations filled with Malala Yousafzais.

We welcome comments from our readers, particularly regarding refining the criteria for inclusion, which incidents we might have missed, and any other contributions you have. Please send them to us in care of ABC-CLIO.

This book is a different writing experience from our previous reference texts and required more patience from family and friends, and the great team at ABC-CLIO. We particularly wish to acknowledge and thank Steve Catalano and Robin Tutt of ABC-CLIO, and Linda Kay Berglund, Susan's sister, who assisted with the indexing.

Introduction

During the last 50 years, the world has seen the rise of a particularly virulent threat to international order—terrorist attacks. The theory and several methods of terrorism have long histories, arguably tracing to the Old Testament with the first political assassination; however, the use of terrorism by nonstate actors on so grand a scale is a comparatively recent phenomenon. The authors have written several volumes chronicling transnational terrorism, and we are often asked to rank events according to most important, worst, deadliest, or an alternative superlative. So far we have refused to do so, being hesitant of trivializing these horrific, shocking, and destructive acts. We changed our minds as we found that the reverse may be a more present danger. As a global community, we are so awash in terrorism—through news, academic articles, government reports, fiction and nonfiction books, films, and television shows—that we are at risk of accepting a general climate of terrorism in which we stop recognizing the individual acts and stop feeling for the reality of the victims. To end terrorism, we must not become inured to terrorist acts. This book attempts to direct attention again to individual acts by listing the most important terrorist attacks in history by year within each decade from 1960 to 2013, including the incidents, key actors involved, victims, and government responses. Both domestic and international terrorist attacks are examined within security and political contexts to shed light on how the events unfolded.

We begin this book's examination of terrorism with the 1960s, because of that decade's importance in the evolution of terrorism on several fronts. The 1960s saw the end of the Algerian insurgency, which featured terrorism on a seemingly unrelenting scale. The rise of the Palestinian struggle, with the commencement of different styles of attacks by Fatah, the leftist Popular Front for the Liberation of Palestine, and various splinter groups, moved international terrorism to the front pages. Turbulence in the West, spurred by a youthful radical leftist movement, led to the rise of major terrorist groups who went on to infamy for their exploits in the following decades. Types of attacks evolved with the growth of the new groups. Aerial hijacking in the 1960s moved from mere lone nut and simple "take me to (name a country)" transportational capers to more complex operations designed to garner media attention and general horror. Kidnappings of political figures and business executives for more than mere financial gain grew.

This book uses the definition of terrorism that we have found useful in our previous books. We consider terrorism to be the use or threat of use of violence by any individual or group for political purposes. The perpetrators may be functioning for or in opposition to established governmental authority. A key component of international terrorism is that its ramifications transcend national boundaries, and, in so doing, create an extended atmosphere of fear and anxiety. The effects of terrorism reach national and worldwide cultures as well as the lives of the people directly hurt by the terrorist acts. Violence becomes terrorism when the intention is to influence the attitudes and behavior of a target group beyond the immediate victims. Violence becomes terrorism when its location, the victims, or the mechanics of its resolution result in consequences and implications beyond the act or threat itself.

Unlike our previous books, we have also included several major domestic terrorist acts whose effects essentially stayed within the borders of one country, although with regional or global media coverage. Listing only international attacks might give a false sense of the extent of terrorism in a country or a period. Much the way incident counts can give a false sense of security or insecurity, so too would merely including international attacks give an inaccurate picture of the *worst*, however defined (Figure 1).

In like manner, looking at trends in outliers, such as the *worst*, can also skew our perceptions. Some have argued that post-9/11 is a new era in terrorism. That may be true for terrorist attacks that can be categorized as *worst* events, but overall trends in "garden variety" attacks have continued throughout the five most recent decades.

In addition to the definition of terrorism, we also need to consider what constitutes a *worst* act. Tallying deaths, injuries, and property damage, while methodologically straightforward, is ultimately unsatisfying. Perpetrators of terrorism are seeking publicity; killing for killing's sake (although increasing in popularity in recent years among the jihadi culture) doesn't quite fulfill our intuitive sense of *worst*. We thus have sought to include incidents that spilled ink and pixels as well as blood and treasure. As a sanity check, we have shared our *50 Worst* list with experts in the field of terrorism,

Figure 1
International Terrorism: 1968–2011

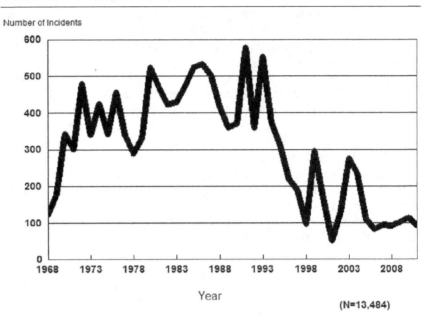

Number of Incidents

(N=13,484)

as well as various worthies in other fields to ensure that the terrorists' message did get through to others beyond the terrorism-watching set. Inherent to such a method, however, is a somewhat Western-centric bias. Many media outlets that we used in putting together the list are Western-based. One also tends to consider *worst* those incidents nearer to one's own interests; an attack that injures you or kills one of your family, colleagues, or friends is for you the worst event possible, although it may recede or vanish statistically when compared with multiple-casualty tragedies.

We have also included some incidents because they created a new technique; attacked a new type of target; crossed a moral, technological, or operational threshold; or otherwise added to the repertoire of terrorism in general. These novel attacks tended not to be as deadly as some incidents that did not make the cut, but are more historically important in the evolution of terrorism as a technique and security problem.

Our criteria for inclusion is limited to single events or events that are so tied together—multiple hijackings or bombings on the same day—as to have been treated as a single incident. Thus, the 1970 Dawson's Field hijackings and the 9/11 attacks, although involving four separate hijack teams, nonetheless had the effect of a single operation. Serial attacks by a single perpetrator or unknown individuals, such as letter bombers sending scores of parcel bombs—consider the Unabomber's 17-year campaign or the Amerithrax attacks of October 2001—while cumulatively important did not include a specific event that rises to the level of others included in the *50 Worst*. In the interests of comprehensiveness, however, we have included such events in a separate section. Similarly, we have included a separate discussion of incidents that were foiled before they could achieve the effects intended by the perpetrators.

Although the *50 Worst* are notable for their deadliness, terrorist attacks overall—at least the 13,000-plus international attacks covered by the ITER-ATE dataset—rarely include casualties in the dozens, much less hundreds. As shown in Figure 2, even the worst year of the half-century tallied just over 4,000 casualties. Given the potential threat inherent in chemical, biological, radiological, nuclear (CBRN), and cyber attacks, terrorists more often than not have kept their attacks under a certain deadly threshold.

Moreover, looking strictly at international attacks, Americans have tended to be disproportionately popular targets of terrorists, whether in garden-variety bombings and shootings or in the *50 Worst* spectaculars. Some of the domestic attacks that rose to the level of *50 Worst*, however, did not include Americans (Figure 3).

Figure 2
International Terrorism Casualties: 1968–2009

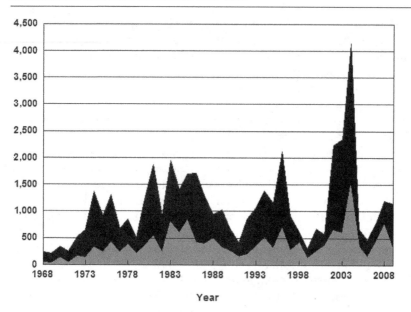

Figure 3
Frequency of International and American Related Terrorist Incidents: 1968–2009

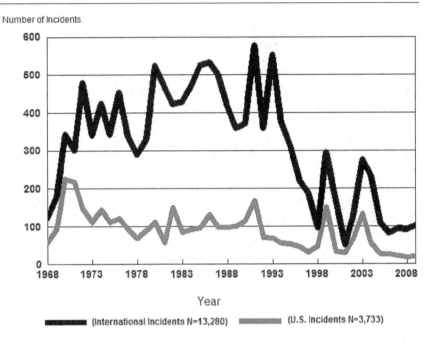

Number of Incidents

Year

(International Incidents N=13,280)   (U.S. Incidents N=3,733)

Expanding the years covered by our list to pre-1960 include proto-terrorist incidents, such as assassinations and anarchist bombing campaigns. Examples include the 1865 assassination of American president Abraham Lincoln by bitter-enders, the 1914 assassination of Austrian Archduke Franz Ferdinand that sparked World War I, and the 1946 bombing of the King David Hotel by Irgun, a Zionist paramilitary group active in the 1930s and 1940s.

We have seen several trends in the *50 Worst* that reflect shifts in terrorist behavior in general over the past half-century. Among them has been a shift in the type of terrorist tactic(s) employed. Terrorism has generally been a battle between offense and defense. Once security forces determine methods to harden a likely target against a certain type of attack, terrorists have generally not thrown in the towel. Rather, they have innovated, constantly putting the burden on the defensive forces to keep up.

There has also been a changing of the guard between terrorist groups and individuals making the list. Although terrorism as a tactic probably cannot be completely eradicated—the existence of evil is part of the human condition—specific terrorist groups have been eliminated, through aging of the principals, their deaths, imprisonment, or maturity beyond their radical youth; changing political fortunes; ending of patron state support; government/private security methods becoming more effective; or other reasons.

We can see this evolution of *worst* group identities most clearly in a ranking of groups whose depredations appear in the *50 Worst* list. Some groups—radical West European leftists, leftist Palestinians—enjoyed their heydays in the 1970s but then dropped off the list—as they did in more "normal" attacks. Most disturbingly, the religious-based Islamist radicals have shown greater staying power than their leftist forebears, most of whom have become extinct. For the moment, al Qaeda and its affiliates have established themselves as the single *worst* group of the half-century in terms of conducting the most spectacular terrorist incidents.

Exclusion of a group from this list does not mean that they were not active, nor a major threat, during this period. Groups such as the Abu Nidal/Black June Organization, the Basque Nation and Liberty, the Armenian Secret Army for the Liberation of Armenia, and scores of other groups conducted numerous attacks during this period. None of their attacks, however, rose to the level of a *50 Worst* event.

50 Worst by Terrorist Group

Al Qaeda and Offshoots

February 26, 1993, World Trade Center Bombing

August 7, 1998, Tanzania and Kenya U.S. Embassy Bombings

October 12, 2000, Yemen USS *Cole* Attack

September 11, 2001, U.S. World Trade Center, Pentagon, and Pennsylvania Hijackings

October 12, 2002, Indonesia Bali Bombings

May 12, 2003, Riyadh Western Complex Bombings

March 11, 2004, Madrid Train Bombings

July 7, 2005, U.K. Subway Bombings

July 11, 2010, Uganda World Cup Bombings

January 16, 2013, Algerian Gas Plant Takeover

September 21–24, 2013, Nairobi, Kenya, Westgate Shopping Mall Attack

Popular Front for the Liberation of Palestine (PFLP) and Offshoots

September 6, 1970, Dawson's Field Multiple Aerial Hijackings

December 21, 1975, Vienna OPEC Hostage-Taking

June 27, 1976, Entebbe

October 13, 1977, Landshut Hijacking and GSG 9 Rescue in Mogadishu

Hizballah

April 18, 1983, U.S. Embassy in Beirut Bombing
October 23, 1983, U.S. Marine and French Paratrooper Barracks in Lebanon Bombing
March 17, 1992, Buenos Aires Israeli Embassy Bombing
July 18, 1994, AIMA Buenos Aires Bombing

Chechens

June 14, 1995, Budennovsk, Russia, Hospital Hostage-Taking
October 23, 2002, Moscow Theater Takeover
August 24, 2004, Russian Planes Bombing
September 1, 2004, Russia Beslan School Takeover
March 29, 2010, Moscow Subway Bombings

Black September

September 5, 1972, Munich Olympics Attack

European Leftists: Baader-Meinhof, Red Brigades

October 13, 1977, Landshut Hijacking and GSG 9 Rescue in Mogadishu
March 16, 1978, Aldo Moro Kidnapping

Latin American Leftists

December 17, 1996, Japan Embassy in Peru Takeover

Irish Republican Army

August 27, 1979, Mountbatten Assassination
August 15, 1998, Omagh, Northern Ireland, Bombing

Japanese Red Army and United Red Army

March 31, 1970, Japan Airlines Flight 351 Hijacking to North Korea
May 30, 1972, Machine Gun Attack in Lod Airport

Indian Nationalists, Leftists, Separatists

June 23, 1985, Air India Flight Bombing

Other Palestinian Groups

May 15, 1974, Ma'alot Massacre
October 7, 1985, Achille Lauro Seajacking

April 5, 1986, Berlin La Belle Discotheque Bombing

September 5, 1986, Pan Am 73 Hijacking

December 21, 1988, Lockerbie Bombing

September 19, 1989, French Airline UTA 772 Bombing

Other Islamists

October 6, 1981, Egypt President Anwar Sadat Assassination

November 17, 1997, Luxor Attack

July 23, 2005, Sharm el-Sheikh Bombing

November 26, 2008, India Mumbai Attacks

For anyone obsessed with counting incidents, this list of incidents by terrorist group does not include eight of the *50 Worst* incidents. These eight do not easily fit into a group-specific category because of suspect attribution, a single attack by an organization that did not appear again, or tenuous ties of the individual perpetrating the attack to a formal terrorist organization. In addition, one incident—the October 13, 1977, Landshut Hijacking and GSG 9 Rescue in Mogadishu—appears twice on the list, because it was a joint operation. To provide context for the environments in which these attacks took place, discussions of each decade introduce that book section.

The 1960s

The decade's *worst* depredations, while chilling for their time, have all fallen off the overall list for the half-century. A *50 Worst* list for the decade of the 1960s could include armed attacks by Algerian insurgents, whose domestic attacks against the continuation of French colonial rule on occasion spilled over into the metropole. Algerian independence was seen by many insurgent theorists as evidence of the possibility of a successful terrorism campaign. Palestinian terrorism, particularly with the establishment of Fatah and the Palestine Liberation Organization under the leadership of Yasser Arafat, began to take root in Israel and the occupied territories, and later spread into the rest of the world by the early 1970s. The decade's *50 Worst* could also include examples from the rash of bombings by leftist groups in the United States—including a failed Weather Underground attempt to bomb the U.S. Capitol—and Western Europe, along with the attacks by various Latin American revolutionary groups encouraged by the success of Fidel Castro's insurgent takeover of the reins of power in Cuba.

Many of these groups resorted to aerial hijacking as an excellent method of publicizing their causes by attracting media attention to a telegenic crisis du jour. Copycats, including mentally disturbed individuals, passengers who wanted to upgrade to a first-class flight to Havana, and domestic U.S. black revolutionaries and their white sympathizers, also added to the rolls of the hijackers. The increase of aerial hijackings, which was then viewed by governments as one of the major sources of nonstate threats to the security of its citizens, led to tentative steps by governments to bolster the defensive side of the issue. Hijackings were not yet viewed as a terrorism problem since the majority of attacks were comparatively nonviolent take-me-to-Cuba and take-me-to-Miami capers. From 1968 through 1972, the U.S. Department of Transportation logged 364 hijackings around the world.

The U.S. administration became fed up after eight planes were hijacked to Cuba in January 1969. The Federal Aviation Administration created the Task Force on the Deterrence of Air Piracy, which developed a hijacker profile for use in screening passengers. Magnetometers (metal detectors) were also introduced at the end of the decade.

The international community chipped in with several antihijacking conventions. In 1963, International Civil Aviation Organization (ICAO) drafted the Convention on Offenses and Certain Other Acts Committed on Board Aircraft (more commonly referred to as the Tokyo Convention), which required states to promptly return hijacked aircraft and passengers. The convention was silent on the fate of the hijackers. The ICAO next met in The Hague, Netherlands, to create the Convention for the Suppression of Unlawful Seizure of Aircraft (Hague Convention), which called for states to extradite or try hijackers. The convention deemed hijacking a criminal rather than a political act. In December 1970, fifty nations signed on, including the United States. The ICAO also drafted a Convention for the Suppression of Unlawful Acts against the Safety of Civil Aviation, which dealt with acts on the ground against aircraft in service. The Montreal Convention was open for signature in 1971 and went into force in 1973.

Nonterrorist hijackings decreased following the coming into force of the three conventions. Terrorists, however, upped the ante, making their attacks increasingly more deadly and diverting planes to countries whose regimes viewed them as conducting legitimate political acts, vice terrorist attacks, and thus making the conventions irrelevant to the episode at hand.

The 1970s

Many of the *50 Worst* of the 1970s involved some form of hostage-taking, including classical kidnapping in which the perpetrators and their hostage(s) move from the original scene of the crime, barricade-and-hostage operations in which the terrorists and their hostage(s) stay put during the bargaining, and aerial, train, vehicular, and naval hijacking, a melding of the previous two types of hostage incidents.

As had been the case in the 1960s, the terrorist spectaculars tended to take place in affluent countries or in capitals with a large media presence that guaranteed coverage of the exploits of the terrorists. News outlets quickly acceded to their demands for publicity of their manifestoes. The terrorists of the 1970s wanted a lot of people watching. They succeeded. The majority (88%) of international terrorist attacks during this period involved no deaths; only 16 percent involved injuries.

The international community's response to these new types of attacks was mixed. Nations directly affected by hostage-taking soon created elite military units designed to conduct daring rescue operations.

The United Nations created a 1973 Convention on the Prevention and Punishment of Crimes against Internationally Protected Persons, including Diplomatic Agents (informally known as the Diplomat Convention). The United Nations went through several fits and starts at drafting a companion International Convention against the Taking of Hostages. Regional efforts included the 1971 Inter-American Convention to Prevent and Punish the Acts of Terrorism Taking the Form of Crimes against Persons and Related Extortion that Are of International Significance (the OAS Convention) and the 1977 European Convention on the Suppression of Terrorism. States sympathetic to various terrorist groups limited the effectiveness of these agreements by raising questions about the definitions of terrorism and hostage-taking, the rights of freedom fighters, extradition and the right of asylum, and sovereignty and territorial integrity.

Foot-dragging on international legal conventions and regional accords was the first stage of a continuum of state support to terrorists, became increasingly worrisome in the 1970s. Allegations of Soviet Union and communist satellite support to Western European and Palestinian revolutionary terrorists were matched by charges against radical Middle Eastern regimes supporting any and all Palestinian terrorist groups. Many terrorist groups, including those who engaged in the sensational incidents that made the *50 Worst* for the decade, benefited from and often owed their existence to the provision of funds, documentation, training, safe haven, arms, explosives, planning, insurance policies for terrorists' families, and other forms of assistance by governments and wealthy nonstate backers. Various sanctions against these patrons led to little change; what change there was usually entailed the support becoming more clandestine and tougher to monitor.

Most of the *50 Worst* from this decade were attributable to the nexus between the West European leftists and the radical Palestinians. Many of the groups cross-trained, shared arms, and even joined each other in collaborative hit teams. The decade also saw a hint of what was to come from Islamist-based terrorist groups with attacks on the U.S. embassies in Tehran and Mecca.

March 31, 1970
Japan Airlines Flight 351 Hijacking to North Korea

Overview: The Japanese United Red Army (URA) and its splinter groups in the late 1960s and 1970s were among the most feared terrorist groups in the world. Led by Fusako Shigenobu (who became one of the few prominent female terrorists of her generation, along with Petra Kraus, Ulrike Meinhof, and Leila Khaled), the group initially spread terror in its homeland before offering its services to revolutionaries throughout the world. Members of the newly formed Japanese Red Army (JRA) went on to develop a partnership with George Habash's Popular Front for the Liberation of Palestine (PFLP), conducting joint and contract attacks for the PFLP. Its membership eventually was picked off by authorities in a worldwide manhunt.

The group came to international attention with the daring hijacking to North Korea of a Japan Airlines (JAL) plane. Its profile increased with machine-gun attacks in airports, bombings, counterfeiting, trafficking in women, and other criminal activities. While playing high-stakes hostage negotiation gambits, the group's attack squads generally had an exit strategy and did not seek martyrdom for Marx.

Incident: On March 31, 1970, a JAL B-727 left Tokyo for Fukuoka, but was hijacked shortly after a 7:30 A.M. takeoff by nine members, ages 16 to 27, of the Japanese URA (Sekigun-ha, Red Army Faction), who wielded samurai swords, daggers, pistols, and pipe bombs and demanded to be flown to Pyongyang, North Korea. The plane carried 3 crew, 4 stewardesses, and 122 passengers, mostly Japanese, including tourists, businessmen, students, a Roman Catholic Maryknoll priest, doctors on their way to a three-day medical conference in Fukuoka, and two Americans, including Herbert Brill. The terrorists tied up the male passengers, while others passed out candy to the children on board. They tied copilot Teiichi Ezaki to his seat. The pilot, Captain Shinji Ishida, claimed that the plane could not reach North Korea without refueling and landed at Itazuke air base outside Fukuoka at 8:59 A.M. Negotiations continued for five hours; the group allowed 12 children, 10 women, and an ailing elderly man to leave the plane in exchange for refueling. Two escort jets accompanied the plane as it left the air base.

The South Koreans attempted to give the impression to the hijackers that the plane had entered North Korean airspace. They fired antiaircraft shells at the plane, scrambled fighter planes, and escorted it to an airfield that identified itself as Pyongyang but was really Kimpo Airport in Seoul. The airport was disguised to look like what Pyongyang might possibly look like, with soldiers and policeman dressed in communist uniforms. Girls sung greetings, and a bullhorn called for them to enter North Korea. The terrorists saw through the ruse when they spotted an American car parked nearby, as well as a U.S. Northwest Airlines plane and a U.S. Air Force DC-3 parked on the runways. The officials could not produce a photograph of Kim Il Sung and were tripped up on several points of communist dogma. The group threatened to blow up the plane if any more attempts to end the hijacking were made.

The plane was moved to a corner of the airfield. The hijackers flicked the passenger cabin lights continually during the night in an attempt to demoralize the occupants. They also denied attempts to send food aboard, accepting only a few sandwiches. When mechanics wheeled a battery cart near one of the engines, the group interpreted this as meaning that the authorities would try to dismantle one of the engines. The hijackers again threatened to set off the pipe bombs that two of them were carrying. Japanese officials had identified two of the group as wanted on explosives charges—Takamaro Tamiya, 27, the group's leader, and Tsuneo Umeuchi, a medical student—which gave credibility to the threat.

The following day the temperature in the cabin rose to 107 degrees, and the hijackers allowed food, water, cigarettes, and blankets on board. They had also let slip their 8:00 A.M. deadline for clearance to fly out of Seoul. They were often extremely agitated and gave the impression that they were serious about harming the passengers despite their general politeness. Japanese Ambassador Masahide Kanayama urged caution on the part of the South Koreans.

Japanese vice minister of transportation Shinjiro Yamamura flew to Seoul to negotiate with the hijackers, along with the ambassador, who had established radio contact with the hijackers, the captain, and two of the passengers. Yamamura offered to become a substitute hostage. When they learned of Yamamura's plan, the South Koreans objected. The hijackers agreed to allow the plane to be moved to a takeoff position, to allow passenger baggage to be removed, to release 50 passengers, to allow Yamamura to board, and to then release the other 50, at which time the plane would fly to North Korea.

During the flight to North Korea, Pyongyang made ominous warnings about the possible incarceration and torture of the hostages. The plane never reached Pyongyang airport but landed in North Korean territory. The hijackers bounded from the plane and struck karate poses, acting as heroes. The North Koreans confiscated their weapons and separated them from the hostages, who were questioned in a local hotel. The communists announced that the hijackers would be given political asylum. On Saturday, they informed Yamamura and the crew that they were illegal immigrants. Yamamura had heard reports from former hijack victims that they had been beaten while held in North Korea and also recalled that the crew of the USS *Pueblo* was still being held. However, his group was allowed to leave. The jet returned to Tokyo on April 5. On April 6, North Korean broadcasts called the hijackers "strangers who came uninvited."

Sources differ as to the identity of the hijackers. During the attack, the 16-year-old identified himself as "Boya," who had played hooky from Kobe High School that day. The Federal Aviation Administration (FAA) identified the group as O. Takeshi, W. Mariaki, A. Shiro, S. Yasumiro, K. Takahiro, A. Kimihiro, Takamaro Tamiya, 27, Yoshizo Tanaka, 25, and Kintaro Yoshida, 24. Various sources claim that Kozo Okamoto, a brother of a hijacker, was involved in the Lod Airport massacre on May 30, 1972.

Two years later, eight of the hijackers met in North Korea with visiting Japanese journalists and informed them that they felt that the hijacking had been a mistake.

Three lawyers representing Yasuhiro Shibata, a URA member indicted for the hijacking, left for Pyongyang on January 8, 1989, to obtain evidence. Shibata's trial was to begin on January 23, 1989. The lawyers planned to contact the six other URA members who had remained in North Korea to determine Shibata's motives for secretly returning to Japan. Shibata, 35, was arrested in Tokyo in May 1988. Tamiya, 45, had sent a note to a Japanese magazine in May saying that all of the hijackers wanted to return to Japan but wanted to reach an agreement with the Japanese government that they be tried without detention when they came home. One of the hijackers had already died in North Korea.

On January 9, 1990, Yukio Yamanaka, head of a support group known for its aid to imprisoned student demonstrators, said that he had met with four of the seven hijackers living in Pyongyang during his visit which began on January 2. Tamiya said that the group had no interest in returning home to be arrested but added that he wanted to negotiate with the Japanese government.

On June 23, 1990, the hijackers wrote a two-page letter to *Mainichi Shimbun* in which the group urged the Japanese government to start negotiations regarding their possible return to Japan. However, they said that they would not surrender only to be arrested in Japan.

On June 13, 1992, five women rejected a Foreign Ministry order to give up their passports. The five were among six Japanese women who went to North Korea to marry the hijackers. The ministry ordered the five women in August 1988 to hand over their passports because they offended the country's interests by having contacts with North Korean agents. The ministry did not seek the return of the sixth woman's passport. The Association in Support of Humanitarian Return of Hijackers of Yodo Airliner called on the government to permit them to return to Japan without being subjected to criminal charges. North Korea continued to reject Japanese requests for extradition.

On January 29, 1994, the news media reported that Takahiro Konishi, 49, ran a letter in a URA sympathizers' newsletter stating that he wanted his eldest daughter, 16, who is stateless, "to study together with her Japanese friends in the land of her ancestors." He became the sixth URA hijacker to express interest in returning to Japan. This was the first time a letter with a hijacker's name reached Japan from North Korea. He thanked the sympathizers for their letters and gifts, and said he "was able to understand the warmness of Japanese relatives" at a meeting three and a half years earlier in Pyongyang. The seven families of the hijackers include 17 children. Konishi said he wanted to send his oldest daughter and her 14-year-old sister to Japan that summer.

On March 24, 1996, Cambodian police arrested a person believed to be Yoshimi Tanaka, 47, wanted for the hijacking. He was arrested on the Cambodian border for possession of several million dollars (face value) of counterfeit U.S. currency. Authorities handed him over to Thai police in Pattaya. Japanese police went there to fingerprint him and confirm his identity. The arrested man attempted to cross the border from Vietnam in a North Korean Embassy Mercedes. He was carrying a North Korean diplomatic passport. Three other North Korean diplomats attempted to bribe a policeman with $50,000 to let them pass through the checkpoint. Warrants had been issued on January 2, 1996, for Tanaka and four Thai men after they used five counterfeit U.S. $100 bills to buy film from a photo shop in Nong Preu village in North Phattaya. Thai police had earlier arrested the four Thais and seized sophisticated counterfeiting equipment from a home in Ang Thong Province. They claimed that Tanaka had hired them to produce the counterfeit notes, which resembled the newly designed $100 bill.

The Japanese terrorist was believed to have worked with Somchai Nanthasan and Prasong Pholthiphet to forge the $100 bills. Police also believed that Tanaka was helped to launder the bills by Kodama International Trading, run by Tang Cheang Tong, alias Shogo Kodama, a Japanese citizen of Khmer–Chinese origin.

Bangkok's *Asia Times* reported that in 1994, the Philippine military arrested Eduardo Quitoriano, 41, the Communist Party of the Philippines international liaison officer to the JRA. He allegedly was involved in a $1.6 million counterfeiting case that was wrapped up in Switzerland in 1990.

On March 26, 1996, Tanaka was extradited to Thailand to face forgery charges. The United States, South Korea, and Japan sought extradition from Thailand. Tanaka was indicted on April 11, 1996. He denied involvement in the case before a court on April 12. He was scheduled to be tried in June 1996.

The hijackers were reported in 2002 by the *Washington Post* to have been involved in efforts to lure Japanese, particularly women, to North Korea. Key to these efforts was Tamiya, leader of the hijackers, who died in 1995. He hoped to use the women to create another generation of revolutionaries in the Japanese Revolution Village in North Korea. In testimony in Tokyo District Court on March 12, 2002, Megumi Yao, 46, former wife of a JRA member, said that she helped lure Keiko Arimoto, 23, a Japanese woman, from Copenhagen to Pyongyang in 1983 as part of the scheme. The *Post* quoted her as saying, "The assignment was to scout for and detain Japanese, and train them into core members of a revolution." Yao was testifying in the trial of another JRA ex-wife charged with passport law violations.

As of this writing, the other hijackers are believed to still be in North Korea.

September 6, 1970
Dawson's Field Multiple Aerial Hijackings

Overview: The Popular Front for the Liberation of Palestine (PFLP) preceded by three decades al Qaeda's 9/11 quadruple aerial hijacking operation. The group dominated world headlines in September 1970 by diverting several European-origin planes to Dawson's Field in Jordan. The Jordanian regime's ultimate reaction to the Palestinian radicals' challenge, eventually dubbed Black September, in turn led to the formation of a rival Black September Organization (BSO).

Incidents

West Germany. On September 6, 1970, at 12:20 P.M., two PFLP members took over Trans World Airlines (TWA) flight 741, a B-707 flying from Frankfurt to New York with 145 passengers and 10 crew. The plane was diverted to Dawson's Field, Zerka, Jordan, a former U.K. Royal Air Force (RAF) landing strip in the desert. This was the first of a well-coordinated series of hijackings carried out by the PFLP. The group demanded the release of three PFLP members held in West Germany for the attack on the airline bus in Munich on February 10, 1970; three held in Switzerland for the Zurich attack on the El Al plane that had resulted in the killing of the copilot on February 18, 1969; and an unspecified number of fedayeen held in Israeli prisons. They later demanded release of Leila Khaled, held in a British jail after an unsuccessful hijacking attempt in the Netherlands. The group threatened to blow up the planes with the passengers inside by 3:00 A.M. on Thursday, September 10, 1970.

A Beirut spokesman for the PFLP explained in a statement to the news media that U.S. planes were seized "to give the Americans a lesson after they supported Israel all these years" and to retaliate for U.S. peace initiatives in the Middle East.

Upon landing, the guerrillas allowed 127 passengers from the planes at Dawson Field, mostly women and children, to go free in Amman. The remaining hostages were men from West Germany, the United Kingdom, Israel, and the United States. The planes were surrounded by commandos, who in turn were surrounded by troops from Jordan's army, including 50 tanks and armored cars. The Swiss and Germans were willing to deal unilaterally with terrorists to free their own nationals, but British Prime Minister Edward Heath called upon all five governments to take a common position. International Committee of the Red Cross (ICRC) representative M. Rochat, who had acted as intermediary in the Athens Seven case on July 22, 1970, told the PFLP in Amman of their stand, which was to release the seven prisoners upon the release of all passengers. The Germans sent Hans-Jürgen Wischnewski, a German Social Democrat party member, to Amman to negotiate on September 7, 1970. On September 11, two more Americans were released from the TWA jet. Another 18 hostages were secretly taken to Zerka and hidden in homes, because the attack squad began to distrust their PFLP leaders in Amman and wanted extra insurance against a double cross.

The Israelis preferred to be observers in the Berne Five, and thus the Red Cross was named by only four of the members as their intermediaries. A three-member liaison group of Red Cross officials went to Amman to confer with PFLP members. The hijacking of the BOAC VC-10 led to an extension of the deadline in hopes that the United States would have more time to pressure Israel to capitulate. On September 12, 1970, the PFLP gave a five-minute warning that women and children would be released in Amman. The planes held at Dawson's Field were evacuated and destroyed by PFLP explosives experts. On September 13, the last West German hostages were freed. Fifty-eight hostages remained, including the 18 secretly held in Zerka.

The activities of the PFLP on Jordanian territory proved too much for King Hussein to tolerate, and Jordanian troops engaged the fedayeen in a series of bloody battles in what became known as Black September, in which approximately 7,000 died. Negotiations became of secondary importance to the embattled PFLP, and hostages were rescued sequentially by Jordanian army troops. On September 29, 1970, the Swiss government announced that seven Arab guerillas would be released by Switzerland, West Germany, and the United Kingdom when the Americans had safely left Jordan. They called upon Israel to release 10 Lebanese soldiers and 2 Algerians taken from an airliner on August 14, 1970, as a humanitarian gesture. The seven were released the next day.

Switzerland. At 1:14 p.m., a Swissair DC-8 carrying 143 passengers and 12 crew was seized over France 30 minutes out of Zurich on its New York–bound flight by two men and a woman belonging to the PFLP. The plane landed in Zerka, almost on the tail of the TWA plane. The PFLP demanded the release of Leila Khaled for the British passengers (this was a bluff because no British passengers were held at the time), three terrorists in West Germany for the German passengers, three terrorists in Switzerland for the Swiss passengers, and an unspecified number of guerrillas in Israeli jails for the Israeli and American passengers. (On August 15, 1970, it was reported that there were 34 Arabs in Israeli jails.) The guerrillas set a 72-hour deadline. The next day, the guerrillas released 127 women and children in return for the Jordanian army's retreating 2 miles from the planes. On September 12, 1970, PFLP operations chief Dr. Wadi Haddad ordered the destruction of the planes in Zerka. A $30 million plane was reduced to rubble in the blast.

During negotiations, the commandos became suspicious of the intentions of their leaders and moved some of the hostages to Amman. They also turned away Red Cross supplies and Palestine Liberation Organization (PLO) buses that had been sent to collect the hostages. However, they did let another 23 hostages into Amman, most of them Indians. Of those hostages remaining, all but 38, including 5 Israeli girls, were allowed to go to the hotel. The 38 were split up and sent to various locations in Amman. These included nationals of Israel, Switzerland, West Germany, the United States, and the United Kingdom.

Netherlands (Pan Am flight 93). At 10:00 a.m., Pan Am flight 93, which was late in getting out of Amsterdam, was hijacked by two Arabs who probably met the FAA profile. They forced the plane to refuel in Beirut before picking up another PFLP member, who flew with the group to Cairo where the plane was destroyed. The trio included Sa'id Ali Ali, Samir Abdel Majid Ibrahim, and Mazin abu Mehanid Khalil, Palestinians whose forebears came from Chad. On board were 152 passengers and 23 crew, including 4 members of a deadheading crew. Two passengers, supposedly students registered in the names of Diop and Gueye, and carrying Senegalese passports, had been denied entry on an El Al plane (which had claimed to have oversold its first-class section). They had booked a flight to New York's John F. Kennedy Airport, from which they would fly to Chile. They were to have been part of a PFLP group that was to hijack the El Al flight, but instead seized the 747. Each carried a revolver and hand grenade and had the plane circle Beirut for two hours because the Lebanese government did not wish to be involved in the incident.

PFLP member Walid Kaddoura talked to the hijackers from the control tower and gave them instructions. A message from Jordan instructed the hijackers to fly to Cairo where the plane was to be destroyed. PFLP Capt. Ali allowed five men to refuel the plane. He was then instructed to separate the Jews from the other passengers, collect their passports, and keep them as hostages after leaving the plane.

Nine PFLP members, including a woman, then boarded the plane armed with .45 caliber pistols and 80 pounds of dynamite. The group's bomb expert stayed on board the plane with a pregnant woman and her husband; the others left. The demolitions expert, in his early twenties, set the fuses before the plane landed. The stewardess activated the emergency chutes and the passengers ran for cover before the $24 million plane was destroyed. In the rush, seven passengers were injured and later hospitalized. The rest went safely to an airport hotel. Egyptian authorities detained the trio of hijackers and began looking for a fourth hijacker they believed had escaped.

The Netherlands (El Al flight 291). The last attempted hijacking of the day was against El Al flight 291, en route from Tel Aviv to New York, 30 minutes out of its stopover in Amsterdam. It was the only airliner of the four that included armed guards among its 145 passengers and 13 crew. However, the sky marshal of the first-class cabin of the B-707 had been mistakenly locked in the pilot's cabin with pilot Uri Bar-Lev when the attack began. The original plan had called for a four-member PFLP team to hijack the plane. However, two members of the group had been denied boarding and instead hijacked a 747 to Cairo (they did not have navigational plans for Zerka). The duo had orders to meet Leila Khaled of the PFLP and Patrick Joseph Arguello, a member of the Sandinista National Liberation Front (Frente Sandinista de Liberación Nacional, FSLN), in the airport lounge after checking in. However, they made no attempt to warn their compatriots of their failure and boarded the 747, leaving Khaled and Arguello to fend for themselves.

The hijacking began 25 minutes after takeoff. Arguello, armed with a grenade and pistol, held his gun to the head of a stewardess and demanded that the crew open a security door leading to the cockpit. A steward seized his gun arm, but was shot in the chest. Arguello's automatic jammed when he tried to shoot him again. Arguello pulled the pin from his grenade and rolled it down the aisle. An Israeli security man stood up with a drawn revolver in the path of the grenade but was not harmed because the fuse was improperly set. Khaled claims that two or three Israeli security men plus three passengers jumped Arguello, beat him, tied him up, and shot him in the back four times. The Israelis claim that the tall security man shot him once. Khaled tried to use two grenades she had hidden in her bra, but was overpowered by two male passengers. An elderly

American disarmed her. One crew member, Sholomo Vider, was injured by five shots. Israel radioed the pilot and pleaded that he return to Tel Aviv with the injured Khaled. However, he proceeded to London to allow prompt medical attention for Vider. Bar-Lev was criticized by his government for this decision. Arguello died under an oxygen mask in an ambulance, but Vider was saved.

Khaled had previously captured headlines with a hijacking on August 28, 1969. When the plane landed in Heathrow Airport, the El Al security guards refused to let her go, and a tug-of-war ensued, with the Israelis pulling at her legs while the British police grabbed her shoulders. She was held in the Ealing police station. Three days later, the Israelis formally informed the British government that they intended to request extradition of Khaled. The same day, a BOAC jet was hijacked and Khaled's name was added to the list of those the PFLP wanted released. She was flown on board a British RAF Comet on September 29, 1970, when it was announced that the British hostages had been flown to the RAF base in Akrotiri, Cyprus. The Comet made stops in Zurich and Munich to pick up other freed terrorists. On October 1, 1970, the seven Palestinians arrived in Cairo in time for Egyptian President Nasser's funeral, but were not allowed to attend, being kept in a government guesthouse. Eleven days later, they flew to Damascus and Beirut.

On April 23, 1996, she set foot on Palestinian soil for the first time in her adult life to attend a meeting of the Palestinian National Council. She refused to recognize Israel's right to exist.

May 30, 1972
Machine Gun Attack in Lod Airport

Overview: After the United Red Army (URA) hijacking on 1970, the Japanese URA splintered into several factions. Some blended into the radical scene in Japan, while a more dangerous Japanese Red Army (JRA) faction reached out to like-minded revolutionaries and anarchists in the Middle East and Europe. Turning its attention to their colleagues' favorite targets—Israel, the United States, and other Western nations—the JRA offered its services in conducting proxy attacks. They garnered international media headlines by attacking Christian pilgrims on a visit to Israel.

Incident: On May 30, 1972, three members of the JRA, on contract from the Popular Front for the Liberation of Palestine (PFLP), fired machine guns and threw hand grenades at passengers arriving at Israel's Lod Airport from an Air France flight, killing 28 and wounding 76. Two of the attackers died in the massacre. The plane, Air France flight 132, had arrived from Paris and Rome when the trio picked up their weapons at the luggage area, opened their suitcases, and pulled out their Czechoslovakian-made

VZ-58 automatic rifles, whose butts had been removed, and six shrapnel grenades. The 116 passengers had just deplaned, and about 300 people were crowding into the waiting lounge. The terrorists fired 133 shots from their 7.63 caliber M43 weapons. Among those killed were 16 Puerto Rican Catholic pilgrims on a visit to the Holy Land. Twenty-seven others of the 68-member tour group were injured. Others killed included Israeli professor Aharon Katchalsky, one of the world's foremost biophysicists. One of the terrorists, identified as Yasuyuki Yasuda, was killed accidentally by bullets from the rifle of Takeshi Okudeira (or Okidoro), 23, who was blown up by a grenade. The surviving member of the squad, Kozo Okamoto, 22 or 24, ran onto the tarmac outside the terminal in an attempt to blow up an SAS plane parked outside. He was tackled with two grenades in his hands by El Al traffic officer Hannon Claude Zeiton.

In reconstructing the movements of the group, police discovered that they had carried tiny paper dolls as good luck charms. The group had also used symbolism in their selection of passports. Okamoto claimed to be Daisuke Namba, who had been executed for the attempted assassination of Crown Prince Hirohito in 1923. His birth date was given as December 7, Pearl Harbor Day. Jiro Sugisaki, whose real name was Takeshi Okidoro, gave his birthday as February 26, 1937, when Japanese army officers had mutinied. The other dead man, who claimed to be Ken Torio, 23, was Yasuiki Yasuda, who claimed to be born on March 30, the date of the URA's 1970 hijacking of a Japanese airliner. Included among those hijackers was Okamoto's brother.

PFLP spokesman Bassam Towfik Sherif (aka Bassam Zayad) claimed credit for the attack, saying that the group were members of the Squad of the Martyr Patrick Arguello, a Sandinista National Liberation Front (Frente Sandinista de Liberación Nacional, FSLN) member who with Leila Khaled staged a foiled hijacking of an El Al plane on September 7, 1970, in the Netherlands. Bassam gave their PFLP names as Bassem, Salah, and Ahmed and said that the attack was in reprisal for the deaths of two Black September terrorists in the Sabena hijacking of May 6, 1972. After his gang had killed eight Israelis, Okamoto told Israeli officers that the group was named the Army of the Red Star.

Okamoto was initially unwilling to talk to the authorities, asking for death. His interrogator, Gen. Zeevi (who had questioned captured terrorists Tannous and Hallasah in the Sabena hijacking), threw his pistol on the table in front of him and told Okamoto that he could turn it on himself if he signed the confession. Okamoto then began talking (it appears that Zeevi never intended to fulfill his part of the bargain). Okamoto studied agriculture at Kagoshima University in Japan. In early 1970, an Iraqi revolutionary, Bassim (who later married Leila Khaled), visited Tokyo and contacted the JRA. There the two organizations made a movie, *PFLP—Red Army Declare World War*. In November 1971, Okamoto was asked to show the film at Kagoshima and was invited to go to Beirut, where his brother was undergoing PFLP training. He said he was directed to depart Tokyo and go to Montreal, New York, and Paris. He was to fly first class on an El Al 717, observing security protocols. Upon arriving in Beirut, he was taxied to Baalbek, Lebanon, and stayed in a safe house with the other two JRA members. He recalled training in Port Said in explosives, shooting pistols and Kalashnikovs, and using hand grenades. On May 17, 1972, they trained for the specific attack.

On May 22, 1972, they left Beirut for Paris and arrived in Rome on May 30, 1972. They booked a night in the Anglo American Hotel and then moved to the Scaligera Pension on the Via Nazionale, where Arabs often stayed. On May 30, 1972, they arrived at Leonardo da Vinci Airport for a flight to Tel Aviv. They passed through a body search, but their baggage was not searched. It appears that their trainer was Abu Hija, who had participated in the Zurich attack on February 18, 1969, under the name of Youssef. Maruoka Osamu was the fourth JRA member to be trained with the group and was wanted as an accomplice in the incident.

Okamoto was charged with the military offense of political terrorism, which carried a death penalty under the 1945 British Emergency Regulations, initially applied to Irgun members. Max Kritzman, a Chicago-born attorney, was appointed to be Okamoto's lawyer. Okamoto at first refused any counsel but accepted when told that the trial could not proceed without one. He sabotaged all attempts by Kritzman to provide a defense and tried to convince the court to sentence him to death. Court records quote Okamoto as saying:

This was out of duty, to the people I slaughtered and to my two comrades, who lost their lives. It is my response with the other soldiers, to the people I killed. I take on myself full responsibility for it. . . . The revolutionary struggle is a political struggle between the classes. It is a just struggle. We strive to build a world where wars will be banished. But it will be a long struggle and we are preparing World War III through our own war, through slaughtering and destruction. We cannot limit warfare to the destruction of buildings. We believe slaughtering of human bodies is inevitable. We know it will become more severe than battles between nations. . . . This incident had been reported worldwide, but it seems to me nobody has grasped the motivation for it. But when a similar operation takes place the next time, what will the world think? When I was captured, certain Japanese asked me, "Was there no other way?" Can that man propose an alternative method? I believe that, as a means toward world revolution, I must prepare the creation of the world Red Army . . . a means of propelling ourselves onto the world stage. . . . The Arab world lacks spiritual fervor, so we felt that through this attempt we could stir up the Arab world. The present world order has given Israel power which has been denied the Arab refugees. This is the link between the Japanese Red Army and the Popular Front for the Liberation of Palestine, with whom we collaborate. . . . I want you to know that the next target may be New York or San Francisco. I would like to warn the entire world that we will slay anyone who stands on the side of the bourgeoisie. This I do not say as a joke. We three soldiers, after we die, want to be three stars of Orion. When we were young, we were told that if we died we may become stars in the sky. I may not have fully believed it, but I was ready to. I believe some of those we slaughtered have become stars in the sky. The revolution will go on, and there will be many more stars. But if we recognize that we go to the same heaven, we can have peace.

Lt. Col. Abraham Frisch, the presiding judge, sentenced Okamoto to life imprisonment.

In interviews since his incarceration, it was learned that Okamoto and his colleagues tore their passports in a lavatory of Lod Airport so that they could not escape, a further expression of their determination to go through with the act. They had also planned to explode their last grenades in their faces to make the job of identifying them much harder. At the last moment, Okamoto apparently decided to attack the SAS plane as well but missed with his last grenades and was captured.

His release was demanded by terrorists in a number of subsequent incidents, including the September 5, 1972, Olympics massacre; a July 20, 1973, JAL hijacking; and the Entebbe affair of July 27, 1976.

Okamoto suffered a mental breakdown in prison. He was part of a swap in May 1985 with Ahmad Jibril's Popular Front for the Liberation of Palestine–General Command (PFLP-GC) in which more than 1,000 Palestinians plus Okamoto were freed in exchange for three Israeli soldiers captured in Lebanon in 1982.

On February 15, 1997, Lebanon arrested six members of the JRA in the Bekaa Valley and West Beirut. (Later reports said eight people, five of them JRA members, were arrested.) They were identified as Kazuo Tohira, 44; Hisashi Matsuda, 48; Mariko Yamamoto, 56, alias Maria; Masao Adachi, 57, alias The Editor, because of his work in pornographic films; Haruo Wako; and Okamoto, 49. Also arrested was acupuncturist Omaya Abboud, 35. Japan said it would send a team to identify the captives and seek their extradition if appropriate. In March 1997, Lebanese state prosecutor Adnan Addoum announced that Lebanon would not extradite the suspects as Japan had requested but would instead try them for forgery and entering the country illegally. The two countries lack an extradition treaty. Japan had recently been involved in the apprehensions of JRA members in Nepal, Peru, and Romania.

National Public Radio reported that other JRA detainees were wanted for bank robbery, hijacking, and a shoot-out.

Okamoto, Yamamoto, and Tohira had frequented a quiet acupuncture clinic in Taanayel. Adachi was often seen being chauffeured in a silver Mercedes. He claimed to be a Malaysian engineer with Solidere, the company rebuilding Beirut's central business district. Yamamoto lived in a two-bedroom apartment in West Beirut's New Street.

On April 3, 1997, a Beirut investigative judge indicted Tohira, Wako, Yamamoto, Adachi, and Okamoto for passport forgery, illegal entry into

Lebanon, and official stamps forgery, which carried 10-year prison sentences. A three-judge panel needed to approve the indictment before the suspects could appear in court. The trial opened on June 9, 1997; 136 lawyers offered to take their cases pro bono. Acupuncturist Umayya Abboud went on trial simultaneously on charges of illegally practicing medicine. On July 31, 1997, a Lebanese court sentenced five JRA terrorists to three years in jail. The sentences came a day after the United States ended a decade-long ban on Americans visiting Lebanon after Beirut pledged to do more to combat terrorism. On March 1, 2000, Lebanon refused Japan's request for Okamoto's extradition. He was granted asylum on health grounds.

September 5, 1972
Munich Olympics Attack

Overview: Before 9/11, arguably the most well-known terrorist attack was the Black September Organization's (BSO's) storming of the Olympic Village in 1972 and taking the Israeli team hostage. The group's name came from the Jordanian government's crackdown on Palestinian extremists in September 1970, following the Dawson's Field multiple hijackings. By attacking an event covered by thousands of journalists and watched worldwide by hundreds of millions of people, the Black September operation dominated world headlines. In the United States, the term "Palestinian" soon became synonymous with "terrorist," all evidence to the contrary. The Black September attack further cemented the effectiveness of barricade-and-hostage operations in the eyes of fellow terrorist groups and presented governments with a wrenching policy decision as to whether to bargain with terrorist hostage-takers. In what later became the stuff of movies and novels, Mossad conducted a years-long assassination campaign against terrorists involved in the attack.

Incident: On September 5, 1972, eight members of the BSO broke into the Israeli quarter at the Olympic Games in Munich, West Germany, killing two Israeli athletes and taking nine others hostage. They demanded the release of 236 guerillas in Israeli jails, including Japanese Red Army (JRA) terrorist Kozo Okamoto, the release of Andreas Baader and Ulrike Meinhof in West Germany, and safe passage to a foreign country. After a shoot-out with police, the hostages were killed, as were five of the terrorists and a West German policeman. The three surviving terrorists, two of whom were wounded, were released after the hijacking of a Lufthansa jet on October 29, 1972.

The group cut through the village's fence and made its way to the dormitory housing the Hong Kong, Uruguayan, and Israeli teams. At 5:30 A.M., the group burst into the Israelis' quarters. Six of the team reached safety. The nine Israelis who were trapped fought their attackers with knives but were soon overcome. Their hands were tied behind their backs, and they were forced to hobble to a central location. Soon after, the terrorists threw a note out of a window with their demands—the release of 236 prisoners within 4 hours and safe passage out of Germany. They threatened to kill two of their hostages every half hour after the 9:00 A.M. deadline. The Germans offered an amount of money to be specified by the terrorists, and German interior minister Hans Dietrich Genscher offered himself and his colleagues as substitute hostages. These suggestions were turned down. The initial negotiations were established between a police officer, Amalise Graes, and the terrorists' leader, Mohammed Masalhah, alias Esa, who trained a machine gun on Graes and kept a hand grenade ready. He told her that his father was Jewish, his mother Jordanian, and his brothers were in Israeli jails.

The police were unsuccessful in plans to trick the terrorists. Manfred Schreiber, the Munich police chief, and Ahmed Touni, the head of the Egyptian Olympics team, repeated their monetary offers to the terrorists, who replied, "Money means nothing to us; our lives mean nothing to us." The terrorists again extended their deadline but threatened to shoot two hostages in front of the building. At 12:30 P.M., a third deadline was postponed when Genscher and Bruno Merck, the interior minister of Bavaria, told the terrorists that they were still talking to the Israeli government. The deadline was then extended to 2:30 P.M., and Tunisian ambassador Mahmoud Mestiri later got an extension to 5:00 P.M. At 4:30 P.M., while the police squad assembled to storm the building, the terrorists demanded to be flown to Cairo, Egypt, with their hostages. They also called for a swap of hostages for the prisoners in Israel when the plane touched down.

The West Germans traced calls made by the terrorists to Beirut and Tunisia. The Beirut number belonged to a Palestinian refugee organization. Mestiri said that the Tunis number belonged to an unnamed "honorable personage." The calls were unanswered. After these calls, at around 3:30 P.M., Mestiri got the deadline extended.

Chancellor Willy Brandt had phoned the Israeli government, who urged that the demands of the terrorists not be granted, although the Israelis were willing to give the group safe passage if their athletes were released. Brandt also attempted to reach Egyptian president Anwar Sadat, but could only get Prime Minister Aziz Sidki, to whom he suggested that the terrorists be allowed to fly to Cairo. Sidki claimed that this was not Egypt's affair and that he could do nothing about it. Egypt later claimed that Brandt misunderstood Sidki, who meant Egypt was powerless to influence the terrorists, as were the West Germans. One last deadline delay was achieved between 6:30 P.M. and 9:00 P.M. During this time, the Libyan ambassador in Munich offered to mediate, but was turned down. He had suggested that he attempt to reduce the demands from the release of 236 to 13 imprisoned guerrillas. At 9:00 P.M., the terrorists agreed to leave the building with their hostages. At 10:10 p.m., using underground corridors, the terrorists boarded a bus with their hostages and were taken to their helicopters, which flew them to Fürstenfeldbruck Military Airport, instead of Riem, Munich's main civil airport. A Lufthansa B-707 was waiting when the helicopters landed at 10:35 p.m. Although Esa had agreed not to hold the four pilots hostage, the Black Septembrists now kept their guns trained on them. Two of the terrorists traversed the 165 yards from their helicopter to the plane. Police had initially been on board the plane disguised as the plane's crew, but this plan was vetoed at the last minute. The two terrorists walked back to the helicopter suspecting a trick by the authorities and were fired upon by five police snipers. Two terrorists standing beside the helicopters and one of the men walking across the tarmac were immediately killed. However, Esa dove for cover. The other terrorists fired on the hostages and control tower, killing a policeman and damaging the tower's radio. At 10:50 p.m., the police called upon the terrorists in English, German, and Arabic to surrender but were fired on. The terrorists were armed with automatic machine guns; the Germans had only single-shot rifles. At 12:04 a.m., a terrorist jumped from a helicopter and threw a grenade into its cabin. Another terrorist emerged from where he had been hiding. Both were immediately shot by the police snipers, but the grenade had already gone off, killing the nine hostages. Armored cars moved in and captured the surviving trio near the undamaged helicopter. One of the volunteer helicopter pilots was badly wounded in the lung. One of the Israelis died of smoke inhalation.

Four days later, the dead terrorists were flown to Libya, where they were mourned at Tripoli's main mosque. Official radio called them martyrs and heroes.

It was rumored that Libya's Col. Mu'ammar Qadhafi paid Black September $5 million for the operation.

In February 1973, Jordanian police arrested and questioned Palestinian Abu Daoud, who told his Jordanian interrogators that in August 1972 he had traveled to Sofia, Bulgaria, to buy arms for Al Fatah, carrying a forged Iraqi passport for Saad ad-Din Wali. Abu Iyad and Fakhri al Umari arrived from Geneva and informed him of the Olympics plan. Daoud was ordered to give Umari his passport because it contained a valid German visa. Daoud claims that he did so after returning from Libya and that he took no other part in the attack. Many observers disagree with this claim and believe that Daoud was a major organizer of the attack.

Daoud's testimony should be compared to the account given by reporter David Tinnin of the activities of Ali Hassan Salameh. According to Tinnin, Salameh assigned Umari, chief of Black September assassins, to the case. Umari collected the weapons, possibly from an Arab diplomatic facility in West Germany, hid them in airline flight bags, and checked them in the luggage room of Munich's train station. When he tried to case the Olympics Village, he was sent away by guards. Mohammed Masalhah, a Libyan architect, was then given the assignment and was later chosen to lead the terrorists. Two other Black September members were told to get Olympic Village jobs. The Syrian embassy vouched for them on their employment questionnaires. The other five terrorists underwent training in a refugee camp near Deraa, Syria, and then left on a circuitous route to Munich. The terrorists were ultimately to take the hostages to Tunis, which accounted for the phone calls. But according to Tinnin, the Tunisian contact apparently panicked and backed out.

On October 29, 1972, Black September hijacked Lufthansa flight 615 flying from Damascus to Frankfurt and successfully obtained the release of the three remaining terrorists—Abdullah Samir, Abdel Kadir el Dnawy, and Ibrahim Badran—picked them up at Zagreb, Yugoslavia, airport and flew on to Libya, where they disappeared.

The Israelis retaliated for the attack by raiding refugee camps in Lebanon on February 21, 1973, killing 31. They later shot down a Libyan airliner that had overflown Israeli air space, killing all 107 aboard. Israeli officials blamed Egypt, Syria, and Lebanon for being behind the Olympics attack. The Israelis established assassination squads (Mivtzan Elohim, The Wrath of God), which killed more than a dozen Black September members in the coming year. Salameh died on January 22, 1979, when a car bomb exploded near his entourage in Beirut.

On August 1, 1981, Daoud was hit by five bullets fired in the evening in the Opera coffeehouse of Warsaw's Victoria International Hotel. On May 3, 1999, he was turned away at Paris's Orly Airport when he tried to enter France to promote his new autobiography. He was now a member of the Palestine National Council and a Ramallah attorney. He acknowledged in the book his role in the Munich attack. On June 13, 1999, Israel banned him from entering the West Bank. The German government had issued a warrant for his arrest the previous week. He reportedly died of kidney failure at age 73 on July 3, 2010 in Damascus, Syria.

In early November 1995, relatives of 11 Israeli athletes and officials killed in the attack filed a $26 million lawsuit against the city of Munich, the state of Bavaria, and the Federal Republic of Germany. In rejecting the claim, a Munich court ruled that the statute of limitations had expired in 1977. The families' attorney said that he planned to appeal, because it was impossible to make a case earlier as police files regarding the incident were classified until 1992. Relatives of the Israelis were paid $1 million in a check issued in 1974 by the Red Cross. Families of the Israeli Olympics athletes murdered by Black September terrorists accepted a $2.98 million compensation package on September 6, 2002.

May 15, 1974
Ma'alot Massacre

Overview: Attacks by various Palestinian terrorist groups against Israeli civilians became commonplace after the formation of Fatah and various

Palestinian Marxist groups. They were later succeeded in the 1990s and 2000s by Hizballah and Hamas, which specialized in suicide bombings. Groups such as the PFLP and its splinters, including the PFLP-Special Operations and PFLP-GC, and the Popular Democratic Front for the Liberation of Palestine (PDFLP), while engaging in high-risk operations, usually took hostages with the intention of trading them for imprisoned colleagues and political concessions. They generally were rebuffed, but their operational aim was to kill a few, take hostage a few, and get out alive to fight again. The Ma'alot operation ratcheted up the terror quotient beyond the simple bombings and shootings, putting children at risk by attacking a school—an operation that was mimicked three decades later by Chechen terrorists in Russia. Publicity around the world regarding the attack focused global attention on the Palestinian issue, giving the terrorists exactly what they sought.

Incident: On May 15, 1974, three members of the PDFLP crossed the Lebanese border into Israel, where they attacked a van bringing Arab women home from work, killing two and injuring one. They then entered the town of Ma'alot, bursting into the apartment of Yosef Cohen, killing three of the family members. A deaf-mute child escaped because he had hidden and did not make a sound. The neighbors sounded an alarm, but there were no troops or effective police forces available to respond in the small border town. An officer in a neighboring city attributed the cry for help as hysteria and ignored it. The terrorists moved on to a nearby school, where they shot a janitor and then herded more than 90 school children from their dormitories, kicking and clubbing them. Three adults and 17 children escaped through windows.

Later that morning, the commandos sent out a female hostage with the demand for the release of 23 Arab prisoners by 6:00 P.M. They demanded that the prisoners go to Damascus, Syria, or Cyprus with French ambassador to Israel Francis Hure and Red Cross representatives, or they would blow up the school. Israeli officials said they agreed to the demands. Defense Minister Moshe Dayan and Army Chief of Staff Lt. Gen. Mordechai Gur arrived to direct rescue operations. The terrorists demanded that Hure and Romanian ambassador Ion Covaci act as mediators. They were to give the terrorists a code word indicating that the prisoners had arrived, at which time half the hostages would be released. The terrorists planned to fly to an Arab capital, preferably Damascus, with Covaci and the rest of the hostages. After the terrorists refused to extend their deadline, the Israelis stormed the building.

Apparently the prisoners, including surviving Lod Airport JRA attacker Kozo Okamoto, had been taken out of their cells in anticipation of the hostage trade when the negotiations broke down. The Israelis decided to attack within half an hour of the deadline. One terrorist was shot as he ran to detonate an explosive, and the two others fired on the children before they died, machine guns in hand. Sixteen of the children were killed immediately, and 5 of the 70 injured children died later. One of the Israeli commandos also was killed in the raid. Premier Golda Meir promised revenge for the attack, and on May 16, 1974, Israeli jets attacked guerrilla camps at Ein el Halweh and Nabatieh in southern Lebanon. Some reports said that 21 were killed and 134 wounded. Later PDFLP leader Naif Hawatmeh claimed that the raid was designed to prevent peace negotiations, which would return the West Bank of the Jordan to the Kingdom of Jordan.

December 21, 1975
Vienna OPEC Hostage-Taking

Overview: Before the rise to prominence of Osama bin Laden, the most famous international terrorist was a Popular Front for the Liberation of Palestine (PFLP) member, Illich Ramirez Sanchez, a Venezuelan known popularly as Carlos the Jackal (named after the assassin in Fredric Forsythe's *The Day of the Jackal*). Carlos developed contacts among the world's major leftist and Palestinian terrorist groups, offering his services to all comers. He was responsible for a laundry list of high-profile attacks throughout Europe, including bombings and assassinations. His signature attack came against the ministers of the Organization of Petroleum Exporting Countries (OPEC), when he led a diverse band of European and Palestinian terrorists in a barricade-and-hostage siege. A worldwide manhunt for Carlos ended in 1994, when he was detained in the Sudan. As of 2013, he was serving his sentence in a French jail.

Incident: On December 21, 1975, six members of the Arm of the Arab Revolution (AAR), believed to be a cover term for the PFLP, attacked a ministerial meeting of the OPEC in Vienna, Austria, seizing 70 hostages, including 11 oil ministers. In the attack and subsequent shoot-out with police, three people were killed and eight injured, including one of the terrorists. The group was led by the famed Venezuelan terrorist, Illich Ramirez Sanchez, alias Carlos the Jackal. According to various popular accounts, although the PLFP-Habash wing denied any connection to the attack, planning was initially engaged in by Carlos and Wadi Haddad of the PFLP. Participants included Hans-Joachim Klein, a Movement 2 June member (a friend of Hanna Elise Krabbe, a Socialist Patients' Collective member who had been involved in the takeover of the West German facility in Sweden), and a woman identified as Gabriele Krocher-Tiedemann, who had been released in the February 27, 1975, kidnapping of Peter Lorenz. Other sources claimed that the woman was Klein's last-known girlfriend, Mechthild Rogali. The group was armed with Beretta model 12 machine pistols, Chinese grenades, plastic explosives, fuse wires, batteries, and detonators and also carried vitamin C tablets and amphetamines to aid them in a siege operation. The identity of three other members of the attack force is less clear, with most accounts making them out to be Palestinians.

In the initial attack, the group members ran up the stairs toward the meeting hall where the OPEC conference was in session. The only security constituted two guards looking forward to retirement, Inspectors Josef Janda and Anton Tichler. Tichler, an Austrian, was killed in the gunfire, and Janda was taken hostage by the group. He managed to get to a phone and relayed a message to his headquarters that OPEC was under attack. The second individual killed was Ali Hassan Khafali, a security officer with the Iraqi delegation, who attempted to surprise Carlos and seize his carbine. He was killed by the woman. The third killed was Yousef Ismirli, a Libyan economist who wrestled with Carlos for control of his weapon and was shot dead by the terrorist. One of the rounds passed through Ismirli and wounded a member of the Kuwaiti delegation in the right arm. By this time, the Austrian security police had sent in reinforcements, and in a gun duel with Inspector Kurt Leopolder, Klein was shot in the stomach. He was taken out of the building on a stretcher, but later returned after demands made by the other terrorists. One of the RGD-5 grenades exploded during the attack, killing no one.

The terrorists rounded up their hostages and barricaded themselves in the conference room, where they discovered that they held 11 ministers: Delaid Abdesselam of Algeria, Jaime Duenas-Villavicencio of Ecuador, Edouard Alexis M'Bouy-Boutzit of Gabon, Lt. Gen. Dr. Ibnu Sutowo of Indonesia, Dr. Jamshid Amouzegar of Iran, Tayeh Abdul-Karim of Iraq, Abdul Mutalib Al-Kazemi of Kuwait, Ezzedin Ali Mabruk of Libya, Dr. M. T. Akobo of Nigeria, Ahmed Zaki Yamani of Saudi Arabia, and Dr. Valentin Hernandez-Acosta of Venezuela. Some reports claim that the original plans were for the assassinations of Yamani and Amouzegar, two of the most important participants in the OPEC meeting, representing countries in disagreement with the Rejection Front of the Palestinian Movement. During the beginning of the 36-hour siege, the hostages were separated into four groups. The Libyans, Algerians, Iraqis, Kuwaitis, and Palestinian OPEC employees were considered friends. Neutrals included citizens of Gabon, Nigeria, Indonesia, Venezuela, and Ecuador. Austrians were placed separately; the rest were considered enemies. The terrorists selected Griselda Carey, the British secretary of Chief M. O. Feyide, the Nigerian OPEC secretary general, to carry their demands to the Austrians. The group's demands included the return of Klein, the publication of a political manifesto over Austrian radio and television, a bus to take them to the airport where a DC-9 with three crew was to be waiting, a rope, scissors, and adhesive tape. The manifesto, translated from the French and published by the news media, read:

Reaffirmation of the 3 fundamentals of the 1976 Khartoum Arab summit: no treaty with, no negotiations with, and no recognition of the state of Zionist aggression. Denunciation of all compromise and all political plans aimed at destroying this anti-capitulation plan and aimed at giving tacit or explicit legality to aggression from any part of the Arab Palestinian land. In the light of this, condemnation of the treacherous agreements over the Sinai and the reopening of the Suez Canal to Zionist trading, with a claim that they be dropped, to allow the heroic Egyptian Arab Army to pursue its victories of the October war by leading a war of total liberation with the armies of the north-east front. Condemnation of attempts to lead Arab states and the Palestine resistance to the negotiating table, and condemnation of treaties and recognition in Geneva, or any other place, of other capitulation formulas. Formation of the north-east front with Syria, Iraq, and the Palestine resistance on the basis of refusal to compromise, and reinforcement of the war of total liberation. The reawakening of the process of Arab unification, whose realization is a fundamental condition for national salvation, by moves towards unification among Arab states who partner each other geographically and politically. The declaration of the principle of full sovereignty over "our" petroleum and financial wealth through nationalization of petroleum monopolies and the adoption of a national petroleum and financial policy which will enable the Arab people to use its resources for its development, its progress, the safeguard of its national interests and the strengthening of its sovereignty alongside the friendly people of the Third World so they can emerge from their economic stagnation, on condition that priority be given to financing the confrontation countries and the Palestinian resistance. Declaration of clear position over the dramatic conflict taking place in Lebanon by condemning and opposing the denominational reactionary-American plot, and the effective equipment and moral support for the Lebanese national Arab forces and the Palestinian resistance who are defending Lebanon and its national Arab adherence.

The Kreisky government agreed to broadcast the manifesto.

During the negotiations, Iraqi chargé d'affaires Riyadh Al-Azzawi served as mediator. Carlos's first choice, the Libyan ambassador, was in Budapest, Hungary, at the time of the attack. The Iraqi obtained the release of several hostages, including an Austrian secretary who had become hysterical, the injured Kuwaiti, and an English interpreter employed by the Algerian oil minister. Later, seven female hostages were allowed to leave to do their Christmas shopping.

A possible rescue attempt failed when the car of two armed Israelis crashed outside the building.

Despite surrounding the building with troops, the Austrian government soon gave in to the terrorists' demands for a flight out of the country. They also granted the demand that a doctor travel with Klein and recruited Dr. Wiriya Rawenduzy, a Kurd who had obtained Austrian citizenship. Forty-two of the hostages, none of them Austrians, were herded onto the DC-9 piloted by Capt. Manfred Pollack and Otto Herold. The plane flew first to Algiers Dar El Beida Airport, where Klein was taken to a hospital in a Red Crescent ambulance. (Later reports claimed that he was transferred to a Libyan hospital, and had been paid £100,000 by Libya's Col. Mu'ammar Qadhafi for his participation in the operation.)

The neutrals were also allowed off the plane. Bruno Kreisky stated that Carlos had agreed to allow all hostages off in Algeria, but the terrorists instructed the pilot to fly on to Tripoli, Libya, and Baghdad, Iraq. The plane flew to Tripoli, where the terrorists instructed air traffic control to have Libyan prime minister Maj. Abdul Salam Ahmed Jalloud ready to meet them. Carlos requested a larger plane but was not given one. Hostages from Saudi Arabia, Iran, United Arab Emirates, Qatar, Algeria, and Libya were released.

Some details of the terrorists' demands are unconfirmed. Some reported that they demanded a large ransom from Saudi Arabia and Iran for the release of their oil ministers. On December 22, 1975, at midnight, the King phoned the Shah from Amman about the situation. An hour later, a Zurich banker was phoned by the Iranian embassy in Geneva and told to transfer an undisclosed sum of money to an Aden bank. A PFLP man in London months later said the sum was $5 million. In Beirut, Fatah sympathizers said it was 10 times that and that Haddad, Habash, and Carlos received much of it (he recouped perhaps $2 million). Three months later, Chancellor Kreisky was reported to have confirmed the ransom tale.

After landing rights were refused in Tunis, the plane flew back to Algiers. Apparently after receiving a code word from Algerian foreign minister Abdel Aziz Bouteflika that Haddad had received the money, the terrorists surrendered and released the hostages. Reporters claimed that the terrorists did not appear to have been arrested, and an Austrian government extradition request was refused on the grounds that no treaty existed between the two countries.

Gabriele Krocher-Tiedemann was captured after a shoot-out with Swiss police on December 20, 1977. A warrant was handed down by the Vienna criminal court on December 23, 1975, for shooting an Austrian policeman at point-blank range during the OPEC attack. She was suspected of involvement in the Entebbe hijacking of June 27, 1976. In October 1983, Carlos threatened to kill Bonn interior minister Friedrich Zimmermann if authorities prosecuted her for her role in the 1975 OPEC attack; she was serving 15 years in Switzerland for seriously wounding two customs officers. On December 18, 1987, Swiss authorities extradited her to West Germany where she was to serve a six-year sentence and answer charges regarding the OPEC attack. In Switzerland she had been sentenced to 15 years in prison.

On September 8, 1998, French police raided the only bar in Saint-Honorine-lal-Guillaume, a Normandy village, and arrested Klein, 50. Klein, living under an assumed name, was a nighttime regular. Townspeople thought "Dick" was a German journalist. He surrendered quietly and was unarmed. After the terrorists fled to Algeria with 35 hostages, Klein was later spotted in Yemen, Libya, and Algeria. In 1978, he told *Der Spiegel* magazine that he had renounced terrorism. Frankfurt prosecutors determined in 1997 that he spent some of his time in France. On February 15, 2001,

Klein was found guilty of murder in the OPEC attack and jailed for nine years by the Frankfurt court. He was paroled in 2003.

On October 15, 1999, Frankfurt police announced the arrest of Rudolf F., 56, a German suspected of being an accomplice in the case. Further details were not released.

Carlos was arrested in Sudan on August 14, 1994, and extradited to France. On December 24, 1997, France found him guilty and sentenced him to life in prison for three murders in 1975. He converted to Islam while in prison. On December 15, 2011, a Paris court sentenced him to another life sentence for organizing four attacks in France in 1982 and 1983 that killed 11 and injured more than 140. As of 2013, he remained in prison.

On November 12, 2013, Sonja Suder, 80, a member of the Revolutionary Cells, was acquitted of a role in the OPEC attack.

June 27, 1976
Entebbe

Overview: Years of giving in to the demands of barricade-and-hostage perpetrators, kidnapers, and hijackers led to increasing frustrations on the part of victimized governments and their citizens who called for tougher measures. Nonnegotiation stances often were not believed credible by terrorists who continued to use these bargaining tactics. A daring and successful Israeli rescue mission into a hostile nation that was directly aiding the terrorists established that governments could indeed get the upper hand and that capitulation need no longer be the default option. Other nations rushed to create their own hostage rescue teams; the Germans' GSG 9 soon showed that the Israeli success was not just a sui generis victory.

Incident: On June 27, 1976, Air France flight 139, an A300 Aerospatiale Airbus carrying 257 people, including 12 crew, from Tel Aviv to Paris, was hijacked out of Athens by seven members of the Popular Front for the Liberation of Palestine (PFLP). In Athens, 56 people boarded, including 14 French, 10 Greeks, 9 Americans, 3 Canadians, 5 New Zealanders, 2 Britons, a Jordanian, a Lebanese, a Cypriot, and a Japanese. The plane first landed in Benghazi, Libya, for refueling. While on the ground, the terrorists allowed a British woman who had been hemorrhaging to deplane. Upon leaving Libya, the plane attempted to land in Sudan, but the government refused. It flew on to Entebbe Airport in Uganda. During the initial seizure, the West German leader of the hijackers announced over the loudspeaker, "This is the Ché Guevara Brigade of the Popular Front of the Liberation of Palestine. I am your new commandant. This plane is renamed *Haifa*. You are our prisoners." The passengers reported that the terrorists attempted to keep their identities secret, referring to each other only by numbers. One passenger, M. Cojot, acted as liaison with the hijackers. Upon landing at Entebbe, the Ugandans provided the hijackers with additional weapons and guarded the hostages while the terrorists left to freshen up. Three additional terrorists joined the original seven.

The demands of the terrorists were initially unclear; there was some question as to the identities of several of the 53 terrorists imprisoned in Israeli, Swiss, West German, French, and Kenyan jails whose release was demanded. Some reports claimed that five terrorists mentioned in Kenyan jails had plotted to assassinate Idi Amin, who added their names to the end of the hijackers' list. Others believe that the group attempted to fire heat-seeking missiles at an El Al plane in January 1976 but had been captured and either killed or turned over to the Israelis. The hijackers named Hashi Abdullan, the Somali ambassador to Uganda, as their representative and instructed France to name an envoy for the side of the governments. However, President Amin refused to allow French ambassador Pierre Renard or a special French envoy to deal with the hijackers directly, claiming that he was negotiating with them.

The hijackers set a deadline of noon on July 1, 1976, for the release of the prisoners, threatening to destroy the plane and all on board. They demanded that the French release Intos Silvia Masmela, a girlfriend of the Venezuelan terrorist Carlos (Ilyich Ramirez Sanchez), and the release from Switzerland of Petra Kraus, the leader of a Baader-Meinhof–type urban terrorist group. West Germany was to release Werner Hopper, Jan-Carl Raspe, Ingrid Shubert, Raphaël Rendat, Inge Viett, and Fritz Tuefel, most of them Baader-Meinhof and Movement 2 June members. They claimed Kenya was holding Abdul Hanafi, Sad, Ibrahim Qasim, Hasan, and Sals. The remaining prisoners were held in Israeli jails; prominent ones included Kozo Okamoto and Melkite Greek Catholic Archbishop Hilarion Capucci (who was being held for smuggling guns to the PFLP). The released prisoners were to be flown to Entebbe International Airport.

None of the governments gave in to the demands. On June 30, 1976, the hijackers released 47 elderly women, sick persons, and children and allowed an Air France 707 to fly them to Nairobi, Kenya. Ugandan officials said that among those released were 33 French nationals, 3 Moroccans, 2 Greeks, 2 Americans, 2 Dutch nationals, a Canadian, a Cypriot, a Paraguayan, a Venezuelan, and a stateless person.

The next day, the Israeli cabinet announced that it was willing to negotiate for the release of some prisoners in return for the release of the remaining hostages. This decision followed a demonstration by 50 relatives of the Israeli hostages, who stormed the office of Prime Minister Yitzhak Rabin. The hijackers extended their ransom deadline to July 4, 1976. On July 1, 1976, the terrorists released 100 more hostages. It was learned from the group that a selection had taken place; the non-Jewish hostages were separated from the Israelis or persons of dual nationality. The crew of the Air France plane decided to stay with the Israeli hostages, who were threatened with death by 7:00 A.M. EDT.

After intervention by France, Yasir Arafat sent a senior Fatah member to Kampala to attempt to secure the release of the hostages. The terrorists refused to meet with him, but allowed Amin to speak to the hostages once more. Israeli Lt. Col. Baruch Bar-Lev telephoned Amin several times, pleading with him to take action to release the hostages, but was unsuccessful.

On July 2, 1976, the terrorists increased their demands, adding $5 million in compensation for the return of the Air France plane. The Israelis also learned from the tapped telephone of Wadi Haddad (PFLP planner of terrorist operations) in Mogadishu, Somalia, that he had ordered the deaths of the Jewish hostages regardless of the Israeli response. With this information, planning for Operation Thunderbolt, a daring rescue of the hostages, began in earnest.

The plan called for flying several C-130 Hercules transport planes 2,500 miles to Entebbe from Tel Aviv, securing the release of the hostages, and returning. The Israelis claimed that no other nations were involved in the rescue operation, although many reports held that the Kenyans allowed the planes to refuel in Nairobi, where the Israelis were allowed to treat the wounded with a 33-doctor medical team. Other reports suggested that 50 Israeli agents had arrived in Kenya a few days before the midnight July 4, 1976, raid to arrange details. It was noted that the hijacking was named "Remember the Kenyan Treachery," making many believe that Kenya had cooperated with the Israelis in the arrest of the five PFLP members in January 1976.

Because of superior intelligence that many believed was derived from questioning the released hostages, overhead photography, and Israeli agents on the scene in Entebbe, the Israeli mission was a success. The operation was commanded by Brig. Gen. Dan Shomron, 30, head of the paratroopers and infantry. The attack force was led by Lt. Col. Jonathan Netanyahu, 30, a U.S.-born officer shot in the back by Ugandan gunfire during the assault.

Flying low to avoid hostile radar, the planes landed at a deserted section of the airfield. A black Mercedes led the first group of commandos, who raced to the airport lounge where the hostages were being held. Some reports claimed that a burly Israeli was made up to look like Amin and confuse the Ugandan soldiers. A second group created a diversion by setting off bombs in another area of the field. They later destroyed 11 Ugandan Air Force MiGs so that their planes could not be attacked while returning to Israel. A third group secured the airfield entrance gate, holding off a squad of Ugandan soldiers. Taken by surprise when the gun battle began, the terrorists did not have a chance to shoot any of the hostages. Several hostages were killed or wounded when they stood up in the crossfire. The operation lasted 53 minutes, and all of the planes successfully returned to Israel.

Israeli authorities believed seven of the terrorists were killed and three who were not present at the airfield escaped. Eleven other Israelis, civilian and military, were wounded. The Israelis believed that about 20 Ugandan soldiers were killed, saying that Amin's claim of 100 deaths was an exaggeration. Amin later claimed that 20 soldiers died, 13 were seriously wounded, and 19 others were hospitalized. Several governments condemned the Israeli action in press statements and during a UN debate, while others, including the United States, congratulated the Israelis. Amin telephoned the Israelis later in July 1976 to add his own congratulations, to request weapons and military spare parts, and to announce that he had broken relations with the Palestinian terrorists. Amin was ignored by the Israelis, although Libya delivered 20 French-built Mirage jet fighters to replace the destroyed MiGs.

Amin was reported to have engaged in a wide-scale purge of individuals connected with the guarding of Entebbe airport, with some claims of 245 killed by Amin's troops as punishment. Among those killed was Dora Bloch, 75, an Israeli British citizen who was left behind in Kampala's Mulago Hospital where she had been taken after choking on some meat at the airport lounge. Israeli officials attempted to obtain her release through the use of third parties, but it has been reported by a number of sources that two to four men dragged her from the hospital and strangled her. Some reports claimed that her burned body was later found in a field. Although a British official had visited Bloch the day after the raid, Ugandan Radio claimed that she had been returned to the airport and was among those freed in the Israeli attack.

The identity of the terrorists is disputed. Most reports agreed that the initial leader of the group was Wilfred Boese, an associate of Venezuelan terrorist Carlos. One of the terrorists who joined the group at Entebbe was Antonio Degas Bouvier, an Ecuadorian associate of Carlos. The identity of the woman, who the hostages claimed had acted "like a Nazi" and mistreated all of them, was subject to much speculation. Many claimed that she was Gabrielle Kroecher-Tiedemann, who had taken part in the OPEC raid of December 1975. Others suggested that she was Turkish-born Barin Acturk, who was arrested in Paris in 1973 for gun smuggling, then released after six months and flown to Baghdad. Still others offered the name of Eleanore Honel-Hausman, the widow of Hugo Muller, who died on May 25, 1976, when his suitcase exploded in the Tel Aviv airport. The identity of the Palestinians was also difficult to ascertain. The PFLP-claimed that one of them was a founder of their group, Al Haj Jayez Jaber, who had also founded the terrorist group Heroes of the Return, which had merged with other groups to form the PFLP. Uganda claimed that the dead were Haji Fayez Jaber, Abdel Razzark Sammarraie, Jayel Arjam, Aboh Khaled Khalayli, and Aboh Ali. The two Europeans were given Arabic pseudonyms, Mahmojud and Halima, saying that the woman was a member of the German Revolutionary Party. French counter espionage said that Boese used the alias Claudius Axel. Others were identified as Jail el-Arja, 39, in charge of South American activities for the PFLP; Faiz

Jaber, 44, a member of the PFLP's military branch in charge of guerrilla operations; and Abd al-Latif Abd al-Razaq, 43, an Iraqi friend of Haddad. Investigative reporters Christopher Dobson and Ronald Payne listed Jayel Naji el Arja as second-in-command of the PFLP's Department of Foreign Relations. They also mentioned that an Abu Ali had contacted the Japanese Red Army in Japan and suggested that the dead terrorist may have been this person.

The terrorists had flown on Singapore Airlines to Athens from Kuwait. They stayed in the Athens transit lounge where they were not subjected to searches, thereby enabling them to board the plane with their weapons. Several suits were filed by hostages against Air France and Air Singapore for these security breaches. Their outcome has not been released.

October 6, 1976
Cubana Flight 455 Bombing

Overview: Anti-Castro Cubans, most of them based in Miami, Florida, dream of one day returning to a post-communist island. While the vast majority of the Cuban diaspora have subsequently settled down in the United States and other countries, assimilated into the local economy and society and quietly wait for the sclerotic Havana regime to fall of its own weight, some fringe groups have used terrorist tactics in the hopes of moving along Havana's history. Among these exile groups was the Coordination of United Revolutionary Organizations (CORU), whose exploits included attacks on Cuba interests and allies throughout the world. One of their most notorious attacks was the bombing of a Cubana airliner that killed 76 people. The search for justice extended over several decades.

Incident: On October 6, 1976, at 2:30 P.M., a bomb exploded on board Cubana Airlines flight 455, a DC-8 flying to Jamaica and Cuba with stops at Georgetown, Guyana, and Port of Spain, Trinidad. The plane had just left Bridgetown, Barbados, when the pilot reported an explosion on board and said that he would try to return. The plane crashed into the ocean, killing all 76 on board. Among them were 59 Cubans, 25 of them Cubana employees, including the crew and 16 members of Cuba's championship fencing team, 11 Guyanese, 5 North Koreans, 2 Trinidadians, and 1 person each from Colombia and Venezuela. An anti-Castro Cuban exile group, El Condor, claimed credit, as did the CORU.

On October 8, 1976, police in Port of Spain questioned two Venezuelans who left the plane in Barbados and returned to Trinidad the same night. On October 18, 1976, Hernan Ricardo Losano, who was carrying Venezuelan identity papers, claimed to have placed the bomb on board the plane. He was accompanied by Freddy Lugo. On October 14, 1976,

Venezuelan authorities arrested Losano's employer, Luis Posada Carriles; CORU leader Orlando Bosch, 49; and three other Venezuelans, identified as Oleg Gueton Rodriguez, Celsa Toledo, and Francisco Nunez.

Bosch had entered the country on a false Costa Rican passport with a tourist visa and also carried a false set of Nicaraguan documents. The U.S. government had tried to extradite him. Bosch had been sentenced to four years in prison for carrying out illegal activities, including firing a bazooka at a Polish ship on September 16, 1968, but had violated his parole and fled to Venezuela on a false passport. It was later learned that Posada was a Cuban who was formerly head of the Venezuelan secret police (DISIP). Losano was an employee of the Caracas detective agency run by Posada. On October 22, 1976, Losano attempted suicide by slashing his wrist. He and Lugo had told police that they were photographers and had traveled to Trinidad to purchase cameras and equipment. There was evidence that they had contacts with Eric Searly, a Barbados political activist and boxing promoter. Trinidad said it would expel the duo. On November 2, 1976, a Venezuelan judge indicted Bosch, Posada, Losano, and Lugo on qualified murder charges, which carry a maximum penalty of 30 years. Five others were released without charges.

The evidence as to culpability was sketchy. A British search team that found the sunken plane determined that the explosive used was C-4. Losano's girlfriend took a call from him in Trinidad and relayed the message to Posada's secretary, "Tell Posada the truck has left with a full load." Venezuelan security police said that they had uncovered CORU plans for terrorist attacks by Cuban exiles in the United States, Venezuela, Trinidad, Barbados, Guyana, Panama, and Colombia. It was also claimed that shortly after the explosion, a caller from Barbados telephoned the office of a private investigation company in Caracas, "The bus is full of dogs."

Havana protested Venezuelan justice minister Fermin Marmol Leon's conditional release of Losano and Lugo.

Posada escaped from prison in 1985. Bosch, the alleged mastermind, was acquitted due to lack of evidence.

On April 12, 2005, Posada, 77, wanted for the Cubana bombing, bombings in Cuban tourist hotels that killed an Italian tourist and injured 11 other people, and a 2000 plot to assassinate Fidel Castro in Panama, applied for political asylum in the United States. On May 17, 2005, U.S. authorities arrested him in Miami after he conducted public interviews with local reporters. On May 19, 2005, the United States charged him with entering the country illegally. On May 21, 2005, Venezuela made a provisional arrest request while thousands throughout the country demonstrated for his return. The United States denied the request on May 27, 2005. A judge ruled on June 20, 2005, that the trial would remain in El Paso and not be moved to Florida. In the fall of 2005, a federal judge ruled that he could not be deported to Cuba or Venezuela. On March 22, 2006,

U.S. Immigration and Customs Enforcement (ICE) said that he would not be released but efforts to deport him to a willing country would continue. On January 11, 2007, he was indicted on one count of naturalization fraud and six counts of making false statements in naturalization proceedings in 2005 and 2006. Also charged were Santiago Alvarez and Osvaldo Mitat, after they refused to testify before a grand jury. They were serving prison sentences on a weapons case. The prosecution said a Federal Bureau of Investigation (FBI) informant claimed that Posada had entered the United States on the *Santrina*, a shrimping boat manned by Alvarez, Mitat, and others. On April 8, 2011, a jury acquitted him of all charges.

Lugo, who had been sentenced to 20 years in prison for the bombing campaign, was released in 1993 after 17 years in prison.

An FBI document filed in the case on May 4, 2007, suggested that the bombing might have been planned in Guatemala.

October 13, 1977
Landshut Hijacking and
GSG 9 Rescue in Mogadishu

Overview: By the late 1970s, cooperation between rejectionist Palestinians and leftist European terrorists had reached a high point. Joint training, weapons exchanges, operational insights, and trading of operational personnel freely flowed among the various wings of the Popular Front for the Liberation of Palestine (PFLP), West German Baader-Meinhof Group and other German leftists, Italian Red Brigades, Irish Republican Army (IRA), Petra Kraus Group, Basque Nation and Liberty, and a host of other now-forgotten organizations. But government forces were similarly banding together against the terrorists, with quick reaction elite forces sharing training, tactics, and doctrine. The Israeli success at Entebbe led to numerous special operations teams armed with clipboards and light weapons to learn the lessons of the Israelis. They were put into practice in October 1977, when a West German team traveled thousands of miles to conduct a similarly daring rescue of its citizens from hijackers. The Entebbe and Landshut rescues led terrorists to all but abandon high-profile aerial hijacking sieges.

Incident: On October 13, 1977, Lufthansa flight 181, a B-737 (called a Landshut) scheduled to fly from the Spanish resort island of Mallorca to Frankfurt, was hijacked 55 minutes after takeoff. Two women hijackers reached into their boots, withdrew guns and hand grenades, and along with two male accomplices, diverted the plane to Rome. On board were 82 passengers and 5 crew. Hostages included a Spanish flight crew, Swedish passengers, an Austrian flight attendant, four West German crew, six West German beauty queens, and two Americans.

Two hijackers identified themselves as Harda Mamoud and Walter Mohammed, who appeared to be their leader. A statement in grammatical and concise Arabic delivered to *Reuters* in Beirut identified them as the Organization of Struggle against World Imperialism, which confirms the "objectives and demands" of the Red Army Faction kidnappers of industrialist Hanns-Martin Schleyer. The group demanded the release of 11 terrorists from the Socialist Patients' Collective and Baader-Meinhof Group in West German jails, as well as the release of two PFLP terrorists held in Turkish jails since an attack on August 11, 1976. They demanded $15 million and 100,000 marks for each prisoner. The terrorists demanded to have the prisoners flown to Vietnam, Somalia, or South Yemen.

The hijackers took off for Cyprus, landing in Larnaca, although the Cypriot government at first barred their arrival. In what came to be known as Operation Oscar X-Ray, Hans-Juergen Wischnewski, Chancellor Helmut Schmidt's troubleshooter, carrying satchels with millions of marks, set off in a German jet trailing the hijacked plane in the hopes of beginning negotiations. Simultaneously, a West German commando unit began practicing assaults on a similar B-737 in the Cologne, West Germany, airport hangar. Two squads of 32 men each boarded a third jet and headed for Cyprus that night. Soon afterward, the German jet carrying the commandos arrived in Akrotiri, Cyprus, 50 miles from Larnaca, Cyprus. Perhaps fearing an Entebbe-type raid, the hijackers took off for Bahrain.

On its way, the plane was refused permission on October 14, 1977, to land in Beirut, Damascus, Kuwait, and Iraq. Bahrain and Dubai, which were next on their itinerary, tried to prevent the plane's landing. Vietnam, Somalia, and the People's Democratic Republic of Yemen, named by the hijackers as candidates to receive the released prisoners, indicated their unwillingness.

The hijackers hoped to increase the pressure by their treatment of the hostages and establish an image of being willing to kill. They consistently refused requests to release sick, young, or female passengers. The leader of the hijackers called out the names of those he believed were Jewish and said they would be killed in the morning. The female hijacker took delight in brushing grenades against the heads of the passengers while the terrorist leader ranted against imperialism and Zionism. Pressure mounted when the hijackers fired three shots at Dubai engineers approaching the aircraft to attach a mobile generator because the plane's lighting system had failed.

The plane now headed for Oman, but the Sultan refused permission to land. They went on to Aden, but Yemen attempted to prevent the landing as well. Pilot Juergen Schumann left the aircraft to inspect damage to the landing gear and wandered into an area cordoned off by security forces. He attempted to convince the authorities not to allow the damaged plane to take off again. When he got back to the cabin, he was forced to kneel in the aisle while a one-question trial was held on whether he tried to escape.

The leaders of the hijackers fired a bullet through his head in front of the passengers.

The terrorists forced the copilot to head the plane for Somalia. When the plane landed at Mogadishu, the pilot's body was dumped onto the runway. The hijackers tied up the hostages, poured alcohol from passengers' gift-shop liquor over them and in the cabin for eventual burning, and collected passports to throw out so that passengers could be identified after the planned explosion.

International recoil at this action grew to recognition of the need for immediate, forceful response. The team members of Grenzchutzgruppe Neun (GSG 9) set off before the Somali government gave permission for the rescue.

The GSG 9 team moved on the plane at 2:00 A.M. on October 18, 1977. Approaching from the rear, the commandos set up four stepladders. They ignited an oil drum and rolled it toward the nose of the plane and away from the craft. The hijackers were drawn to the cockpit for a better look, allowing the commandos to open the plane's doors simultaneously. The raiders threw in specially designed British flash-bang grenades. Rushing in, the commandos yelled, "Get down!" Two terrorists were killed in the cockpit. A third in the first-class compartment opened fire. Although hit by two bullets, he hurled a grenade toward the rear of the plane. Hit by more bullets, he detonated another grenade while falling, injuring several hostages. The fourth terrorist, a woman, opened fire through the door of the lavatory in the rear of the plane. She was quickly subdued. Six minutes after the beginning of the operation, the passengers were safely out of the plane. One commando and four passengers were slightly injured.

The euphoria of the Germans was tempered by the embarrassment to the government over the prison suicides of Baader-Meinhof members Andreas Baader, Jan-Carl Raspe, and Gudrun Ensslin, and the attempted suicide of Irmgard Moeller.

On October 27, 1977, the PFLP-Special Operations claimed credit, saying that the hijack leader was Zuhair Akkasha, whose fingerprints matched those of the killer of North Yemen's former prime minister, Al Jehri, on April 10, 1977. The two other dead hijackers were identified as Nadia Shehade Doebis and Nabi Ibrahim Harb. Many suggested that the hijackers were members of an Iraqi-based group PFLP wing headed by Wadi Haddad.

In the wake of Japan's embarrassment over caving in to hijackers during a September 28, 1977, incident in India and Germany's jubilation over its success, many other nations felt pressed to establish similar commando rescue squads.

On March 20, 1993, Monika Haas was arrested for involvement in the Landshut hijacking. A warrant was issued for hostage-taking, kidnapping for the purpose of blackmail, and disrupting air traffic. She had been under investigation since March 4, 1993. She had written a book entitled *The Red Army Faction–Stasi Connection*. Haas was tried in 1996 for providing the weapons. She was sentenced in 1998 to five years in prison. A federal court dismissed her 2000 appeal.

On October 31, 1994, *Der Spiegel* reported that Palestinian Soraya Ansari, 41, was arrested in Norway and provided investigators with details of the Landshut hijacking of which she was the sole survivor. She stated that she knew Haas, who lived in Frankfurt, Germany. She said that Haas was the former wife of a Palestinian leader. Germany's request for Ansari's extradition was rejected by a lower court judge on December 9, 1994, citing humanitarian considerations. The decision was reversed a week later by an intermediate level court. She was freed just before Christmas.

As of January 6, 1995, Ansari, alias Souhaila Sami Andrawes, was fighting extradition. She admitted her role in the hijacking. A Somali court convicted her of air piracy and terrorism and sentenced her to 20 years. She was placed on a cargo plane to Baghdad and freedom in 1978. Beirut-born Ansari had been on Interpol's wanted list since the early 1980s. Norwegian authorities said they did not know of her past when she, her husband Ahmed Abu-Matar, and daughter received residency permits after arriving from Cyprus in 1991.

Ansari claimed that Germany could not try her because of double jeopardy; she had already served time in Somali jails for the same crime. German officials said that a new German trial would be lawful because Somalia is not a signatory to international judicial conventions and that a year in jail fell far short of justice.

On November 19, 1996, Hamburg's State Supreme Court convicted Suhaila Sayeh, a Palestinian woman, of murder and other crimes and sentenced her to 12 years in prison for her role in the Landshut hijacking. She was one of the four hijackers, but claimed she had no role in killing the plane's pilot. The court ruled that she had been complicit. Sayeh was the only hijacker to survive the German GSG 9 rescue operation in Somalia that freed 87 hostages. She was arrested in 1994 in Oslo, Norway, and extradited to Germany.

March 16, 1978
Aldo Moro Kidnapping

Overview: Leftist terrorists plagued Italy during the 1970s, conducting thousands of attacks during that period. Although the Italian Left was badly splintered, the main terrorist worry for the government was the Red Brigades, whose tentacles spread to various other European leftist and Palestinian revolutionaries. The Red Brigades conducted numerous bombings, assassinations, and bank heists during its long history. Its major claim to infamy came with the kidnapping, two-month hostage negotiation, and murder of former Italian premier Aldo Moro. An embarrassed government conducted a massive manhunt for the killers and dismantled the Red Brigades along the way.

Incident: On March 16, 1978, a dozen members of the Red Brigades killed five bodyguards while kidnapping Aldo Moro. The Rome abduction took place at 8:15 A.M. when Moro's sedan, accompanied by a police car, was ambushed as he was on his way to meet with Christian Democratic Premier Guilio Andreotti, who was going to request a vote of confidence for the first communist-supported government in 31 years. Moro, 61, president of the ruling Christian Democrats, was cut off by two stolen cars from which three to five terrorists jumped out and fired machine guns. The two policemen in Moro's car died immediately and two of the three in the following car died later. The fifth bodyguard died after undergoing surgery. Police found 710 bullets at the scene; some came from a rarely seen Soviet-made weapon and a Czechoslovakian pistol. The escape vehicle was later found with stolen diplomatic plates.

The kidnappers demanded the release of jailed comrades and a suspension of the Turin trial of 15 Red Brigades leaders, including founder Renato Curcio. They also called for the release of Armed Proletarian Nuclei (Nuclei Armati Proletari) members. On March 18, 1978, the group announced a "people's trial" of Moro, who was photographed in front of a Red Brigades flag. Because the government refused to negotiate, the Moro family requested Caritas International, a Roman Catholic relief organization, to act as an intermediary. In one of their nine communiqués, the Red Brigades said they would deal only with the government. On April 15, 1978, the group announced that Moro had been sentenced to death. Three days later, a message claimed that Moro's body could be found in Duchess Lake, a mountain lake 100 miles northeast of Rome. Police, soldiers, firemen, and skin divers found nothing after a three-day search. On March 20, 1978, a newspaper received a photo of Moro in apparently good health, holding the previous day's newspaper. On April 22, 1978, the government allowed a 9:00 A.M. deadline to pass without granting the terrorists' demands. Two days later, a new terrorist ultimatum called for the release of 13 terrorists. On April 24, 1978, Luis Carlos Zarak, Panama's ambassador, said that his president had offered asylum to the prisoners in return for Moro's safe release.

On May 9, 1978, Moro's bullet-riddled body was found in the trunk of a car parked in downtown Rome. The burgundy Renault R-4 was parked on a small street around the corner from the headquarters of both the Christian Democrats and Communists. Moro's hands and feet were chained, and at least 10 bullets were found in his chest and head. The car was found after police intercepted an anonymous call to one of Moro's secretaries at 1:00 P.M.

On May 18 and 19, 1978, police discovered three Red Brigades hideouts. One of them was believed to be the printing headquarters of the kidnappers. On September 14, 1978, police in Milan arrested Corrado Alunni, reputedly the new Red Brigades leader, in connection with the kidnapping and murder. By then, 17 people had been charged, although 11 suspects were still at large. The next day, Marina Zoni, 31, was arrested. On October 3, 1978, Lauro Azzolini, 35, and Antonio Savino, 27, were arrested in a gun battle with police, in which Savino and two police were injured. On April 16, 1979, Italian judiciary officials released new evidence implicating 12 people in the case. Several of them had been imprisoned for the previous nine days. Among them were educators, journalists, professors sympathetic to leftists, and Antonio Negri, professor of political science at Padua University. Ultraleftist Professor Franco Piperno, 36, was arrested in Paris on August 18, 1979, and charged with murder. On September 14, 1979, after giving a press conference denying involvement in the case, Lanfranco Pace, 32, was arrested by Paris police in a hotel. On September 24, 1979, after a gun battle with Rome police, Prospero Gallinari, 28, believed to have driven the car with diplomatic plates that blocked Moro's car, was arrested, along with Mara Nanni. Gallinari was hit twice in the legs, twice in the lower abdomen, and once in the left temple.

On January 3, 1980, Rome's public prosecutor asked for trials for several individuals arrested in the Moro case. Alunni, Gallinari, Franco Bonisoli, Azzolini, Teodoro Spadaccini, and Giovanni Lugnini were charged with the kidnapping and killing of Moro and with the slaying of his five-man escort. Adriana Faranda, Valerio Morucci, Mario Moretti, Enrico Triaca, Gabriella Mariani, Antonio Marini, and Barbara Balzerani were accused of crimes connected to the ambush. Toni Negri was believed to have phoned Moro's wife on April 30, 1978, to announce that Moro would be killed. An eyewitness claimed that Negri was at the scene of the ambush and that a woman congratulated him on the attack. Three Red Brigades members were sentenced to life in 1983.

On June 8, 1988, in Lugano, Switzerland, police arrested Alvaro Lojacono, 33, who had been convicted of terrorism in Italy and was believed involved in the Moro kidnapping and murder along with Alessio Casimirri, who remained at large. He was tried in 1975 and initially acquitted of murdering a young rightist extremist, but subsequently was found guilty of the charge by a higher court in 1980. He was sentenced to 16 years. He had vanished by the time of his second trial.

On October 9, 1990, construction workers found 421 photocopies of handwritten and typed letters written and signed by Moro hidden inside a window sill. They also found a machine gun, a pistol, and 60 million lire ($50,000) in a Milan apartment previously used by the terrorists as a hideout. Carabinieri had discovered the Milan hideout at 8 Via Montenevoso on October 1, 1978, and arrested nine Red Brigades members. More than 30 letters written by Moro were delivered to his family and leading Italian politicians during the 55-day kidnapping. The money was part of the ransom paid to the Red Brigades for the January 12, 1977, kidnapping of industrialist Pietro Costa.

On November 5, 1995, former prime minister Giulio Andreotti, 76, was indicted in Perugia on charges of complicity in the 1979 murder of journalist Mino Pecorelli. The charge said that he and former trade minister Claudio Vitalone conspired with the Mafia to kill the journalist because they feared he would publish damaging revelations concerning the kidnapping and murder of Moro.

On July 16, 1996, an Italian court sentenced to life Germano Maccari for the kidnapping and murder of Moro. Maccari was convicted of shooting Moro. In 1993, another Brigades member convicted as an accomplice led police to arrest Maccari as the fourth kidnapper.

Twenty years after the kidnapping, the newspaper *Corriere della Sera* hosted a roundtable on the topic that included the former terrorists. Triggerman Moretti said that Moro would have been spared if the government had given "just a signal, the recognition of the existence of political prisoners." However, former Red Brigadist Anna Braghetti said that the 200 members of the gang were polled and could not justify keeping him alive because the government had refused to compromise.

August 27, 1979
Mountbatten Assassination

Overview: Tens of thousands of attacks were attributed to the Irish Republican Army (IRA) and its various splinters, the Irish National Liberation Army (INLA), and various Unionist forces during the decades of "The Troubles" in Northern Ireland. Most of the attacks were low-level bombings and shootings, and involved attacks against suspected civilian supporters of the government, Protestants, or Catholics (depending upon the group). The Provisional IRA did not limit its operations to small-scale attacks, however, on occasion targeting the senior most level of the British government, and in this instance, the royal family. The successful assassination of Earl Louis Mountbatten caused widespread consternation within the United Kingdom, with the man on the street fearful of his own safety if that of the royals could not be guaranteed. Police and paramilitary operations against the IRA and its adherents increased dramatically in the aftermath of the attack. While as of this writing most of the IRA adherents are dead, in jail, retired, or have given up the fray, on occasion diehards claim a bombing.

Incident: On August 27, 1979, Earl Louis Mountbatten of Burma, 79, second cousin of Britain's Queen Elizabeth, was killed shortly after noon when a bomb exploded on his 29-foot *Shadow V*, a green and white fishing boat that had just pulled out of Mullaghmore, Ireland, a fishing village in County Sligo near the border. Lord Mountbatten died instantly when 50 pounds of explosives went off. His grandson, Nicholas Knatchbull, 14, and his friend, Paul Maxwell, 15, also died. The dowager Lady Brabourne, 82, mother-in-law of Lord Mountbatten's daughter, Lady Patricia Brabourne, died of her injuries the next day. Lady Patricia was seriously injured. Her husband, film and television director Lord Brabourne (John Ulick Knatchbull), and son Timothy, Nicholas's twin, were reported in satisfactory condition at a nearby hospital. The INLA and the IRA claimed credit, the latter saying that the execution was part of a "noble struggle to drive the British intruders out of our native land."

Two patrolmen in a separate car had accompanied the Earl on the half-mile drive from his home to the mooring, a standard procedure for them. However, they did not regularly inspect his boat or accompany him on it. The local police superintendent told the news media, "It was at his own request that he was not guarded constantly." Police officials speculated that the bomb may have been planted in his boat, which was left at an unguarded mooring a few yards from a stone jetty, and then set off either by remote control from the nearby hills or by a timing device. The bomb may have been placed in one of the Earl's lobster traps, which then exploded when pulled out of the water. Two skin divers had been reported in the area. Witnesses disagreed as to the speed of the boat and whether the trap was being pulled up at the time of the explosion. This was to have been the last weekend of a three-week trip to Classiebawn Castle where Lord Mountbatten spent part of the summer for the previous three decades.

The Irish Republic offered a £100,000 reward for information leading to the arrest of the perpetrators, while the Ulster Defense Association threatened to "take the law into its own hands" if IRA violence was not stopped. A few hours before the bomb went off at 9:30 A.M., an Irish police patrol had arrested two individuals who were suspected of being involved. Thomas McMahon, 31, an upholsterer, and Francis McGirl, 24, a farmer, were stopped in their car 80 miles away from Mullaghmore near the town of Granard, County Leitrim, in a routine police inspection. They seemed unusually nervous, and McGirl used a fictitious name and address. Police records indicated that McMahon was an IRA expert in bomb mechanisms and McGirl came from a family of IRA activists. Both had Eire addresses. They were held on charges of IRA membership, but were later released on a technicality. They were immediately rearrested and taken to Dublin's special no-jury criminal court, where they were charged with murder. Traces of nitroglycerin and seawater were found in their clothing. On November 23, 1979, a Dublin court found McMahon guilty and sentenced him to life in prison. The presiding judge refused to allow an appeal. McGirl was found innocent of the slaying, but was charged to stand trial on January 21, 1980, on charges of belonging to the outlawed IRA. Irish police believed seven other men were involved in the murder.

Mountbatten, an uncle of Prince Phillip, was England's leading World War II hero. He had been chief of the British Defense Staff, last viceroy of

India, admiral of the fleet, Allied commander-in-chief in Southeast Asia, and First Sea Lord. Burma, where he had governed, declared a week of mourning.

On August 7, 1998, McMahon, 50, was released from an Irish prison as part of the peace process. He had served 19 years of his life sentence. McMahon has since dissociated himself from the IRA.

November 4, 1979
Iran Hostage Crisis

Overview: The overthrow of the Shah by followers of the relatively obscure, elderly, Paris-based Ayatollah Ruhollah Khomeini caught the Western world by surprise. Iran quickly changed from a pro-U.S. oasis to an unrelentingly hostile base protecting anti-U.S. terrorists. The takeover and subsequent ineffective negotiations were marked each day on television news with headlines of "Iran Hostage Crisis: Day X." A failed rescue attempt modeled along the lines of the successes of the Israelis and the Germans further added to the American public's perception of President Jimmy Carter's administration as feckless in handling the crisis. The Iranians waited to release the hostages until the inauguration of President Ronald Reagan, further taunting Carter until the last possible moment of his presidency, thus ending the 444-day national ordeal.

Incident: On November 4, 1979, 500 radical students attacked the U.S. Embassy in Tehran, seizing 100 hostages after a two-hour battle in which 14 U.S. Marine guards lobbed tear-gas canisters. The terrorists later picked up Jerry Plotkin, a California electronics businessman, at a Tehran hotel, and brought him to the embassy. The students called for the extradition of the exiled Shah of Iran, who 13 days before traveled to New York to be treated for lymphatic cancer.

The students claimed that they were armed with only 10 pistols, although they later said that they had mined the embassy grounds and had placed explosive charges throughout the buildings. They threatened to kill the hostages and blow up the embassy compound if the United States attempted a military rescue.

There was some question as to who was in charge of the attack and with whom the United States could negotiate. The Bazargan cabinet resigned on November 6, 1979, leaving all formal authority in the Khomeini-led Revolutionary Council. A series of foreign ministers—Ibrahim Yazdi, Abol Hassan Bani-Sadr, and Sadegh Ghotzadeh—followed and were frequently defied by those holding the embassy. It appeared that there may have been up to five different groups of students involved—fundamentalist Phalange, Qom theological students, Tehran university students, leftists, and Communists. *ABC News* reported that the Central Intelligence

Agency (CIA) believed some of the students may have been trained by the Popular Front for the Liberation of Palestine (PFLP). Although the students said that they were loyal only to Khomeini, many observers suggested that the PFLP was directing the negotiations.

While the takeover initially appeared to be student-led, the government quickly moved to back the demands of the students. On November 12, 1979, Bani-Sadr upped the ante, saying that Iran demanded U.S. recognition that the Shah is a criminal and must be extradited, the return to Iran of the Shah's fortune, and an end to "American meddling" in Iranian domestic affairs. He announced an oil embargo on the United States at the same time President Carter was announcing that the United States would no longer buy Iranian oil. It was also noted that L. Bruce Laingen, the U.S. chargé, and two other U.S. diplomats were being held at the foreign ministry.

On December 15, 1979, the Shah was flown to Panama from San Antonio, Texas, after successful surgery. Iran requested extradition from Panama, and the students said that this would not affect the freedom of the hostages, whom they threatened to try as spies.

The American response consisted of incrementally increasing pressure on Iran, as well as diplomatically isolating Tehran. Numerous anti-Iranian protests in the United States underscored widespread support for the president's actions. On November 14, 1979, the United States froze Iranian government assets and blocked Iran's call for a UN Security Council debate. The United States had previously banned the sale of military spare parts to Iran. On November 23, 1979, Finance Minister Bani-Sadr said Iran would refuse to honor $15 billion worth of foreign debts involving loans from 28 private banks. On November 23, 1979, the U.S. Department of Defense canceled pilot training for Iranians. On December 12, 1979, the United States ordered all but 35 of the 218 Iranian diplomats in the United States to leave within five days.

Internationally, the United States focused on obtaining condemnations of Iran's actions by governments and international organizations. Scores of governments agreed that Iran had violated fundamental international legal norms. On November 9, 1979, UN Security Council president Sergio Palacios de Vizzio of Bolivia asked that the hostages be released. On December 4, 1979, the council again called for the release of the hostages, and said that the United Nations could be used as a forum for the settlement of Iran's dispute with the United States. UN secretary general Kurt Waldheim was authorized to use his "good offices" in settling the crisis. On December 31, 1979, the council approved a U.S.-sponsored resolution calling for economic sanctions if Waldheim's trip to Iran was not successful in obtaining the release of the hostages by January 7, 1980. Waldheim met with hostile demonstrations and was not allowed to meet with the hostages. The United States agreed to temporarily postpone consideration of a sanctions resolution when Iranian UN diplomats claimed to have a proposal to solve the crisis. On January 13, 1980, the Soviet Union vetoed a U.S.-sponsored sanctions resolution.

In Geneva on November 29, 1979, the United States announced that it would petition the International Court of Justice (ICJ) for interim measures, noting that Iran had violated three international agreements on protection of diplomats, the UN Charter, and the 1955 U.S.–Iran Treaty of Amity. Iran refused to participate in the deliberations. On December 15, 1979, the ICJ unanimously ruled in favor of the U.S. position, calling upon Iran to release the hostages and remove all unauthorized personnel from the U.S. Embassy grounds.

Tehran claimed that the issue was not its holding of hostages but rather the crimes of the Shah and alleged American intelligence collusion with the former regime. Numerous demonstrations involving tens of thousands of individuals underscored support for this position by Tehran residents. On November 13, 1979, the Revolutionary Council called for the interrogation of the Shah by a team of Iranian-picked investigators to prepare for his eventual trial in Iran. Khomeini repeatedly referred to the embassy as a "nest of spies" and claimed that the hostages had lost their diplomatic immunity due to their actions. On December 8, 1979, the foreign minister said Iran would form an international tribunal to review "the crimes of the U.S. government in Iran," and that the "spies" would be displayed before the tribunal. This was a departure from previous Iranian statements that the hostages would be tried in Islamic courts or possibly by the students.

The Iranians sequentially released several of the hostages, ultimately holding only those whom they claimed were spies. Thirty Iranian employees were freed shortly after the students seized the embassy. Three other non-Americans were released the next week. On November 18, 1979, as part of their careful attempts to exploit the heavy media coverage of the embassy siege, the students brought forward three hostages before television cameras. The trio—Kathy Gross, 22, a secretary, and two black U.S. Marine security guard sergeants, Sgt. Ladell Maples, 23, and Sgt. William Quarles, 23—were released the next day. On November 18, 1979, the director of Iranian media said women and blacks would be released. Khomeini so ordered on that day, saying "Islam reserves special rights for women" and that "blacks for a long time lived under oppression and pressure in America and may have been sent [to Iran under duress]." Four white women and six black men flew to Paris on November 20, 1979. The female secretaries were identified as Lillian Johnson, Elizabeth Montagne, Terry Tedford, and Joan Walsh. The blacks were U.S. Marines Sgt. David Walker and Cpl. Wesley Williams, contracting officer Lloyd Rollins, and three U.S. Air Force administrators, S. Sgt. James Hughes, Capt. Neal "Terry" Robinson, and M. Sgt. Joseph Vincent. On November 23, 1979, the students released a Bangladeshi, a Korean, a Pakistani, and two Filipinos. Those remaining, including blacks and a woman, were dubbed spies.

Visits by outsiders to the hostages were carefully orchestrated as media events by the students. Visitors were not allowed to see all of the hostages, leading observers to suggest that some of the hostages had been removed from the U.S. Embassy grounds.

Letters from several hostages, including some of those who had been accused of being spies, trickled out of the embassy to the hostages' families and the *Washington Post*.

In late January 1980, the Canadian government helped smuggle out six Americans who had escaped from the U.S. Embassy during the initial attack. The group first hid in the Tehran home of Robert G. Anders, a consular official, and then moved to the Iran–American Society to establish a telephone link with Washington, D.C. They hid at several locations before being given shelter at the Canadian Embassy. Under cover of a general personnel drawdown at the Canadian Embassy, the Americans used Canadian passports to slip out of the country with the rest of the embassy staff. The Canadian heroism triggered an outpouring of pro-Canadian sentiments in the United States and led to the making of the 2012 Oscar-winning movie "Argo."

On March 23, 1980, the Shah flew from Panama City to final asylum in Egypt.

On April 7, 1980, the United States broke diplomatic relations with Iran, imposed an economic embargo banning all exports to Iran except food and medicine, ordered a formal inventory of Iranian financial assets in the United States, and canceled all future visas for Iranian travel in the United States. On April 22, 1980, the European Community agreed informally not to purchase Iranian oil priced above Organization of Petroleum Exporting Countries (OPEC)-set prices. On May 18, 1980, the European Community agreed to cancel contracts signed with Iran after November 4, 1980, except for food and medicine.

Visits to and interviews with the hostages continued during the second quarter of 1980. On April 14, 1980, Red Cross officials claimed that they had been permitted to see all of the hostages. Three U.S. clerics were allowed to perform Easter services at the U.S. Embassy. On April 21, 1980, Barbara Timm was permitted to visit her son, U.S. Marine Sgt. Kevin Hermening, 20.

On April 24, 1980, an attempt by U.S. military forces to rescue the hostages failed when three of the eight helicopters assigned to the mission became unavailable due to mishaps in the desert near Tabas, Iran. During the preparation for the flight from Tabas to Tehran, the rescue team was forced to detain a busload of 50 Iranians who came onto the scene. After a decision to call off the mission, a helicopter crashed into a transport plane, killing eight. After being displayed by an Iranian cleric at the U.S. Embassy, the remains of the men were returned to the United States. Secretary of State Cyrus Vance resigned over the wisdom of the mission. The Iranian students claimed that they would prevent future rescue attempts by moving the hostages out of the embassy to other locations, including Mashad, Tabriz, Isfahan, Shiraz, Qom, Qazvin, Najafabad, Jahrom, Arak, Mahallat, Yazd, Gorgan, Zanjan, and Hamedan.

On May 24, 1980, the ICJ unanimously ordered Iran to release the hostages and said in a 12–3 decision that Iran must pay damages to the United States.

On January 20, 1981, with the release of frozen Iranian bank assets and the help of Algeria negotiators, the 52 remaining Americans gained their freedom. They flew home by way of Algeria and Germany and 10 days later were honored with a New York City ticker tape parade.

On February 4, 1998, Vice President Massoumeh Ebtekar, the seniormost woman in the Iranian government, admitted that she was the interpreter and spokeswoman for the hostage-takers.

On April 18, 2002, U.S. district court judge Emmet G. Sullivan ruled that the Algiers Accords meant that the hostages could not sue Iran. Hostages' attorney Thomas V. Lankford said they would appeal, which he did on May 12, 2003, in the U.S. Court of Appeals for the Washington, D.C. Circuit. Various groups of hostage families pursued judicial remedies; to date, Tehran has not paid a dime in compensation.

On November 4, 2002, an Iranian court jailed Abbas Abdi, one of the hostage-takers, for activities of a polling institute he founded. He asked the elected president, Mohammad Khatami, to resign in protest if conservatives blocked two reform bills.

November 20, 1979
Mecca Grand Mosque Takeover

Overview: While the primacy of the sacred places of Islam is not disputed among Muslims, disputes regarding the appropriateness of what governmental authority and sect should have sway over the sites has pockmarked Islamic history. The sanctity of the sites has been a centerpiece of Saudi policy since the Wahhabi-dominated kingdom's inception. One of the King's most cherished titles is Custodian of the Two Holy Mosques (referring to Mecca and Medina). Disagreements with Riyadh's royal family's Western connections on occasion bubble to the surface in the form of terrorist attacks. The most noteworthy attack came on the heels of the Iranian students' attack on what they termed the Great Satan days earlier. While the Saudis were successful in putting down the insurrection, the attack rattled Muslim notions of the safety of the sites for years to come.

Incident: On November 20, 1979, between 200 and 500 heavily armed rebels raided the Grand Mosque at Mecca, Saudi Arabia, during dawn prayers, seizing hundreds and perhaps thousands of worshippers of

30 nationalities. The attackers said that they sought reversal of Saudi modernization and the abolition of television, professional soccer, and the employment of Saudi women outside the home, in favor of a fundamentalist society based upon conservative Shia tenets.

The raiders closed the doors leading out of the courtyard and presented Mohammed ibn-Abdullah Qahtani as the Mahdi, the enlightened one long awaited as the final prophet. An Islamic prophecy says that the Mahdi will be proclaimed at dawn prayers at the Grand Mosque and that fighting in the streets of Mecca will accompany his coming. The attack took place on the Muslim year 1400's first day.

Saudi Arabia initially clamped down on all reports of the takeover, leading to the spread of numerous rumors. Several sources blamed the Iranian regime for the attack. Ayatollah Khomeini of Iran claimed that the United States was behind the sacrilege, leading to anti-U.S. riots in several Muslim countries. Responding to a request from Washington, D.C., Saudi interior minister Nayef bin Abdulaziz declared that the United States was not involved.

Saudi National Guardsmen blew up the mosque gates and fought their way inside against the rebels, who were armed with submachine guns, rifles, and pistols. The commander leading the Saudi assault was killed. Most of the hostages escaped or were freed by the Saudis several hours after the takeover, but the rebels held out for two weeks. Saudi troops used tanks, heavy artillery, snipers, and tear and asphyxiating gases against the attackers, who had taken up sniper positions in the mosque's minarets. Frequent Saudi claims of victory were proven premature, and it was not until December 3, 1979, that Saudi troops routed the last of the rebels occupying the mosque's basement.

Casualty figures vary. Some accounts indicated that 300 rebels, 65 soldiers, and 20 pilgrims were killed, and that at least 200 people were wounded. The Saudis announced that they had captured 170 rebels, most of whom were expected to be beheaded after questioning. Sheikh Mohammed Bin Sebil, a Grand Mosque imam, said a guard was killed and two were seriously injured in the takeover. The self-appointed Mahdi was killed in the final battle. He was identified as a 27-year-old dropout Islamic law student previously known to police as a religious agitator.

In questioning the surviving terrorists, the Saudis learned that the attack was to be part of a general uprising against the Saudi regime. A simultaneous attack on a shrine in Medina was aborted when the raiders discovered that troops were coincidentally praying there. A large demonstration of foreign workers in the oil fields was also to take place. The raiders had hoped to take hostage King Khalid, who cancelled a planned appearance at the mosque due to illness. The intruders fanned out at the mosque, searching the faces of the faithful in hope of finding the king. One of the captured rebels was a National Guard colonel. Most were Saudi nationals, with the rest coming from Pakistan, North and South Yemen, Morocco, and Kuwait. Some prisoners admitted that they had been trained in South Yemen.

The previously unknown Union of the Peoples of the Arabian Peninsula (UPAP) later claimed credit, saying the attack was part of a "national progressive Islamic Arab revolution."

In the early morning of January 9, 1980, 63 of the 170 militants arrested in the mosque were beheaded. The locations of the executions and nationalities of those executed were

- Mecca: nine Saudis, two South Yemenis, one Egyptian, one Kuwaiti, one Sudanese, one Iraqi
- Riyadh: seven Saudis, two Egyptians, one Kuwaiti
- Medina: one South Yemeni, two Egyptians, four Saudis
- Damman: three Saudis, one Kuwaiti, one Egyptian, one South Yemeni, one North Yemeni
- Buraydah: five Saudis, one South Yemeni, one Egyptian
- Tabuk: three Saudis, one South Yemeni, one Egyptian

As the executions were held in the early morning, few Saudis witnessed the carrying out of the Koranic sentences, which were not televised. Juhaiman Bin Seif, the military commander of the group, was among those executed. The 107 other individuals, including 23 women and boys, were given various prison and reeducation center terms. Another 38 people were found not guilty and were released.

The Saudis reported that 12 officers and 115 noncommissioned officers were killed in the mosque battle. Another 49 officers and 402 noncommissioned officers and soldiers were injured. Officials reported 75 terrorists were killed during the siege; another 27 later died from their injuries. Fifteen bodies were found when the mosque vaults were cleared. The final government tallies indicated that 270 people were killed and more than 550 wounded. At least 117 rebels and 26 pilgrims were among the dead.

The 1980s

The 1980s were the last hurrah of communist state sponsorship, and concomitantly, of the European Left, many of whom died, were detained, stayed in jail, stayed in hiding, or renounced terrorism and effectively retired. The end of communist control of Eastern Europe at the end of the decade led to the winnowing away of the European leftist terrorist movement as well. The breakup of the Soviet empire left The Left with few revolutionary regimes to serve as role models—few saw Cuba, Vietnam, North Korea, or China as saviors of the Marxist revolution, with China moving economically, if not declaratively, toward aggressive capitalism.

The leftists were replaced in the next decade by al Qaeda, whose antecedents arrived in 1981 with the assassination of Egyptian president Anwar al-Sadat. The al-Gama'at al-Islamiyyah assassins later melded with al Qaeda at the behest of Gama'at leader Ayman al-Zawahiri. Zawahiri later became Osama bin Laden's deputy and then his successor following his death.

The key focus of Western government responses to terrorism in the 1980s was the debate over the extent of Soviet and satellite assistance given to terrorists. Radical Middle Eastern regimes were also in the conversation over how to stop terrorism by stopping patron state support. The bombing of La Belle disco, although not particularly bloody, led the United States to use its military might to retaliate. The air raid on Tripoli did not dent Mu'ammar Qadhafi's willingness to attack Western targets, however, and just over two years later, Libyan-sponsored bombers struck against Pan Am 103 and a year later, a French Union des Transports Aériens (UTA) flight.

Successes by governments against hijackings and barricade-and-hostage operations led terrorists to again shift tactics. Hijackings went down in part because countries revamped airline security after the United States publicized the names of international airports that were inadequate in their antiterrorist security measures. The *worst* in the 1980s tended to be attacks that caused dozens of deaths, usually involving methods of transportation, including planes, trains, and ships, with the occasional diplomatic or official facility included. Pressure against state support to some terrorist groups led them to coordinate operations with each other, as seen with Direct Action, the Combatant Communist Cells, and the Italian Red Brigades in the middle of the decade.

While many of the *worst* involved multiple deaths, of particular note for the decade is that deaths and injuries from all terrorist attacks had outrun the body counts of previous decades. The more spectacular terrorism events appeared to have a trickle-down effect on "normal" attacks.

August 2, 1980
Bologna Train Bombing

Overview: Separatist, left-wing, and Palestinian terrorists received the bulk of media attention and conducted most of the terrorist attacks in the 1980s. In Italy, the Red Brigades, Communist Fighting Cells, Organized Communist Movement, and like-minded revolutionaries were responsible for thousands of low-level attacks. Right-wing terrorists were not silent, just not as prolific in explosives and media ink. That said, one of the most devastating attacks in all Europe was conducted by a right-wing Italian group at the beginning of the 1980s, presaging mass casualty train attacks in following decades by al Qaeda and Indian groups.

Incident: On August 2, 1980, a bomb containing 200 pounds of TNT exploded in the crowded waiting rooms and restaurant of Bologna, Italy's main rail station, killing 84 and injuring more than 400 people. Most of the victims of the 10:25 A.M. blast were Italians. The bodies of a Japanese man and a French woman were also found in the rubble. Two American brothers were injured. Callers claimed the Red Brigades were responsible, but later calls denied the charge. The Organized Communist Movement also denied credit. Another caller said the neofascist Armed Revolutionary Nuclei (Nuclei Armati Rivoluzionari, NAR) set the bomb in retaliation for a Bologna judge's decision that morning to try eight people for the August 4, 1974, bombing of a passenger train inside a tunnel between Bologna and Florence, which killed 12 and injured 35. Police suggested that the crash of the Italian domestic airlines DC-9 in the Tyrhenian Sea on June 27, 1980, may have been caused by a rightist bomb, as was claimed in the same phone call. All 81 on board the flight died.

On August 4, 1980, French police arrested Marco Affatigato, 24, an Italian neofascist. He was extradited on September 5, 1980. He had been wanted by Rome since 1978 and had been sentenced in absentia the previous month by a Pisa court to three and a half years for helping Mario Tuti, one of the train bombers, escape from prison. (Tuti was recaptured.)

On August 16, 1980, an arrest warrant was issued against neo-Nazi Luca de Orazi, 17, who was charged with subversion. On August 29, 1980, police raids in Rome and two other cities netted a dozen suspects. Warrants for 16 others were issued. On October 11, 1982, Bolivia expelled to Italy Pier Luigi Tagliari.

On February 17, 1983, Spain arrested seven people suspected of being involved in the Bologna bombing and the bombing of a Paris synagogue.

On December 12, 1985, Bologna magistrates issued warrants for 16 people. Included were three former chiefs of the Italian Intelligence and Military Security Service (Servizio per le Informazioni e la Sicurezza Militare, SISMI): Gen. Pietro Musumeci, former assistant director; Col. Giuseppe Belmonte; and Francesco Pazienza, currently imprisoned in the United States. A warrant was also issued for Licio Gelli, the head of the underground P-2 Masonic Lodge. Gelli, who allegedly was involved in tax frauds and financial scandals that brought down the Christian Democratic government in 1982, escaped from a Swiss prison in 1983. The three service chiefs were sentenced to heavy prison terms in July 1984 in connection with illicit SISMI activities on charges of conspiracy, embezzlement, arms and explosives infringements, and "interference in magistrates' investigations." Police arrested Professor Fabio de Felice, who was believed to be the right-wing terrorist leader who organized the bombing. Others charged with "complicity in a massacre and forming an armed gang" included Paolo Signorelli, leader of the NAR, Italy's principal right-wing terrorist group; Massimiliano Facchini; and Stefano Delle Chiaie, sought abroad for the past 15 years. Some of those charged were already serving prison sentences, including Valerio Fioravanti and Francesca Mambro, who had been recently married in prison.

On July 11, 1988, a Bologna court sentenced Valerio Fioranvanti, Mambro, Facchini, and Sergio Picciafuoco, all members of extreme rightist groups, to life sentences for setting off the bomb. Gelli was acquitted of the charge of masterminding the attack for lack of evidence. He was sentenced to 10 years in jail on charges of trying to throw investigators off the track, as were Pazienza and ex-SISMI officers Gen. Musumeci and Col. Belmonte. The court then reduced the sentences by five years for Gelli and three for the other trio. Right-wing extremists Delle Chiaie, Facchini, and Signorelli were acquitted of subversion charges for lack of evidence.

On July 13, 1988, the neofascist group Comrades in Jail bombed central Rome's Piazza Independenza near the central train station, injuring Emilio Manni, 46, a sanitation worker who was emptying the bin in which the bomb was placed inside a Coca-Cola can.

On May 15, 1989, the British government announced that it had no reason to expel Roberto Fiore, Marcello de Angelis, Massimo Morzello, and

Stefano Tiraboschi, all members of the neofascist Third Position (Terza Posizione), who were sentenced in absentia by an Italian court on charges of participation in an armed gang. They were also suspected of involvement in the Bologna bombing.

On July 19, 1990, the Bologna assizes appeals court overturned four of the life sentences. Cleared of any involvement in carrying out the bombing were neofascists Fioravanti, Mambro, Facchini, and Picciafuoco, who were all sentenced to life in the first trial. Gelli, 71, and former Secret Service agent Pazienza were both acquitted of slander and planting false evidence to mislead investigators. Former SISMI officials Gen. Musumeci and Col. Belmonte saw their 10-year sentences for subversion dropped. The court also reduced the sentences for armed insurrection against Fioravanti to 13 years, Mambro to 12 years, Gilberto Cavallini to 11 years, and Egidio Giuliani to 8 years. Others cleared by the ruling included Signorelli, who was up for a life sentence, and Roberto Rinani. For the appeals court, the act of association for subversion did not exist and thus cleared of all charges Gelli, Musumeci, Belmonte, and fascist extremists Delle Chiaie, Paolo Tilgher, Marco Ballan, and Maurizio Giorgi.

On April 13, 1993, shortly after midnight, Interpol agents arrested Italian right-wing terrorist Augusto Caucci, 42, in an apartment at 2400 Sarmiento Street in the Once District of Buenos Aires. He was charged with involvement in the attack at the Bologna rail road station. He was believed to be an explosives expert. He had lived in Argentina for a decade.

October 6, 1981
Egyptian President Anwar
Sadat Assassination

Overview: Egyptian president Mohammed Anwar al-Sadat's signing of a peace accord with Israel made him anathema to radical Arabs across the Middle East and in Egypt. Numerous groups denounced the treaty and Sadat personally. Ayman al-Zawahiri, who three decades later rose to the leadership of al Qaeda, led a fledgling band of Islamist militants in opposition to Sadat's lean to the West and Western political and cultural touchstones. Recruiting coreligionists across a wide spectrum of Egyptian society, including the armed forces, the radicals were able to plot a successful assassination of a Nobel Peace Prize winner. A crack down on the oppositionists by Sadat's successor, Hosni Mubarak, was soon in coming, but the group continued its string of antiregime attacks for decades to come. Mubarak ruled the country for another 30 years before his ouster by the Arab "street" in the Arab Spring of 2011.

Incident: On October 6, 1981, at about 12:40 P.M., Egyptian president Sadat was assassinated in a hail of automatic rifle fire and grenade explosions as he stood in review of a military parade in Nasr City celebrating Egypt's crossing of the Suez Canal in 1973. At least 9 others, including government officials and foreign diplomats, were killed, and 38 others injured.

While the attention of those in the reviewing stand was diverted by a spectacular air show of overflying Mirages, a Soviet truck hauling a new South Korean–manufactured field artillery piece came to a stop parallel to the stand, 15 yards away. The assassination team forced the driver to stop. Lt. Khaled Ahmed Shawki Islambouli (also identified as 2nd Lt. Khaled Attallah) led the assassins off the truck. He had given his assigned men a vacation and recruited in their place two civilians with past military service and an officer on inactive reserve. The group advanced on the reviewing stand unmolested by the bodyguards, who ran for cover. The terrorists fired at almost point-blank range, hitting Sadat with 28 bullets. Sadat was rushed onto a helicopter, still alive, but pronounced dead at 3:00 P.M. Three of the terrorists were reported killed at the scene, while other media reports said three were captured.

The press reported that the dead included chief chamberlain Hassan Allam; Sadat's official photographer Mohamed Rashwan; an Omani battalion commander; Bishop Samuel, member of the caretaker Papal Council of the Coptic Orthodox Church; Samir Hilmi, chairman of the Central Accounts Administration; Army Chief of Staff Gen. 'Abd Rabb an-Nabi Hafiz; a security guard; and two unidentified persons.

The wounded included the North Korean ambassador, presidential assistant Sayyid Mar'I, Sadat's private secretary Fawzi Abdel Hafez, Belgian ambassador Claude Ruelle, Irish defense minister James Tully, Egyptian defense minister Abdel Hamlim Abu Ghazala, CBS News correspondent Mitchell Krauss, several other Egyptians, U.S. Air Force Capt. Christopher Ryan, U.S. Marines Maj. Gerald R. Agenbroad, U.S. Air Force Lt. Col. Charles D. Loney, and Richard McCleskey, a Raytheon employee. Vice President Mubarak, who succeeded Sadat and was seated next to him, was uninjured, despite the assassins' plans to mount a coup by killing the members of the administration seated at the reviewing stand. Maj. Gen. Mahmoud Masri, commander of the Republican Bodyguard, claimed that 12 members of his staff were wounded. He was unable to explain why the security forces turned and ran during the attack, nor how civilians snuck onto the trucks with live ammunition, which was not to be issued for the parade.

The next day, 54 policemen were killed and more than 100 wounded in clashes with Muslim fundamentalists in Asyut after the group launched coordinated attacks from 10 cars at dawn against two police stations, security headquarters, and a police unit guarding a mosque. Six militants died and four were wounded. The extremists were part of a group that had seen 1,500 of their number arrested the previous month by Sadat in an anti-insurgent move against al-Gama'at al-Islamiyya.

On October 17, 1981, investigators linked Lt. Col. Abu Abdel Latif Zomor, who was captured in a gun battle between police and Muslim extremists at the Giza pyramids, with the attack. His brother and three others were also arrested.

One of the assassins, a major, had a brother who had been arrested in the September 1981 crack down.

The group Takfir wa Hijra (Repentant and Holy Flight) was blamed, as was Libyan leader Qadhafi and the Muslim Brotherhood. In Beirut, the exiled Egyptian opposition group known variously as the Independent Organization for the Liberation of Egypt and the Rejection Front for the Liberation of Arab Egypt, headquartered in Tripoli, Libya (and, according to the Egyptian press, given $3 million by Qadhafi), claimed credit. The group was headed by Saadeddin Shazli, a former Egyptian general who was chief of staff of the Egyptian Armed Forces between 1971 and 1973 and who subsequently broke with Sadat.

The assassins admitted that the ammunition had been purchased in the Upper Nile town of Deshna, 325 miles south of Cairo.

Police later arrested 356 Muslims affiliated with the terrorist organization that killed Sadat.

On November 12, 1981, twenty-four people were indicted for the murder. Sadat's assassins were listed as Lt. Islambouli, the commander of the artillery squad; Atta Tayem Hamida Rahim, an engineer and former reserve officer in the Egyptian Air Defense Command; Sgt. Hussein Abbas Mohammed, a member of the Home Guard; and Abdel Halim Abdel Salim Abdel Ali, a stationery store owner. Abdel Salam Farag, 27, a Cairo engineer and civilian leader of the El Jihad terrorist group, was charged with "complicity and instigation" for publishing the book *Absent Duty*, of which only 500 copies have been printed and which served as the assassins' ideological guide. A furniture dealer, three university students, and an 18-year-old high school student were accused of conspiracy. A blind mullah, Sheikh Omar Ahmed Abdel Rahman, 43, a theology professor from Cairo's Al-Azhar University who had recently taught at Asyut, was also indicted for saying "It is God's will," when told of the assassination plot. Rahman later figured prominently in the bombing of the World Trade Center in New York City and a plot to bomb other New York City landmarks in 1993.

On March 6, 1982, chief judge Maj. Gen. Samir Fadel Attia announced that the 3-man military court had convicted and sentenced 22 of the 24 defendants. The blind sheikh was acquitted. Lt. Col. Zomor, 35, a member of the army's intelligence service, and his student brother, Tariq Zomor, were sentenced to life. Defendant Mohammed Salamouni read a statement in English, saying "Sadat made of himself the last pharaoh in our country. He made of himself the last shah. Sadat killed himself by his behavior here in Egypt." At the noisy trial, the defendants—who were eventually caged for their outbursts—claimed that they had been tortured while in prison. Ignoring all clemency appeals, President Mubarak accepted the death sentences for the four assassins and Farag. On April 15, 1982, Lt. Khaled Ahmed Shawki Islambouli, 24, and Sgt. Hussein Abbas Mohammed, 28, were killed by a firing squad, while the three civilians were hanged.

On July 17, 1988, three members of the Jihad Organization who were serving life sentences for the assassination escaped from Turrah prison at dawn after attacking two prison guards. The trio were identified as Khamis Muhammad Musallam, Muhammad Mahmud Salih al-Aswani, and 'Isamal-Din Muhammad Kamal al-Qamari. The interior ministry offered a large financial reward. On July 25, 1988, Egyptian police fatally shot Qamari in a gun battle in the Shobra district of Cairo. Two policemen were wounded when Qamari fired a submachine gun and threw two grenades at the police, allowing the two other fugitives to escape. Police found grenades and explosives at their hideout, owned by another Muslim fundamentalist.

On November 5, 1993, Montasser Zayyat, defense lawyer for several militant Muslims standing trial in military courts, said in an interview that Switzerland had granted political asylum to Egyptian militant leader Zawahiri, accused by Egypt of relaunching the Vanguards of Conquest (New Jihad) group that assassinated President Sadat. Zayyat said his client applied for asylum six months earlier, and it was granted the previous week. Corinne Goetschel, a Swiss justice ministry spokeswoman, told the press, "This is not true. There is no one of that name who has applied for political asylum nor been granted political asylum in Switzerland." She did not know whether Zawahiri had used another name in such a request. Zawahiri served three years in jail in connection with Sadat's murder. He had no other legal charges pending against him in Egypt.

On February 22, 1994, Copenhagen's *Politiken* ran an article on Tal'at Fu'ad Qassim, one of the leaders of the organization that killed Sadat and who still conducted terrorist attacks in Egypt. Qassim was identified as instigating terrorist attacks against Danish firms and Danish tourists in Egypt from his home in the Copenhagen area. He was under a death sentence for his part in the Sadat case. In 1981, he was arrested as a leader of the banned Holy War (Jihad). In 1989, he escaped while being moved with other prisoners. Traveling through the Sudan and Peshawar, Pakistan, he reached Afghanistan, where he became one of the leaders of the Muslim fundamentalist volunteers aiding the mujahideen in fighting the Russians. Egypt had requested his extradition, but Qassim was given asylum from the death sentence by Denmark. He was known for his links to al-Gama'at al-Islamiyya. The Egyptian newspaper *al-Ahali* interviewed him, noting that he threatened foreign tourists and investments in Egypt, including Danish firms operating in Egypt and the 2,000 Danish tourists who holiday there each year. Qassim told the paper, "Tourism is a non-Islamic source of income which helps keep the present government in power, and foreigners have been warned to stay away from Egypt."

April 18, 1983
U.S. Embassy in Beirut Bombing

Overview: By the early 1980s, law in Lebanon had broken down and Beirut, often referred to as the Paris of the Middle East, had deteriorated into
an ungovernable city, split between various factions that held turf rather
than governed. Snipers and bombers roamed the city at will, threatening
locals and foreigners alike. Hizballah, Islamic Jihad, and their adherents
often targeted Westerners, kidnapping them and holding them for years
until releasing them, sometimes dead, sometimes alive. In 1983, anti-U.S.
militants upped the ante with massive car bomb attacks against the U.S.
Embassy and U.S. Marine barracks.

Incident: On April 18, 1983, a U.S. Embassy car, which had been stolen
in southern Lebanon, broke through a security barrier in front of the U.S.
Embassy in Beirut, Lebanon. An unidentified man then abandoned the
vehicle just before it blew up, causing the collapse of the central section of
the seven-story embassy building. Sixty-four people, including the fleeing terrorist, 17 Americans, 32 local embassy staffers, and 14 visa appli-
cants and passersby, were killed in the blast. Another 123 people were
wounded. The top Mideast expert from the Central Intelligence Agency,
Robert Ames, and the deputy director of the Agency for International
Development, William McIntyre, were among the dead, which also included members of the Departments of Defense and State. Even though
Iran dissociated itself from the bomb attack, the Iranian-based Islamic
Jihad (Muslim Holy War) claimed responsibility. The booby-trapped car
was filled with 330 pounds of Hexogene, equivalent to 1,320 pounds of
TNT. Many of the injured were in the visa applications section of the
embassy.

On July 26, 1985, a Lebanese military magistrate charged four extremists: Hussein Saleh Harb and Mahmoud Moussa Dairaki, both Lebanese;
Muhammad Nayif al-Jada', a Palestinian; and Sami Mahmoud Hujji, an
Egyptian. Harb and Hujji were also charged with the 1981 bombing of
the Iraq Embassy in Beirut that killed 48. By May 1986, Harb had been
freed on £200,000 bail, after having been captured and held for some time.
In November 1986, the military court magistrate called for the death sentence for six extremists accused of the U.S. Embassy bombing, including
the four just named, all of whom were at large. At least eight others were
suspected of having aided the accused in the bombing.

On April 30, 1993, a military court ruled that the suicide truck bombing of the U.S. Embassy was a political crime and could not be punished
under the political amnesty law. The ruling protected the accused, identified as Hussein Saleh Harb, Sami Mahmud al-Hijjah, Mahmud Musa
al-Dirani, Muhammad Nayif al-Jada', Hasan Muhammad Harb, and 'Ali
Mustafa Haydar. The ruling also considered the assassination of French

military attaché Christian Gouttiere on September 18, 1986, as covered by the political amnesty law.

The United States announced that it would close the U.S. offices of the Lebanese-based Middle East Airlines.

On May 12, 1993, a military appeals court presided over by Judge Shaykh Amin Nassar overruled the lower court. The case was to be submitted to the Judiciary Council.

On May 14, 1993, the Islamic Jihad protested the Lebanese government's decision to repeal the military court's ruling on the bombing of the U.S. Embassy in Beirut. Munif' Uwaydat, attorney general at the Court of Appeals, prepared the request for repealing the ruling regarding military court's standing in the case of the bombing. The military appeals court said in its repeal that crimes committed against foreign diplomatic missions were not covered by the law.

On April 7, 2003, U.S. Agency for International Development official Anne Dammarell took the stand in U.S. District Court in Washington, D.C., as the lead plaintiff in a $5 billion lawsuit against Iran, identified as the sponsor of the bombing. Dammarrell was blown through a wall and sustained 19 broken bones, glass embedded in her skin, and post-traumatic stress disorder. More than 90 plaintiffs joined the suit. On September 8, 2003, U.S. district judge John D. Bates ruled that Iran had sponsored the bombing and awarded $129 million to 29 American victims and family members. Dammarell was awarded $6.7 million. Yvonne Ames, wife of Robert Ames, and their six grown children were awarded $38.2 million. Bates ruled that the plaintiffs were not entitled to punitive damages.

October 23, 1983
U.S. Marine and French Paratrooper
Barracks in Lebanon Bombing

Overview: Soon after the bombing of the U.S. Embassy in Beirut, Hizballah followed up with a coordinated attack against two military forces they deemed hostile. Hizballah exceeded the previous body count, and the U.S. administration contemplated pulling out of Lebanon.

Incident: On October 23, 1983, a yellow Mercedes truck, packed with 2,000 pounds of a plastic explosive equivalent to 6 tons of TNT, drove through a barbed-wire perimeter fence and then passed a sandbag sentry post before coming to rest in the lobby of the Battalion Landing Team building, housing some of the U.S. Marines at Beirut International Airport. The ensuing blast created a crater 30 feet deep and 120 feet across and caused the four-story building to collapse instantly into smoldering rubble. Windows over a half mile away were shattered by the explosion.

The 6:20 A.M. blast killed 241 American servicemen and injured over 80. Marine sentries were unable to fire on the truck because their weapons were kept unloaded per orders. A heavy iron gate placed between the barbed-wire fence and the ill-fated building had apparently been left open, allowing easy access for the suicide bomber.

About 20 seconds after the blast, a second suicide bomber drove his car into the eight-story apartment building housing 110 French paratroopers. When the bomb detonated, the building folded, one floor upon the other, killing 58 soldiers and injuring at least 15 others. The second blast was 2 miles to the north of the airport in the Ramel el-Baida district in central Beirut.

In a phone call to Agence France-Presse (AFP) offices in Beirut and Paris, Islamic Holy War (Islamic Jihad) claimed responsibility for both blasts. The caller issued the following statement:

> We are the soldiers of God and we crave death. Violence will remain our only path if they [foreign forces] do not leave. We are ready to turn Lebanon into another Vietnam. We are not Iranians or Syrians, or Palestinians. We are Lebanese Muslims who follow the dicta of the Koran.

Islamic Jihad is closely linked to Hizballah (Party of God), whose leader was the radical Shi'ite Muslim Mohammed Hussein Fadlallah. Fadlallah's headquarters were in Baalbek, Lebanon. Husayn Musawi, Fadlallah's strongman, headed the Islamic Amal faction, which was associated with Hizballah. The Islamic Amal had ties to Iran's Ayatollah Khomeini. Newspaper reports linked the Islamic Amal, Fadlallah, and Musawi to the two blasts.

In an anonymous call to AFP, the suicide bombers were identified as Abu Mazin, 26, and Abu Sijan, 24. In another call to AFP, the Free Islamic Revolution Movement (aka the Islamic Revolutionary Movement) claimed responsibility for the bombings. The linkage between Hizballah, Islamic Jihad, Islamic Amal, and the Free Islamic Revolution Movement is difficult to untangle.

On November 9, 1994, First Investigating Military Judge Riyad Tali' issued judicial warrants to the Lebanese Army Intelligence Directorate, the State Security Intelligence Department, the Internal Security Forces, and the Judicial Police, asking them to search for and apprehend the bombers of the U.S. and French Marine barracks. Hizballah condemned the decision. The decision removed the protection of a civil war amnesty covering all acts of violence between 1975 and 1990.

On March 17, 2003, some 600 relatives of the U.S. servicemen killed in the bombing filed suit in U.S. District Court in Washington, D.C., alleging Iranian culpability. U.S. district judge Royce C. Lamberth ruled that Iran could be sued because the Marines were on a peacekeeping mission under peacetime rules of engagement, not rules of combat. He cited a

1996 law that permits U.S. citizens to take legal action against state sponsors of terrorism. The judge had entered default judgments against Iran on December 18, 2002, because of its failure to respond to the lawsuit. On May 30, 2003, Judge Lamberth ruled that Iran was behind the bombing, thereby permitting the relatives to collect damages against Iran. Lamberth said a court-appointed master would consider the financial claims. On September 7, 2007, Lambert ordered that Iran pay $2,656,944,877 to the circa 1,000 family members and survivors, specifying individual awards down to the dollar. The largest award of $12 million went to Larry Gerlach, who sustained a broken neck and became a permanent quadriplegic. As of late 2013, payment has yet to be made.

June 23, 1985
Air India Flight 182 Bombing

Overview: Sikh militants generally confined their operations to the region of conflict between India and Pakistan. Seeking revenge for the Indian army's storming of the Sikhs' holiest shrine, the Golden Temple in Amritsar in 1984 in which hundreds died, some Sikhs in Canada expanded their operations to conduct a high-profile airliner bombing campaign that presaged the al Qaeda simultaneous mass-casualty, multiple-target attack template.

Incident: On June 23, 1985, Air India flight 182, en route from Toronto to Bombay with intermediate stops in Montreal, London, and New Delhi, disappeared from Shannon Airport radar at 31,000 feet altitude, 90 miles from the Irish coast. The B-747 carried 329 people, including 4 infants and 77 children. Passengers included 279 Canadians and 7 Americans; most of the rest were Indian. Four helicopters of the Royal Air Force searched for survivors and debris. Everyone had perished in the worst airplane crash over water and the third worst in aviation history.

An hour earlier, a bomb placed in a suitcase aboard Canadian Pacific Airlines flight 003, en route from Vancouver to Tokyo with 374 passengers and 16 crew, exploded after being unloaded at Tokyo's Narita International Airport. The suitcase was in a baggage container waiting to be loaded onto Air India flight 301 to Bombay. Baggage handlers Hideo Asano and Hideharu Koda were killed when the bomb prematurely exploded in the baggage area of Narita Airport; four other airport employees were injured. The baggage aboard the Canadian Pacific flight had not been given X-ray surveillance for explosives. Authorities at the Toronto airport confirmed that the surveillance equipment was malfunctioning on June 23, 1985, and that many pieces of luggage placed aboard flight 182 had not been screened for explosives.

In two anonymous phone calls to the *New York Times*, self-proclaimed spokesmen took credit for the Air India crash on behalf of two Sikh separatist groups—the Sikh Student Federation and the Kashmir Liberation Front. In a call to the Canadian Broadcasting Company, a self-proclaimed spokesman claimed credit on behalf of a third extreme Sikh group.

India conducted the investigation into the crash. Experts from the United States, the United Kingdom, and Canada assisted. Evidence included 50 video films of the aircraft wreckage, the results of autopsies performed on the bodies, 4,000 photographs, the cockpit voice recorder, the digital flight data recorder, and recovered pieces of the wreckage. The overwhelming evidence pointed to a mid-air bomb blast:

- The wreckage was strewn over a 5-mile area.
- The autopsies revealed that many of the victims suffered injuries caused by a sudden deceleration.
- The two black boxes stopped functioning the moment that the plane left the radar screen.
- A large piece of the lower skin of the forward luggage hold, recovered by Canadian salvage teams on October 22, 1985, contained 30 holes, pierced from the inside.
- A second piece of wreckage had burn marks on it.
- The flight data recorder and the cockpit voice recorder recovered on July 11, 1985, in 6,600 feet of ocean indicated that an explosion had occurred.

On November 21, 1985, India's director of air safety, H.S. Khola, issued a report that concluded that a bomb had caused the crash. On February 26, 1986, a judicial inquiry in New Delhi concluded that a suitcase planted by a terrorist caused the explosion. The 212-page report submitted to the Indian Civil Aviation Ministry indicated that a bomb had been placed aboard the ill-fated plane's forward luggage compartment in Toronto. The report accused two Sikh extremists—Lal Singh and Annand Singh—of having placed the bomb on board. The Singh brothers had booked tickets on flight 182. Even though they had checked luggage on the flight for Bombay, neither of them boarded the flight. The report also implicated the brothers in the explosion at the Tokyo Airport. On June 20, 1985, the brothers booked tickets on the Canadian Pacific Airlines flight 003 to Tokyo. In Tokyo, they were scheduled to transfer to Air India flight 301, the flight for which the suitcase bomb had been intended. At Vancouver, a man named A. Singh checked in one or more bags for flight 003, which were to be transferred to Air India flight 301 in Tokyo. Neither L. Singh nor A. Singh boarded flight 003.

The Singh brothers had attended a mercenary training camp in Birmingham, Alabama, in the early part of 1985. They had told the camp director, Frank Camper, that they were preparing an "offensive" that summer. In the training camp, they were taught the use of weapons and explosives. Investigators believed that a time bomb had been used in each incident. The bomb at the Tokyo Airport had exploded prematurely, causing the death of the two baggage handlers.

Lal Singh and Annand Singh were also wanted for a plot to assassinate Rajiv Gandhi during his scheduled visit in June 1985. As of November 1988, the Singh brothers were at large.

Prosecutors said Sikh militants built the bomb in British Columbia.

On June 10, 1991, Justice Raymond Paris of Canada's British Columbia Supreme Court sentenced to 10 years in prison Inderjit Singh Reyat, 39, a Canadian Sikh who was convicted on May 10, 1991, on two counts of manslaughter and four explosives offenses for making a bomb that exploded at the Tokyo airport. Justice Paris said that the former auto electrician at the very least helped others build a suitcase bomb that was to have been used to blow up an Indian airliner. Reyat was the only person charged with the blast. He was a devout Sikh who aided members of the militant Babbar Khalsa, a Sikh nationalist organization. On February 10, 2003, Reyat pleaded guilty to manslaughter in the Air India 182 case. He was sentenced to five years for helping acquire the materials used to make the bomb. Prosecutors said he did not know who made the bomb and thought the material would be used for bombs in India. The surprise plea came less than two months before he and two other men were to stand trial on murder charges in the case.

On October 27, 2000, Royal Canadian Mounted Police officers in Vancouver arrested Ripudaman Singh Malik, a millionaire who ran a Vancouver radio station, and Ajaib Singh Bagri, a sawmill worker from Kamloops, British Columbia. They faced eight charges, including first-degree murder, conspiracy, and attempted murder in the killing of the 329 people on the Air India flight 182 bombing. They were also charged with the attempted murder of the passengers and crew in the Tokyo explosion. On April 28, 2003, their trial began. On March 16, 2005, British Columbia Supreme Court justice Ian Josephson acquitted Malik and Bagri of murder and other charges in the Air India 182 case and of the bombing in Tokyo. The judge said key witnesses were not credible.

October 7, 1985
Achille Lauro Seajacking

Overview: A dizzying blizzard of Palestinian terrorist groups jockeyed for position in the 1970s and 1980s to gain leadership of the Palestinian struggle against Israel and its allies. Groups conducted campaigns of bombings, assassinations, hijackings, and barricade-and-hostage operations against primarily European targets throughout Europe and the Middle East. The Palestine Liberation Front (PLF) garnered extensive publicity with its shipjacking and brutal murder of a wheelchair-bound American, whose body they threw off the ship. Post-incident handling of the case strained U.S.–Egyptian relations and led to the resignation of the Italian government. The search for the Abu Abbas–led group took years, but eventually the perpetrators were rendered to justice.

Incident: On October 3, 1985, the Italian cruise ship *Achille Lauro* set sail from Genoa, Italy, carrying 754 passengers and 331 crew. As scheduled, the ship made calls at Naples and Syracuse. When it docked in Alexandria, 634 passengers disembarked for an overland trip to the Pyramids with plans to reboard the ship at Port Said. Thirty miles from the next port-of-call, on October 7, 1985, four terrorists armed with Kalashnikov assault rifles, eight grenades, and other weapons seized the ship. The takeover took place at 1:00 P.M. when the terrorists fired warning shots in the main dining room. Two hostages were slightly injured by gunfire during the initial takeover. The hijackers held 331 crew and 116 passengers hostage, including 12 Americans. The terrorists collected the passengers' passports and grouped people according to nationalities. The Americans were ordered onto the top deck, where for four grueling hours of heat, they were not given water. Hostages included people from West Germany, Austria, Switzerland, Belgium, Portugal, Italy, the United States, the United Kingdom, Poland, and the Netherlands. The hijackers ordered Capt. Gerardo de Rosa to head to Syria. On the morning of October 8, 1985, the ship was off the coast of Tartus, Syria. By radio, the hijackers, who identified themselves as members of the PLF, requested permission to dock. Syria denied the request. The hijackers demanded the release of 50 Palestinian terrorists imprisoned in Israel. At 2:42 P.M., one hijacker radioed Syrian authorities, saying "We have no more time. We will start executing at 3:00 P.M. sharp." At 2:55 P.M., they warned, "We have five minutes only." The hijackers singled out Leon Klinghoffer, 69, an American confined to a wheelchair. Klinghoffer was shot in the head and chest. The hijackers then ordered two of the hostages to dump Klinghoffer in his wheelchair overboard.

Israel responded to the hijackers' demands by reiterating its policy of not conceding to terrorists. The United States announced that the USS *Saratoga*, an aircraft carrier, and the USS *Scott*, a guided-missile destroyer, were steaming to the vicinity of the *Achille Lauro*. The Delta Force was also dispatched to the region.

Israel believed that the four hijackers—Bassam Ashqar, 17; Majid Yusuf al-Mulki, 23; Mar'uf Ahmad al-As'adi, 23; and 'Abdal-Latif Ibrahim Fatayer, 20—had been sent by Mohammad Abbas Zaidan (Abu Khalid) on a suicide mission to Ashdod, Israel. In an interview with CBS Radio after the incident ended, Abbas confirmed that the terrorists were, indeed, en route to a suicide mission inside Israel when the boat hijacking occurred.

When Syria refused their request to dock, the hijackers ordered the captain to head back toward Port Said. On October 9, 1985, the ship was 12 miles off the coast of Port Said. During the early afternoon, the terrorists communicated with Egyptian officials by ship-to-shore radio. Egyptian defense minister Mohammad Abu Ghazala headed the negotiations. Two Palestine Liberation Organization (PLO) representatives—Hani Hassan and Zahdi Qoudra—in Cairo assisted with the negotiations. The PLF interests were represented in Cairo by Abbas. At 4:20 P.M., the negotiators agreed in principle on a deal with the hijackers, where by the hostages would be freed in exchange for safe passage to Tunis for the hijackers. The incident ended at 5:00 P.M. when Abbas and Egyptian authorities took a small boat to the ship and boarded it.

The United States immediately requested that Egypt turn the hijackers over to them to face trial.

On the morning of October 10, 1985, Egyptian president Mubarak announced that the hijackers had already departed Egypt.

The *Washington Post* reported that U.S. intelligence sources used electronic eavesdropping devices to establish that the terrorists were still in Egypt. At 7:00 P.M., the USS *Saratoga*, off the coast of Albania, turned around, and seven F-14 fighter jets took off, supported by E2C Hawkeye electronic surveillance planes. At 9:15 P.M., a chartered Egyptair B-737 left Cairo with Abbas, Hani Hasan, and the four hijackers. The surveillance planes intercepted the B-737, which had been refused permission to land in Tunis and Athens. The F-14s flashed their lights to convince the Egyptair pilot that he was surrounded. The F-14s ordered the B-737 to follow them to Sigonella, a U.S.–Italian air base in Sicily. U.S. commandos, Italian soldiers, and police took the four hijackers and two Palestinian officials into custody. Seventeen Egyptian passengers were also on the plane.

The four hijackers were arrested by Italian authorities, but the two Palestinian officials were only detained for questioning. On October 12, 1985, Abbas and Hasan boarded the Egyptair B-737 and took off from Ciampino Airport to Leonardo da Vinci Airport in Rome. At 7:10 P.M., the two boarded a Yugoslav JAT Airways jet for Belgrade and freedom. The United States protested the escape of Abbas, whom the United States wanted to charge with sea piracy. At the time of his release, the United States was preparing papers asking Italy to extradite Abbas and the four hijackers. U.S. attorney general Edwin Meese characterized Abbas as "an international criminal" and vowed that the United States would do everything possible to bring Abbas to justice.

A fifth Palestinian—Muhammad Isa Abbas, 25—was charged on October 14, 1985, with complicity in the hijacking. Abbas, a cousin of the Abbas who masterminded the operation, was arrested as he disembarked from a ship from Tunis on September 28, 1985, five days before the departure of the *Achille Lauro*. A sixth Palestinian, who departed the *Achille Lauro* in Alexandria, was also being sought.

On October 16, 1985, the Israeli government released a partial transcript of a ship-to-shore telephone conversation between the hijackers and Abbas. The transcript clearly indicated that Abbas had been in control of the terrorists during the hijacking.

On October 17, 1985, Italian prime minister Bettino Craxi announced the resignation of his cabinet in the wake of the government's handling of Abbas.

On October 23, 1985, hijacker Mur'uf Ahmad al-As'adi turned state's evidence. As'adi identified Abbas as having masterminded their mission. Majid Yusuf al-Molqi was identified as the head of the terrorist squad and as the one who murdered Klinghoffer.

On October 26, 1985, Italian authorities revealed that a sixth suspect—Yusef Ali Yuseb Ismail—had been arrested.

On November 3, 1985, Agenzia Nazionale Stampa Associata (ANSA) wire service revealed that a senior aide to PLF leader Abbas had been aboard the *Achille Lauro*. Abd al-Rahim Khalid traveled under a stolen Greek passport bearing the name Petros Flores. Khalid was believed to have left the ship at Alexandria.

On November 13, 1985, Italian authorities issued arrest warrants for 16 PLF members connected with the hijacking. Only seven were in custody—the four hijackers, Muhammad Isa Abbas, Yusuf Ali Ismail, and Ibrahim Husari. Arrest warrants were also issued for:

- Mohammad Abbas Zaidan (alias Abu Khalid)
- Izz al-Din Badra Khan, PLF military chief
- Ziyad al-Umar, the PLF member who bought the cruise tickets
- Muhammad Jarbu', a PLF member scheduled to be aboard the ship but who fell ill before the ship departed
- Abu Kifah, who helped smuggle the arms
- Al-Khadrah, who helped smuggle the arms
- Abd al-Rahim Khalid, 49, who got off the ship at Alexandria
- Abu' Ali Kazim, a bodyguard for Abbas Zaidan
- Yusuf Hishamal-Nasir, a PLF informer in Italy

On November 18, 1985, the four hijackers and Mohammad Isa Abbas, who allegedly smuggled the Kalashnikov rifles into Italy, were tried on arms smuggling charges. All were found guilty. Isa Abbas was sentenced to nine years in prison, and Yusuf al-Molqi was sentenced to eight years. The others were sentenced to between four and five years.

On June 18, 1986, the murder and kidnapping trial opened in Genoa. Al-Molqi, As'adi, and Fatayer were in the courtroom, along with accused accomplices Isa Abbas and Mohammad Gandour, 37. Gandour had been arrested in Rome in early September 1985 for possession of fake documents. He was an alleged courier and financier for the hijackers. Ten others, including Abbas, were tried in absentia.

On July 10, 1986, the Italian court sentenced 11 men convicted in the trial. PLF leader Abbas was sentenced to life imprisonment. Al-Molqi was sentenced to 30 years. Izz al-Din Badra Khan and Ziyad al-Umar were sentenced to life. Fatayer was sentenced to 24 years. As'adi was sentenced to 15 years and 2 months. Isa Abbas received a six-month sentence for using a false passport. Gandour was sentenced to eight months and freed because he had already served the time awaiting trial.

On August 1, 1986, Yusuf Hisham al-Nisir was arrested in Viechtach, West Germany. Al-Nisir had been sentenced, in absentia, to six and a half years for providing weapons to the hijackers.

On December 6, 1986, Ashqar was found guilty of complicity in the murder of Klinghoffer and was sentenced to 16 years and 3 months by a juvenile court.

On May 19, 1989, Swedish police arrested a Palestinian believed to have been involved in the case.

On December 24, 1990, three weeks before the opening of the Allied air attacks on Iraq occupation forces in Kuwait, a Genoa magistrate freed Isa Abbas and Yusuf Ahmed Saad—who were jailed in the case—under an amnesty program. Their lawyers said that they were immediately expelled from Italy and apparently went to Algeria.

On March 5, 1991, Athens police arrested Khalid, 57, one of three masterminds of the attack, and three Greeks in the home of Petros Floros, a friend in central Athens, who had been acquitted in the *Achille Lauro* case. (Floros had been accused of giving Khalid his passport so that he could board the ship.) Police said that they had been planning to bomb a Barclays Bank branch; they found dynamite and a gasoline bomb on the premises of the house. Police also found drugs in Khalid's home. A court in Genoa, Italy, had convicted Khalid in absentia in 1986 and sentenced him to seven and a half years in prison. After prosecution protests, in May 1987 a Genoa appeals court increased the sentence to life imprisonment. Rome requested extradition. On March 20, 1991, Athens police said that Khalid admitted to having planned the attack. On May 6, 1991, Khalid, using the name Mohammed Nouami, was sentenced to 10 years in prison for drug dealing.

On May 29, 1991, an Athens appeal council decided to extradite to Italy Khalid. He tried to escape from Koridhallos maximum security prison near Piraeus with 31 others on May 12, 1991, but was arrested.

On October 25, 1991, the Greek Supreme Court ruled in favor of Italy's extradition request. Khalid was serving a 33-month sentence for trying to escape from Koryda prison.

On February 21, 1994, a Swedish court issued a warrant for the arrest of Samir Muhammad al-Qadir, an operations officer of the Abu Nidal group suspected of being the mastermind in the *Achille Lauro* case.

On January 26, 1995, Warsaw's *Gazeta Polska* reported that the terrorists were armed with Kalashnikovs supplied by three Polish generals.

On April 13, 2003, U.S. Special Operations troops captured Abu Abbas in southern Baghdad. He died of natural causes on March 8, 2004, in U.S. custody in Iraq.

On July 7, 2008, Fatayer, 43, was ordered freed, having served his 25-year sentence (reduced for good behavior).

On April 30, 2009, al-Molqi was released early from a prison in Palermo, Italy. He had served nearly 24 years of his 30-year sentence.

April 5, 1986
Berlin La Belle Discotheque Bombing

Overview: Libyan leader Col. Mu'ammar al-Qadhafi supported numerous Palestinian and other Middle Eastern terrorist groups during his 40-plus year reign. Guns, money, safe haven, and other operational support were easily available to itinerant terrorists visiting Benghazi and Tripoli. Qadhafi's efforts to expand his idiosyncratic ideology throughout the Middle East and Africa fell on deaf ears, but terrorist groups were willing to make appropriate statements of agreement in return for aid. Evidence of Libyan involvement in a direct attack against U.S. interests in Europe was more than the Reagan administration was willing to take. In the absence of stronger Western support against Libya, the bombing of La Belle Disco sparked an airstrike by the United States that quieted Qadhafi's attacks, but for a short time only.

An attack on an airliner carrying Americans two years later showed that Qadhafi was not easily deterred from his dreams of rule by his Green Book. Increased sanctions against his support of the bombings of Western aircraft eventually led to his renunciation of terrorism and dismantling of his weapons of mass destruction programs. Qadhafi and his rule came to a violent end as part of the extended Arab Spring of 2011, in which numerous despotic regimes were overturned by popular uprisings.

Incident: On April 4, 1986, at 1:45 A.M., a 4.5-pound bomb placed near the dance floor destroyed La Belle Discotheque located in Friedenau in the West Berlin's Schoeneberg district. At the time of the explosion, about 500 people packed the discotheque. The blast blew a hole through the ceiling and the cellar below, and destroyed the walls. A female survivor recalled, "The lights suddenly went out and then a deafening explosion, and the ceiling and all these cables came down on my head and I thought, 'Oh, God, now I die.' There was blood all over, legs sticking out of the debris and people were walking on my head." The blast killed three people—Sgt. Kenneth Terrance Ford, 21; Nermine Haney, 28; and S. Sgt. James E. Goins, 26. The 231 wounded included 62 Americans, plus West Germans, Turks, and Arabs. Ford and Goins were U.S. servicemen; Haney was a Turkish woman.

On April 5, 1986, three groups claimed credit. One was the hitherto unknown Anti-American Liberation Front. The other two were the Holger Meins Commando, an offshoot of the Red Army Faction (RAF), and the RAF.

On April 7, 1986, Richard Burt, the U.S. ambassador to West Germany, told the *Today* show, "There is very clear evidence that there is Libyan involvement." Burt said that the evidence was "hard" that the perpetrator operated out of the Libyan People's Bureau in East Berlin.

On April 8, 1986, the United States gave decoded messages between Libya and its East Berlin embassy to the West German government. Prior to the attack, the intercepted messages appeared to indicate that an operation was planned. Following the attack, a message was received that appeared to offer praise for a job well done.

On April 8, 1986, the *Bild Zeitung* reported that a Libyan diplomat posted in East Berlin, Al-Amin 'Abdullah al-Amin, was suspected by West German police as having organized the bombing.

President Ronald Reagan said in an April 9, 1986, news conference that the United States was prepared to retaliate militarily if there was proof linking Libya to the discotheque bombing.

On April 11, 1986, U.S. officials told of a warning of an attack against U.S. servicemen in West Berlin. The officials said that the so-called warning came too late to alert military personnel.

On April 12, 1986, the United States, Britain, and France agreed to ban suspected terrorists from entering West Berlin from the east. A series of security measures were installed.

On April 14, 1986, U.S. war planes left air bases in Britain to launch retaliatory strikes against targets in Libya. The raid started on April 15, 1986, at 2:00 A.M. local time. U.S. government officials cited the La Belle bombing as motivating the strikes.

On April 20, 1986, West German police arrested Ahmed Nawaf Mansour Hasi, 35, as a suspect. Evidence gathered from the London-based investigation into the April 17, 1986, attempted bombing of an El Al plane by Nezar Hindawi led to the arrest of Hasi, the brother of Hindawi. During a police lineup, "about a hundred witnesses" present at the La Belle bombing identified Hasi as being at the discotheque, according to newspaper reports. During interrogation, Hasi admitted responsibility for the March 29, 1986, bombing of the Arab–German Friendship Society but denied any involvement in the La Belle bombing. Hasi's confession led to the arrest of two alleged accomplices—Farouk Salameh and Fayez Sahawneh—for the March 29, 1986, bombing. Hasi and Salameh were found guilty of the March 29, 1986, bombing but were never charged in the La Belle bombing.

On August 27, 1986, Italian police arrested Jordanian citizen Gassan Belbeasi, 25, on suspicion that he belonged to an international terrorist group linked to the Berlin bombing. Belbeasi, a student at the medical school of the University of Genoa, was questioned. His two roommates were also arrested and questioned.

On January 18, 1987, the *Berliner Morgenpost* reported that a letter found on Awni Hindawi, a cousin of Nezar Hindawi, suggested a link between Nezar Hindawi and Syrian contacts in the discotheque bombing.

On January 11, 1988, authorities arrested Kristine Endrigkeit in Lubeck, West Germany. She was charged with planting the bomb in La Belle Discotheque. According to authorities, she was following the orders of Hasi and Hindawi.

On April 19, 1993, the trial opened at the Twenty-Ninth Grand Criminal Bench of the Berlin Region Court, where Imad Mugniyah, 37, pleaded not guilty to charges of planning attacks on members of the U.S. military. The stateless Palestinian said that he would probably rely upon his right to remain silent in the case. He had been in custody since November 16, 1992. Prosecution lawyers accused Mugniyah of planning attacks on a U.S. military bus and on an unspecified bar frequented by U.S. soldiers in West Berlin in March 1986. Members of the Libyan People's Bureau (embassy) in East Berlin delivered weapons to his flat in West Berlin. Threats from Libya against the United States resulted in the police tightening controls and caused the would-be attackers to drop their plans. Instead, they set off an incendiary in La Belle.

In August 1993, German federal authorities began trying to obtain the extradition of stateless Palestinian Yusef Shuraydi, who was arrested in Lebanon, on charges of being involved in La Belle Disco attack. In 1986, he was a diplomat at the Libyan People's Bureau in East Berlin. In 1992, he was detained in Lebanon pending extradition.

On January 12, 1994, Beirut's *al-Diyar* identified him as Yasir al-Shuraydi (variant Shuraydi), a Palestinian being held in Tyre prison on charges of attempted murder and forgery. He could face other charges in seven pending cases. Several charges were dropped due to insufficient evidence. He was due to face public trial later that month. The paper noted:

> In 1983, when al-Shuraydi lived in Libya, Germany called on that country to extradite him. He was later implicated in the murder of a Libyan citizen called Mustafa al-'Ashiq. Al-Shuraydi, born in 1959 and a resident of 'Ayn al-Hulwah camp, hails from the al-Safsaf, a village in northern Palestine.

On June 21, 1994, a Sidon, Lebanon tribunal acquitted Shuraydi on charges of murdering a Libyan dissident in West Berlin in 1984. The chief witness recanted testimony.

On August 2, 1994, Lebanese authorities released Shuraydi to the consternation of the Germans, who claimed the Americans were slow in providing material crucial to the extradition request. The *Washington Post* reported that Stasi documents indicated that he had told a Lebanese court that he began working in 1984 as a driver in the East Berlin Libyan People's Bureau, which provided him with a Libyan passport for the alias Yussef Salam. German officials believed he was tied to Abu Nidal and the Popular Front for the Liberation of Palestine (PFLP). Stasi files noted that a planning meeting was held on March 26, 1986, in a Vienna Street apartment in West Berlin's Kreuzberg section.

Shuraydi was extradited from Lebanon to Germany on May 23, 1996, after Bonn agreed not to send him for trial to the United States or Turkey, where he faced the death penalty.

On June 17, 1996, former East German Stasi Lt. Col. Rainer Wiegand, the star witness against Shuraydi, died in a head-on collision with a meat truck in Portugal. Police suspected foul play.

On January 8, 1997, Greece said it would extradite Andrea Hausler, 31, in connection with the bombing. She was arrested in October 1996 at the request of German authorities while she was vacationing in the Chalkidiki resort near Thessaloniki. Justice Minister Evanghelos Yanopoulos signed the extradition order on January 7, 1997.

On February 7, 1997, state prosecutor Dieter Neumann accused the Libyan intelligence service of having instigated the bombing. Five people, including a Libyan, were indicted.

On August 25, 1997, Italian police arrested Musbah Abulgasem Eter, 40, a Libyan wanted in Germany and believed to be the only remaining fugitive with a direct role in the bombing. He had shown up at the German Embassy in Malta in 1995, offering to blame everything on Libya. He claimed he had seen cables between the Libyan People's Bureau and Said Rashid, the head of Libyan intelligence, who had also been tied to the 1988 bombing of Pan Am 103 over Lockerbie. Eter claimed Rashid ordered the bombing after U.S. planes sank two Libyan patrol boats in the Gulf of Sirte in March 1986. Eter said Shuraydi was the mastermind. Eter later flew to Libya unmolested. He flew to Berlin to await trial but ran off again. He was arrested in Rome at a hotel across from the Libyan Embassy, where he was found with a suitcase full of cash.

Shuraydi denied prosecution claims that he had been a member of the Popular Front for the Liberation of Palestine—General Command (PFLP-GC) since 1976. They said he had assassinated a Libyan exile in Berlin in 1984.

On November 18, 1997, Eter, two other Libyan Embassy employees, and two German sisters went on trial. The embassy employees were Ali Chanaa, 39, a German citizen of Lebanese origin, and Shuraydi, 39. The two German sisters were Ali's ex-wife Verena, 39, and Hausler. The charge sheet said Verena, accompanied by her sometime-prostitute sister, carried the bomb in her purse and planted it at the edge of the dance floor. They left five minutes before the explosion. Shuraydi and the Chanaas were charged with three counts of murder, nine counts of attempted murder, and causing a fatal blast. Eter and Hausler were charged as accessories. Everyone faced life in prison.

The Chanaas were apparently Stasi informants. Verena had been convicted of spying by a Berlin court in 1993. She had received 6,000 marks for carrying the bomb; Ali received 9,000 marks. Prosecutors said Shuraydi and Ali made the bomb; Eter passed the Libyan Embassy's money to them.

On December 2, 1997, Eter recanted his confession implicating the other defendants and Libya.

On November 13, 2001, German judge Peter Marhofer convicted and sentenced four defendants to 12–14 years for the bombing. He ruled that charges that Qadhafi ordered the bombing personally were not proven. Libya refused to extradite five other suspects.

Verena Chanaa was found guilty of murder and sentenced to 14 years. Hausler was acquitted. Shuraydi was convicted of multiple counts of attempted murder and sentenced to 14 years.

On August 10, 2004, Libya agreed to pay $35 million in compensation to 170 of the non-U.S. victims, including Germans who were wounded, and to the family of a Turkish woman who was killed. Libya refused to accept guilt, saying it was a "humanitarian gesture."

September 5, 1986
Pan Am 73 Hijacking

Overview: Terrorist hijackers from this era generally used their hostages for negotiations, at times killing one or more to establish their commitment to their negotiation position but with an eye to getting out of the situation alive and with some or all of their demands met. The Pan Am 73 incident was a rare case in which the terrorists turned their guns and grenades on the passengers before institution of a rescue operation by the authorities. Fatah renegade Abu Nidal's organization, using cover names such as Black June, often reached new levels of ferocity in their attacks and at times turned on their own members. Court testimony of the hijackers presaged the 9/11 use of airplanes as weapons; the terrorists had planned to explode the plane, with themselves in it, over Israel.

Incident: On September 5, 1986, the Libyan Revolutionary Cells and the Organization of the Soldiers of God–Martyr Zulfikar Ali Bhutto Group separately claimed credit when four gunmen took over Pan Am flight 73 (*Clipper Empress of the Seas*), a B-747 that had just loaded passengers at Karachi, Pakistan, airport at 5:55 A.M. The plane was to fly from Bombay to New York via Karachi and Frankfurt. The hijackers stormed aboard dressed in security guard uniforms, killing American crew member Rajesh Kumar and injuring two Pakistani baggage handlers. Kumar had objected to the terrorists' rough handling of the flight attendants. The hijackers shot him in the back of the head and threw him out of the plane. The three chief American crew members escaped out a hatch in the pilots' compartment, there by grounding the plane with 399 people, including 44 Americans, 16 Italians, 15 Britons, 12 West Germans, 84 Pakistanis, 195 Indians, and 16 crew.

The director general of Pakistan's civil aviation department established contact with the hijackers, who demanded to be flown to Larnaca where they wished to secure the release of their friends in Cyprus—Briton Ian Davison, 27; Syrian Khalid 'Abd al-Qadir al-Khatib, 28; and Jordanian 'Abdal-Hakim Sa'du al-Khalifah, 29, who were convicted of the massacre on September 25, 1985, of three Israelis on a yacht at Larnaca marina in Cyprus. The group threatened to kill one of the 399 on the plane every 10 minutes if their demands that the cockpit crew return were not met by 7:00 P.M. Air marshal Khurshid Anwar Mirza won an extension of the deadline of several hours at 6:30 P.M. when he promised that a new Pan Am crew was en route. The group also demanded the release from Cyprus of Amin Sulayman Za'rur, 25, from Lebanon, who was arrested on August 14, 1986, 10 days after the rocket and mortar attack on the U.K. base at Akrotiri, in which two servicemen's wives were slightly injured.

Cyprus and Iran refused to allow the plane to overfly their air space or to land.

The group was unable to find any American passports among those collected by the flight attendants—they had hidden the U.S. passports—but the hijackers selected that of a British school teacher from London, Michael John Thexton, 27, who they forced to come forward and stay with them for the next 14 hours.

One of the hijackers, who went around barechested and called himself Rambo, identified himself as Zeba Hamid and claimed that it was his birthday. Another hijacker forced passengers to walk to the bathroom on their knees.

As the hostage siege moved into evening, 16 hours after it began, the airplane's lights began to dim as main and auxiliary generators began to run out of power. Thinking that the Pakistanis might be planning a rescue raid, the hijackers herded all of the passengers into the front compartment at 9:20 P.M. A few minutes later, Zayd Hassan Abd al-Latif Masud al-Safarini (at first only known as Mustafa and later as Mohbar Hussain), the hijackers' leader, yelled, "Are you ready for the final episode? Prepare yourself! Jihad!" The hijackers then threw their grenades and fired two clips of ammunition into the hostages, killing 22 and injuring 100 others. An American passenger pushed a terrified flight attendant out of the way and opened one of the emergency doors. The passengers scrambled out of the plane.

Safarini, who had explosives strapped to his body, ordered one of his compatriots to shoot him in the stomach to set off the explosives and kill everyone else on board. His colleague missed, winging him, and then fled. Pakistani security forces arrested the four hijackers. Alessandra Bettolo, a student from Italy, and her friend from Milan, Michele Colombo, 21, pointed out a hijacker who was trying to escape by posing as a passenger. Passengers attacked the hijacker, but the police rescued and arrested him.

Pakistan claimed that it had sent a rescue squad, but some passengers disputed the claim. On September 14, 1986, the *Washington Post* reported that Pakistani snipers may have sparked the bloodbath by attempting to shoot the hijackers' leader through the cockpit windows, which the bullets could not pierce.

Twenty-five ambulances sped toward the plane, narrowly missing running over escaping passengers. Two of the ambulances carrying wounded passengers collided on the main road, injuring both drivers.

Autopsies determined that 10 passengers died from gunfire, 7 from grenade shrapnel, and 4 from injuries suffered as they leaped from the wing of the plane. Among those killed were 3 Americans, 13 Indians, 2 Pakistanis, a Mexican, and an unidentified child. The injured included Americans, an Indian, a West German, a Briton, an Australian, and an Italian.

Police arrested 100 Arabs residing in Pakistan for questioning.

Three of the hijackers were held at the Malir Army Base 4 miles from the Karachi airport. A fourth gunman unsuccessfully attempted to escape from the hospital.

The hijackers claimed after being arrested that they belonged to the International Revolutionary Organization. Safarini said he was a Palestinian and that two of the attackers were a Lebanese and a Syrian. A man with falsified Bahraini passport 250257 was also interrogated. Each hijacker gave six different names. Police learned that the hijackers purchased a Suzuki van in Karachi and were searching for its renter, a man named Joseph who met with Safarini several times. They had stayed in Karachi's Taj Mahal Hotel, where they paid for 19 days accommodation and had security uniforms tailored locally. President Zia ul-Haq said that three of the hijackers were 19, 23, and 25 years of age.

On September 8, 1986, the hijackers were charged with hijacking, murder, attempted murder, and several other crimes. They were identified in court as Bomar Hussein (Mustafa), Abdullah Khalil, Nasir Husain, and Fahad. All carried Bahraini passports.

On September 10, 1986, police arrested Wadoud Muhammad Hafiz al-Turki (known at the time as Salman Tariki or Sulman Taraqi), who had a valid Libyan passport with a visa obtained at the request of the Libyan People's Bureau and held a job with a maritime company that had offices in Tripoli. Hong Kong AFP reported that a companion of Turki fled into the Palestine Liberation Organization (PLO) office in Islamabad, but a PLO spokesman denied that his group was involved. (On September 13, 1986, PLO leader Yasir Arafat offered to help track down the attackers. Pakistan declined his offer.) Turki had been in Pakistan for six weeks, arriving from Larnaca, Cyprus, where the gunmen had demanded to be taken. Pakistan said that Turki had masterminded the assault by the four Palestinians, who grew up in the Lebanese refugee camps. The four traveled to Pakistan separately after arriving in the country two weeks before the hijacking. Turki and the leader arranged for weapons and cased the airport. Turki led the authorities to a cache of East European weapons on the coast near Karachi that had not been used.

The Civil Aviation Authority in Karachi reported on September 11, 1986, that threats had been made to hijack a Pakistan International Airlines jet to obtain the release of the four detained terrorists. On October 1, 1986, Pakistan's Federal Investigation Agency detained Yahya Abdus Salam, a Libyan commercial pilot trainee, who was suspected of being an associate of Turki.

Abu Nidal sent a message to Pakistani president Zia ul-Haq, denying that his group was involved.

On January 5, 1988, during their trial in a courtroom at Adiyala prison, the five accused hijackers (Safarini, Turki, Jamal Saeed Abdul Rahim, Muhammad Abdullah Khalil Hussain ar-Rahayyal, and Muhammad Ahmad al-Munawor) admitted taking over the plane with the intention of blowing it up over Israel after securing the release of Palestinians from Israeli prisons. However, they claimed that Pakistani commandos were responsible for the deaths of those on board and said that they had intended to release the passengers. In a statement read by the Pakistani defense counsel the group said:

> We came to Pakistan to hijack an American airplane to instantly draw the whole world's attention towards Palestine. Our aim was to hijack the plane, free all the hostages, and take the plane to various countries to get the release of 1,500 Palestinian freedom fighters. Our aim was to fly the plane toward some sensitive strategy center of the Zionist enemy and to blow it up with us inside. . . . We wanted to destroy the sensitive strategic center of the Zionists through an American weapon—the explosion of the American plane. By this we would have struck at American imperialism. We wanted to strike at both enemies with one weapon at one time.

They claimed that they became frustrated by alleged delaying tactics of the Pakistani commandos, who "attacked the airplane without caring for the lives of the innocent passengers on board except the Americans. It was done only to please America, although many innocent passengers . . . were killed." They claimed they chose the Pakistani location:

> due to the policies of the present regime, which maintains close relations with the great Satan, America . . . pro-American policies of this regime are detrimental not only to the Pakistani nation but to the Palestinian nation so. . . . All the Arab and Moslem governments maintain that they support the cause of Palestine. . . . In fact they support American imperialism and Israel. They declare they are friends of Palestine but the fact is that the jails of many Arab and Moslem countries are full of Palestinian prisoners.

On September 28, 2001, Abu Nidal member Safarini was arrested after his release from a Pakistani prison where he had served 14 years for hijacking the plane. The Kuwaiti-born Safarini shot U.S. passenger Rajesh N. Kumar in the head. President George Bush announced on

October 1, 2001, that he had been brought into Alaska and that he would be charged with murder. Safarini was arraigned in U.S. District Court on charges contained in a 126-count indictment issued in 1991. His trial began in federal court in Washington, D.C., in September 2001; he was accused of being the ringleader who ordered the other gunmen to shoot the passengers and throw grenades at them. Prosecutors sought the death penalty. On November 12, 2003, he pleaded guilty to the charges to avoid the death penalty. U.S. district judge Emmet G. Sullivan announced on December 16, 2003, that Safarini, 41, would be sentenced to life after Safarini pleaded guilty to 95 counts of murder, air piracy, and terrorism. On May 13, 2004, Safarini was given three consecutive life sentences plus 25 years. The judge recommended he be sent to a super-maximum security prison in Florence, Colorado, which also houses Unabomber Ted Kaczynski and 1993 World Trade Center bombing mastermind Ramzi Ahmed Yousef.

On January 9, 2010, Rahim, a Palestinian member of Abu Nidal with suspected al Qaeda ties, was killed in an air strike in North Waziristan, Pakistan. He had been tried and convicted in Pakistan in the Pan Am 73 attack, but he and three accomplices were freed in January 2008. The four made the Federal Bureau of Investigation's (FBI's) Most Wanted Terrorist List in 2009.

December 21, 1988
Lockerbie Bombing

Overview: The midair explosion of Pan Am 103 sparked one of the most puzzling whodunits in modern terrorism investigations. Initial theories looked at Iranian-sponsored Popular Front for the Liberation of Palestine— General Command (PFLP-GC) terrorists out for revenge for the shoot-down of an Iranian civil airliner in July 1988 by the USS *Vincennes*. Further investigation, however, pointed to two Libyans who worked at the behest of Qadhafi's intelligence service. The United States eventually decided that Libyan perfidy was once again at play, and Tripoli had earned its inclusion on the list of patron state sponsors of terrorism.

Incident: On December 21, 1988, a pressure-sensitive time bomb exploded on Pan Am flight 103 as it was flying from London to New York. The B-747 crashed into the Scotland town of Lockerbie, 15 miles north of the English border, killing all 258 on board plus 15 people in the town. Another 12 seriously burned villagers were hospitalized. The plane had left London's Heathrow Airport at 6:25 P.M. It disappeared from radar contact at 7:15 P.M. when it was cruising at 31,000 feet.

Investigators initially believed that the Iranian Revolutionary Guard Corps (IRGC) and the PFLP-GC were responsible for the attack. The Guardians of the Islamic Revolution claimed credit, saying it was retaliating for the downing in July of an Iranian airliner by a U.S. warship in which 290 people died. A spokesman for the IRGC also claimed credit, although Iran denied responsibility. Fadl Shrourou, chief spokesman for Ahmed Jibril, leader of PFLP-GC, denied responsibility, although some observers noted that 13 members of the group had been arrested in Frankfurt on October 27, 1988.

U.K. and U.S. investigators examined the theory that the bomb was unwittingly taken on board by Khalid Jaafer, 21, a U.S. citizen of Lebanese Shia origins, who was returning to Michigan after a visit to Lebanon and Frankfurt. They thought he may have carried the brown Samsonite bag containing the bomb, believing it contained heroin. He traveled from Beirut to Germany, where he stayed with a Lebanese friend who had a relative in Hizballah.

On December 21, 1989, Muhammad Abu Talib was sentenced by the Uppsala, Sweden, town court to life imprisonment for attempted murder and gross destruction dangerous to the public for setting off two bombs in Copenhagen in July 1985 against the synagogue and against the Northwest Orient Airlines office, in which one person was killed and several others injured. Talib was also suspected by British police of participating in the Lockerbie bombing. Believed to be a member of PFLP-GC, Talib was one of 14 Arabs arrested on October 26, 1988, in Neuss, West Germany, where police found a weapons cache. The cache included altitude-sensitive detonators and three bombs built into Toshiba Bombeat 453 radio-cassette recorders. The Lockerbie bomb fragments exactly matched these components.

A fragment of the detonator found in the Scottish countryside differed from the Neuss cache. The Pan Am 103 detonator lacked an altimeter and had only a timer. This type of detonator matched timers seized from two Libyan intelligence agents arrested in Dakar, Senegal, in February 1988 on an Air Afrique flight en route to the Ivory Coast.

Bits of clothing in the suitcase in which the bomb exploded were traced to a clothing shop in Malta, a hangout for Libyans. The shopkeeper recalled selling it in November 1988 to a man with a Libyan accent. Investigators suspected the suitcase was sent to Frankfurt via Air Malta flight 180, then transferred unaccompanied to Pan Am 103.

On June 26, 1991, French authorities announced evidence that senior Libyan officials, including Abdullah Senoussi, Qadhafi's brother-in-law and de facto chief of Libyan intelligence, and Moussa Koussa, vice minister of foreign affairs, were involved in the September 1989 French UTA bombing and the bombing of Pan Am 103.

On November 14, 1991, a federal grand jury in Washington issued 193 felony counts against Libyan intelligence officers Abdel Basset Ali al-Megrahi, 39, and Lamen Khalifa Fhimah, 35. They were accused of planting and detonating the bomb and were believed to be in Libya. The U.S. indictment included 189 counts for killing the 189 U.S. citizens. It also included one count of conspiracy, one count of putting a destructive device on a U.S. civil aircraft resulting in death, one count of destroying a U.S. civil aircraft with an explosive device, and one count of destroying a vehicle in foreign commerce. The United Kingdom issued similar arrest warrants.

Authorities said the evidence was built up after FBI agents and Scottish police combed 845 square miles of territory. One clue was part of the Toshiba's circuit board. Another was part of a timing device traced to Meister and Bollier, a Zurich-based Swiss company that had sold it in a consignment of 20 prototypes made in 1985–1986 to a high-level Libyan intelligence official. Moreover, according to the State Department, the Pan Am 103 bomb had been activated by a sophisticated electronic timer, in contrast to the PFLP-GC bombs, which had altimeter switches and relatively crude timers.

On December 4, 1991, Libya's new intelligence chief, Col. Yusuf al-Dabri, announced the detention of Megrahi and Fhimah. The United States and United Kingdom demanded their extradition, but Qadhafi declined.

On December 8, 1991, Libya announced that it would try the two men charged by U.S. and U.K. authorities and that it would deliver the death penalty if they were found guilty.

On December 29, 1991, the *Washington Post* cited a CNN report that a Libyan who defected to the United States could serve as a witness in the case, testifying that Fhimah fabricated the Air Malta luggage tags. He was in the Justice Department's Witness Protection Program and was living under an assumed identity on the West Coast. The low-level defector, who did not have an intelligence affiliation, obtained Fhimah's Malta diary. The December 15, 1988, diary entry said, "Take tags from Air Malta." The defector had arrived in the United States several months earlier, but had left some family members in Libya. He could be eligible for up to $4 million in a federal reward system.

On January 14, 1992, Libya proposed that an international commission of legal experts decide whether the UN Security Council should rule on who was responsible for the UTA and Pan Am cases. Maj. Abdul Salaam Jalloud said that his government would abide by the decision of such a panel, although Libya questioned whether the United Nations had jurisdiction.

On January 20, 1992, the UN Security Council strengthened draft Resolution 731 urging Libya to surrender the six suspects wanted for the Pan Am and UTA bombings. The resolution, which passed unanimously on January 21, 1992, included a lead role for UN secretary general Boutros Boutros-Ghali and called for a "full and effective response" to requests for the suspects. Libya denounced the resolution as an infringement on its sovereignty.

On March 31, 1992, the UN Security Council imposed via Resolution 748 an air and arms embargo on Libya, which took effect on April 15, 1992, when Libya refused to hand over the duo. The sanctions were far milder than those in place against Iraq and permitted oil exports. Libya thus became the sixth country in UN history to be hit with sanctions, joining Rhodesia, South Africa, Iraq, Yugoslavia, and Somalia.

On May 6, 1992, the Argentine interior ministry canceled the residence permit and Argentine passport granted to Syrian citizen Monzer al-Kassar, 46, accused narcoterrorist and weapons smuggler. He was also suspected of financing the Lockerbie bombing. Buenos Aires *Clarin* reported that the Israeli secret service was following an "al-Kassar clue" regarding the March 17, 1992, bombing of the Israeli Embassy in Buenos Aires. On June 3, 1992, officers of Spain's general intelligence department arrested al-Kassar and two other men as they were deplaning at Madrid–Barajas airport as they arrived on a flight from Vienna.

On September 28, 1993, Lord Macaulay suggested that an international court be set up to deal with such cases. It would have judges from Libya, the United Kingdom, the United States, and France, and it would be chaired by a judge from another country. The prosecution could be conducted by Scotland's lord advocate and the U.S. attorney general.

On September 29, 1993, Libyan foreign minister Omar Muntasser told UN secretary general Boutros-Ghali that it would turn over the duo to Scotland.

On January 23, 1994, the *London Observer* reported that Edwin Bollier, who had changed his testimony on the timers, admitted receiving expenses from Libya to include his travel to and from Libya, hotel bills there, and telephone and fax expenses, as well as Lockerbie-related legal bills. He also hoped Libya would pick up the £1.2 million in lost business Mebo had suffered.

On March 23, 1995, the FBI announced a $4 million reward for the capture of the two Libyans and placed them on its Ten Most Wanted List.

On March 31, 1995, the UN Security Council extended the sanctions against Libya. U.S. UN ambassador Madeleine K. Albright urged other nations to join in an oil embargo. The council reviewed the sanctions every 120 days. No formal vote was taken on the automatic extension. On October 29, 1988, the UN Security Council, for the 20th time in seven years, extended the sanctions against Libya.

The United Nations and the Libyans eventually agreed to a trial to be hosted by the International Court of Justice in The Hague using Scottish law with a Scottish judge. On April 5, 1999, the Libyans handed over the duo to UN officials, who took them to Camp Zeist outside The Hague. Their arrival automatically suspended the sanctions against Libya. The two appeared in court the next day charged with murder, conspiracy to commit murder, and violations of international aviation security laws. The trial opened on May 3, 2000.

On January 31, 2001, the court found Megrahi guilty of murder; he lost an appeal on March 14, 2002. Fhimah was acquitted and immediately returned to a hero's welcome in Libya. The court said the Libyan government was involved in planning and carrying out the bombing. Megrahi was sentenced to life in prison with the possibility of parole after 20 years. The court cited the identification of the Swiss-made Mebo MST-13 timer as a key piece of evidence linking the bomb to the Libyans. Testimony of a prosecution witness was deemed not credible enough to link Fhimah to the blast.

On August 15, 2003, Libya formally accepted responsibility and agreed to pay as much as $10 million to each victim's family. The first $4 million would be paid upon lifting of UN sanctions, the next $4 million after the United States lifted sanctions, and the final money after the State Department removed Libya from the patron state list. On September 20, 2004, President Bush lifted the ban on commercial air service to Libya and released $1.3 billion in frozen Libyan assets. Libya was expected to use $1 billion of the money to compensate the families. On June 26, 2006, Libya announced that it was no longer legally bound to its agreement to make final payments of $2 million each to the families of the victims. Libya said that although it had recently been dropped from the State Department's list of terrorism sponsors, the United States had until the end of 2004 to do so to and thereby trigger the final payment.

On December 19, 2003, Libya announced that it would abandon weapons of mass destruction, freeze its nuclear program, and permit international inspectors into the country.

On August 4, 2008, President Bush directed the State Department to settle the final lawsuits against Libya in the bombing. Libya would receive immunity from future proceedings once compensation was paid.

Megrahi, claiming to have three months to live from terminal prostate cancer, was permitted to return to Libya on August 20, 2009. He gave a media interview from his death bed in October 2011. The following month, U.S. State Department said it would make a formal request for extradition. Meghrahi died at his home in Tripoli, Libya, on May 20, 2012.

September 19, 1989
French Airline UTA 772 Bombing

Overview: While the Pan Am 103 bombing received greater publicity in the United States, the Libyan hand was also seen behind the bombing of a French airline Union des Transports Aériens (UTA) plane from Chad that killed 171 people. Libya government officials eschewed responsibility, but Tripoli ultimately paid millions in compensation to the victims' families.

Incident: On September 19, 1989, the Clandestine Chadian Resistance claimed credit for setting off a bomb in French UTA flight 772, a DC-10 flying from N'djamena to Paris, killing all 171 passengers and crew when it crashed in eastern Niger's Tenere Desert.

Among the dead were 49 Congolese, 29 Chadians, and French passengers. All of the crew were French. There were eight children, including three infants, on board. The victims included seven Americans, including Bonnie Pugh, wife of Robert L. Pugh, U.S. ambassador to Chad. Mrs. Pugh was traveling to help plan the wedding of her daughter in October. Also on the plane was Margaret Schutzius, 23, a Peace Corps volunteer who had completed a two-year tour in Chad as an English teacher; Patrick Huff, 38, of Franklin Texas; Donald Warner, 25, of Terry, Montana, of Parker Drilling Company; and Mihai Ali Manestianu. Also on board were James Turlington, 48, of Bellville, Texas, and Mark Corder, 35, of Houston, who had worked for Esso and an Exxon subsidiary.

The dead included Dominique Mavoungou, managing director of Congo's Housing Promotion and Management Company; his wife; child; and seven members of another family. Other victims were the leader of Congo's theatrical troupe, Roca do Zulu; Jean-Pierre Klein of France; the daughter of Jean-Michel Bokamba Yangouma, secretary general of the Congolese Trade Union Confederation; and son of Norbert Dabira, secretary of the Central Committee of the ruling Congolese Labour Party. One of the Frenchmen, Jacques Renaudat, 53, had been alleged to be trafficking arms. Mahamat Soumahila, Chad's minister for planning and cooperation, also died. Two British employees of Parker Drilling perished. The Capuchin Roman Catholic order announced in Lucerne that Monsignors Antoine Gervais Aeby, who heads the order in Switzerland, and Gabriel Balet, a Swiss bishop in Chad, were on the flight. Also dead was the brother of Renaud Denoix de Saint Marc, the French government's secretary general.

Reports said 77 of the 155 passengers boarded the plane in Brazzaville.

The group sent a typewritten statement in French to a Western news agency in Beirut saying that the "struggle will continue until the total departure of colonial military troops from Africa." Shia Muslim activists in Africa were suspected.

French authorities denigrated two telephoned claims by callers from the Islamic Jihad. One caller demanded the release of Sheikh Abdul Karim Obeid, the Shi'ite cleric who was captured by Israel in 1989, in southern Lebanon. The caller accused the French government of sharing information on him with Israel.

The flight began in Brazzaville, Congo, and was flying to Charles de Gaulle Airport in Paris. *Le Parisien* and *Liberation* reported that 10 kilograms of Semtex plastic explosives were planted on the plane's fuel tanks in Brazzaville.

On September 22, 1989, the French government denied reports that it had received warnings of the attack. On September 15, 1989, the Lebanese magazine *Ash Shiraa* had quoted pro-Iranian Islamic militants as accusing France of reneging on a May 1988 deal that led to the release of three French hostages in Lebanon. The group threatened to attack French interests in Africa.

On October 1, 1989, Hamburg's *Bild Am Sonntag* claimed that Libyan leader Mu'ammar Qadhafi paid the killers and provided the Semtex-H to the PFLP-GC. *Bild* reported that Libyan diplomats provided cash to PFLP offices in France, Spain, Yugoslavia, and Romania for explosives, weapons, plane tickets, hotels, and expenses.

The paper said Qadhafi was getting back at the French for aiding the Chadians in their border skirmishes with Libya. *Bild* attributed the UTA and Lockerbie bombings to Palestinian engineer Muhamad al-'Umari (alias Abu Ibrahim), founder of the terrorist group 15 May in 1979. He was the first to develop an easily moldable explosive that cannot be identified by the X-ray instruments at airports and explodes in planes through self-ignition with the help of an altimeter.

The next day, Libreville's *Africa No. One* cited Rene Lapautre, UTA's managing director, as saying that the bomb was placed on the plane in Brazzaville in a sugar container in the front baggage compartment.

On October 6, 1989, Salah Khalaf (alias Abu Iyad), the PLO's number two, told *Le Journal Du Dimanche* that Iranians were cooperating with the PFLP-GC, who had been involved in the bombing.

On October 31, 1989, Gabon's *Africa No. One* reported that a Samsonite attaché case was discovered with a double depth lining with deposits of 150–300 grams of pentryl between the layers. The bomb had a simple quartz alarm clock for a detonator to automatically set off the explosion at 10,000 meters. The paper noted that the suitcase was the same as used in the February 1985 attack on the British Marks and Spencer store in Paris. The perpetrator, arrested a year later, was Habib Amal. While awaiting sentencing, he admitted to being a member of Abu Ibrahim's group of Fatah dissidents, which was linked to Hizballah.

On August 25, 1990, Paris AFP reported that a trio of Congolese armed by Libyan diplomats placed the bomb. *Le Point* quoted investigating judge Jean-Louis Bruguiere as concluding that the mastermind was a Libyan diplomat in Brazzaville, Abdallah al-Azrag. AFP added that one of the passengers, Apollinaire Mangatany, had taken explosives training in Libya. It was not clear whether he was one of the nine passengers who deplaned in Ndjamena. In January 1990, according to *Le Point*, Congolese police arrested Mangatany's friend, Bernard Yanga, who had taken him to the Brazzaville airport. Yanga confessed, and provided the name of accomplice Jean-Bosco Ngalina, believed to have gone to Zaire. Yanga told French and Congolese authorities that Mangatany was to leave the plane in Chad, where the bomb was to explode on the tarmac, mimicking a 1984 attack.

On October 26, 1990, the Zairian paper *Elima* reported that Ngalina had been arrested two weeks earlier and held in the Kinshasa central prison of Makala on suspicion of masterminding the bombing. He fled to Zaire immediately after the bomb was planted on the plane. He was arrested after 12 investigators from Zaire, Paris, and Interpol finished their work. The paper reported that he had confessed to fabricating the bomb. Jean-Louis Bruguiere, a French examining magistrate, arrived in Kinshasa on October 25, 1990, to hear Ngalina's case. Paris AFP reported that Ngalina was a native of Zaire's Equateur Province, from which President Mobutu hailed.

On June 26, 1991, French authorities announced that it had evidence that senior Libyan officials, including Abdullah Senoussi, Qadhafi's brother-in-law and de facto chief of Libyan intelligence, and Moussa Koussa, vice minister of foreign affairs, were involved in the UTA bombing and the 1988 bombing of Pan Am 103. Attacks against U.S. and French targets were discussed at a meeting at Libyan intelligence headquarters in Tripoli in September 1988. *L'Express* cited the confessions of two terrorists who took part in the UTA bombing. Judge Bruguiere was near to issuing charges against the Libyans. The UTA bomb was reportedly brought into the Congo in a Libyan diplomatic pouch and delivered to the three Congolese by an official of the Libyan Embassy in Brazzaville. Mangatany brought it onto the plane. Fragments of the bomb led investigators to believe that it was one of five bought by the Libyans from terrorist bomb-maker Abu Ibrahim in the mid-1980s.

On October 30, 1991, Bruguiere issued arrest warrants for Senoussi; 'Abdallah al-Azraq, Libya's chief diplomat in Brazzaville who also led Libyan intelligence there; and Ibrahim Naeli and Musbah Arbas, two members of the Libyan intelligence service. Naeli left Brazzaville on the day of the bombing. All four were charged with violations of French law by conspiring to commit murder, destroying property with explosives, and taking part in a terrorist enterprise. Bruguiere also issued wanted notices for Koussa and 'Abdessalam Zadma, No. 3 in the Libyan intelligence service and chief of Qadhafi's bodyguards. The United States was also investigating a Libyan intelligence official named Mohammed Naydi, who at times used the name Naeli. (Naydi and another Libyan intelligence officer were arrested in February 1988 in Dakar, Senegal, but released four months later. They were carrying timers which matched the Pan Am timer. Clothing found in the bombed-out suitcase was purchased in a Silema, Malta, clothing shop by one of Naydi's lieutenants.)

On January 13, 1992, at Cotonou, Benin, police arrested French citizen Ahmed Bouzid in the UTA investigation.

Yanga showed up at the French Embassy in Kinshasa, Zaire, on March 18, 1992, saying that he was ready to help with inquiries. He had been arrested early in 1990, after which he had accused the Libyan chargé d'affaires in Brazzaville of giving him explosives, which were made into a parcel and then handed to a passenger later thought to have left the plane during a stop in Chad. Yanga named two Congolese as his accomplices. All three were members of an opposition party financed by Libya. Yanga later retracted his accusations against Abdallah Elazragh, the Libyan chargé. On the basis of his evidence and other findings, however, Bruguiere issued an international arrest warrant against four Libyans in October 1991.

On February 3, 1993, Congolese police arrested Mohamed Emali, managing director of the Congolese Arab Libyan Lumber Company, in a Brazzaville hotel. He was released on February 11, 1993, after interrogation by French and Congolese police.

On December 1, 1994, French authorities detained Libyan intelligence officer Ali Omar Mansour for questioning in the UTA case. Bruguiere ordered him released on December 5, 1994.

Bruguiere visited Libya on July 5–18, 1996, and questioned 40 people.

On March 10, 1999, a French antiterrorism court sentenced in absentia Abdesslam Issa Shibani; Abdesslam Mamouda, who purchased the bomb timer in Germany; Senoussi; Elazragh; Ibrahim Naeli; and Arbas to life in prison.

On July 16, 1999, Libya gave $33 million to France to compensate families of the victims. On January 9, 2004, the Qadhafi Foundation said it would add $170 million in compensation in four installments.

The 1990s

The final decade of the millennium saw a new tactic tried by Western governments—renditions of terrorists. Rather than await foot dragging and recalcitrant governments to arrest and extradite terrorists, many of whom enjoyed substantial freedom of movement on the turf of sympathetic and/or cowed regimes, fedup terrorist targets took the battle to the perpetrators. With a series of stings and straightforward extrajudicial operations, Western governments quietly snatched terrorists off the streets, from their yachts, and from their safe houses and whisked them off to Western jails for trial on a host of charges.

The 1990s saw perhaps the most diverse group of perpetrators of the *worst*, including Latin American leftists, classical Irish Republican Army (IRA) separatists, radical and religious-based Palestinians, right-wing bands, dispossessed Third Worlders with no clearly articulated ideology, radical Islamists, oddball cults, separatist Chechens, and the rise of what became the most well-known terrorist group of the new millennium—al Qaeda.

The decade saw the use on a mass scale of chemical weapons by a terrorist group against the Tokyo subways. Aum Shin Rikyo explored the use of a host of nontraditional weapons—biological, chemical, and nuclear—and by example established that causing widespread deaths and injuries via this type of weapon was now a viable part of a terrorist arsenal.

The fledgling al Qaeda established a reputation for willingness to attack major targets, be they supposedly hardened embassies or symbols of Western wealth, and to continue to do so until they succeeded. Transient initial failures to set off bombs and create mass casualties just meant a return to the drawing board and recruitment of a new batch of willing bombers. Al Qaeda's operations in the 1990s showed tremendous patience for planning, logistics, fund-raising, recruitment, and surveillance of targets, often taking years of attention to detail.

The decade also saw a more difficult challenge to the defense forces—the rise of the suicide bomber. Although known in the West mostly as a Middle Eastern phenomenon with initial attacks against Israelis and down the road against Westerners, the technique was used throughout the world, most notably by Sri Lanka Liberation Tigers of Tamil Eelam, whose rolls of suicide bombers included women, heretofore not known for taking their lives in no-return operations.

March 17, 1992
Buenos Aires Israeli Embassy Bombing

Overview: The 1994 bombing of the Argentine–Israel Mutual Aid Society (AIMA) in Buenos Aires and the 1992 bombing of the Israeli Embassy illustrated the global reach of jihadis. Concerns about the South America triborder area—home to a large Lebanese expatriate population—serving as a safe haven and jumping-off point for Palestinian terrorists appeared justified when these two attacks occurred. Their investigation was headed by a determined judge, although progress was slight in the intervening years.

Incident: On March 17, 1992, at 2:47 P.M., a Ford Fairlane with 100 kilograms of explosives detonated at the Israeli Embassy in Buenos Aires, Argentina, killing 29 people and injuring 252. Windows were shattered within a five-block radius. Many of the injured, including several children in a school yard across the street, were hit by flying glass from a school, a museum, an apartment house, a church, a senior citizens' center, and other embassies and buildings. Only a corner of the three-story building remained standing. At least 20 cars were gutted. Gas mains were ruptured, forcing government officials to cut power to the area for fear of sparking another explosion.

The blast killed 10 Israelis, including 2 diplomats and the wives of 2 others. The rest were Argentines and one Uruguayan passerby.

Argentine president Carlos Menem blamed "a suicide commando" and attributed the bombing to an Argentine Islamic convert. He had also suggested involvement by individuals who staged a failed coup on December 3, 1990.

On March 19, 1992, the Islamic Jihad Organization (IJO) claimed credit, saying that this was Operation Child Martyr Husayn—the son of Sayyid 'Abbas al-Musawi, the prince of the Islamic resistance martyrs. The statement, heard on Ba'labaak Voice of the Oppressed, attributed the attack to Abu Yasir, an Argentine who converted to Islam. On March 23, 1992, the IJO in Beirut reaffirmed that it was responsible. Accompanying the Arabic typewritten statement was a video showing the embassy building before the suicide operation. IJO said that it was retaliating for Israel commandos killing Hizballah leader Musawi.

On March 25, 1992, the Palestine Liberation Organization (PLO) representative in Brasilia denied involvement, as had a Palestinian spokesman in Buenos Aires. The Buenos Aires magazine *Noticias* claimed that the Chui Palestine colony in Rio Grande do Sul, 600 kilometers from Argentina, may have served as a stopover for the terrorists. The magazine noted that PLO representative Ahmad Subhi visited the colony the previous week.

On March 20, 1992, Juan Carlos Montero, a spokesman for the Uruguayan interior ministry, said that Annette Klump was in Uruguay until four or five days before the bombing. She might have crossed over into Argentina via the bridge linking Fray Bentos, Uruguay, with Puerto Unzua, Argentina, 300 kilometers northwest of Montevideo. Her sister, Andrea Martina Klump, 34, is believed to be an explosives expert for the German Red Army Faction. Andrea was wanted in Germany for a 1989 bombing that killed a German banker. The German government had offered a $47,000 reward for her capture. The next day, Annette and the Argentine interior ministry denied involvement of the women.

On March 21, 1992, the federal police antiterrorist brigade raided a downtown apartment in Bulnes Street 260 and arrested four men for possible involvement. Chief Justice Ricardo Levene, Jr. ordered the release of four Pakistani citizens on March 23, 1992. The Pakistanis had testified before Court Secretary Alfredo Bisordi. A taxi driver, an eyewitness to the case, was unable to identify them in the police lineup. Their release order was suspended after chemical tests on their clothing indicated the presence of suspicious substances. The four were released on March 28, 1992, for lack of evidence, although charges had not been dropped. Mohammed Azam, Mohammed Nawaz, Mohammed Nawaz Chaudhary, and Azhar Igbal appeared shaken as they climbed into a Fiat Duna outside the courthouse with attorneys Federico Figueroa and Jorge Kent.

Police were still searching for the Pakistani owner of the apartment. He was abroad, although his Argentine wife was in town. Police were also looking for the former valet of Pakistani ambassador Raja Trivid Roy. The valet was reported to have driven by the embassy on a motorcycle at a high speed minutes before the blast. Some of his documents were found in the raided apartment.

Federal Police and Secretariat for State Intelligence officials said that an individual carrying a false Brazilian passport purchased the pickup truck used to trigger the explosionby.

The next day, United Press International (UPI) reported the arrest of five men and a woman in a city 300 kilometers north of Buenos Aires.

Teams removing rubble discovered that the embassy's armory was intact. They extracted 15 Uzi submachine guns, 10 handguns, and 1,000 bullets, all of which matched a list provided by the ambassador. This disproved the view that there were explosives inside the armory. Meanwhile, rescuers gave up on finding more survivors; the raps heard the previous day were not heard again.

Observers searched for reasons why the attack took place on Argentine soil. Some noted that Argentina has the largest Jewish population in Latin America, estimated at 300,000, along with 1 million people of Arab descent. Argentina also participated in Operation Desert Storm.

On March 27, 1992, Tel Aviv's *Yedi'ot Aharonot* claimed that the Iranian Embassy had assisted the Hizballah terrorists. On March 31, 1992, Hizballah secretary general Hasan Nasrallah denied that his group was involved. The previous day, Sheikh Husayn al-Musawi, head of the Islamic Amal Movement, also denied Hizballah involvement.

On March 29, 1992, *Noticias Argentinas* reported that police in several countries were searching for a former Argentine military man and a Brazilian citizen for their involvement. They were on a list of 10 suspects still at large. Eight fugitives were of Arab descent. The Argentine had reportedly traveled to the Middle East several times in the last two years. The Brazilian was identified as Elias Ribeiro da Luz, who on February 21, 1992, had purchased the station wagon that carried the explosives at a Villa Luro dealership for $3,000.

On March 31, 1992, Border Guards experts told the Supreme Court that the bomb was made of nitrogen triiodide, one of the most powerful explosives known, which is manufactured only in France. This report contradicted that made by the Federal Police, which said the bomb was made of pentrite.

The same day, retired Maj. Arnaldo Luis Bruno denied press reports linking him to the blast.

On May 2, 1992, Ecuadoran police detained seven suspected Middle Eastern terrorists in Quito in connection with the blast. Six Iranian citizens, including two women, and a seventh man who used an Italian passport but was believed to be Iraqi, were identified by Interpol as Hizballah terrorists. Their passports were issued to Iranian citizens Mohammad Reza, Maryan Remesani, Siamac Adjitchac, Maryan Morak, Saragot Sardi, Abumason Sali, and Italian citizen Bertan Valentino. *Noticias Argentinas* later reported that they intended to go to Canada via the United States.

The seven boarded a Lufthansa flight in Frankfurt, Germany, earlier in the week. Interpol officials in Germany alerted counterparts in Venezuela, Colombia, and Ecuador, where the flight stopped. The seven bought tickets to Quito but attempted to deplane in Bogota, Colombia. A heavily armed police contingent forced them back on the flight. They were arrested upon deplaning in Quito. Interpol said that Islamic extremists were targeting the Israeli ambassador in Bogota and an Israeli-owned business in Cali. On May 9, 1992, the Crime Investigation Division in Quito said that the group was not involved in the bombing but would be deported to Iran through Bogota and Caracas anyway. The Iranians said that on the date of the attack, they were in Iran and had left Iran due to restrictions on freedom in that country. As no country had outstanding charges against them, they were released on May 12, 1992, and given 17 hours to leave the country.

On May 6, 1992, the Border Police ruled out the suicide commando theory, saying that no human remains were found in the car. The police said that the bomb contained between 55 and 60 kilograms of exogenous explosives and plasticizers, and that the perpetrator escaped along Arroyo Street toward Suipacha Street. Police also said that the bomb was in the left side of the bed of a pickup truck. The terrorist evaded the embassy's two cameras and walked along Arroyo, Suipacha, and Juncal Streets.

On June 4, 1992, at Marbella, Spain, police arrested Mundhir al-Kassar, a Syrian believed to have financed the attack and who was also linked to drug deals and arms trafficking. He was held by Judge Garzon in Spain. A Mendoza investigating judge was preparing an extradition request. Police searches uncovered arms, jewels, and cars with false registration plates. The next day, three other people were arrested in Marbella in the al-Kassar case. Searches of homes in Madrid, Malaga, and Marbella yielded arms, passports, and false vehicle registration plates. Al-Kassar had obtained Argentine citizenship through questionable procedures. Al-Kassar's brother, Ghassan, had been expelled from Argentina to Spain on May 20, 1992, for having a false Brazilian passport.

On May 1, 1993, *EFE News* reported that the terrorists were trained in countries bordering Argentina, including Paraguay.

On May 4, 1993, police in Asuncion, Paraguay, reported that they had no information that the Lebanese Shi'ites involved in the attack had trained in Paraguay.

On July 27, 1995, Argentina federal judge Roberto Marquevich released six Lebanese and a Brazilian who had been extradited from Paraguay on July 23, 1994, in connection with the discovery of an arsenal near Buenos Aires. The judge said there was no connection between the group and the cache discovered in 1994 in the possession of former Argentine intelligence agent Alejandro Sucksdorf. Three of the seven admitted to pro-Hizballah sentiments, but denied involvement in the embassy bombing or the July 18, 1994, bombing of an Argentina–Israeli facility. The suspects were identified as Sergio Rodrigo Salem, Luis Alberto Nader, Johannie Moraes Baalbaki, Mohammed Hassan Alayan, Fadi Abdul Karim Chekair, Roberto Riveiro (or Ribiero) Ruiz, and Brazilian citizen Valdirene Vieira Ferguglia.

On May 19, 1998, the Argentine government expelled seven Iranian Embassy officials and detained another eight Iranian civilians in Buenos Aires for interrogation. Absolhassem Mesbahi, an Iranian defector, had claimed that former Iranian cultural attaché Mohsen Rabbani was the bombing planner.

On December 5, 1998, Argentina issued an arrest warrant for Imad Mughniyeh, a Hizballah leader, believed to have ordered the bombing. Mughniyeh was killed on February 12, 2008 by a car bomb in Damascus, Syria.

The bombing remains an open case.

February 26, 1993
World Trade Center Bombing

Overview: New York City's World Trade Center (WTC) was a symbol for many terrorists of American economic might, and by extension, its cultural and political reach. Jihadi terrorists saw its potential destruction as a major psychological boost in their war for the fealty of the ummah. Homegrown Islamist radicals, led by a radical Egyptian preacher, pre-saged al Qaeda as an organization and developed a daring plan to attack the WTC, UN building, New York subway, and other landmarks. The not-quite-successful WTC bombing led to their arrest by federal officials before the rest of the plot could be put into play. Al Qaeda established that it would not rest until its goal had been achieved. Although it took more than eight years of patient planning, it achieved the aims of its pre-decessors with the 9/11 attack.

Incident: On February 26, 1993, 7 people, including 4 Port Authority workers, were killed and more than 1,000 injured when a car bomb ex-ploded 17 minutes after noon in the garage of the WTC in New York City. The bomb left a crater measuring 100 feet in diameter and 60 feet deep in the three-story garage. Shock waves collapsed the ceiling of the Port Authority Trans-Hudson (PATH) metro station underneath the complex.

At least 50,000 people fled the 110-story building as black smoke quickly filled all floors. Emergency power supplies went out, plunging the build-ings into darkness and preventing alarms from going off. The building's operating control center was just above the garage, where the blast was centered. Some people smashed windows so they could breathe. Helicop-ters were called in to rescue people trapped on the roof. Seven schoolchil-dren were trapped in elevators for hours when the power went off.

Nearly 750 firefighters—the equivalent of a 16-alarm fire—along with 40 percent of the city's firefighting equipment responded, as did hundreds of other police and federal law enforcement officers. Firefighters found steam pipes bursting, cars burning, concrete walls collapsing, support col-umns buckling, and miles of electric cables strewn randomly over floor and ceiling. The force of the bomb was magnified, because it was con-tained inside the huge structure.

New York Downtown Hospital treated 139 people, primarily for smoke inhalation, laceration, and burns. St. Vincent's Hospital in Greenwich Vil-lage treated 103 patients, including one with a fractured hip and one with cardiac arrest. One was pronounced dead on arrival. Bellevue Hospital said that 2 of 53 patients under its care were in serious condition; 1 was in critical condition.

Police received 56 phone calls claiming credit. No calls were made prior to the explosion.

One letter claiming credit for the previously unknown Liberation Army Fifth Battalion was received by the *New York Times* four days after the bombing. It was believed to have been written by Nidal A. Ayyad, a Palestinian chemical engineer born in Kuwait, who was later charged with the bombing. The original text of the letter was found on one of Ayyad's computer disks. Saliva on the envelope containing the letter was traced to Ayyad. The letter demanded the United States to stop all military, economical, and political aid to Israel; stop all diplomatic relations with Israel; and stop interfering with any Middle East countries' interior affairs.

On March 4, 1993, the Federal Bureau of Investigation (FBI) charged Mohammed A. Salameh, 26, a Jordanian-born Palestinian living in Jersey City, with, according to the charge sheet, "aiding and abetting" the bombing "by use of an explosive device causing the death of at least five individuals." The handyman was arrested that morning after investigators determined that he had rented the bomb-carrying Ford Econoline van on February 23, 1993. Police searching his apartment found bomb-making equipment and explosives residue. Salameh had given the apartment's address on the van rental slip found at the Ryder truck rental agency in Jersey City. Several hours after the bombing, He returned to the agency with a companion and reported that the Econoline E-350 had been stolen from a nearby grocery store parking lot. He also went to a Jersey City police station to report the theft. Investigators had found pieces of the van in the rubble, saw it listed in the nationwide computer directory of stolen vehicles, and followed the lead to Ryder trucks and ultimately to Salameh. The rental documents had traces of chemical nitrates, which are often found in explosives. When Salameh returned to the agency with the police documents confirming that the van had been stolen, he asked for return of the $400 security deposit. The FBI arrested him as he walked to a nearby bus stop.

The FBI linked Salameh to a rental space at the Space Station Self Storage area in Jersey City. Employees identified him as a man who rented a shed in November 1992 using the name Kamal Ibraham. When the unit was searched on March 5, 1993, agents discovered several hundred pounds of urea and nitric acid that, if combined and triggered correctly, could produce an explosion. Kamal Ibraham had also purchased the chemicals in November 1992. Employees said that the day before the bombing, they saw Salameh and several other men make trips to the storage unit using a yellow Ryder van. They also saw Salameh make several calls from a nearby pay phone, whose records showed four calls made February 25, 1993, to the office of Ayyad, with whom he had a joint bank account.

Police also searched other New York area apartments, including the Brooklyn apartment of Egyptian-born Ibrahim Elgabrowny, 42, the cousin of Sayyid A. Nosair, who was acquitted of the murder in 1990 of Rabbi Meir Kahane.

Elgabrowny was arrested on March 4, 1993, and charged with possessing five fraudulent passports and with obstruction of justice after hitting an FBI agent during the search. Agents found a licensed handgun, 150 rounds of ammunition, two stun guns, and false Nicaraguan passports for Nosair and his wife and three children in Elgabrowny's apartment.

Nosair and Salameh belonged to the Masjid al-Salam mosque in Jersey City. Among its preachers was the fiery fundamentalist Sheikh Omar Abdel-Rahman, 54, a blind anti-Western cleric with a huge following in his native Egypt. Abdel-Rahman, despite being suspected of involvement in terrorism, had entered the United States on a tourist visa from Sudan, and had lived in New Jersey since 1990. He had issued a fatwa (religious edict) condoning the 1981 assassination of Egyptian president Anwar Sadat. He was believed to be the spiritual leader of the al-Gama'at al-Islamiyya, an Egyptian terrorist group.

On March 10, 1993, the FBI arrested Ayyad, 26, a Kuwaiti-born chemical engineer, at 60 Boyden Avenue, Maplewood, New Jersey, and held him on charges of aiding and abetting the bombing.

On March 14, 1993, Egyptian police arrested another suspect, Egyptian-born former Brooklyn cab driver, Mahmud Abu Halima, 33, now a German citizen. He was a friend of Nosair and Salameh.

Ayyad and Salameh were indicted on March 17, 1993, before a federal grand jury in New York for "aiding and abetting" in the explosion and "knowingly and maliciously did damage and destroy, by means of fire and an explosion . . . the World Trade Center complex." Officials released a second indictment of Elgabrowny for obstruction of justice.

On March 24, 1993, police arrested Bilal Alkaisi, 26, a resident of New York and New Jersey, and charged him with using explosives to cause the bombing. He was arraigned in U.S. District Court in Manhattan, where he pleaded not guilty. His case was joined with those of Halima, Ayyad, Salameh, and Ramzi Ahmed Yusuf.

On March 31, 1993, federal prosecutors in Manhattan indicted Yusuf, 25, a fugitive who was believed to have escaped to Egypt. He had resided at the same Jersey City address once occupied by Salameh. Yousef was arrested in Pakistan and deported to the United States in February 1995.

On May 5, 1993, Mohammad Ahmad Ajaj, 27, a Palestinian refugee who sought U.S. asylum, was placed in a cell attached to the U.S. attorney's office in Manhattan. He entered the United States illegally at John F. Kennedy Airport on September 1, 1992, carrying 12 bomb-making and chemical manuals. Two manuals bore the fingerprints of Yusuf.

On May 26, 1993, Halima, Ajaj, Alkaisi, Ayyad, and Salameh were named with Yusuf in an eight-count indictment accusing them of planning and carrying out the blast.

The trial of Salameh, Halima, Ayyad, and Ajaj began in September 1993. Prosecutors said Ajaj brought the manuals, Ayyad was the chemical engineer, Halima "mixed and transported the chemicals," and Salameh rented the warehouse, the laboratory apartment, and the van.

On October 15, 1993, a handcuffed Sheikh Abdel-Rahman was charged under a federal sedition law for encouraging the bombing and other plots.

On March 4, 1994, after five days of deliberation, the jury found the four Arab defendants guilty on all counts of conspiracy, explosives charges, and assault. They faced maximum sentences of life in prison without parole.

On May 24, 1994, U.S. district judge Kevin Duffy sentenced each of the convicts to 240 years in prison, a life term calculated by adding the life expectancy of each of the 6 people killed in the blast, plus 30 years for 2 other counts.

On February 7, 1995, Pakistani police arrested Yusuf from Sokawa rest house in Islamabad. The Islamabad-based *Pakistan* paper reported that Yusuf planned to bomb the Israeli Consulate in Bombay and the Israeli Embassy in New Delhi. He reportedly was also involved in the bombings of the Israeli embassies in London and Buenos Aires, and had contacts with the Afghan mujahideen and Kashmiri nationalists. Pakistani police also said that he intended to kill Prime Minister Benazir Bhutto on December 24, 1993. Bhutto had earlier claimed that Yusuf had tried to kill her in September 1993 when he drove a car with explosives toward the Bilawal House in Karachi. On April 1, 1995, Philippine authorities indicted Yusuf on charges of plotting to assassinate the Pope and bombing the Philippine Airlines B-747 in December 1994. On April 13, 1995, U.S. prosecutors indicted Yusuf for the bombing of an airliner on December 11, 1994, that killed Japanese passenger Haruki Ikegami and injured 10 people, and of planning to bomb other U.S. airliners. Yusuf's group also planned a series of bombings of U.S. airliners and considered loading a plane with explosives and crashing it into the Central Intelligence Agency's headquarters.

On April 12, 1994, *Newsday* reported that the FBI had identified seven men—including three Egyptians and one Moroccan—with ties to Hamas and the Islamic group who helped to plan the WTC bombing. They lived in Denmark and were arrested in April 1994 by Danish police on suspicion of complicity in various arsons, attempted bombing, and plotting to disrupt a UN conference in Copenhagen. They were released. Fingerprints of two of the Egyptian men—Abdel Halim Mohammad Atim Soliman and Mohammed Shauban Mohammed Hassanein—were found on manuals and magazines confiscated from Ajaj when he was arrested at John F. Kennedy Airport on September 2, 1992. The others were Mohammed Abdel Halim Mohammed Fahim, Talat Fouad Kassem, Mohammad al-Banar, and Hassan Fathallah.

On April 13, 1995, federal officials in New York charged Yusuf and Abdul Hakim Murad (alias Saeed Ahmed) of conspiring with others to plant bombs on "numerous" commercial U.S. aircraft.

On April 10, 1996, the United States demanded the expulsion of Sudanese U.N. diplomat Ahmad Yusuf Mohamed for involvement with the WTC bombers and the New York landmark plotters.

On August 1, 1996 a Kuwaiti-born Palestinian who carried a Jordanian passport, Eyad Mahmoud Ismoil Najim, 24, was arrested in Jordan. On

August 3, 1996, he was charged in a New York federal court with planning and executing the WTC bombing.

Yusuf was charged with mixing the bomb's chemicals and organizing the bombing. Najim was charged with driving the van. They were found guilty on November 12, 1997. Yusuf was sentenced on January 8, 1998 to life plus 240 years, fined $4.5 million, and ordered to pay $250 million in restitution.

Prosecutors indicted Khaled Sheikh Mohammed, possibly a relative of Yusuf, who helped Yusuf finance and develop the bomb plot. Mohammed is currently in the Guantanamo Bay military prison, awaiting trial on numerous terrorism charges, including several related to the September 11, 2001 attacks.

July 18, 1994
Buenos Aires AIMA Bombing

Overview: The 1994 bombing of the Argentine–Israel Mutual Aid Society (AIMA) has been linked to the 1992 bombing of the Israeli Embassy in showing that even South America can host Middle East-based violence. Foreign terrorists able to blend into a prosperous local expatriate community can prove difficult to deter or apprehend. The Iranian hand was suspected in the case, but efforts to arrest and try top Iranian officials proved futile.

Incident: On July 18, 1994, at 10:00 A.M., a Renault Trafic van bomb loaded with more than 200 kilograms of ammonal exploded at the AIMA in Buenos Aires, killing 96 and wounding 231. The Partisans of God (Al Sad Allah or Ansar Allah) claimed credit. Observers believed this was a cover name for Hizballah. The Islamic Command also claimed responsibility.

Al-Kabir Talcan (or Balkan), 33, a Moroccan, was arrested in the AIMA neighborhood. On July 20, 1994, Uruguay arrested an Iranian citizen, 30, on suspicion of involvement. The individual, whose residence documents had expired, had resided in Montevideo for the past six years.

On July 24, 1994, the Argentine government instructed Attorney General Oscar Fappiano to request that Judge Juan José Galeano issue an extradition for Sheikh Subhi al-Tufayli, the leader of the Followers of God, who lived in Lebanon. On July 29, 1994, London's *Al-Hayah* reported that Lebanon had rejected the request.

An individual in Caracas claiming to be a former Iranian diplomat, Manuchehr Motamar, 38, claimed that Iran was behind the blast. He said that he had been kidnapped by Iranian diplomats in Caracas, but escaped. Caracas declared Iranian ambassador Seyyed Reza Zargarbashi persona non grata. Motamar said an Iranian military officer was responsible for planning the attack and that the explosives entered the country via the diplomatic pouch.

On July 31, 1994, *La Nacion* reported that two people were arrested in Ciudad del Este, Paraguay. Argentine police, the evening before, had captured two intermediaries who bought the van from Carlos Alberto Telledin under the false name of Ramon Martinez. Telledin was the last buyer of the van, and asked Ariel Nitzcaner and Marcelo Jouce, two mechanics, to repair it. The description of Ramon Martinez coincided with the description of the purchaser of the Ford F-100 pickup used in the bombing of the Israeli Embassy in Buenos Aires on March 17, 1992.

On August 1, 1994, police compiled an Identikit likeness of an alleged religious fanatic who may have driven the Renault Trafic van used as the car bomb. He was believed to be an Iranian member of Hizballah. His remains were found near the engine of the car.

On August 9, 1994, based on Motamar's testimony that they were Hizballah members, Galeano ordered the arrest of Iranian diplomats Third Secretary Ahmad Allameh Falsafi, Mahvash Monsef Gholamreza, Akbar Parvaresch, and First Secretary Abbas Zarrabi Khorasani.

Galeano noted that by the end of 1993, Mohsen Rabbani, an Iranian cultural attaché, visited car rental companies, looking to acquire a Trafic van.

Galeano also ordered proceedings and preventive arrest of Telledin for "concealment," illegal replacement of an engine, and forgery of a private document. Telledin's assets were confiscated up to 100,000 pesos. Galeano also ordered criminal proceedings against the two mechanics for illegal replacement of a car engine.

On October 8, 1994, Argentine police detained 'Ali al-Hasan, 25, a Syrian, who was carrying four sticks of dynamite and Iraqi Embassy military attaché credentials. The Iraqi Embassy denied knowledge of him. According to his passport, he had toured the Arab world over the past few years. He was arraigned in the Moron court headed by Judge Susana Morris Douglas for possession of explosives. Police were investigating whether he was involved in the July AIMA bombing; he was in possession of a large quantity of newspaper clippings on the blast. Al-Hasan told police that he did not know of the explosives and that a person who had stayed in his home might have left them there.

The next day, police arrested Syrians Ernesto Tanuz, 64, and his son Julio, 24, owners of the premises and the house where al-Hasan was arrested. So far, police had detained 20 individuals in connection with the bombing. The only person still under arrest was Telledin, the Argentine mechanic who sold the station wagon that was used as a car bomb. He was charged as an accessory.

Between January 25 and 27, 1995, following accusations by Telledin, Judge Galeano ordered the arrest of the man who allegedly purchased the Trafic van. Police in Mar del Plata arrested Jose Ramon Juan (or Juan Ramon) Martinez, 50, a Spaniard.

On January 29, 1995, five Lebanese and two Brazilians were detained in a suburb of Asuncion, Paraguay. All seven had entered through Ciudad del Este on Brazilian passports and had overstayed their 30-day tourist visas. Police believed the three who were Hizballah members were linked to the AIMA bombing. Police confiscated an unlicensed .38 caliber Taurus revolver, ammunition, and 6 grams of cocaine. Valdirene Vieira Ferguglia, 23, had an Iberia airline ticket valid for Madrid and Brussels. They were charged with drug trafficking, violating immigration law, and illegal possession of weapons. Argentina requested extradition on February 24, 1995, for stockpiling explosives and combat weapons on an island in the Tigre River Delta. On March 23, 1995, Principal Superintendent Enrique Martinetti, chief of the Police Intelligence Department in Paraguay, told the press that Interpol had confirmed that one of the Lebanese had given a false name while another, Luis Alberto Nader, 22, a Brazilian of Lebanese origin, was a contact of the Cali cocaine cartel in Italy and Russia. Johannie Moraes Baalbaki, 24, was carrying a false birth certificate and illegal identity card. The other Lebanese in detention were Roberto Riveiro (or Ribiero) Ruiz, 22; Mohammad Hassan Alayan, 41; Fadi Abdul Karim Chekair, 23; and Sergio Rodrigo Salem, 26. Buenos Aires' *Telam* reported that Baalbaki, Nader, and Alayan were Hizballah members. Extradition of the seven was approved by Paraguayan Criminal Court Justice Jose Emilio Yaluk on May 30, 1995. On July 14, 1995, Argentine interior minister Carlos Corach announced that the extradition had been approved.

On January 31, 1995, Judge Galeano indicted Hugo Antonio Perez and Miguel Gustavo Jaimes on charges of "harboring" in the AIMA case. He embargoed their assets for 500,000 pesos, but released them. Galeano also released Martinez.

In February 1995, Buenos Aires Province police discovered a cache of weapons and empty shells similar to the caliber of rifles found in the home of Nazi sympathizer Alejandro Sucksdorf, a former civilian intelligence officer attached to the army, located in the Tigre River Delta. Police also found 25 kilograms of TNT, antitank grenades, and munitions. They determined that he was connected to six Lebanese males and one Lebanese female who were extradited from Paraguay. Police found a blank identity document that contained a small piece of ragged paper with the words "For Sergio." The name belonged to Sergio Rodrigo Salem, one of the Lebanese arrested on drug trafficking charges. The land on which Sucksdorf's home is located is close to the island of businessman Mario Falak, which police believed was used for military exercises by Middle Easterners. Sucksdorf's estranged wife had implicated him in the 1992 attack on the Israeli Embassy.

On February 19, 1995, Asuncion's *Noticias* reported that the Intelligence Department found a "red diary" in a luxurious house on Santisima Trinidad Street. Portions were decoded by Mossad, which learned that the seven Lebanese were planning a new attack on the Israeli Embassy in Argentina and another one against government officials, including President Carlos Menem, and members of the Jewish community.

On May 25, 1995, Tel Aviv's *Ma'ariv* reported that Israeli intelligence believed that three of the extradited Lebanese were involved, but another trio, possibly Iranian officials, had fled to Iran.

On June 25, 1995, Buenos Aires police arrested Erik Deprez (alias El Frances), who had in his possession a double-barrel shotgun, a "ballester Molina" 11.25-caliber pistol, and ammunition. He also had documents on vehicles and ID documents. Judge Galeano levied a fine of 60,000 pesos on him, concluding that "he knew about the illegal origin of the documents." On July 18, 1995, Galeano ordered the preventive detention of Deprez and Antonio Avelino Aguero, who were connected with Telledin. The magistrate believed they were responsible for a cover-up. Tradesman Oscar Castro (alias El Sapito) was indicted on charges of violating the motor vehicle law, but was ordered released. Aguero was accused of being an accessory by helping Telledin "obtain, arm, and prepare the van used for the car bomb." Three other suspects—Juan Carlos Almiron, Geronimo Agapito Martinez, and Roberto Jose Uhrig—were released for lack of evidence.

On July 19, 1995, Buenos Aires police chief Pedro Klodcczyk admitted that Buenos Aires Province police officers Diego Barreda and Mario Barreiro were linked to Telledin but had not been arraigned. The press in September 1995 noted that Telledin, a massage parlor operator, was involved with corrupt police officials in a car theft ring and that he had earlier lied about who had purchased the van. The press now claimed that corrupt policemen had bought the van.

On October 21, 1995, four plainclothes police arrested a colleague of Telledin, Cesar Antonio Fernandez, 24, outside a Gualeguaychu teacher training college.

On October 30, 1995, Judge Galeano issued an arrest warrant for Carlos Irigoytia for his links with the AIMA detainees. Irigoytia was arrested in his home. Later that day, police arrested Roberto Valdez, 34, who was linked to Telledin and Alejandro Victor Monjo. Galeano ordered the release of Rodolfo Setau and Antonio Quiroga due to lack of evidence that they were involved with Telledin and Monjo in obtaining the van. Setau had been held since October 19, 1995. An agent for Alejandro Automotores, Setau was suspected of being Monjo's direct link to Telledin. Quiroga also worked for the car firm.

On November 2, 1995, Judge Galeano indicted on charges of unlawful association all those who had been held in the AIMA case. He declined to remand anyone but Telledin into custody. Monjo, Gabriel Melli, Edgardo Yema, Marcelo Delacour, Jaimes, Perez, and Fernandez were set free. Pablo Ibanez was indicted for possession of drugs.

In 1996, former chief inspector Juan Jose Ribelli and two other senior provincial police officers were charged with assisting in the bombing. Local press reported that Ribelli received a $2.5 million payment a week before the attack.

On July 14, 1996, Judge Galeano heard testimony of two deputy police superintendents (Raul Idilio Ibarra and Antastasio Ireneo Leal) and two former police inspectors (Barreda and Barreiro) who allegedly sold the car bomb.

On September 24, 2001, the trial began of 20 people charged with helping to arrange the bombing. On September 2, 2004, a federal court in Buenos Aires acquitted five men of being accessories in the case, clearing four former provincial police officers and a former used car salesman.

On March 8, 2003, Judge Galeano indicted four Iranian diplomats: Ali Fallahian, serving as Minister of Security and Intelligence when the attack occurred; Mohsen Rabbani, Iranian cultural attaché; Ali Akbar Parvaresh, former minister of education and former speaker of the Iranian Majlis; and Ali Balesh Abadi, former embassy spokesman. On October 25, 2006, Argentine prosecutors asked for the arrest of former Iranian president Akbar Hashemi Rafsanjani and seven others for plotting the bombing.

On May 20, 2009, Argentina issued an international arrest warrant for Samuel Salman el-Reda, a Colombian of Lebanese descent.

The case remains open.

March 20, 1995
Tokyo Subway Sarin Gas Attack

Overview: While much of the speculative literature on the future of terrorism worries about the use by terrorists of weapons of mass destruction, including chemical, biological, radiological, or nuclear materials, the overwhelming number of international and domestic attacks have involved conventional methods. Reasons for this hesitancy to move into a new type of weapon have included lack of skill, fear of scoring "own goals," likely public revulsion at the deaths of thousands, and difficulty of acquiring and weaponizing the materials. These limitations were not a concern for Aum Shin Rikyo, a millennial cult that attracted tens of thousands of adherents in the 1990s throughout Asia and Russia.

Aum Shin Rikyo's membership included sophisticated chemists, biologists, and nuclear engineers, who were encouraged to experiment with the use of all of these potential weapons. The group conducted tests, some affecting, some directly against, the local population. On July 2, 1993, more than 100 residents of the Koto district of Tokyo complained of noxious white fumes coming from buildings owned by the group. On June 27, 1994, seven people died from a sarin attack in the resort city of Matsumoto, 125 miles northwest of Tokyo. At least 264 people were hospitalized. A week later, residents of the small village of Kamikuishiki, near Mount Fuji south of Matsumoto, had the same symptoms, although all recovered. On September 1, 1994, more than 230 people in seven towns in Nara State suffered rashes and eye irritation from fumes. Authorities found a by-product of sarin in Kamikuishiki in December 1994.

Aum upped the ante for all terrorists in March 1995, when it attempted to kill thousands via a sarin gas attack on the Tokyo subway. Twelve commuters died and 5,511 people were hospitalized. Strict Japanese laws regarding the rights of religious groups, even those advocating violence, hampered the authorities' investigation and response to the case, but eventually those responsible were brought to justice.

Incident: On March 20, 1995, Aum Shin Rikyo (Aum Supreme Truth), a fringe cult headquartered in Japan, simultaneously released sarin gas into 6 trains involving 16 substations of the Tokyo subway system during the 8:00 A.M. rush hour, killing 12 and injuring 5,511 people. Affected stations included Nakano-Sakane, Kasumigaseki, Tsukiji, Kamiyacho, Hongosanchome, Kodenmacho, Hibiya, Marunouchi, Ebisu, Yotsuya-Sanchome, Shinkoenji, Higashi Koenji, Ogikubo, Nakano Fujimicho, Hatchobori, Kayabacho, Ochanomizu, Kokkaigijidomae, Akasaka Mitsuke, Ningyocho, Korakuen, and Chiyoda. The three affected subway lines (Hibiya, Marunouchi, and Chiyoda) crossed each other at the Kasumigaseki terminus, site of the headquarters of several Japanese national government ministries.

Sarin's chemical name is isopropyl methyl phosphoro fluoridate. It was developed by the Nazis in the late 1930s, but apparently not used by them in battle. It is one of the least persistent nerve agents, dispersing rapidly. It is fairly simple to manufacture.

The cult was led by Shoko Asahara, 40, self-described Venerated Master, who in 1985 wrote that he had conducted successful antigravity experiments. He had failed as an acupuncturist and health tonic salesman. During his career, he had railed against the Japanese military and the United States, predicted that the world would end in 1997, and said that it was now "time for death," without specifying if it was for himself, his followers, or Tokyo subway riders. Asahara was born Chizuo Matsumoto, the fourth son of a tatami mat maker. He was jailed in 1982 for selling counterfeit medicines. He founded three cults. In 1982, he and his wife created the Heavenly Blessing Association. He next tried the Aum Divine Wizard Association, claiming that Buddhist principles would permit him to fly. In 1987, he came out with the Aum Supreme Truth, in which he praised the Hindu god Shiva (god of destruction and renewal), Buddhist saints, and Adolf Hitler. The cult has branches in the United States, Germany, Russia, and Sri Lanka.

On March 22, 1995, police raided Aum facilities in Kamikuishiki Village, Yamanashi Prefecture, and found a large quantity of peptone, used to culture germs. Police found germ-culture equipment, electron microscopes, and other experimental equipment used in germ research. The cult had purchased large quantities of botulinus bacillus. The next day, Japanese police seized huge supplies of sarin precursor chemicals, including phosphorous trichloride and sodium fluoride. Police also found atropine, a chemical agent antidote. Police found 22 pounds of gold ingots and $7 million in cash at Asahara's mountain stronghold. Raids by 2,500 police at two dozen of their installations turned up gas masks and acetonitrile, which can dilute sarin. Police also found a Russian chemical agent detector and a Russian MI-17 helicopter capable of carrying 30 people. Fifty malnourished, drugged people, apparently being held against their will, were freed by police. Some were Aum members and refused medical assistance. Five people were arrested.

One day before the subway incident, leaflets publicizing Asahara's book *Disasters are Approaching the Country Where the Sun Rises*, which hinted at the Tokyo gas attack, were distributed in the Ginza shopping area. Three months after the Matsumoto attack, a threatening letter sent to news organizations hinted at the use of organic solvents in the subway.

On March 27, 1995, police found a hidden chemical lab behind a secret door behind a huge Hindu statue of Shiva in the group's main building near Mount Fuji. Police found 40 kinds of chemicals, including those used to make sarin and tabun, glycerine compounds for explosives, and drugs precursors.

On March 29, 1995, Japanese police searching the Mount Fuji site found 160 barrels of peptone, suggesting that the Aum was also experimenting with biological warfare agents. Police had earlier discovered a powerful ventilation system that could have removed toxic gases and agents during the experiments. Police found an incubator and a library of 300 books on bacteriological research. Police discovered empty syringe vials of sarin. Police said that the sarin production facilities were "seemingly larger, more sophisticated, and of better quality than Iraq's chemical gas plants, and are good enough to produce highly-purified sarin," according to the *Mainichi Shimbun*.

By April 1, 1995, police had confiscated 650 drums filled with enough chemicals to make 5.6 tons of sarin. The group had purchased huge quantities of a sarin antidote from a Tokyo hospital.

On April 1, 1995, police found a major heavy machine maker's classified document on uranium enrichment technology among the belongings of an Aum member who had been arrested in Shiga Prefecture.

On April 13, 1995, police arrested Tomomitsu Nimii, Aum's home affairs minister, on suspicion of kidnapping a nurse who had tried to leave the cult. During the previous week, police had arrested the ministers of defense, finance, and treatment, the latter who drugged dissenters into submission.

On April 14, 1995, police arrested Masanobu Iwao, 35, for breaking and entering the facility of Sagamihara, Kanagawa Prefecture, on November 6, 1994. The facility is the firm's major laser research lab. Aum was allegedly interested in laser weapons.

On April 15, 1995, thousands of police officers raided 130 Aum buildings, removing 53 children from the group's main compound. Many of the children, ages 3–14, were wearing head gear with wires that Aum members claimed sent brain waves from Asahara. Some of the children were malnourished; eight were hospitalized. Police found a Russian military helicopter, gun-making materials, biological warfare supplies, and chemical warfare plants.

On April 19, 1995, police arrested Kiyohide Hayakawa, 45, Aum "construction minister" and allegedly number two in Aum. He reportedly was involved in attempts to purchase six Russian tanks.

Police at Los Angeles International Airport apprehended two Japanese Aum members a few days before Easter, who were carrying information on sarin manufacture. Police believed they were planning an attack on Disneyland.

Kyodo reported that 58 present and former members of the Self-Defense Forces had been Aum members. On May 25, 1995, police announced the arrest of Aum adherent Sgt. Tatsuya Toyama, on charges of trespassing at a research facility operated by Mitsubishi Heavy Industries, Japan's largest defense contractor.

On April 23, 1995, Hideo Murai, Aum's minister for science and technology, was stabbed to death in front of Aum's Tokyo headquarters by a man who claimed to be a rightist.

On April 26, 1995, police arrested Masami Tsuchiya, 30, Aum's top chemist. Tsuchiya told police that he produced sarin.

On April 28, 1995, the Japanese Self Defense Force announced that two army sergeants who are Aum members had tipped off the cult's leaders in advance of the March 22, 1995, raid, permitting group members to escape with incriminating evidence. One of the sergeants also admitted throwing a Molotov cocktail at the group's Tokyo office in an attempt to distract police and win public sympathy.

On May 6, 1995, guards thwarted a cyanide gas attack in a Tokyo subway station, defusing a device in a restroom.

Australia announced on May 11, 1995, that Aum had tested sarin on livestock at a sheep ranch in Western Australia. Police found sarin residue in the carcasses of 24 sheep and on the soil of a 48,000 acre sheep ranch that Aum had purchased in 1993.

By May 14, 1995, police had arrested 200 Aum members.

On May 16, 1995, police arrested Asahara, who was hiding with his wife, Tomoko Matsumoto, 36, and 6 children at the Mount Fuji complex. Police had to search for three hours in the underground tunnels and secret passages before finding him in his meditation chamber.

Prosecutors indicted Asahara and six followers on murder charges on June 6, 1995, saying that he masterminded the attacks. Prosecutors said that the Aum members packed the sarin into 11 sealed plastic bags and used umbrellas with sharpened tips to puncture them in five subway cars. Another nine Aum members were indicted on charges of "preparation for murder" for building the chemical plants where sarin was produced.

On June 6, 1995, the government announced that it would move to disband Aum, revoke its status as a religious corporation, and not permit it to enjoy tax advantages or own property in its own name. It would still be able to make converts and hold meetings.

On June 14, 1995, Asahara was also charged with ordering the strangling of Kotaro Ochida, 29, a pharmacist in a cult hospital. He was killed by Hideaki Yasuda, a former Aum member, in January 1994. Yasuda told police that Asahara and 10 other senior cult members witnessed the strangling at the commune at Kamikuishiki.

On July 5, 1995, Asahara was charged with ordering the production of LSD, truth serums, amphetamines, and other illegal drugs.

On October 30, 1995, a Tokyo District Court judge ruled that the cult must forfeit its status as a religious corporation, which could lead to a liquidator selling the group's holdings, estimated at between $300 million and $1 billion.

On October 31, 1995, U.S. Senator Sam Nunn reported that Aum tried to purchase material for nuclear and chemical weapons in the United States and Russia, and had developed numerous front companies. The cult tried to obtain a $500,000 laser system and 400 Israeli-made gas masks, along with Russian nuclear materials.

On December 4, 1995, Asahara was served a warrant for involvement in the VX gas murder of Osaka businessman Tadahito Hamaguchi, 28, on December 12, 1994.

On May 26, 1998, Ikuo Hayashi was sentenced to life in prison for murder. The same day, court testimony indicated that Aum had conducted at least nine germ attacks in the early 1990s in an effort to kill millions of people throughout Tokyo and thousands of American service people and their families at a nearby military base. The group sprayed pestilential microbes and germ toxins from rooftops and trucks at the Diet, the Imperial Palace, the surrounding city, and the U.S. base at Yokosuka. In June 1993, cult members sprayed anthrax from the top of their building, but no one became ill. The group also sprayed anthrax via a truck around central Tokyo and sprayed botulinum toxin in the Kasumigaseki Tokyo subway in 1995.

On September 29, 1999, Aum announced it would close its branches and cease using that name.

Between 1998 and 2000, courts sentenced to death Kazuaki Okazaki, Masato Yokoyama, Yasuo Hayashi, and Satoro Hashimoto.

Asahara was sentenced to death on February 26, 2004.

April 19, 1995
Oklahoma City Bombing

Overview: The public wants to *know*. So analysts shuffled before television cameras and radio microphones speaking hurriedly and so soon after an incident and can be way off the mark in surmising what is really going on. From the famous Dewey Beats Truman headline to the fog of war, pundits frequently speculate beyond the data and miss the call. So it was in the case of the Oklahoma City bombing—and the later bombings of Madrid subways in 2004. Pundits rushed to judgment and declared that the mass casualty bombing had all the hallmarks of al Qaeda and that Middle Eastern terrorism had come to the heartland of America. Cursory investigation soon put the lie to that theory, as authorities determined within hours that the bombing was the handiwork of a small band of right wingers inspired by racist literature. The case of a decorated army veteran dragged on for years but ultimately led to the execution of bomber Timothy James McVeigh and the jailing of his coconspirators.

Incident: On April 19, 1995, a bomb in a 1993 Ford truck exploded at 9:02 A.M. at the nine-story Alfred P. Murrah Federal Building at Fifth and Hudson Streets in Oklahoma City, Oklahoma, killing 169—including 19 children—and injuring over 500. Among the dead were 15 children who were in the America's Kids day care center, which was destroyed when the second story of the building collapsed. Two people were found dead in a neighboring building that had been damaged. People heard the blast from 50 miles away. At least 75 buildings were condemned and at least 312 damaged. Ten buildings collapsed. Damage estimates ranged from $750 million to $1 billion.

The dead included Baylee Almon, 1, who was carried away bleeding by a fireman. The photo, sent worldwide, became a symbol of the horror of the bombing.

Approximately 250 children lost one or both of their parents in the blast.

Among the injured was a man on a Russian ice-dancing team, which had been camping out on the floor of the YMCA across from the federal building.

The bomb likely contained at least 4,800 pounds of explosives, probably including fuel oil and ammonium nitrate, a fertilizer ingredient.

Federal employees in the building worked for the Social Security Administration; the Departments of Health and Human Services, Labor, Agriculture, Veterans Affairs, Defense, Housing and Urban Development; the Secret Service; the Drug Enforcement Administration; the General Services Administration; the U.S. Customs Service; the Bureau of Alcohol, Tobacco and Firearms; and the General Accounting Office.

Rebecca Anderson, 37, a nurse helping at the scene, was killed by falling rubble. Her heart was transplanted into a 55-year-old Oklahoma man.

A caller to Brussels RTL-TVI claimed membership in the Nation of Islam and said it was responsible. He gave his name as Mohammed Ali. Hamas (the Islamic Resistance Movement) and the Islamic Jihad in Gaza denied involvement. The FBI received hundreds of calls claiming credit for the blast.

Federal facilities around the country were evacuated when several hoax bomb threats were received. Calls were received at federal buildings in Los

Angeles, Orange and Ventura counties, at a county office building in San Diego, and at city halls in Riverside, Anaheim, and Santa Ana. Banks, post offices, and businesses received similar calls. The John F. Kennedy Federal Building in Boston was evacuated after an Internal Revenue Service (IRS) employee found several doors open that should have been locked. Federal buildings in Dallas and Fort Worth, Texas; Wilmington, Delaware; New York City and Rochester, New York; Cincinnati, Dayton, and Steubenville, Ohio; Miami, Florida; Spokane, Washington; Washington, D.C. (including the FBI, the Department of Justice, and the Capitol buildings); Omaha, Nebraska; Kansas City; Portland, Oregon; and Boise, Idaho were also evacuated after phone threats.

Pundits initially suspected Middle Eastern terrorists after a man flew to London with bags in Rome checked on to Jordan was found carrying what appeared to be bomb-making materials. U.S. citizen Abraham Abdullah Hassan Ahmad, 31, had flown to Chicago on an American Airlines flight and was to go from Chicago to Rome and Amman on an Alitalia flight. Customs officials in Chicago questioned him for so long he missed his flight. Italian authorities opened his luggage, which contained needle-nosed pliers, spools of electric wire, kitchen knives, photographic materials, a video recording device, aluminum foil, and silicon that could be used in making a bomb. Also included was a photo album with pictures of military weapons, including missiles and armored vehicles. Police also found three gym suits similar to those worn by a person seen near the site of the bombing. British authorities returned him to the United States. After questioning, he was released. On November 9, 1995, he filed a $1.9 million suit against the federal government. The FBI issued an all-points bulletin for three men seen speeding from the city in a brown pickup truck.

Attorney General Janet Reno announced a $2 million reward for information leading to the arrest of the bombers.

On April 21, 1995, the U.S. Department of Justice reported the arrest of McVeigh, 27, a member of the right-wing Michigan Militia, which views the U.S. government as the enemy of the common man. McVeigh was angry with the federal raid on the Branch Davidian compound in Waco, Texas, two years earlier, in which scores died. Eight minutes after the bomb went off, he was picked up in a 1977 Mercury Marquis 20 miles from the bombing site on a traffic offense; federal authorities did not know until later that he was in custody. Police found residue of ammonium nitrate and high explosives inside the car.

According to records unsealed on November 3, 1995, McVeigh was also carrying political documents and a note citing the right to kill political oppressors. The package included a copy of the Declaration of Independence, material on the Branch Davidian raid, material on the battles of Lexington and Concord, an antigovernment leaflet, and quotations from political philosophers, including 17th-century philosopher John Locke.

McVeigh had served in the army, and was decorated for his service as a gunner on a Bradley fighting vehicle in Desert Storm. After returning from the Gulf War, an injury prevented him from successfully competing for a position with the Green Berets. He was discharged as a sergeant on December 31, 1991. He developed contacts with various militia groups in Michigan and Arizona, and stayed with his friends, the Nichols, on their Dexter, Michigan, farm. He supported himself buying and selling guns as "T. Tuttle."

The truck used in the attack was rented from the Ryder rental agency in Junction City, Kansas, by two white men using aliases. John Doe One, later identified as McVeigh, was described as 5 feet 10 inches tall, of medium build, weighing about 180 pounds with light, close-cropped hair, and right-handed. John Doe Two was of medium build at 5 feet 9 inches tall, 175 pounds, with brown hair and a tattoo on his lower left arm, and possibly a smoker. Months later, investigators were uncertain of his identity, or whether he even existed.

On April 25, 1995, federal authorities charged Terry Lynn Nichols, 40, and his brother, James Douglas Nichols, 41, with conspiring with McVeigh to build explosives at their farm in Michigan. The charges were unrelated to the specific Oklahoma bombing, but permitted federal officials to keep them in prison while they investigated further leads. Terry Nichols was charged with involvement in the bombing on May 9, 1995.

Michael Fortier, 26, of Kingman, Arizona, told federal investigators that he and McVeigh drove to the Murrah building a few days ahead of time, apparently on a reconnaissance mission. McVeigh told him that he was going to blow up the building. His wife, Lori, testified before a grand jury after being given immunity, as did Jennifer McVeigh, 21, Timothy McVeigh's sister. Fortier had sold one gun apparently stolen in a November 5, 1994, robbery from a Royal, Arkansas, gun dealer, Roger E. Moore, that may have funded the Oklahoma bombing. The thief stole $60,000 worth of property, including 60 firearms, precious metals, and ammunition, some of which was recovered in the home of Terry Nichols.

Jennifer McVeigh told the FBI that Timothy had said that he had robbed a bank and drove around the West in a vehicle loaded with explosives. She was initially considered as a principal suspect, but the federal authorities later decided to use her as a witness.

On May 2, 1995, FBI agents arrested Gary Alan Land and Robert Jacks as material witnesses. Their movements in Kingman, Arizona, and Perry, Oklahoma, mirrored those of McVeigh.

On May 12, 1995, Steven Garrett Colbern, 35, a California biochemist and acquaintance of McVeigh, was arrested after he pulled a loaded revolver and scuffled with U.S. marshals in an Arizona mining town. He knew McVeigh by the alias Tim Tuttle. Police raiding his residence seized four rifles, three handguns, and 16,000 rounds of ammunition, including 4,000 bullets used in assault rifles. Documents suggested that the residence was used to produce methamphetamine, known on the street as "crank." Colbern has ties to the Arizona Patriots militia group.

Michael E. Tigar, Terry Nichols's court-appointed lawyer, said McVeigh rented the Herington, Kansas, storage shed in the name of Shawn Rivers. The Ryder truck was seen backed up to the shed on April 18, 1995. Fortier had claimed that Nichols had helped mix the explosives.

By August 8, 1995, Fortier, McVeigh's army buddy, had reached a tentative deal to turn state's evidence in return for not being named a principal in the case and facing a death penalty. Under the agreement, he would plead guilty to illegal firearms trafficking, knowledge of the bombing, and lying to federal agents.

On August 15, 1995, McVeigh and Terry Nichols were arraigned before U.S. magistrate Ronald L. Howland. They pleaded not guilty to an 11-count indictment that charged that they carried out a terrorist attack. A grand jury formally accused them on August 10, 1995. Fortier was charged in a separate indictment of knowing of the plan and concealing it from law enforcement authorities, lying to the FBI, and involvement in a robbery that financed the attack. Prosecutors said they would seek the death penalty against McVeigh and Nichols.

The indictment said "McVeigh attempted to recruit others to assist in the act of violence" and noted that McVeigh and Terry Nichols "conspired with others unknown to the Grand Jury." The indictment did not mention John Doe Number 2, nor did it discuss any motive or where the bombing was plotted. It said the duo planned and "caused" the robbery, but did not specify who committed it. The duo were charged with conspiring to use a weapon of mass destruction to kill people and destroy federal property, with using a truck bomb to kill people, and with malicious destruction of property resulting in death. The other eight counts cited the murders of federal law enforcement officers.

On June 2, 1996, the jury found McVeigh guilty on all 11 counts of murder, conspiracy, and using a weapon of mass destruction. The jury recommended execution on June 13, 1996; Judge Richard P. Matsch sentenced him on August 14, 1996. On June 11, 2001, an unrepentant McVeigh was executed by chemical injection.

On December 24, 1996, a jury acquitted Terry Nichols of first-degree murder, but convicted him on eight counts of involuntary manslaughter and conspiracy to blow up the building. On June 4, 1998, Judge Matsch sentenced Nichols to life in prison with parole. On May 25, 2004, a jury found Nichols guilty of all 161 counts of murder; he was sentenced on August 9, 2004, to 161 consecutive life sentences without parole.

On May 12, 1998, Fortier was sentenced to 12 years in prison and fined $200,000, a sentence echoed on October 8, 1999. He was released early on January 20, 2006, for good behavior.

June 14, 1995
Budennovsk, Russia, Hospital Hostage-Taking

Overview: Chechen separatist terrorists tended to engage in high-profile, high-risk, high-casualty attacks. Waves of bombings against apartments and airliners routinely caused scores of casualties, while barricade-and-hostage operations secured hundreds of hostages, many of whom later died in rescue operations or at the hands of nervous terrorists. Although never formally becoming an affiliate or franchise of al Qaeda, the group nonetheless developed ties to the more famous terrorist network and certainly matched al Qaeda for conducting large-scale operations with little regard for an exit strategy for the attack force.

The leader of the attack team, Shamil Basayev, believed in leading from the front. He became a key rebel commander during the first Chechen war of 1994–1995, having returned to Russia after hijacking an Aeroflot flight to Turkey in 1991. Although he escaped at the end of the incident, authorities had not heard the last of him. On August 22, 1995, he threatened to carry out terrorist attacks using radioactive substances. On November 8, 1995, he told Independent Television Network where there was a buried container of cesium isotope and said that four containers were wrapped in TNT and could be detonated. He led the Islamic International Peacekeeping Brigade, which was established in 1998, and the Riyadus-Salikhin Reconnaissance and Sabotage Battalion of Chechen Martyrs (Requirements for Getting into Paradise). He claimed credit for the May 14, 2003, suicide bombing of an Islamic prayer meeting in Iliskhan-Yurt, a village outside Gudermes, killing 18 people and injuring between 45 and 150; and the September 1, 2004, attack on the school in Beslan in which hundreds were killed. He also directed two suicide bombers onto two Russian jets in 2004. The Federal Security Service on March 15, 2005, offered a $10 million bounty.

Incident: On June 14, 1995, some 75 Chechen rebels invaded the town of Budennovsk, Russia, killed scores of people, and then took over the local hospital, seizing more than 1,300 hostages. The rebels announced that they had killed five hostages and demanded that Russia withdraw troops from the region. The next day, they executed on the street another six captives, including two Russian pilots and some police officers. During tense negotiations with Russian authorities and following two failed rescue attempts by the armed forces elite Alpha Group, the rebels released 400 hostages. The rescuers managed to free 200 hostages, but fire spread through the hospital and the troops withdrew. More than 20 troops were injured in the firefight, which included the use of heavy machineguns, rocket-propelled grenades, cannons, and assault rifles. At least 20 hostages died—some reports say 100—and dozens were wounded in the rescue attempt, which was bitterly protested by their families. Prime Minister Viktor Chernomyrdin initiated publicly televised telephonic negotiations with Basayev, 30, a Chechen guerrilla leader, who demanded to give a news conference. On June 19, 1995, the rebels were permitted to go by bus to Zandak with 139 volunteer hostages, including 9 members of parliament and other politicians, 16 journalists, and local residents. The terrorists then fled to the Caucasus Mountains after freeing the final hostages. Another 764 hostages left the hospital; many did not wait to be tallied. Moscow agreed to a cease-fire in its six-month efforts to end the Chechen independence movement and to begin negotiations to settle the conflict.

President Boris Yeltsin refused to return from the G-7 meeting in Halifax, Nova Scotia, Canada, saying he would not bow to terrorist threats. He called Chechnya the center of world terrorism.

Many of the hostages were criticized for identifying with the attackers and saying that they had been well-treated—classic Stockholm syndrome behavior. The freed hostages pointed out that the rebels donated their own blood for the wounded.

Basayev's wife and six children had been killed by Russian forces earlier in the month.

On June 22, 1995, Russian and Chechen negotiators agreed that the rebels would begin to disarm and Russian troops would partially withdraw from the region. The accord called for an immediate cease-fire, an exchange of prisoners, and the establishment of a demilitarized zone. The Chechen delegates agreed to help the Russian authorities search for and arrest the Budennovsk hostage-takers. General Anatoly Kulikov, head of Russian forces in the region, said the accord would be jeopardized if Basayev and his men were not handed over. He was quoted by the news media as observing, "We reserve the right to resume military actions and adopt measures to detain or destroy the criminals."

The Russian Duma (parliament) urged Yeltsin to fire his aides, threatening a no-confidence motion. On June 29, 1995, the leading hawks in Yeltsin's government offered to resign. They included Defense Minister Pavel Grachev; Sergei Stepashin, chief of the Federal Security Service; Internal Affairs Minister Viktor Yerin; Oleg Lobov, secretary of the Security Council; Deputy Prime Minister Nikolai Yegorov; and Yevgeny Kuznetsov, governor of the Stavropol region. On June 30, 1995, Yeltsin accepted the resignations of Stepashin, Yerin, Kuznetsov, and Yegorov.

By June 26, 1995, rebels and police were still searching for Basayev, who many believed had fled to Pakistan.

On July 10, 2006, a dynamite-laden truck exploded around midnight near Ekazhevo in Inguishetia amidst the convoy of Chechen terrorists, killing Basayev, 41. It was unclear whether the government had placed the 220 pounds of dynamite on the truck or whether it was dynamite mishandled by the terrorists. Another dozen terrorists died in the explosion, which destroyed the truck and three cars in the convoy.

November 23, 1996
Ethiopian Airlines ET961 Hijacking

Overview: Hijackers generally tried to use planes to get them to a destination originally unscheduled and to use the passengers as bargaining chips to obtain political, monetary, or other demands. In the 1960s, individuals or small groups of friends hijacked planes as an alternative form of transportation. The 1970s ushered in the era of terrorist hijackings. Increased security measures made this type of terrorist operation rare, although on occasion, terrorist hijackings occurred on flights with minimal screening. The hijackers of Ethiopian Airlines flight 961 appeared to not be as bright as more sophisticated members of terrorist organizations. They showed that it is never a good idea to let hijackers inside the cockpit, but locking the cockpit doors did not become standard practice until after 9/11.

Incident: On November 23, 1996, Ethiopian Airlines flight ET961, a B-767 carrying 163 passengers and 12 crew, was hijacked at 11:20 A.M. after take-off from Addis Ababa. It was scheduled to fly to Nairobi, Kenya; Brazzaville, Congo; Lagos, Nigeria; and Abidjan, Ivory Coast, but the hijackers demanded to go to Australia to obtain political asylum. They were armed with an ax, a fire extinguisher, and a device they claimed was a bomb. At one point, a drunken hijacker forced copilot Yonas Mekuria away from his seat and played with the joystick controls, putting the plane into steep turns and banks. The hijackers refused to believe that the plane was running out of fuel, claiming that the plane could fly for 11 hours without stopovers. Rekha Mirchandani, 29, an Indian passenger, said crew members told her that the hijackers had responded, "If we die, we want others to die with us. We want to make history." The plane crashed at 3:20 P.M. into the Indian Ocean near the Grand Comore Mitsamiuti tourist beach in the Comoros Islands, killing 127 people, most of them Africans and Asians. The pilot, Capt. Leul Abate, tried to minimize casualties by landing in the sea near the shore, where rescuers could more quickly find survivors. However, the plane bounced and flipped before breaking apart. This was the third hijacking Abate had survived.

Police initially arrested two men for the hijacking, but determined that they were innocent when the copilot said that he did not recognize them.

The hijackers were Ethiopians who had lived in Djibouti for years before coming to Addis Ababa five weeks before the hijacking. Authorities were unable to determine the motives of Alamayhu Bekele, Mateias Solomon, and Sultan Hussein, who did not belong to any political party. Kenyan survivor Kanaidza Abwao, a young hotel executive whose hand was broken in the crash, said in a press interview that the hijackers used the plane's public address system to read a statement in Amharic, French, and English: "There is a problem with the government. We were prisoners, and now we have changed the destination. If anyone tries to attack us we are going to blow the plane up. I have a grenade."

Among the dead was Mohamed Amin, 53, a Reuter Television camera-man whose 1984 photos alerted the world about the Ethiopian famine. He was returning home to Nairobi with Brian Tetley, who wrote the texts for Amin's photo books. Also killed was Leslianne Shedd, 28, a commercial officer with the U.S. Embassy, who was headed for Kenya to meet friends for Thanksgiving. Also missing was Ron Farris, 46, a missionary doctor returning from India to Abidjan.

No one was charged in the case.

December 17, 1996
Japan Embassy in Peru Takeover

Overview: Most leftist Latin American terrorists had seen their heyday in the 1970s, but remained a security concern for many nations, notably Colombia and Peru, for decades. While the Shining Path had proven a more active terrorist threat for Peru, the most spectacular operation was conducted by the Tupac Amaru Revolutionary Movement (Movimiento Revolucionario Túpac Amaru, MRTA), which resurrected the barricade-and-hostage style attack. Patient negotiations gave the government time to prepare for a dangerous but ultimately successful raid on the terrorists, who had wearied in the months-long siege. The rescue broke the back of the MRTA.

Incident: On December 17, 1996, two dozen MRTA gunmen blew a hole in a concrete wall at 8:20 P.M. and stormed a birthday party for Japanese emperor Akihito at the residence of the Japanese ambassador in Lima, Peru, seizing 700 diplomats, business leaders, and government officials. The gunmen told the hostages to lie on the ground and to keep silent. One hostage saw six or seven guerrillas dressed in green army fatigue pants. They covered their faces with red and white bandannas and carried small arms. Some barricaded the doors and windows with furniture. When Peruvian police fired tear gas into the residence, the terrorists pulled gas masks from small backpacks. The gunmen joined comrades who were disguised as waiters for the cocktail reception. Cartridges had been smuggled inside flowers and the Christmas cake. The rebels had rented an adjacent house three months earlier and tunneled into the grounds.

The rebels included two young women and appeared to have automatic weapons and night-vision equipment. They told hostages the garden was mined and the back door booby-trapped.

A rebel was injured in the initial firefight.

The rebels said they were protesting the Japanese government's support to the Peruvian regime. The hostages included at least 60 Japanese, including 17 Japanese Embassy staff members and representatives of

17 Japanese firms doing business in Peru, as well as guests from at least 28 countries.

The terrorists threatened to kill the hostages one by one, starting with Peruvian foreign minister Francisco Tudela, unless the government freed 400 or 500 hundred jailed insurgents, including their leader Victor Polay and Lori Helene Berenson, a New Yorker serving a life sentence in Yanamayo prison. The Marxist rebels also called on the government to change its economic policies "to benefit the poor," a monetary "war tax" ransom, and safe passage to the Amazon jungle, where their last hostage would be released. A deadline passed without bloodshed.

Among the hostages were the president of the Peruvian Supreme Court; President Alberto Fujimori's brother; the Speaker of Parliament; Agriculture Minister Rodolfo Munante Sanguineti; the current and past chiefs of the antiterrorism police; an admiral; generals; senior intelligence officials; several congressmen; 19 foreign ambassadors, including those from Japan, Cuba, South Korea, Panama, Austria, and Spain; and other senior diplomats from Argentina, Brazil, Bulgaria, Egypt, Spain, the United Kingdom, Guatemala, Honduras, Poland, and Venezuela. During the event, the rebels released scores of women, including Peruvian president Fujimori's mother and sister. Seven Americans were taken hostage, including four officials of the Agency for International Development. Also held were executives from Mitsui, Marubeni, Kanematsu, Fujita, Japan Water Works, Japan Airlines, Nissho Iwai, Ajinomoto, Matsushita Electric Industrial, NGS Consultants, Toyota, Nissan, NEC, Asahi Chemical Industry, and Tomen, plus employees of several Japanese trade associations and Japanese teachers. Representatives from Malaysia, the Dominican Republic, the European Union, and Uruguay were also held.

The rebels' Communique No. 1, from the Edgar Sanchez Special Forces commanded by Comrade Edigiro Huerta, issued the group's demands to end the "military occupation." The group contacted radio and television stations throughout the day. They asked to see Jorge Santistevan, Peru's human rights ombudsman, and Reverend Hubert Lanssiers. The duo were turned back from the residence by Peruvian authorities.

The rebels permitted all female hostages and four elderly Japanese guests to leave on December 17, 1996.

The Peruvian government refused to negotiate, although the Japanese government announced that the hostages' safety was its first priority.

The gunmen, who included at least three non-Peruvians, permitted family members to send in fresh clothing to the hostages via the Red Cross. The guerrillas asked for cellular telephones from a specific company, toothbrushes, toilet paper, sutures, bandages, and an X-ray machine. Captives were permitted to make brief phone calls.

Michael Minnig, a Swiss Red Cross official, led the negotiations. Four ambassadors were released on December 18, 1996, to serve as "hostages on parole" and were to "act as a link for communications," according to

Canadian ambassador Anthony Vincent, who often shuttled between the residence and the outside world during the negotiations.

On December 19, 1996, two shots were fired at 4:30 P.M. inside the compound. At 6 P.M., four men—two Japanese businessmen and two Peruvians, one of them a businessman—were freed for medical reasons.

Apoyo pollster Alfredo Torres, one of 38 hostages released on December 20, 1996, reported that the terrorists "classified" the hostages by their "value," sending the more valuable 180 upstairs. Torres released the results of a poll of the first floor hostages, indicating that 78 percent thought their treatment was favorable, 83 percent said that the worst thing was uncertainty, and 87 percent said that the attack revealed a serious security lapse.

Also freed were the ambassadors of Brazil, Egypt, and South Korea, who were chosen by the remaining diplomats to "establish channels of communication." The rebels also sent out a 12-point communique.

The press reported that the rebel leader was Nestor Cerpa Cartolini (alias Comrade Evaristo or Commandante Huertas), a Marxist ideologue and the only MRTA leader at large. A former textile union official, he was one of the group's founders in 1984 and served as its military commander. He demanded to talk to the prisoners and the media, but a speech by President Fujimori seemed to rule out both options.

On December 22, 1996, in a "Christmas gesture," the MRTA released 225 hostages, among them all of the Americans; the ambassadors of Panama, Cuba, and Venezuela; along with Elmer Escobar, the representative to Lima of the Washington-based Pan-American Health Organization. Until his release, Escobar had served as the principal coordinator for health care inside the residence. The freed Austrian ambassador reported that each terrorist had 15 kilograms of explosives strapped to his body.

On December 24, 1996, the rebels freed Uruguayan ambassador Tabare Bocalandro Yapeyu. Uruguay later confirmed that a Uruguayan appeals court had released Sonia Silvia Gora Rivera and Luis Alberto Miguel Samaniego, two MRTA members imprisoned in December while entering the country with false passports, but denied that it had arranged for the ambassador's release.

On Christmas Day, the rebels freed a Japanese Embassy first secretary, who was led out in a wheelchair.

On December 26, 1996, at 1:45 A.M., an explosion was heard inside the residence. Observers suggested that an animal had set off a mine.

The Peruvian government suspended a March 1993 accord that permitted the Red Cross to visit 4,000 accused or convicted terrorists, including the 404 MRTA prisoners. Police also detained 28 people, including 6 women, on suspicion of being involved in the siege.

The rebels freed another 20 hostages on December 28, 1996, after having their first direct talks in the residence with Education Minister Palermo. The freed hostages included the ambassadors of Malaysia and the

Dominican Republic and a Peruvian businessman. After they were released, Minnig used a bullhorn to read a rebel communique, in which the MRTA criticized the rival Shining Path terrorists. The freed hostages said that the guerrillas had strapped explosives to their bodies and had booby-trapped the entrances.

Other hostages were sequentially released during the following months. On January 7, 1996, at 4:00 A.M., a rebel fired his gun; no injuries were reported. Negotiations had been suspended for the previous five days.

Four shots rang out inside the residence on January 10, 1996, at 3:00 A.M.

Later that day, Fujimori said in an interview that his government had conducted only three direct conversations with the rebels. One country had offered asylum. The government had proposed that an independent commission might find an "exit" for surrendering rebels.

Three bursts of gunfire were heard from the residence on January 13, 1996, at 11:20 A.M. Police believed they were shooing away helicopters that ventured too close.

The rebels agreed to a mediation commission on January 15, 1996. Cerpa requested representatives from Guatemala and a European country.

On January 27, 1996, during a police show of force that included armored vehicles, a volley of shots fired into the air rang out from the compound.

After the two-hour meeting with Japanese prime minister Ryutaro Hashimoto on February 1, 1996, Fujimori announced that as long as the hostages were unharmed, he would not use force to rescue them and end the incident. Fujimori announced that Cerpa had given up on the demand for prisoner release; Cerpa angrily denied the claim.

On February 10, 1996, the rebels said they were willing to restart face-to-face talks with the government, but would not drop their prisoner release demand. The next day, the government and rebels discussed terms of the talks for four hours.

Following Fujimori's visit to Havana, Cuban president Fidel Castro offered asylum to the rebels on March 3, 1996; the rebels rejected asylum in the Dominican Republic the next day. Cerpa said that the rebels wanted to stay in Peru. Talks between the rebels and government resumed on March 3, 1996, but were suspended by the rebels on March 6, 1996, when they claimed that they heard tunneling by security forces. Japanese vice foreign minister Masahiko Komura visited Lima for two days, then met with Fidel Castro in Havana on March 19, 1996, to formalize a request for granting asylum.

The government conducted a surprise raid at 3:17 P.M. on April 22, 1996, freeing 71 hostages. The 140 rescuers from the army, air force, and navy killed all 14 terrorists after setting off explosives under a rebel soccer game. One hostage, Peruvian Supreme Court justice Carlos Giusti Acuna, died from a heart attack; 25 others, including Japanese ambassador Mori-hita Aoki, Foreign Minister Francisco Tudela, and Supreme Court Judge Luis Serpa Segura, were slightly injured. Two soldiers died in the gunfire that ended the 126-day standoff. President Fujimori was at the scene to give the orders to attack. The soldiers swarmed through tunnels secretly dug by local miners. Hours after the hostages had been taken, Fujimori had ordered the military to begin training for the rescue operation at a secluded naval base on Fronton Island, off the port of Callao.

The news media reported that the Peruvians used several methods to gather information about the whereabouts and intentions of the terrorists. A transmitter was smuggled in for the use of the hostages to keep in touch with the government. The *Associated Press* said that microphones were hidden in a chess piece, crutches used by terrorist Eduardo Cruz, a thermos, a guitar, and a Bible. The rescuers used periscopes to keep tabs on the terrorists. The rescuers tipped off some of the hostages 10 minutes ahead of time that they would swarm in via a network of tunnels.

On May 17, 2002, a forensic report on the 126-day hostage siege indicated that at least eight terrorists were incapacitated and then shot from behind. The government issued arrest warrants for a dozen commandos who participated in the raid, accusing them of executing several MRTA hostage-takers. The military refused to turn over any of them, including Brigadier General Jose Williams, saying they were only doing their duty in protecting Peru. The warrants were revoked following nationwide protests and calls in Congress for a blanket amnesty.

November 17, 1997
Luxor Attack

Overview: Before he joined Osama bin Laden to form and lead al Qaeda, Egyptian physician Ayman al-Zawahiri led al-Gama'at al-Islamiyya, an antiregime Egyptian terrorist group that conducted numerous attacks throughout the country. Its claims to infamy included the assassination of Egyptian president Anwar Sadat on October 6, 1981. Its most deadly attack was on foreign tourists at Luxor, Egypt.

Incident: On November 17, 1997, at 9:30 A.M., six Muslim militants dressed in black sweaters similar to the winter uniforms of the Egyptian police got out of a car and fired on foreign tourists at Luxor, killing 58 foreigners and 4 Egyptians, including 2 policemen. The terrorists were armed with six machine guns, two handguns, and police-issue ammunition. They also had two bags of homemade explosives. Witnesses differed as to whether they arrived by taxi or on foot. Some wore red bandannas with black lettering that said, "We will fight until death."

Ahmed Ghassan, 40, a police guard at the ticket booth, told the news media that he stopped the six men and asked for their tickets. The last man pulled out a gun and said, "This is the ticket." He then shot Ghassan in the elbow and leg. Ghassan said several other guards were also shot and fell on top of him. The terrorists later slit the throats of wounded tourists.

An early tally of the dead included 14 Japanese, 34 Swiss, 3 Egyptians, 5 Germans, 6 Britons including a child, a Bulgarian, a Colombian, and several French tourists (there was some double counting and confusion about nationalities). Eight of the 24 wounded were in critical condition. A doctor removed a bloody al-Gama'at al-Islamiyya (Islamic Group) pamphlet from a wound in the abdomen of a dead Japanese man. A Japanese woman was missing an ear. A European man's nose had been cut off. Robyn Du Plessis, 22, of Durban, South Africa, said that the tourists hid in the tombs for three hours.

After an hour-long gun battle in which one terrorist died, the five surviving terrorists hijacked the tour bus of Hagag Nahas, 36, who had dropped off 30 Swiss an hour earlier. The terrorists forced him to drive "to another place so they could shoot more people," according to press accounts. He drove for an hour before he stopped near the access road to the Valley of the Queens, half a mile away from the temple. A terrorist clubbed Nahas in the chest with the butt of his rifle. Police fired on the gunmen, killing one terrorist. The rest fled into nearby mountains. Police said they had caught up to the bus and killed all five gunmen, who had fired into the crowds along the plaza facing the 3,400-year-old Hatshepsut temple.

One of the dead terrorists was identified as Midhat Abd-al-Rahman, who had left Egypt in 1993 for Pakistan and Sudan, where he received military training and was involved with Islamic Group leaders.

In a November 20, 1997, fax to foreign news agencies, the Islamic Group said it would quit its attacks if its leader was released from a U.S. jail, several of its members were released from prison, and the government severed relations with Israel. One leaflet said that the attack was a gesture to Mustafa Hamza, an exiled mastermind of the June 1995 assassination attempt against Egyptian president Hosni Mubarak.

The Islamic Group said that it had not intended to kill the victims but had planned to take them hostage to force the United States to release its leader, Sheikh Omar Abdel-Rahman, from a New York federal prison. However, witnesses said that there was no evidence that the terrorists attempted to take hostages. Rather, they chased the tourists, made them get down on their knees, and systematically shot them. Rosemarie Dousse, who was wounded in the arm and leg, told Swiss television that a heavy man fell on top of her and a woman behind her also covered her. The terrorists shot those who were still alive in the head. Other Swiss survivors said that the gunmen beat children with guns, raped and mutilated women, and danced for joy as they slaughtered the tourists.

Egyptian president Mubarak deemed Luxor security "a joke" and fired his interior minister, the Luxor police chief, and several other security officials. On November 22, 1997, new Interior Minister Maj. Gen. Habib Adli told Parliament that the armed forces would join police in protecting tourist sites. Mubarak ruled out a dialogue with the Islamic Group.

On November 24, 1997, Tala'eh Al-Fath (the Vanguards of Conquest) told *USA Today* that orders "have already been given for attacks against

Americans and Zionists not only in Egypt but elsewhere." They claimed to be the successors of the Jihad group that assassinated Egyptian president Anwar Sadat in 1981. Meanwhile, Sheikh Salah Hashem, 44, of the Islamic Group, said the government should be prepared for more attacks.

Within a week, tourism in Egypt had halved and had dropped 90 percent in Luxor.

On June 28, 1998, in the first trial of its kind, a police disciplinary tribunal fired former Luxor police chief Maj. Gen. Medhat Shanawani and his deputy, Maj. Gen. Abul-Atta Youssef Abul-Atta, for ignoring security warnings that the sites in Luxor could be targeted. Their police pensions were also reduced.

In February 1999, Uruguay arrested Said Hazan Mohammed (variant al-Said Hassan Mokhles), while he was trying to enter the country from Brazil with a fake Malaysian passport. In July 2003, Uruguay extradited him to Egypt, which said that he was an Islamic Group member and possible al Qaeda associate. Egypt agreed that he would not be subjected to the death penalty, permanent imprisonment, or charged for document fraud, for which he already had served four years.

In April 2002, the Brazilian Federal Police arrested Egyptian Mohammed Ali Aboul-Ezz al-Mahdi Ibrahim Soliman in the tri-border city of Foz do Iguazu. He was arrested on the basis of an Egyptian government extradition request in the Luxor case. The Brazilian Supreme Court released him on September 11, 2002, due to insufficient evidence to extradite him. On September 14, 2002, Brazil arrested another Islamic Group suspect, Hesham al-Tarabili, at Egypt's request in connection with the case. His judicial status was not reported.

August 7, 1998
Tanzania and Kenya U.S. Embassy Bombings

Overview: The Middle East and Europe had historically been the most likely locations for attacks by jihadi and other Middle Eastern terrorist groups. Attacks in Africa, by anyone, against foreign nationals were more statistical oddities than considered an ongoing security threat. That perception changed when al Qaeda again showed its penchant for complex, coordinated attacks against multiple targets; this time against U.S. embassies in Nairobi and Dar es Salaam. In an address to the nation, President Clinton vowed:

> No matter how long it takes, or where it takes us, we will pursue terrorists until the cases are solved and justice is done. The bombs that kill innocent Americans are aimed . . . at the very spirit of our country and the spirit of freedom, for terrorists are the enemies of everything we believe in and fight

for: peace and democracy, tolerance and security. As long as we continue to believe in those values and continue to fight for them, their enemies will not prevail. Our responsibility is great, but the opportunities it brings are even greater. Let us never fear to embrace them.

An initial set of airstrikes was followed by a worldwide manhunt. As of this writing, many of the planners await trial in Guantanamo.

Incidents: Some 253 people, including 12 Americans, were killed and more than 5,500 wounded, including 80 non-Africans, when a car bomb went off in the Ufundi Cooperative Building in Nairobi, next door to the U.S. Embassy, at 10:35 A.M. Five minutes later, a truck bomb exploded at the U.S. Embassy in Dar Es Salaam, Tanzania, killing 10 Tanzanians and injuring at least 70 people.

Several groups claimed responsibility. The previously unknown Islamic Army for the Liberation of Holy Places demanded the release of detained Islamic militants, that the U.S. military leave Saudi Arabia, and that the United States end support to Israel. It said Osama bin Laden and Sheikh Omar Abdel-Rahman served as its inspiration. A communique sent to Agence France Press claimed credit for the Dar es Salaam bombing for the Abdallah Azzam Battalion.

Most observers believed that terrorists from outside the countries were responsible. Many suspected exiled Saudi terrorist financier Osama bin Laden of being behind the attacks. Others suggested Ayman al-Zawahiri, the exiled leader of the Egyptian Islamic Jihad Organization. The previous week, the group had threatened to attack the United States for the June 28, 1998, capture in Albania and extradition to Egypt of three Islamic militants connected to the ethnic Albanian separatist in Kosovo, Yugoslavia. One of the captured individuals was Ahmed Ibrahim Najjar, who was under sentence of death in Egypt for his role in the attack on Cairo's Khan el Khalili bazaar. Both suspects were believed to be hiding out in Afghanistan.

Kenya. An embassy guard said that someone got out of a truck and threatened him with a grenade. The guard ran away, but the terrorist threw the grenade. There apparently were some shots before the vehicle exploded in a parking lot at one of the city's busiest intersections. It flattened the Ufundi Cooperative Building and seriously damaged the U.S. Embassy. Numerous cars were destroyed and windows a mile and a half away were broken. Damaged buildings included the Cooperative Bank House, the Extelcoms telecommunications headquarters, the Kenya Railways Headquarters, and the Pioneer House. Passengers in a bus were incinerated where they sat. At least 12 U.S. citizens were killed, along with 14 Kenyans who worked at the U.S. Embassy. Some 153 Kenyans were blinded. The rest of the dead were Kenyans. Among those injured was Kenyan trade minister Joseph Kamotho.

The bodies of 11 dead Americans were brought home to U.S. soil on August 14, 1998, accompanied by Secretary of State Madeleine Albright, who had announced a $2 million reward for information leading to the capture and conviction of the killers.

Tanzania. Most of the dead had been working at the guard post at the embassy entrance near where the bomb exploded. All either worked at the embassy or for a security company that guarded the gate. The bomb apparently was attached to an embassy-owned tanker truck delivering water. After it was waved through the security gates, it exploded several feet from the embassy's southeastern edge, tearing a large crater in Laibon Street. The blast destroyed the guardhouse and killed the driver, Yusuf Shamte Ndange. It was unclear whether the bomb was remotely detonated or had exploded when it was discovered by guards. Nearby cars were badly damaged. The home of the British high commissioner two blocks away had broken windows and damage from debris. A multicar pileup ensued when cars were hit by the debris. The nearby French and German embassies were damaged, but no injuries were reported there. At least 22 cars were destroyed.

On August 11, 1998, the Tanzanian police announced that they had arrested 30 foreigners in connection with the blast. They included six Iraqis, six Sudanese, a Somali, and a Turk. The Sudanese included a teen and a man who claimed to work for the Saudi Embassy. The Iraqis included a teacher, a civil servant, a telecommunications technician, an engineer, and an agricultural engineer (the sixth Iraqi was not identified). Fourteen lacked passports and could not give a reason for being in the country.

Epilogue. Pakistani officials arrested a Jordanian-born Palestinian, Mohammed Saddiq Odeh, an engineer, at Karachi Airport the day of the bombings and returned him to Kenya on August 14, 1998, for traveling on a false Yemeni passport with a fake visa, using the name Abdul Bast Awadah. He had flown to Pakistan on August 6, 1998. He said his spiritual guide was bin Laden and that he was attempting to seek refuge with him in Afghanistan. He claimed that the bomb contained 1,760 pounds of TNT and was assembled over several days at the hotel under his direction. Police held three other people in connection with the attack. Two names given were Mohammed Saleh and Abdullah (identities uncertain). Odeh also claimed that his group had taken part in the October 1993 attack on U.S. forces in Mogadishu, Somalia, which killed 18 Americans.

On August 18, 1998, authorities raided two rooms in the seedy Hilltop Hotel that had been occupied by two Palestinians, a Saudi, and an Egyptian from August 3 to August 7, 1998. Odeh said the bomb was made between August 4 and August 6, 1998, in the rooms.

On August 19, 1998, the Taliban refused to turn bin Laden over to the West, even if the West had proof that he was behind the bombings.

On August 20, 1998, the United States fired 79 Tomahawk cruise missiles at the Zhawar Kili al-Badr paramilitary training camps in Afghanistan and Sudan's Shifa pharmaceutical plant that was believed to be developing EMPTA, a VX chemical weapons precursor. All facilities were suspected of being used in planning new anti-U.S. attacks. Bin Laden's terrorist training complex in Khost, Afghanistan, 94 miles southeast of Kabul, just inside the border with Pakistan, was deemed by President Clinton as "one of the most active terrorist bases in the world." Initial damage was reported to be moderate to heavy. Afghanistan said 21 people were killed and more than 50 wounded in the camps around Khost, near the Pakistan border.

On August 21, 1998, the Nairobi *Daily News* reported that Khalid Mohammed was identified as the man who threw the grenade at the guards before escaping. He was picked out of a police lineup by witnesses.

On September 5, 1998, Tanzania arrested two suspects. A Nairobi suspect, Fazul Abdullah Mohammed (alias Harun Fazul), is an explosives expert.

On September 16, 1998, German police arrested Mamduh Mahmud Salim, an al Qaeda member who was described as a major financial operative who also procured weapons. A sealed warrant seeking his arrest was recently filed in Manhattan.

On December 19, 1998, the FBI arrested U.S. citizen Wadih el-Hage, a Lebanese Christian who once served as bin Laden's personal secretary. He lived and worked with Mohammed while working in the gem business in Kenya until 1997. He helped Odeh obtain an identity card and sent him to Somalia in 1997 for bin Laden. The U.S. State Department announced a $2 million reward for the capture of Mohammed, who was charged in the Kenya attack. On September 21, 1998, el-Hage was indicted with eight counts of perjury. Federal prosecutors said that he once purchased guns in Texas for one of the 1993 WTC bombers, and that he had contacts with Sayyid A. Nosair, who helped plan the WTC bombing and who killed Jewish Defense League leader Meir Kahane in 1990.

On September 21, 1998, Egyptian Mustafa Mahmoud Said Ahmed (alias Said Ahmed and Saleh Aben Alahales) and Tanzanian Rashid Saleh Hemed, Zanzibar native, were charged in a Dar es Salaam courtroom with 11 counts of murder.

On October 7, 1998, a federal grand jury in New York handed down a 238-count indictment, charging several of bin Laden's disciples of planning to kill Americans. The plot included the Tanzania and Kenya bombings and the training of militias that attacked U.S. soldiers in Somalia in 1993. The plot named U.S. citizen el-Hage, Mohammed Rashed Daoud al-Owhali, Azzam (who apparently died in the Nairobi blast), Odeh, Mohammed, and Salim. Unindicted coconspirators included Zawahiri; Ahmed Refai Taha, Gama'at leader; and former Gama'at leader Sheikh Abdel-Rahman. Prosecutors also sought the extradition of Khaled al-Fawaz, a bin Laden spokesman who was arrested in September 1998 in London. Mohammed, Odeh, and Owhali were charged with 224 counts of murder. Odeh and Mohammed were charged with training the Somalis. On October 8, 1998, el-Hage, Odeh, and Owhali pleaded not guilty.

On November 5, 1998, the U.S. State Department offered a $5 million reward for bin Laden's arrest. Bin Laden and his top military commander, Muhammed Atef, were indicted by a New York federal grand jury in U.S. District Court on 238 counts for the August 7, 1998, bombings and for conspiracy to kill Americans overseas.

On December 16, 1998, the U.S. District Court in Manhattan issued a 238-count indictment against fugitives Mustafa Mohammed Fadhil, an Egyptian; Khalfan Khamis Mohamed, a Tanzanian; Ahmed Khalfan Ghailani, a Tanzanian; Fahid Mohammed Ally Msalam, a Kenyan; and Sheikh Ahmed Salim Swedan, a Kenyan, on charges of bringing the vehicles, including the 1987 Nissan Atlas truck that carried the bomb and the oxygen and acetylene tanks used in the Dar es Salaam attack.

On July 5, 1999, President Clinton signed Executive Order 13129 that banned all commercial and financial dealings between the United States and Afghanistan's ruling Taliban militia, which was providing refuge to bin Laden. The order froze all Taliban assets in the United States, barred the import of products from Afghanistan, and made it illegal for U.S. firms to sell goods and services to the Taliban.

London police arrested Ibrahim Hussein Abd-al-Hadi Eidarous and Adel Meguid Abd-al-Bary on extradition warrants on July 11, 1999, at a request from the United States. Their fingerprints appeared on originals of faxes that claimed credit for the bombings.

On October 8, 1999, Khalfan Khamis Mohamed, a Tanzanian whose house was used as a bomb factory and who was arrested in South Africa on October 5, 1999, was charged in federal court in New York on charges of murder and conspiracy in the two bombings.

On December 22, 2004, the Tanzanian High Court freed Hemed, even though a bomb detonator was discovered in his house and he admitted knowing people involved in the bombing.

On April 13, 2006, Egyptian explosives expert Muhsin Musa Matwalli Atwah was killed in a helicopter strike in North Waziristan.

On March 12, 2007, Tawfiq bin Attash told a U.S. military tribunal in Guantanamo that he organized the USS *Cole* attack and the Africa embassy bombings.

On November 17, 2010, Ghailani was found guilty of one count of conspiracy to damage or destroy U.S. property but acquitted of 284 counts of murder and attempted murder.

Osama bin Laden died in a SEAL raid in Abbotabad, Pakistan, on May 2, 2011.

On June 7, 2011, Somali officials killed Mohammed and a second al Qaeda operative in a shoot-out at a Mogadishu checkpoint.

Several suspects awaited trial in Guantanamo Bay military prison in late 2013.

August 15, 1998
Omagh, Northern Ireland, Bombing

Overview: Efforts to end the decades-long Irish Troubles came in fits and starts as various legal parties and underground factions of Catholics and Protestants faced off, often demanding irreconcilable terms. The Provisional Irish Republican Army (IRA) often saw tiny but recalcitrant groups of thugs refuse to accept negotiated agreements and start up their own terrorist campaigns. One of the most active was the Real IRA, which conducted a record mass-casualty attack in Northern Ireland. Omagh became a rallying cry for peace activists on both sides of the dispute and both sides of the border.

Incident: On August 15, 1998, the Real IRA, an IRA splinter group, set off a 500-pound car bomb in the Omagh town square during the afternoon, killing 29 people, including babies, grandfathers, and a pregnant woman, and wounding more than 350 others. The bombing was the bloodiest single incident in three decades of sectarian violence. The group said it was "part of an ongoing war against the Brits," but that "it was not our intention . . . to kill any civilians." The group claimed that it had given a 40-minute warning. However, police said that the warning said the bomb was near the courthouse at the west end of town. Shoppers were directed to move east down Market Street, where the bomb really was. Police believed that the bomb might have been placed by a young terrorist who did not know the town's layout. Several thousand people representing Catholics and Protestants conducted an outdoor memorial service.

The maroon Vauxhall sedan used for the bomb was stolen in Ireland the previous week.

On August 17, 1998, police arrested five suspected Real IRA members, including Shane Mackey, son of Francis Mackey, an Omagh city council member and chairman of the 32-County Sovereignty Committee, a group opposed to the peace plan and believed to be the political arm of the Real IRA. The group was headed by Mickey McKevitt, 49, a former senior IRA member. He had served as the IRA's quartermaster. He had been shot in both legs by the IRA in 1975 for breaking rules. However, he never revealed the names of his attackers.

The United States refused a visa to Bernadette Sands-McKevitt, a spokeswoman for the Real IRA's political front. She is the sister of the late Bobby Sands, an IRA member who died during a prison hunger strike in 1981. Store owners demanded her eviction from a local mall where she had a print shop.

Britain and Ireland vowed to institute a severe crackdown on terrorists. On September 3, 1998, the British and Irish parliaments approved emergency legislation making it easier to arrest suspected terrorists and hold them without bail. Judges were authorized to order the jailing of suspects without bail if a police official testified that they are believed to be terrorists; corroborating evidence was no longer needed. The statutes also permit courts to consider an accused's refusal to answer questions as evidence of guilt.

On September 7, 1998, the Real IRA declared "a complete cessation of all military activity," although it did not apologize for the bombing.

On September 21, 1998, police arrested nine people in dawn raids on both sides of the Irish border. Irish police grabbed three men aged 19–34, while Northern Ireland authorities detained another 6. Northern Ireland authorities released the six on September 27, 1998.

Sinead O'Connor, U2, Liam Neeson, Boyzone, and Van Morrison joined several other rock stars in releasing an album entitled *Across the Bridge of Hope* on November 30, 1998; the profits went to the victims. Neeson read a poem written by Shaun McLaughlin, 12, who was killed in the bombing.

On February 22, 1999, Belfast police began interrogating nine men on suspicion of involvement in the bombing. The Royal Ulster Constabulary said they were questioning six men in a crackdown on the IRA. Irish Republic police released two of five men they arrested on February 21, 1999, in a related operation. On February 23, 1999, a spokesman for the Garda Siochana, Ireland's national police, said it would charge a man with two offenses in Dublin's three-judge no-jury Special Criminal Court that hears terrorist offenses. He would be accused of being a member of an illegal paramilitary group that broke away from the IRA, and another, unnamed charge.

On February 27, 1999, Irish police questioned two more male unnamed suspects, who were detained in Dundalk. Another man was arrested in connection with the inquiry in another border town. The next day, Dublin police arrested a woman in connection with the case. She was held and questioned under Section 30 of Ireland's Offenses Against the State Act, which allows suspects to be held for up to 72 hours.

On February 24, 1999, Irish authorities charged Colm Murphy, 46, a building contractor and pub owner. He appeared in Dublin's Special Criminal Court three days after police arrested him at his Dundalk farmhouse, 50 miles north of Dublin.

Police in both parts of Ireland arrested 10 suspected IRA dissidents on June 20, 1999. They had arrested but freed without charge nearly 100 people in the case. The next day, Irish police arrested two women in Cavan and Monaghan counties and a man in his twenties in Dundalk. On June 23, 1999, Irish police detained two more men in Dundalk.

As of August 14, 1999, no one was in jail for the crime. Two dozen people had been arrested, some more than once, all but one had been released without charges. Murphy was charged with conspiracy but was free on bail; no trial had been scheduled. On January 2, 2002, Murphy was convicted of conspiracy. On January 25, 2002, he was sentenced to 14 years in jail by a three-judge panel in Dublin. The panel called the wealthy pub owner a "republican terrorist of long standing." Murphy won his appeal and was freed after posting bail on January 28, 2005. The judge said that detectives had lied about the evidence.

On September 3, 2003, a 34-year-old IRA dissident was arrested in Newry on suspicion of involvement. He was charged with conspiracy to cause explosions and possession of explosives. Police charged him on February 8, 2005, saying he stole the car used by the bombers.

On May 26, 2005, Belfast prosecutor charged suspected IRA dissident Sean Gerard Hoey, 35, an unemployed electrician, with 29 counts of murder. On December 20, 2007, he was found not guilty of all 50 charges related to Omagh.

On June 9, 2009, the Belfast High Court ruled that the victims' families could collect $2.4 million in damages from organizers and bombers McKevitt, Liam Campbell, Murphy, and Seamus Daly.

The 2000s

While al Qaeda had established itself among terrorism-watchers as a major threat to Western security, it had not permanently grabbed the headlines until the hijacking and use of jetliners as weapons on September 11, 2001. The 9/11 body count of just under 3,000 victims broke all records. Records for economic impact were also topped, including damage estimates in the billions and secondary effects on stock markets, which saw a $1.3 trillion loss in the days after the attacks. More than a hundred thousand jobs were lost. Significant financial and social costs were incurred from new and heightened security measures. The attacks led to the United States and like-minded nations invading two nations—Afghanistan and Iraq—believed involved in the attacks, or at least neck-deep in supporting some form of international terrorists. Preventive security measures—profiling, pat downs, magnetometers, U.S. creation of a new Cabinet Department of Homeland Security and Transportation Security Administration, and reorganization of the Intelligence Community—in response to the attacks were matched with terrorist adaptation of methods. Although "classical" hijacking was probably stopped—there are still rare instances—terrorists nonetheless tried to attack airliners with shoe and underwear bombs and binary explosives, and to use planes as methods to deliver bombs. The success of any of these methods would have added the event(s) to the *50 Worst* list.

In the 1990s, al Qaeda tended to take several years to develop spectacular *50 Worst*-worthy attacks and rarely took credit for the attacks. Post-9/11 affiliates became far more ready to claim responsibility, even for comparatively amateurish attacks and attempts.

With the main leadership—Osama bin Laden, Ayman al-Zawahiri, and a succession of third-in-commands whose life spans were comparable to fruit flies—of al Qaeda on the run or in graves following the incursions into their Afghan safe havens, the group continued its strategy of evolving rather than giving up. The group soon created a series of offshoots, some with formal franchise arrangements with al Qaeda in their names—al Qaeda in Iraq, al Qaeda in the Islamic Mahgreb, al Qaeda in the Arabian Peninsula, etc.—and some with extensive ties but no official command-and-control agreements, such as Jemaah Islamiyah (JI) and various Philippine groups. Still other cells trained and sometimes obtained weapons from al Qaeda and Taliban remnants, then went on to conduct their own independent operations. Yet other lone wolves who on occasion had met with some flavor of al Qaeda leaders or franchisees, or were merely "self-radicalized" by studying the writings and YouTube videos of al Qaeda, popped up around the world. While the latter are in theory especially difficult to find, inept operational tradecraft of the loners, support for societal stability of peaceful Muslim communities who were quick to point out potential miscreants to government officials, and patient sting operations led to foiling numerous plots that would otherwise have added to the list of *50 Worst*.

International revulsion at the 9/11—and later 3/11 and 7/7—attacks led to an extensive coalition working to "find, fix, and finish" terrorists around the world. This in turn led to the arrests of thousands of terrorist suspects, including numerous "high value" terrorists, who were initially held in local prisons before being turned over to U.S. authorities. The cooperative efforts were so successful in taking terrorists off the streets that the United States was faced with a growing inventory problem. It was at least temporarily resolved with the opening of a terrorist detainee facility at Guantanamo Bay military base on Cuban shores. The detention without trial of scores of major threats to security caused constant tension between civil libertarians and potential prosecutors regarding the ultimately juridical disposition of these individuals. As of this writing, the debate continues.

As in earlier decades, the *worst* of the 2000s included attacks against transportation modes—planes, trains, ships—and symbolic soft targets, including mosques, schools, and theaters. Body counts, particularly of those who were simply in the wrong place at the wrong time, continued to rise. While the literature of academic studies of terrorism debates whether "everything changed" after 9/11—and most garden variety attacks continued to mimic previous patterns of few casualties and exit strategies for the terrorists—suicide bombings and tactics difficult to defend against continued to increase in popularity. That said, the *worst* for this decade, except for occasional Chechen barricade-and-hostage situations causing hundreds of deaths, shows a virtual extinction of end-game calculations by the terrorists. Those that conducted more spectacular incidents were looking to kill, not bargain. Hostage-takers tended to go for a quick headline, then kill the hostages, rather than wait patiently, sometimes years, for negotiations to develop, as had been the case with Hizballah in the 1980s.

Women appeared more frequently as suicide bombers. RAND researcher Karla Cunningham determined that by mid-2008, female suicide bombers were responsible for 21 attacks in Iraqi markets and other Shi'ite civilian venues. State Department intelligence analyst Heidi Panetta added that between 2005 and 2010, women conducted more than 50 suicide attacks in Iraq, accounting for 10 percent of the group's attacks in-country. Between 2002 and 2012, women conducted half of the suicide bombings in Chechnya, Turkey, and Sri Lanka, including some of the *50 Worst* in Russia. Some observers suggested that this is a generational shift in how religious-based radical women now participate in their struggles against established authority. While women have previously been heavily involved in attacks—including in Morocco, Palestine, Lebanon, Israel, Egypt, Japan, Western Europe (especially the 1970s-era groups led by women, including the Petra Kraus Group in Switzerland, the Baader-Meinhof Group in West Germany, and the Japanese Red Army of Fusako Shigenobu)—the lack of an exit strategy is new. Women also appeared in the legions of lone wolves who were caught, including Colleen R. La Rose (alias Jihad Jane) and Jamie Paulin-Ramirez, who attempted to support the jihad at the turn of the decade. Other U.S. women were indicted for supporting terrorists in Somalia, Afghanistan, Egypt, and the United Kingdom.

Terrorists developed use of the Internet, but not in the way that pundits had initially thought. Rather than conduct cyber-attacks that could potentially cripple infrastructure and economies of "the far enemy," al Qaeda and other terrorists found that the Internet was helpful in recruitment and directing overall strategies from afar. While the centralized al Qaeda was rapidly becoming a bad memory, individuals flocked to the jihadi websites to "self-radicalize," publicize their exploits through posted videos of attacks, publish eulogies for their fallen comrades, and share operational tips. Rather than continue with multiyear meticulously planned attacks that had been the watchword of al Qaeda in the 1990s and early 2000s, the new lone wolves could continue the fight, with the enemy now pecked to death by ducks, rather than by one or two spectacular hits.

Finally, although the body and incident counts did not reach the high bar of the *worst*, a spate of beheadings in Iraq marked a new phase in terrorist violence during the decade. Begun initially as a headline-grabbing threat against American hostages, the tactic soon proliferated to threats against Kenyans, Turks, Somalis, Egyptians, Filipinos, Iraqis, and the gruesome murders of Nepalese. The beheaders again broke previous mores with their callous disregard for what had heretofore been commonly accepted norms of decency, and appalled publics wondered what the next group could devise that could be even worse. They soon had their answer when Chechen terrorists shot to death hundreds of fleeing children on their first day of school.

October 12, 2000
Yemen USS *Cole* Attack

Overview: Osama bin Laden's fatwa to attack Americans around the world proved troubling to U.S. policymakers, but did not become of general public concern until the bombings of the two U.S. embassies in Tanzania and Kenya in August 1998 and the bombing of a U.S. Navy destroyer in Aden in 2000. While other terrorist groups were content to set off late-night bombs with no casualties, with these two operations, al Qaeda established itself as the world's preeminent terrorist group, willing to tackle complex terrorist operations. American determination to bring the perpetrators to justice has lasted more than a decade as of this writing, with debates continuing over the venue for the trial of those detained for this and other attacks.

Incident: On October 12, 2000, a 20-foot Zodiac boat laden with explosives came alongside the 8,600-ton USS *Cole*, a 505-foot Arleigh Burke-class guided-missile destroyer, and detonated, ripping a 40 × 40 foot hole in the hull's half-inch-thick armored steel plates near the engine rooms and adjacent eating and living quarters, killing 17 American sailors and injuring another 44. No Yemenis were killed in the Aden port blast.

A Syrian-born cleric living in the United Kingdom, Sheikh Omar Bakri Muhammad, said that the Islamic Army of Aden (alias Aden-Abyan Islamic Army) of Yemen had claimed credit.

Yemeni president Ali Abdullah Saleh told CNN that some detainees belonged to the Egyptian al-Jihad, whose leader, Ayman al-Zawahiri, was with bin Laden in Afghanistan. Saleh said a 12-year-old boy told investigators that a bearded man with glasses gave him 2000 rials ($12) and asked him to watch a four-wheel drive vehicle parked near the port on the day of the attack. The man took a rubber boat off the top of the car and headed into the harbor, never to return. The car led investigators to a modest house in the Madinet al-Shaab suburb of Aden.

On October 16, Yemeni investigators discovered bomb-making material in an apartment used by individuals believed involved. Yemeni security said they were non-Yemeni Arabs; others said they were Saudis who stayed for six weeks in a house near Aden's power station. Another house, close to the Aden refinery and oil storage facilities in the al-Baraiqa neighborhood, was discovered by October 21. The suspects apparently had briefly left and then reentered Yemen before the bombing. They had parked a fiberglass boat in the driveway; the boat was now missing. Police tracked the car to a house in al-Baraiqa, or Little Aden, west of Aden.

The Navy revised its theory of the bombing on October 20, saying that the destroyer had been moored for two hours and was already refueling when the bomb boat came alongside. The boat blended in with harbor workboats and was not suspected by the gun crews on the ship.

By October 24, the investigators were looking at three safe houses that served as the terrorists' quarters in Little Aden, workshop in Madinet ash-Shaab, and lookout perch in the Tawahi neighborhood. A lease for the lookout apartment was signed by Abdullah Ahmed Khaled al-Musawah. Binoculars and Islamic publications were found in the apartment. The same name was found in a fake ID card in personal documents seized in the safe houses. Yemeni investigators detained employees of the Lajeh civil registration office in the northern farming region. Investigators looked at a possible Saudi connection—one of the individuals had a Saudi accent. Others looked at the mountainous province of Hadramaut—one suspect used a name common to the area. The press also indicated that the terrorists' wills dedicated the attack to the al-Aqsa mosque in Jerusalem.

On October 25, Yemeni president Saleh said that the bombing was carried out by Muslims who fought against the Soviet Union in Afghanistan and then moved to Yemen. Egyptian Islamic Jihad terrorists affiliated with bin Laden remained the key suspects; a witness identified one of the bombers as an Egyptian. Yemeni authorities arrested Islamic activists originally from Egypt, Algeria, and elsewhere, as well as local Yemenis. A local carpenter confessed that he had worked with two suspects in modifying a small boat to hold explosives and helped them to load the explosives on board. He had rented the suspects the building where they prepared the boat. A Somali woman who owned a car used by the suspects to haul the boat was questioned. Yemeni investigators believed the terrorists had given her money to buy the car.

The Taliban in Afghanistan said that bin Laden was not responsible. Osama bin Laden welcomed the attack.

Yemen arrested four men living in Aden on November 5 and 6 after tracing them via phone records that showed that they had been in contact with the suspected bombers. Officials in Lahej had provided the bombing suspects with government cars for use in Aden. The bombers knew the officials from their time together in Afghanistan in the 1980s.

On November 11, Yemeni investigators said that at least three plots against U.S. targets in Yemen had failed in the past year. Yemeni officials said a detainee claimed that terrorists had planned to bomb the U.S. destroyer USS *The Sullivans* during refueling in Aden on January 3, 2000. The explosives-laden small boat sank instead from the weight of the explosives.

On November 16, Yemeni prime minister Abdel-Karim Ali Iryani said that the two Yemeni bombers were veterans of the Afghan war. One was a Yemeni born in the eastern province of Hadramaut. (Osama bin Laden had Yemeni citizenship because of his father's birth in the Hadramaut region.)

On November 19, Yemeni authorities said that they had detained "less than 10" suspected accomplices out of the more than 50 people still held for questioning.

An explosives expert reconfigured the charge using lightweight C-4 plastique. The *Yemen Observer* reported that the fiberglass boat was brought in from another country.

On November 21, U.S. officials said that the bombing appeared to be linked to the bombings of the U.S. embassies in Africa in 1998. A composite sketch of one of the bombers appeared to match that of a man wanted for questioning in the Africa bombings.

The State Department announced on December 7 that it supported Yemen's decision to prosecute three and possibly six Yemeni suspects in January, following the end of the holy month of Ramadan. One of them, Fhad al-Qoso, reportedly told investigators that an associate of bin Laden gave him more than $5,000 to finance the *Cole* attack's planning and video-taping of the suicide bombing. Suspect Jamal al-Badawi admitted that he was trained in bin Laden's camps in Afghanistan and was sent with bin Laden's forces to fight in Bosnia's civil war. He was believed to have obtained the boat. Yemen had also identified Muhammad Omar al-Harazi, a Saudi born in Yemen, as a planner of the attack and a member of al Qaeda. He may also have played a role in the truck bombings in Tanzania and Kenya in 1998.

On January 30, 2001, *ABC News* reported that U.S. African embassies bombing defendant Mohamed Rashed Daoud al-Owhali allegedly told the Federal Bureau of Investigation (FBI) in 1998 about a plan for a rocket attack on a U.S. warship in Yemen.

On February 17, 2001, Yemen detained two more suspects when they returned from Afghanistan.

Bin Laden applauded the attack on February 26, 2001, saying the *Cole* was a ship of injustice that sailed "to its doom." His comments were made at a family celebration in Afghanistan and broadcast on Qatar's satellite channel *Al Jazeera*. He recited a poem to celebrate the January marriage of his son, Mohammed, in Qandahar, saying "In Aden, the young man stood up for holy war and destroyed a destroyer feared by the powerful." He said the *Cole* sailed on a course of "false arrogance, self-conceit, and strength."

On March 31, 2001, Yemeni police announced the arrests of several more suspects believed to be Islamic militants. The main suspect apparently fled to Afghanistan. Ali Mohammed Omar Kurdi was arrested; his house had been searched the previous day.

Yemen arrested five suspects with ties to Islamic terrorist cells on April 14 and 15, 2001, bringing the total in custody to 28. Two jailed suspects had informed security officials about terrorist cells operating in the country. The cells had two or three members each and were directed by leaders of Yemen's Islamic Jihad (YIJ) who were based in several countries outside Yemen, including Afghanistan. The cells assisted non-Yemeni Arabs with ties to YIJ by providing forged Yemeni passports, safe houses, and information on Yemeni security.

A 100-minute videotape made by Al-Sahab Productions (The Clouds) circulated in Kuwait City by Muslim terrorists shows bin Laden for several minutes and suggests that his followers bombed the USS *Cole*. His followers training at the Farouq camp in Afghanistan included them singing "We thank God for granting us victory the day we destroyed *Cole* in the sea."

On October 26, 2001, Jamil Qasim Saeed Mohammed, 27, a Yemeni microbiology student and active member of al Qaeda, was handed over to U.S. authorities by Pakistani intelligence, according to Pakistani government sources. Pakistan bypassed the usual extradition and deportation procedures. He was the first suspect captured outside Yemen. He arrived in 1993 in Pakistan from Taiz, Yemen, to study microbiology at the University of Karachi. He was asked to leave in 1996 after failing to qualify for the honors program in which he had enrolled. Pakistani authorities arrested him later that year in connection with the November 1995 bombing of the Egyptian Embassy in Islamabad, but he was released without being charged. He was brought to Karachi International Airport in a rented white Toyota sedan by masked members of the Inter-Services Intelligence (ISI) agency, and handed over to U.S. officials who put him on a Gulfstream V jet. Government authorities detained two other Yemeni university students with ties to Mohammed.

On January 29, 2011, Yemen announced it had tracked down Mohammed Hamdi al-Ahdal and Qaed Salim Sunian al-Harithi, wanted for questioning in the case.

After a $250 million repair, the USS *Cole* returned to service on April 14, 2002.

On November 3, 2002, a Hellfire missile hit a car in Yemen carrying a group of al Qaeda terrorists, killing all six of them, including Abu Ali al-Harithi, a *Cole* suspect. Around that time, authorities captured a suspected planner of the *Cole* attack, al Qaeda member Abd-al-Rahim al-Nashiri, who was believed to have also planned the USS *The Sullivans* attack and the thwarted attack on U.S. and U.K. warships in the Strait of Gibraltar in 2002.

On April 11, 2003, 10 of the main suspects, including Jamal al-Badawi, escaped from an Aden prison.

On May 15, 2003, a federal grand jury indicted on 50 counts Jamal al-Badawi and Fahd Quso; they faced the death penalty. The indictment named as unindicted coconspirators Osama bin Laden; Saif al-Adel, head of al Qaeda's military committee; Muhsin Musa Matwalli; Abd-al-Rahim al-Nashiri; and Tawfiq bin Attash. On July 7, 2004, a Yemeni court charged Nashiri and five other Yemenis in the bombing. On September 29, 2004, a Yemeni judge sentenced Nashiri and Badawi to death.

On February 3, 2006, 23 al Qaeda convicts, including Badawi, broke out of a Sana'a prison. Yemeni forces recaptured him on July 1, 2006. Yemen freed him on October 25, 2007. He remained on the FBI's Most Wanted List.

On March 12, 2007, Tawfiq bin Attash told a U.S. military tribunal in Guantanamo that he organized the USS *Cole* attack and the 1998 U.S. African embassies bombings.

On July 25, 2007, a U.S. judge ordered Sudan to pay circa $8 million to the families of the 17 dead sailors. In mid-April 2010, another 61 grieved relatives sued Sudan for $282.5 million.

Fahd al Qoso reportedly died in an air strike in Pakistan in October 2010, although a photo of him surfaced afterward.

In April 2011, Nashiri was charged by U.S. military prosecutors with murder, terrorism, and other violations of the laws of war regarding the USS *Cole* attack and others.

As of late 2013, many of the accused were held in Guantanamo Bay military prison, awaiting trial.

September 11, 2001
Al Qaeda U.S. World Trade Center, Pentagon, and Pennsylvania Hijackings

Overview: And then the world changed forever. Every American who lived through that day can tell you where they were when they heard the news. The attacks killed nearly 3,000 people from more than 80 countries. American response to the attacks included a massive reorganization of the U.S. government, creation of the 180,000-person Department of Homeland Security and the Office of the Director of National Intelligence, and a host of airline passenger screening measures. The U.S. military and a coalition of the willing soon flushed al Qaeda and the Taliban from the safety of Afghanistan. Suspicion of Iraqi involvement with al Qaeda led the Bush administration to invade Iraq in 2003 as part of the War on Terrorism.

Incidents: On September 11, 2001, terrorists hijacked four U.S. air liners and crashed them into the twin towers of the World Trade Center (WTC), the Pentagon, and a field in Pennsylvania, killing nearly 3,000 people.

American Airlines Flight 11. A B-767 carrying 92 people, including 9 flight attendants and 2 pilots, and traveling from Boston's Logan International Airport to Los Angeles International Airport was hijacked shortly after its 7:59 A.M. takeoff by terrorists armed with box cutters and knives. The plane was diverted over New York and crashed into New York City's 110-story WTC North Tower at 8:45 A.M., killing all on board. A fireball engulfed the tower as millions watched on television, certain they were seeing a horrible accident. Dozens of people jumped out of WTC windows. The building collapsed at 10:29 A.M., sending a 10-story cloud of smoke and ash throughout Manhattan. The fires burned for weeks.

The hijackers were identified as Mohamed Atta, Waleed M. Alshehri, Wail M. Alshehri, Satam M.A. al Suqami, and Abdulaziz Alomari. In February 2001, Atta inquired about crop dusters at Belle Glade State Municipal Airport in Belle Glade, Florida. (This piece of information, developed in September 2001, led the United States to ground all crop dusters in the country in hopes of stopping a possible chemical–biological attack.) The terrorists apparently had been told to blend in with U.S. society, not appearing to be too devout as Muslims and cut their beards to U.S.-style lengths.

United Airlines Flight 175. A B-767 flying from Boston's Logan International Airport to Los Angeles International Airport with 65 people, including 7 flight attendants and 2 pilots, was hijacked shortly after its 7:58 A.M. takeoff by terrorists armed with box cutters and knives. The plane was diverted across New Jersey, pulled sharply right, and just missed crashing into two other airliners as it descended toward Manhattan. The hijacker maneuvered to avoid colliding with a Delta flight; a third U.S. Airways aircraft descended rapidly after being notified of an imminent collision. United Airlines flight 175 crashed into New York City's 110-story WTC South Tower at 9:05 A.M. The second crash was captured on television, which was covering the North Tower fire, further horrifying millions. No one on board survived the crash. The building collapsed at 11:10 A.M., burying thousands, including hundreds of police officers and firefighters. At 5:00 P.M., WTC Building No. 7, a 47-story tower, was the third structure to collapse. The rest of the WTC complex buildings collapsed during the day, and numerous neighboring buildings were damaged. The dust clouds from the collapsed buildings raced down major New York avenues.

The hijackers were identified as Marwan al-Shehhi of the United Arab Emirates; Fayez Rashid Ahmed Hassan al Qadi Banihammad, a Saudi; Ahmed Alghamdi; Hamza Alghamdi; and Mohand Alshehri. The "muscle" for the attacks had Saudi ties.

Circa 20,000 people were inside the WTC towers at the time of the attacks. Photos of the missing could be found throughout the streets of New York, taped onto walls, mailboxes, and telephone poles. The media ran dozens of biographies of the victims.

American Airlines Flight 77. A B-757 headed from Washington's Dulles International Airport to Los Angeles with 64 people, including 4 flight attendants and 2 pilots on board, was hijacked shortly after its 8:10 A.M. departure. The hijackers, armed with box cutters and knives, forced the passengers and crew to the back of the plane. Barbara K. Olson, a former federal prosecutor and prominent television commentator who was married to Solicitor General Theodore Olson; a Senate staffer; three DC school children; three teachers on an educational field trip; and a University Park family of four headed to Australia were ordered to call relatives to say they were about to die. The plane made a hairpin turn over Ohio and Kentucky and flew back to Washington, D.C., with its transponder turned off. It aimed full throttle at the White House but made a 270 degree turn at the last minute and crashed at 9:40 A.M. into the Pentagon in northern Virginia. The plane hit the helicopter landing pad adjacent to the Pentagon, sliding into the west face of the Pentagon near Washington Boulevard. The plane cut a 35-foot wedge through the building's E, D, C, and B rings between corridors 4 and 5. A huge fireball erupted, as 30,000 pounds of jet fuel ignited. The federal government shut down within an hour; hundreds of local schools closed.

Officials determined that 189 people, including all of the plane's passengers and crew, died, and scores were wounded. Dozens of Pentagon employees were hospitalized. The Pentagon crash displaced 4,800 workers, destroying 4 million square feet of office space. Virginia's economy took a $1.8 billion economic loss and a sharp increase in unemployment, including the loss of 18,700 jobs from the temporary closing of Reagan National Airport.

The hijackers used the names Hani Hanjour, Majed Moqed, Nawaf Alhazmi, Salem M.S. Alhazmi, and Khalid al-Midhar. In January 2000, Nawaf Alhazmi and Midhar were videotaped meeting with operatives of the Osama bin Laden organization al Qaeda in Malaysia. The Central Intelligence Agency (CIA) put them on a watch list in August 2001, but the Immigration and Naturalization Service (INS) and FBI were unable to find them.

United Airlines Flight 93. A B-757–200 flying from Newark International Airport to San Francisco's International Airport with 45 people, including 5 flight attendants and 2 pilots, was hijacked sometime after its 8:01 A.M. departure by terrorists armed with box cutters. At 9:31 A.M., the pilot's microphone caught screaming as two men invaded the cockpit. A hijacker got on the microphone to tell the passengers, "Ladies and gentlemen, it's the captain. Please sit down. Keep remaining sitting. We have a bomb aboard." The hijackers subdued the pilots, then forced several passengers to phone their relatives to say they were about to die.

Passengers saw two people lying motionless on the floor near the cockpit, with their throats cut. Passenger Jeremy Glick, a national judo champ, told his wife during a cell phone call that the passengers would go down fighting. He said the terrorists, wearing red headbands, had ordered everyone to the rear of the plane. Business executive Thomas Burnett Jr. said during four cell phone calls that the terrorists had stabbed and seriously injured one of the passengers. He later called to say that the passenger or pilot had died and that "a group of us are going to do something." Todd Beamer indicated to a GTE colleague that the passengers were about to fight the terrorists, ending his conversation with "Let's roll." The plane made a hairpin turn over Cleveland and headed for Washington; some pundits believe that the plane was aiming at the White House. The plane crashed in Stony Creek Township, Pennsylvania, midway between Camp David and Pittsburgh and 14 miles south of Johnstown, at 10:06 A.M., killing all on board. Air Force fighter pilots were ordered to down the plane if it neared Washington, believed to be its intended target.

The hijackers were identified as Ziad Samir Jarrah, Ahmed Alnami, Ahmed Ibrahim A. al-Haznawi, and Saeed Alghamdi.

Epilogue. U.S. law enforcement and intelligence agencies began the country's most extensive investigation in history and quickly developed leads and detailed information about the hijackers and their supporters. Osama bin Laden's al Qaeda organization soon became the major suspect; bin Laden was linked to the previous bombing of the WTC on February 26, 1993. The hijackers were linked with those of several other hijackings that day. At least one hijacker on each plane received flight training in the United States, and several had received pilot's licenses; others studied martial arts so that they could subdue the passengers.

The United Nations listed 86 countries as having lost its citizens in the attacks.

The monetary costs of the series of attacks were staggering. The American commercial airline system was grounded—for the first time in U.S. history—for several days, and many major airlines lobbied Congress for immediate assistance to prevent bankruptcy of the industry. On September 29, 2001, New York City officials estimated that cleanup and repair of WTC Ground Zero would cost $40 billion and take at least one year. That figure rose to $105 billion in early October 2001. The stock market lost $1.3 trillion in paper assets during the first week it was open after being closed the week of the attacks. The casualties were greater than those tallied from all international terrorist attacks recorded during the previous decade.

The world responded with an outpouring of sympathy, holding candlelight vigils, leaving thousands of flowers in front of U.S. embassies, and sending donations. Paris Le Monde's editorial observed, "Today, we are all Americans."

The hijackers differed from the normal al Qaeda terrorists in Europe, who tended to be disaffected, poorly educated youths who lived in slums. Atta was a city planner; fluent in German, English, and Arabic; and who earned advanced degrees. German police tracked members of a cell created by the hijackers in Hamburg.

On November 14, 2001, the FBI concluded that Yemeni economics student Ramzi Binalshibh was meant to be the fifth hijacker on flight 93. The FBI concluded that Zacarias Moussaoui was not to be the fifth hijacker, but may have been part of a wave of chemical–biological weapons attacks. Germany indicted fugitives Binalshibh, Said Bahaji, and Zakariya Essabar, part of an al Qaeda cell that operated in Hamburg since 1999.

In 2004, the FBI also noted that Moshabab Hamlan, a Saudi, was meant to be a hijacker but lost his nerve.

War on Terror. The coalition military retaliation began on October 7, 2001, around noon EDT, with U.S. and U.K. air strikes—principally cruise missiles—against command and control/radar air defense installations near Kabul, Herat, Jalalabad, Mazar-e-Sharif, Kunduz, and Kandahar. U.S. troops remained in Afghanistan a decade later. Czech officials confirmed on October 27, 2001, that Atta had contact with Ahmed Khalil Ibrahim Samir al-Ani, an Iraqi intelligence officer, on a trip to the Czech Republic earlier in the year. This news led members of the Bush administration to advocate the invasion of Iraq as part of the War on Terror.

Key Prosecutions. On August 19, 2005, a German court convicted Mounir el-Motassadeq and sentenced him to seven years as a member of the Hamburg cell, but found him not guilty of more than 3,000 counts of accessory to murder in the 9/11 attack.

On September 26, 2005, a Spanish court convicted and sentenced Imad Eddin Barakat Yarkas to 27 years for conspiring with the hijackers.

On April 4, 2011, Attorney General Eric Holder dropped the Manhattan civilian court option for the 9/11 trial and announced that key figures Khalid Sheik Muhammad, Ramzi Binalshibh, Walid Muhammad bin Attash, Amar al-Baluchi, and Mustafa Ahmed al-Hawsawi would be tried before a Guantanamo Bay military commission. Charges included conspiracy, murder, attacking civilians, intentionally causing bodily injury, destruction of property, terrorism, and material support for terrorism. As of late 2013, the accused were awaiting trial.

Finale. On May 2, 2011, U.S. Navy SEAL Team 6 raided a compound in Abbotabad, Pakistan, during the night and shot to death Osama bin Laden, whose body was given a Muslim funeral aboard the USS *Carl Vinson* before burial at sea.

October 12, 2002
Indonesia Bali Bombings

Overview: Following the operational successes of the attacks against the U.S. African embassies, USS *Cole*, and 9/11 targets, radical Islamist groups were eager to establish some connection to the core al Qaeda leadership. Various types of relationships developed, including formal merger of a group with al Qaeda (as seen with Ayman al-Zawahiri's joining of his Egyptian al-Jihad group to al Qaeda), franchises with formal *bayat* pledged to bin Laden (as seen with al Qaeda in Iraq, the Islamic Maghreb, and in the Arabian Peninsula), and affiliates in the Far East (including Abu Sayyaf in the Philippines and Jemaah Islamiyah (JI) in Indonesia). JI conducted numerous attacks in the region, the most deadly of which were the Bali nightclub bombings. In the aftermath,

Southeast Asian governments arrested most of the first generation of
JI leaders.

Incident: On October 12, 2002, at 11:10 P.M., two bombs exploded at the
Sari Club and Paddy's, two Bali nightclubs popular with foreign tourists,
on Legian Street near Bali's Kuta Beach strip, killing at least 202 people,
including 88 Australians, 4 French citizens, and at least 7 Americans, and
injuring more than 300.

The first small bomb went off in front of Paddy's disco. The second
larger bomb was in a Toyota Kijang SUV in front of the Sari Club.

Victims represented 21 nationalities—including Canadians, Britons, Germans, Swedes, New Zealanders, Norwegians, Italians, Swiss, and French—
from six continents. Four Americans, seven French citizens, and at least
five Britons were injured. JI terrorists were suspected. The blast shattered windows 400 yards away and set alight numerous cars. It left a hole
6 feet deep and 15 feet wide and destroyed 20 buildings.

On October 17, 2002, local authorities summoned to Jakarta for questioning JI spiritual leader Abubakar Baasyir, 64. They wanted to discuss
a series of church bombings by al Qaeda–linked militants. He collapsed
and was hospitalized after a press conference. Jailed al Qaeda operative
Omar al-Farouq told local investigators that Baasyir was involved in the
bombings.

On November 5, 2002, Indonesian authorities arrested two suspects.
Two days later, police released composite sketches of four other suspects.
Amrozi bin Nurhasyim, an East Javanese car repairman and the owner
of the Mitsubishi L-300 minivan that exploded, said he was part of the
group. He was arrested at an Islamic boarding school, Al Islam, in Lamongan, where he had attended a lecture by Baasyir. Amrozi said he was
involved in the August 2000 remote-controlled bombing of Philippine
ambassador Leonides Caday's house in Jakarta. He said the Bali bombings were "revenge for what Americans have done to Muslims." He said
he was trying to kill as many Americans as possible and that the terrorists were unhappy that large numbers of Australians had died instead.
Amrozi said he had met with Riduan Isamuddin (alias Hambali), the
leader of JI and al Qaeda's leader in the region. He said he was also involved in the bombing of the Jakarta stock exchange in 2000 that killed
15 people and the October 12, 2002, bombing of the Philippine Consulate
in North Sulawesi.

Amrozi claimed to have purchased a ton of ammonium chlorate in
Surabaya, East Java. The seller was detained by police. Amrozi led police
to a home in Denpasar, Bali, where explosive residue was found.

Amrozi's older brother, Mukhlas Amrozi (alias Ali Ghufron), was a JI
operative wanted for the bombing. Police were seeking three other relatives, including two other brothers belonging to JI. Police believed Mukhlas

was the Malaysia chief of JI and was involved in a failed plot to blow up pipelines that supply Malaysian water to Singapore. Younger brother Ali Imron was believed to have helped detonate the car bomb. Mukhlas attended an Islamic boarding school founded by Baasyir. Brother Ali Fauzi was also wanted in connection with the bombing. Brother Khozin founded Al Islam, the Islamic boarding school.

On November 10, 2002, police detained Tafsir, whom they said had driven Amrozi in his Mitsubishi L-300 van to Bali.

On November 11, 2002, Indonesian police arrested a forest ranger in Tenggulun, Komarudin, on suspicion of storing weapons and explosives for Amrozi. Police found two canisters, one of which contained five weapons, including two M-16s and an AK-47.

Amrozi told police that Imam Samudra (alias Hudama) asked him to buy the chemicals to make the bomb.

Meanwhile, police named four new suspects—Samudra, already in custody one, and three of his brothers (Umar, Idris, and another Umar), who remained at large. Amrozi claimed that he, Samudra, and another man named Martin met more than once in Solo, Java, to discuss the bomb plan. Amrozi said Idris gave him more than $5,000 in U.S., Singaporean, and Malaysian currency.

On November 17, 2002, police said a computer engineer from West Java, Imam Samudra, was the ringleader. The radical intellectual had received arms training in Afghanistan. The JI member had helped build the bomb. In a meeting in central Java on August 8, 2002, he decided to target the Sari Club in hopes of killing Americans. Police said the man suspected of setting off the car bomb was Amar Usman (alias Dulmatin), an electronics expert from central Java. On November 22, 2002, police reported that Samudra had confessed to the Bali bombings a day after his arrest and had admitted involvement in the Christmas Eve 2000 church bombings. Police said two terrorist cells totaling a dozen people were involved. One group of militants, including Amrozi, from Lamongan in eastern Java set off the remote-detonation bombing of the Sari Club. Another group from Serang in western Java set off the smaller Paddy's bar bomb, which involved a suicide bomber named Iqbal, who had an explosives-laden backpack. Samudra was following the directives of Mukhlas, an Islamic teacher and JI strategist and older brother of Amrozi.

Mukhlas was arrested on December 3, 2002, and confessed to helping plan the Bali bombings.

On January 14, 2003, two more suspects, including field coordinator Ali Imron, were arrested on Berukan Island in eastern Kalimantan Province.

On January 28, 2003, Indonesian National Police chief Dai Bachtiar said that detained cleric Abubakar Baasyir had given a blessing to the "jihad operation" in Bali. Baasyir approved the plan that was developed by senior militants at a meeting in Bangkok in February 2002 to strike U.S. and other Western targets in Indonesia and Singapore. Bachtiar also said

Hambali provided $35,000 to finance the attacks, giving the money to Malaysian operative Wan Min Wan Mat, who forwarded the funds to Mukhlas. Other Indonesian security officials believed the money came from Seyam Reda, a German held on immigration charges.

On February 3, 2003, Indonesian police announced the arrest of JI members Mas Selamat Kastari, a Singaporean wanted in Singapore for participating in a hijacking plot, and Malaysian citizen Noor Din, who was suspected of helping plan the Bali bombings. Kastari had fled Singapore in December 2001 and planned to hijack a U.S., U.K., or Singaporean jet flying out of Bangkok and crash it into Singapore's Changi Airport. Din was grabbed in Gresik on Java Island, where police seized an M-16 rifle and ammunition that belonged to Ali Imron.

On February 21, 2003, the trial began of Silvester Tendean, the store owner accused of selling the chemicals used in the bombing.

On March 11, 2003, the government announced that the August 1, 2000, car bombing of Philippine ambassador Leonides Caday's home in Jakarta was carried out by the same JI terrorists accused in the Bali blasts. The government said the attack was ordered in July 2000 by Hambali during a meeting in Kuala Lumpur, Malaysia. Two of the terrorists were Amrozi, who purchased the Sari Club van, and Hutomo Pamungkas (alias Mubarok), who distributed the money that financed the attacks and helped assemble the Jakarta bomb. Amrozi purchased the explosives for the two attacks at a shop in Surabaya, East Java. Ali Imron was also indirectly involved in the Jakarta bombing, according to police. Philippine investigators said JI was trained by the Moro Islamic Liberation Front (MILF) of the Philippines in the attack.

On April 14, 2003, Indonesian prosecutors filed treason charges against Abubakar Baasyir.

On April 23, 2003, the national police announced the arrests of 18 JI members, including Mohamad bin Abas (alias Nasir Abbas), Malaysian leader of the Mantiqi 3 cell that operates in the southern Philippines and northern Indonesia. Three of them were linked to the Bali bombings. The Mantiqi 3 includes the Philippines, Brunei, eastern Malaysia, and Kalimantan and Sulawesi in Indonesia. It was based in Camp Abubakar, run by the MILF, before the Philippine military overran it in 2000. Police also arrested Abu Rusdan, who had been JI's temporary leader.

Baasyir's trial began on April 23, 2003. He was charged in a 25-page indictment with involvement in church bombings on Christmas Eve 2000 that killed 19 people, a failed plot to bomb U.S. interests in Singapore, and a plot to assassinate President Megawati Sukarnoputri in 2001 when she was vice president. The government said Baasyir is JI's leader. The charges carry a life sentence. He was not charged with the Bali bombings. On May 28, 2003, Ali Imron and Mubarok, both suspected of involvement in the Bali bombings, testified that they believed Baasyir was JI's leader.

On April 30, 2003, prosecutors charged Amrozi with buying the explosives and driving the van that exploded. The charges carry the death penalty.

On June 26, 2003, Faiz bin Abu Bakar Bafana, 41, a Malaysian and treasurer of JI, told the court via teleconference from a Singapore jail that bin Laden had set in motion a series of plots that JI pursued in Singapore and Indonesia in 2000. Bafana said Baasyir approved of the planned attacks and appointed Mukhlas as an operations chief of JI; Mukhlas was charged with organizing the Bali bombings.

On June 30, 2003, police arrested Idris, one of the organizers of the Bali bombing, who had also helped in a bank robbery on Sumatra to fund terrorist operations.

On August 7, 2003, Amrozi was found guilty and sentenced to death.

On September 2, 2003, Chief Judge Muhammad Saleh announced that an Indonesian court had convicted Baasyir of treason for involvement in the JI and attempting to overthrow the government, sentencing him to four years in prison. On December 1, 2003, an Indonesian appeals court overturned the treason charges and reduced Baasyir's sentence from four to three years. He was cleared of charges of leading the JI. The court upheld his conviction of immigration violations. On March 9, 2004, the Indonesian Supreme Court further reduced Baasyir's sentence, permitting him to go free by April 4, 2004. On March 3, 2005, Baasyir was sentenced to two and a half years for conspiracy for the Bali bombings. He was freed in June 2006.

Meanwhile, also on September 8, 2003, a Bali court sentenced three militants to 15–16 years for a robbery that funded the bombing.

On September 10, 2003, a court in Bali sentenced Imam Samudra to death by firing squad for his masterminding of the bombing. Prosecutors said he chose the recruits and financed the attack. Samudra said the bombing was revenge for U.S. tyranny.

On September 18, 2003, a court sentenced to life in prison Ali Imron, finding that he had participated in making the bomb and driving the minivan to the area.

In 2003, one of the 17 Indonesians who took terrorist training in the Philippines in April 2000 was arrested for hiding a Bali bomber.

On November 8, 2008, the Indonesian government executed Imam Samudra, Amrozi, and Mukhlas.

On March 9, 2010, police raided an Internet cafe and killed Dulmatin (alias Joko Pitoyo), a senior member of JI who they believed was behind the Bali bombings. His group claimed to be the Aceh branch of al Qaeda for Southeast Asia.

On January 25, 2011, Pakistani security officials arrested al Qaeda operative Umar Patek in connection with the Bali bombings. His trial began in February 2012. He was convicted on six terrorism charges and sentenced on June 21, 2012, to 20 years in prison for murder and bomb-making.

On June 9, 2011, Indonesian authorities in central Java arrested Heru Kuncoro, who was suspected of buying electronic equipment used in the bombings. He was among 16 people arrested in early June 2011 on suspicion of plotting cyanide attacks against police, according to *Fox News*. He was charged in late October 2011. His case remains open.

October 23, 2002
Moscow Theater Takeover

Overview: Chechen terrorists became more brazen during the late 1990s and early 2000s, refusing to buckle in the wake of massive crackdowns against them by the Moscow regime. Attacking planes, subways, apartment complexes, and government officials, the Chechen rebels posed the greatest terrorist threat to the Russian regime since the breakup of the Soviet Union. An especially daring attack took place in the heart of Moscow in October 2002, when Chechens resurrected an attack type rarely seen in the 2000s—a large-scale barricade-and-hostage operation with a laundry list of demands posed to the authorities. Exceptionally long and fanciful names designed to sow confusion and fear were trotted out by various self-appointed terrorist spokesmen. A bungled Russian rescue attempt left 170 people dead, sparking a firestorm of internal and international protests regarding the government's handling of the incident and of the rebellion in general. Russian attempts to equate the Chechens to al Qaeda's depredations, despite evidence of links between the two groups, fell on deaf ears.

Incident: On October 23, 2002, at 9:00 P.M., scores of masked Chechen gunmen and women armed with automatic weapons took over a Moscow theater on the corner of Dobrovskaya and Melnikova, holding nearly 900 people hostage. About 100 people escaped in the initial attack; another 46 were freed in stages. The House of Culture for the State Ball-Bearing Factory theater was showing a popular musical, *Nord-Ost* (Northeast). The terrorists demanded that Russian troops leave Chechnya within a week and end the war in the separatist region. They threatened to kill all the hostages if their demands were not met. At least one and perhaps two hostages were killed and two wounded in the initial assault by the gunmen, who had grenades strapped to their bodies. The Chechens said they were holding 650 people after having released 150. They claimed to have placed land mines around the theater's perimeter.

Tatyana Solnishkina, an orchestra member, used her cell phone to say that the rebels were threatening to kill 10 hostages if one of them was harmed. The news media quoted her as saying that the terrorists had explosives.

Alevtina Popva, an actress, escaped from backstage, and told the news media that the terrorists were chanting like kamikazes. She and some colleagues used curtains and scarves to climb out windows. Terrorists later fired rocket-propelled grenades at two teen girls who were attempting to run to safety, injuring a Russian soldier.

Rebel Abu Said claimed that the rebels were all *shahids* (Arabic for martyr). An *Interfax* reporter called from his cell phone to say that the rebels claimed membership in the Suicide Commandos of the 29th Division.

The rebels separated the men and women, and later separated out the foreign citizens into a third group. Some Muslim audience members were permitted to leave.

Several children were freed by the rebels. One boy said that his mother and sister were still being held, as were dozens of other children.

The hostages included citizens of the United States, the United Kingdom, Germany, Austria, Switzerland, Australia, France, Belarus, Azerbaijan, Georgia, Bulgaria, Ukraine, Israel, and the Netherlands. At least 3 Americans, a Russian with a U.S. green card, and 70 other foreigners were being held.

President Vladimir Vladimirovich Putin said that the attack was planned by foreign forces and was connected with the attacks in Bali and the Philippines. A police source said that the rebels were contacting accomplices in Turkey and the United Arab Emirates.

Aslan Maskhadov, former president of Chechnya, denied involvement with the hostage-takers, blaming a splinter faction with links to Muslim terrorists. *Al Jazeera* played a tape that showed the hostage-takers in front of an Arabic-language banner. A Chechen website said the attackers were led by Movsar Barayev, 25, nephew of Arbi Barayev, a Chechen rebel leader who died in 2001. The younger Barayev said he headed a group of Islamic radicals he called the Islamic Special Purpose Regiment of the Chechen State Defense Committee (Majlis al-Shura) with 400 active fighters and as many in reserve. His second-in-command was Abu Bakr. *Al Jazeera* later said the group was the Sabotage and Military Surveillance Group of the Riyadh al-Salikhin Martyrs (aka the Riyadus-Salikhin Reconnaissance and Sabotage Battalion of the Chechen Martyrs). A group member said in a recorded statement, "Our demands are stopping the war and withdrawal of Russian forces. We are implementing the operation by order of the military commander of the Chechen Republic."

The State Department said that the attack was by three groups:

• The Islamic International Peacekeeping Brigade: It was established in 1998 by Shamil Basayev, who led the group with Saudi-born Ibn al-Khattab until the latter's death in March 2002. Arab mujahideen leader Abu al-Walid had since taken over al-Khattab's position.

- The Riyadus-Salikhin Reconnaissance and Sabotage Battalion of Chechen Martyrs (Requirements for Getting into Paradise), also led by Shamil Basayev.
- The Special Purpose Islamic Regiment, led by Movzar Barayev, who died in the attack. Leadership was picked up by a Chechen who used the alias Khamzat.

Singer and politician Yosif Kobzon, the Duma member from Chechnya, claimed he had established communications with the hostage-takers, and was going to negotiate with the gunmen. Kobzon, accompanied by a Red Cross representative, was permitted into the theater and obtained the release of five hostages after 1:30 P.M. on October 24, 2002. They included a sick Briton in his fifties or sixties, a woman, and three children. During Kobzon's second visit, he was accompanied by parliamentarian Irina Khakamada. The terrorists refused to free anyone else, saying that they did not want to deal with intermediaries, only with decisionmakers. Parliamentarian Grigory Yavlinsky was permitted inside the theater later that day, as was another group of negotiators. Other negotiators included Sergei Govorukhin, a film director; U.S. ambassador Alexander Vershbow; Duma member for Chechnya Aslanbek Aslakhanov; journalist Anna Politkovskaya; and former prime minister Yevgeny Primakov. Another two hostages fled at 6:30 P.M.

During one visit, Kobzon was accompanied by Mark Franchetti of the *Sunday Times of London*, who interviewed the rebel leader.

On October 26, 2002, the Chechens freed seven more hostages at 6:00 A.M. At noon, eight children were freed.

A male hostage threw a bottle at a Chechen woman and charged her. She shot him dead, along with a nearby woman.

On October 25, 2002, the Chechens called for antiwar demonstrations in Red Square. That day, the rebels released 19 hostages, including some children.

The terrorists refused to improve the conditions of the hostages, who were starving and who had to use the orchestra pit as a toilet.

On October 26, 2002, in the early morning, the terrorists reportedly killed two male hostages and wounded a man and a woman. The hostages had attempted to escape, but only two made it. The sound of gunfire and explosions was heard at 3:30 A.M., when Russian Special Forces raided the theater in a battle that led to the deaths of 42 rebels, including rebel leader Movsar Barayev and 18 female suicide bombers with explosives strapped to their stomachs, and 117 hostages who were killed by the incapacitating gas used by the rescue force. Some of the women were shot. A man with head wounds and a woman with stomach injuries were taken away by ambulance. Several rebels were captured. Most of the freed hostages were hospitalized due to the effects of the gas that was pumped into the ventilation system. Russian soldiers refused to identify the gas, even to the attending physicians. At least 600 hostages were treated for bullet wounds and gas inhalation. The gas came in so quickly that the terrorists did not have time to put on their gas masks. Pentagon sources suggested that the gas was opium-based. Other U.S. doctors suggested it was fentanyl, an opiate derivative. Still others said it was an aerosol form of carfentanil, a potent narcotic used to sedate big game animals, or halothane, an inhalational anesthetic used in surgery for 50 years.

Among the dead hostages were 115 Russians, an American, an Azerbaijani, a Dutch citizen, 2 Ukrainians, an Armenian, an Austrian, a Kazakh, and a Belarussian.

On October 28, 2002, the Russians arrested a pair of Chechens in connection with the attack.

On October 29, 2002, Denmark arrested Akhmed Zakayev, an aide to Chechen separatist leader Aslan Maskhadov, for possible involvement in the attack. He was held until November 12, 2002, pending investigation. He had been attending the final session of the World Chechen Congress in Copenhagen. Russian officials detained dozens of possible accomplices.

On January 25, 2003, the theater officially reopened after $2.5 million in renovations, including a new security system with metal detectors, a new audio system, and new orchestra pit. Elsewhere, Russian police detained three Chechens in Penza, 310 miles southeast of Moscow, on suspicion of involvement in the attack.

Nord-Ost reopened on February 8, 2003.

In June 2003, Zaurbek Talkhigov was sentenced to eight and one half years for tipping off terrorists about police attempts to rescue the hostages.

By July 17, 2003, 793 former hostages and families of the 129 dead hostages were having a difficult time seeking redress in Russian courts. The 135 former hostages or family members who had agreed to sue were represented by Attorney Igor Trunov. As of that date, Russian courts had rejected 35 of the 65 lawsuits filed against the state. On July 28, 2003, a Moscow court rejected appeals in 21 compensation cases; attorneys argued that the law applies only to material damages for loss of income.

May 12, 2003
Riyadh Western Compound Bombings

Overview: Because fifteen of the nineteen 9/11 hijackers were Saudis, many observers suggested that the Saudis were supportive of al Qaeda, at least passively, and that not enough had been done to combat the group. Views of the Saudi regime's stance on terrorism changed dramatically when a wing of al Qaeda began attacking Saudi interests at home. A significant slap at the House of Saud occurred when al Qaeda conducted a major suicide bombing against a residential complex. The Saudi government engaged in a two-pronged attack on domestic terrorists, establishing an extensive Most Wanted Terrorist List, while also creating a terrorist rehabilitation program. Western leaders praised Saudi efforts.

Incident: On May 12, 2003, at 11:25 A.M., suicide bombers set off three truck bombs in a residential complex in Riyadh, Saudi Arabia, killing 34 people, including 8 Americans, 2 Britons, 7 Saudis, 2 Jordanians, 2 Filipinos, 1 Lebanese, 1 Swiss, and 9 terrorists. Another 190 people were injured. The facilities were identified as the Cordoval, Gedawal, and Hamra residences. The terrorists first fired at the sentries before pushing a button that opened the gates and permitted them to drive deep into the compounds. A member of the Saudi National Guard was killed in a gun battle. Two Filipino employees of Vinnell Corporation were also killed, and several employees were injured, two critically. Jordanian children Zeina Abassi, 10, and her brother Yazan, 5, were killed. A ninth American died on June 1, 2003. The 2-week-old niece of Jim Young, 41, an entrepreneur from Dalton, Georgia, was badly injured in the face. Also injured was British citizen Erika Warrington, 15.

In an initial attack, the terrorists fired at guards, detonated the bomb, and then escaped. The compound houses several Britons; a British school is on the grounds. The terrorists worked their way through three levels of security, including Saudi National Guards. The Dodge Ram truck contained 400 pounds of plastic explosives and damaged every building in the compound. The terrorists also drove a white Ford Crown Victoria, which they left outside; it was impaled on the gate in the explosion. Two attackers died; three escaped on foot.

At Al Hamra, two cars, including a car bomb, drove up to the main entrance at 11:30 P.M. The terrorists shot the security guards. As one car drove toward the recreation area, the terrorists continued firing, wounding or killing several people on the street. The car bomb went off outside a pool area where a barbecue party was under way. The car landed in the pool. At least 10 people died and dozens were wounded. Saudi officials worried that some of the attackers were still on the grounds hours later. The press reported that gunfire could be heard in the early morning in Riyadh. Injured were Saudis Berkel, husband Jelal, and their 3-year-old son; two little girls from Jordan—their father was in a coma—and a Lebanese man. Al Hamra and Gedawal are home to workers from Turkey, Lebanon, the United States, and United Kingdom. Two attackers died; three escaped on foot. Mohammed Atef al Kayyaly was killed.

Gedawal facility housed Americans working for a local subsidiary of the Fairfax, Virginia-based Vinnell Corporation, a subsidiary of Northrop Grumman Corporation. The firm is jointly owned by U.S. and Saudi interests, and trains the Saudi National Guard. U.S. ambassador Robert W. Jordan had asked the Saudi interior ministry for more security on April 29 and May 7, 2003, and on May 10, 2003, specifically requested more security for Gedawal. (The house raided on May 6, 2003, is just across the street from Gedewal.) The compound's elaborate security system minimized the effect of the bombing of the 408 six-bedroom, two-story villas in the complex. At 11:25 P.M., a guard posted at one of the four towers at the corners of the facility went to a small room below to have tea with other guards. Shortly thereafter, a GMC pickup and a Ford sedan drove up to that gate. The terrorists shot to death two guards and wounded two other guards and another employee. They raised a gate by hand. Guards at a nearby interior gate heard shooting and keyed in a security code that prevented the metal gate from opening. The car and truck stopped outside the second gate. The three men in the Ford left the car, while the duo in the truck set off the truck bomb, killing them and the other three terrorists, who had grenades strapped to their waists. No residents died. The blast destroyed the gates, sewage tanks, and the terrorists' vehicles.

At least some of the attackers wore Saudi Arabian National Guard uniforms and drove vehicles commonly used by residents and guards. When the sentries requested ID, the terrorists opened fire.

Ali al-Khudair and two other new-generation radicals called on Saudis not to cooperate in the investigation. They were rebuffed and forced to retract their statements.

President Bush vowed "American justice" would be given the terrorists.

The Saudis said the 50- to 60-member al Qaeda cell that attacked on May 6, 2003, was responsible. It was led by Khaled Jehani, 29, who had left the country at age 18, and fought in Bosnia and Chechnya. He served in Afghan camps.

The bombings came hours before U.S. secretary of state Colin Powell was due to arrive in Riyadh.

Only three dead terrorists were positively identified via DNA. Possibly among the dead was Abdul Kareem Yazijy, 35, who was suspected of membership in the terrorist cell. His younger brother, Abdullah, called on him to turn himself in and noted that he had disappeared 18 months earlier. He had a long history of "emotional instability," according to Abdullah. His brother went to Afghanistan for a few months in 1990 and later worked for two years in Sarajevo for the Saudi charity Supreme Committee for the Collection of Donations for Bosnia–Herzegovnia, which was raided in 2002 for al Qaeda ties.

Saudi officials said three al Qaeda cells with 50 active members were operating in the country before the bombings. The cells were set up by Abd-al-Rahim al-Nashiri, the former head of operations for al Qaeda in the Persian Gulf. He was captured in November 2002 and is in U.S. custody. He was involved in the USS *Cole* attack in October 2000 and planned other attacks on U.S. and Western ships. He was succeeded by Khaled Jehani, 29, a Saudi Afghan war veteran, who was in charge of planning the attack. The bombing team leader was Turki Mishal Dandani, another Saudi Afghan veteran who remained at large.

Saudi officials suggested that all of the dead terrorists came from the list of 19 who were sought in the May 6, 2003 case.

On May 14, 2003, the Saudis said they were holding a suspect who turned himself in to authorities the day of the bombings.

On May 18, 2003, Saudi interior minister Prince Nayef said that four al Qaeda suspects detained in the last three days knew in advance of the attacks.

On May 24, 2003, the Bush administration suspended contacts with Iran over reports that an al Qaeda cell in Iran was involved in the bombings. Saif al-Adel, an Egyptian serving as the group's military commander, was believed to have given the order to attack. He was believed hiding in Iran along with Abu Mohammed Masri, the group's training chief; Saad bin Laden, Osama's son; and Abu Musab al-Zarqawi, who had been in Baghdad. Iranian foreign ministry spokesman Hamid Reza Asefi told *IRNA* that Tehran had arrested several al Qaeda members, "but we don't know who these people are to be able to say whether they are senior or not. They need to be identified and interrogated." Iran claimed it had deported 500 al Qaeda members in the past year. Saudi foreign minister Prince Saud said the kingdom will seek to extradite anyone who had a role in the bombings.

A second command group was believed to be on the Pakistan–Afghan border.

Saudi oil and security analyst Nawaf Obaid wrote in the May 18, 2003, *Washington Post* that a captured senior member of the cell said they rushed the attack because the May 6, 2003, group feared it was about to be picked up by the authorities. He noted that two leaders of the cell and most of the explosives had come through Yemen.

On May 20, 2003, Saudi officials said that some al Qaeda members fled the country to the United States before the attacks.

Saudi officials arrested Ali Abdulrahman Gamdi, 29, a key figure in the bombings in Riyadh, on May 27, 2003. The Saudi had attended al Qaeda camps in Afghanistan and was in contact with bin Laden at Tora Bora. He was picked up with two other Saudis after they left an Internet cafe; authorities said the trio were planning an attack on a major hotel and commercial center in Riyadh. Authorities confiscated the computers they were using. Ali Aburahman Gamdi was the first of the 19 people Saudi officials said were involved in the bombing. As of that date, Saudi officials had arrested 44 people, including 4 women picked up in Mecca.

Saudi authorities announced on May 28, 2003, that they had captured nine al Qaeda suspects in Medina during the previous 24 hours, along with Ali Khudair and Ahmed Khalidi, two clerics who had called on their followers not to cooperate with the investigation. The London-based Movement for Islamic Reform in Arabia said that the two clerics were shot dead in Medina. A third cleric, Nasser Fahd, remained at large. Those detained included two Moroccans and a Moroccan woman stopped at a checkpoint. Saudi Special Forces also surrounded two groups of seven extremists in Medina. Police found explosives and bomb-making equipment at one of the Medina buildings.

In a gun battle on May 31, 2003, Saudi authorities killed Youssef Saleh Eiery, a Saudi national who belonged to the 19-member gang and arrested another after the duo threw hand grenades at a police patrol, killing two policemen.

The United States asked the Saudis to arrest Ahmed Abu-Ali in the case. His family's residence in Falls Church, Virginia, was searched by the FBI. He was represented by attorney Ashraf Nubani, who also represented some of the defendants in the June 25, 2003, arrests in northern Virginia against Lashkar-e-Taiba.

On July 3, 2003, following a five-hour standoff, Saudi police killed Turki Mishal Dandani and three associates when the terrorists ran out of ammunition in a shootout in a house in Suweir in the north.

On September 23, 2003, Saudi forces killed three terrorists, including Zubayr Rimi, a suspected al Qaeda militant believed involved in the attack, who was named in an FBI terror alert on September 5, 2003. The gun battle occurred at a housing complex in Jizan, near the Yemen border. One security officer died. Two suspects were arrested.

On January 8, 2004, 100 Swiss police officers raided homes throughout the country and arrested eight foreigners suspected of being al Qaeda supporters who aided the attacks. They questioned 20 other people in five states. The detainees were held on suspicion of providing logistical support to a criminal organization, but were not formally charged.

By April 2004, Saudi security forces had arrested more than 600 individuals on counterterrorism charges.

As of late 2013, the case remained open, with Abd-al-Rahim al-Nashiri in Guantanamo Bay military prison awaiting trial.

February 27, 2004
Philippines Superferry 14 Bombing

Overview: The Philippines was the scene of various terrorist insurgencies for decades. The Moro National Liberation Front, the Moro Islamic Liberation Front (MILF), Abu Sayyaf, the Sparrow assassination teams of Communist Party of the Philippines radicals, and numerous other groups have operated, often with impunity, on the islands. Ramzi Yusuf's hopes to attack the Pope, fly planes into buildings, and other plots took shape in Manila. Bombings, targeted assassinations, kidnappings, and murders—including beheadings—became common in the 2000s. The Abu Sayyaf group's al Qaeda ties led to stepped-up bilateral efforts by the United States to improve Filipino security response capabilities. Abu Sayyaf's bloodiest incident to date was its bombing of the Superferry, putting the death toll in the triple digits.

Incident: On February 27, 2004, an explosion sank the Superferry 14, killing 118 people an hour after it left Manila, Philippines. In March 2004, Abu Sayyaf member Redendo Cain Dellosa confessed to hiding TNT in a TV set he carried onto the ferry before escaping. He later claimed he was tortured into signing the confession.

On October 11, 2004, authorities charged six men, two of whom were arrested shortly after the explosion, with setting off the bomb. President Gloria Macapagal Arroyo said the six were also responsible for the 2001 kidnappings of 17 Filipinos and 3 Americans in Dos Palmas; one of the Americans was beheaded and another killed during a rescue attempt. Arroyo said the government was hunting for the attack organizers— Khadaffy Janjalani and Abu Sulaiman—and two accomplices. Police said Janjalani had demanded $1 million from the ferry company as protection money, which it said was "unhampered use" of the waters in the southern Philippines. Janjalani died in a September 2006 gun battle with Philippine security forces.

March 11, 2004
Madrid Train Bombings

Overview: Although Spain had a long history of attacks by Euskadi ta Askatasuna (ETA, Basque Nation and Liberty separatists, terrorists from the First of October Anti-Fascist Resistance Groups (GRAPO)—the armed wing of the illegal Communist Party of Spain—and various right-wing groups, its most wrenching attack came at the hands of al Qaeda–inspired Islamic radicals who killed more than 200 and injured another 2,000 in a morning attack on commuter trains in Madrid. Ten million people marched in Madrid, Zaragoza, Valencia, Bilbao, and elsewhere in protest of the terrorist attacks. Public reaction to the attacks led to the March 14, 2003, electoral victory of the opposition Socialist Workers Party. Many voters said they had voted for the opposition because of the discovery that al Qaeda was responsible for the bombings and that most of the electorate was against Spanish involvement in Iraq. This appears to have been the first time a terrorist group had directly influenced the outcome of an election. Prime Minister–elect Jose Luis Rodriguez Zapatero promised to withdraw Spain's 1,300 troops from Iraq but make terrorism the government's chief priority.

Incidents: On March 11, 2004, between 7:35 and 7:55 A.M., 10 bombs hidden in backpacks exploded on four packed commuter trains in three Madrid train stations during rush hour, killing over 200 people and injuring another 2,000. Victims included at least 47 people from 10 other countries, including Ecuador, Peru, the Philippines, and Romania.

Three bombs went off at 7:39 A.M. on a train entering Atocha station. Another four blasts hit a train arriving from Alcala de Henares at Atocha at 7:44 A.M. A bomb went off on a train entering Santa Eugenia station at 7:49 A.M. Two bombs went off on the platform of the El Pozo station at 7:54 A.M., killing 70 people on a double-decked train. Police detonated several unexploded devices. Police said there were 13 bombs, all containing 28–33 pounds of explosives. Police also destroyed a suspicious car near one of the stations.

The government initially blamed the Basque Nation and Liberty (ETA), but later changed its focus to al Qaeda affiliates.

A van discovered outside Madrid in Alcala de Henares later in the day contained seven detonator caps and a cassette with Koran verses.

A sports bag found in one of the trains at El Pozo station contained a timed detonator, a mobile phone, wires, and explosives that were commonly available. The explosives had not gone off because the terrorists had mistakenly set the timer to 7:40 P.M., instead of 7:40 A.M.

The al Qaeda–affiliated Abu Hafs al-Masri group claimed credit in an e-mail to the *al-Quds al-Arabi* newspaper, saying that Spain was a U.S. ally. Spain had been part of the coalition in Iraq. The group said, "Operation Death Trains . . . a way to settle old accounts with Spain, crusader and ally of America in its war against Islam." The group warned that "the expected 'Winds of Black Death' strike against America is now in its final stage." However, the group had also claimed credit for the East Coast blackout of 2003. Osama bin Laden had warned in an October 2003 tape that al Qaeda would attack Spain. The group later sent a videotape, which some officials suggested was filmed in Brussels or Amsterdam. Police were also investigating the movement of a large amount of money to Morocco to finance Islamic extremist operations. In a message following the election, the group said it would suspend operations to permit Spain time to fulfill the new government's promise to pull troops out of Iraq.

In a video found in a trash can in a parking lot on March 13, 2004, Abu Dujan al-Afgani, who claimed to be head of al Qaeda's European military wing, said the bombings were to protest Spanish "collaboration with the criminal Bush and his allies. . . . If you do not stop your collaboration, more and more blood will flow." Police later believed him to be Rachid Oulad Akcha, a Moroccan immigrant.

On March 13, 2004, the government announced the arrest of three Moroccans and two Indians, possibly with links to Muslim extremists. Two Spaniards of Indian descent were also being questioned. Several buildings and houses were searched. The group had been linked to the cell phone and cell phone card found in the gym bag. The Moroccans were identified as Jamal Zougam, who had been listed as an al Qaeda operative in a 9/11 indictment; Mohamed Bekkali; and Mohamed Chaoui.

They had criminal records in Spain. Zougam apparently had been under surveillance since the May 2003 bombings in Casablanca, Morocco. The investigating judge also questioned Imad Eddin Barakat Yarkas (alias Abu Dahdah), who had been in prison since November 2001 on suspicion of leading the al Qaeda cell in Spain. Zougam was an associate of Yarkas. The suspects purchased 100 prepaid calling cards for mobile phones 15 days before the attack. Zougam owned a cell phone shop in Madrid.

The government also announced that it had received a videotape from the self-described al Qaeda military spokesman in Europe, who said "We declare our responsibility for what happened in Madrid exactly two and a half years after the attacks on New York and Washington."

On March 31, 2004, the investigating judge issued international arrest warrants for five Moroccans and a Tunisian. A wealthy Moroccan, Abdelkarim Mejjati, was thought to be the organizer of the attacks. He was also wanted for the bombings in 2003 in Casablanca and Riyadh. Police were now investigating the involvement of the Moroccan Islamic Combatant Group in the attacks. The Tunisian was identified as Sarhane Ben Abdelmajid Fakhet, the leader and coordinator of the plot. All were wanted for murder and belonging to a terrorist group. The warrant said Fahket had rented a house 25 miles southeast of Madrid, where the explosives were prepared.

Police cornered seven terrorist suspects in the Madrid suburb of Leganes on April 3, 2004, at 7:00 p.m. The terrorists yelled, "Allah is great" and "We will die fighting." After a two-hour gun battle, the terrorists committed suicide by setting off bombs in their apartment. A Special Forces policeman died and 15 were injured in the nighttime bombing. Police said that four suspects might have escaped. Among those killed were Sarhane Ben Abdelmajid Fakhet (alias The Tunisian); Abdennabi Kounjaa, a Moroccan; Asri Rifaat Anouar; and Jamal Ahmidan, a Moroccan (alias The Chinese), the suspected operational commander. Police said on April 7, 2004, that the dead terrorists had planned another major attack in Madrid, possibly during Easter, and possibly against Jewish sites. Police found 200 copper detonators, 22 pounds of Goma 2 Eco explosives, money, and other evidence of plans in the apartment debris.

By April 11, 2004, investigators believed that the cell leader, Fakhet, sought out al Qaeda for assistance but that the group did not directly participate. He traveled to Turkey in late 2002 or early 2003 to meet with senior al Qaeda European operative Amer Azizi, to whom he outlined plans for the attack. He asked for manpower and other support to carry it out. Azizi had fought in Bosnia and Afghanistan. He said al Qaeda could not offer direct aid, but it supported the plan and Fakhet could use al Qaeda's name in claiming credit. Azizi also suggested contacting Jamal Zougam, a follower of Yarkas, imprisoned since November 2001 on suspicion of being al Qaeda's Spanish cell leader.

Interior Minister Angel Acebes told reporters that the 3/11 financing came from drug deals. Police cited testimony by Khayata Kattan, a Syrian member of al Qaeda who was extradited from Jordan earlier in 2004 on a warrant issued for the 9/11 attacks.

On April 28, 2004, Azizi was indicted on charges of helping to plan the 9/11 attacks by organizing a meeting in northeastern Spain in July 2001 in which key plotters Mohamed Atta and Ramzi Binalshibh finalized details, according to Judge Baltasar Garzon. He had also been charged in a September 2003 indictment against bin Laden and 34 other terrorist suspects. Azizi was charged with belonging to a terrorist organization. He was charged with multiple counts of murder "as many deaths and injuries as were committed" on 9/11. He allegedly provided lodging for the Tarragona meeting and acting as a terrorist courier. He was a close friend of Yarkas. Azizi fled Spain in November 2001.

On June 8, 2004, police in Belgium and Italy arrested 17 individuals with suspected links to al Qaeda, including Rabei Osman el Sayed Ahmed (aka Mohamed the Egyptian and Mohamed Abdul Hadi Fayad), believed involved in the bombing. The press reported that Ahmed was a former army explosives expert who conducted training courses at al Qaeda camps in Afghanistan. He was in Spain in 2003 and in touch with the ringleader, Fakhet. Ahmed recruited Fakhet at a Madrid mosque and may have supplied the explosives expertise. He was traced to Italy via intercepted phone calls. Spain requested extradition so he could face 190 counts of murder, 1,430 counts of attempted murder, and 4 counts of terrorism. A Palestinian and a Jordanian arrested in Belgium were known lieutenants of Ahmed and were believed involved in the 3/11 attacks. Police believed Ahmed and Fakhet were in a house in Morata de Tajuna where the bombs were made. On December 1, 2004, Italy's top appeals court informed Spain's High Court that it had approved the extradition of Ahmed, who was being held in the Voghera prison near Milan.

Spanish authorities believed that the overall organizer was Syrian-born former journalist Abu Musab Suri (alias Mustafa Setmarian Nasar), who was once the overall commander of al Qaeda training camps in Afghanistan and who once headed the group's propaganda operations.

On November 16, 2004, a court sentenced a 16-year-old Spaniard to six years in a juvenile detention facility after he pleaded guilty to helping steal and transport the dynamite used in the bombings.

In 2005, Azizi, who had recruited the leaders of the bombers' cell, died in a missile strike on Haisori village near Miranshah in North Waziristan, Pakistan.

In June 2005, forensic experts suggested that Mohamed Afalah, a Moroccan wanted in the Madrid bombings, conducted a suicide attack in Iraq in May 2005.

On April 11, 2006, Judge Juan del Olmo charged six people with 191 counts of terrorist murder and 1,755 attempted murders. Another

23 people were indicted for collaborating in the plot. The trial began on February 15, 2007. On October 31, 2007, a Spanish court convicted 21 of involvement but cleared 3 of being masterminds. Two Moroccans and a Spaniard who provided the explosives were sentenced to 42,924 years in prison. Jamal Zougam was convicted of membership in a jihadist terrorist cell and of terrorist murder. Moroccan citizen Othman el-Gnaoui was convicted of membership in a jihadist terrorist cell, terrorist murder, and helping to get explosives to the house where the bombs were made. Spanish citizen Jose Emilio Suarez Trashorras was found guilty of providing the explosives. Ahmed was cleared of all charges. His acquittal was upheld by the Supreme Court on July 17, 2008.

On November 6, 2006, a Milan court found Ahmed guilty of conspiracy to participate in international terrorist activities and sentenced him to 10 years. He was extradited to Madrid on November 17, 2006. He would remain in prison on these charges following his acquittal in the 3/11 case.

In November 2009, Judge Eloy Velasco indicted seven Islamic militants—including four Moroccans, an Algerian, and a Tunisian—for providing money, housing, food, and forged documents to the bombers.

August 24, 2004
Two Russian Planes Bombing

Overview: Chechen terrorists continued to conduct mass-casualty attacks, stepping up their operations by introducing women—heretofore less likely to attract the attention of security screeners—to attack squads.

Incident: On August 24, 2004, two Russian passenger jets that left the same Moscow airport within 30 minutes of each other disappeared on radar screens around 11:00 P.M. They crashed within three minutes of each other, killing all 90 on board.

The Islambouli Brigades claimed credit, saying it was avenging Russian abuses in Chechnya. The group said on a website that five attackers were on each plane, adding:

> Russia continues to slaughter the Muslims and will not stop unless a war starts where there will be bloodshed. Our mujahideen, thanks to God, were able to make the first strike, which will be followed by a series of other operations in a wave of support to our brothers, the Muslims of Chechnya and other Muslim areas that suffer the blasphemy of Russia.

The crashes occurred four days before an election to choose a Chechen president. Chechen rebel leader Aslan Maskhadov's London representative, Akhmed Zakayev, denied involvement.

At 9:30 P.M., Sebir flight 1047, a TU-154 carrying 38 passengers and 8 crew, left Moscow for Sochi. It disappeared from radar at 11:00 P.M. The pilot activated a distress and hijack signal. Four hours later, investigators found the debris 82 miles north of Rostov-on-Don.

At 10:00 P.M., Volga-Avia Express flight 1303, a Tupolev TU-134, took off from Moscow's Domodedovo Airport heading for Volgograd (former Stalingrad) with 36 passengers and 8 crew, including the chief of the airline. It disappeared from radar at 10:56 P.M. Witnesses in Tula said they saw an explosion before the plane hit the ground near Buchalki village.

On August 27, 2004, authorities announced that investigators had discovered traces of hexogen explosives (also known as RDX or clyclonite) in the wreckage of the TU-154 that crashed near Rostov-on-Don. The next day, investigators reported finding RDX traces on the TU-134 that crashed in the Tula region south of Moscow. Police believed two Chechen women bought tickets at the last minute to board the two planes at Moscow's airport. They were the only people whose family members did not inquire about the bodies.

Investigators reported on August 31, 2004, that two Chechen women had accompanied the suspected bombers to Moscow in the days before the crashes. The duo remained at large in Moscow.

On September 17, 2004, Chechen rebel leader Shamil Basayev, 39, took credit on Kavkaz-Center, an Islamic website based in Lithuania.

Investigators said that a Chechen woman bribed an airline ticket agent with 1,000 rubles ($34) to put her on a different flight; the agent scrawled, "Admit on board flight 1047." The two women paid 5,000 rubles to a black market dealer for tickets for the flights. They had initially been stopped by police but were inexplicably let go. They were identified as Satsita Dzhebirkhanova and Aminat Nagayeva, although some Russian newspapers said that the passports were faked.

On September 24, 2004, police Captain Mikhail Artamonov was charged with negligence that led to fatalities. Airline employee Nikolai Korenkov and accused ticket scalper Armen Arutyunian were charged with complicity in terrorism. On April 12, 2005, a Moscow regional court charged the latter two with aiding and abetting terrorism and commercial bribery. On June 30, 2005, Artamonov was sentenced to seven years for negligence.

September 1, 2004
Russia Beslan School Takeover

Overview: Chechen terrorists' preference for large-group attacks and the holding of large groups of hostages was seen two years earlier with the takeover of a Moscow theater. The organization, with other ethnic groups joining them, increased the pressure on the government and the public by taking over an elementary school on the first day of classes.

Incident: On September 1, 2004, at 9:00 A.M., 32 terrorists, including Chechens, Kazakhs, Russians, Ingush, Ossetians, and at least 10 Arabs, drove up in a military-style GAZ-66 truck and shot their way into School No. 1 in Beslan in North Ossetia, Russia, near Chechnya, during the morning and took 1,200 people, including hundreds of students and parents, hostage on the first day of school. At least 11 adults died in the initial shootout with the terrorists, who were wearing camouflage. At least two female terrorists wore explosive belts. The terrorists set up a pedal mechanism to an explosive and threatened to blow up the school if rescuers attacked them and said they would kill 50 hostages for every kidnapper killed, 20 for each wounded.

The school had been defended by only three security guards; one was killed and the two others were injured in the initial shootout.

By mid-afternoon, 15 children, who were hidden in the boiler room by their English teacher, ran to safety. The terrorists had attempted to open the heavy iron door with two grenades, with no success.

The hostage-takers demanded the release of 30 Chechen prisoners and Russian withdrawal from Chechnya. By phone, the terrorists asked to talk to the presidents of Ingushetia and North Ossetia.

The terrorists initially refused to permit medicine, food, and drink to be brought in for the hostages. By the third day, the tap water was running short, and some children drank urine. Many of the children stripped to their underwear to try to escape the suffocating heat in the school. The terrorists also rejected safe passage.

Some of the hostages later said that the terrorists were Wahhabis, wearing long beards and prayer caps.

Hundreds of Russian troops surrounded the school with armored vehicles. The perimeter broke down, however, and numerous armed townspeople joined the siege. In the afternoon of September 2, 2004, the terrorists fired rocket-propelled grenades (RPGs), setting a car alight. They again fired RPGs the evening of September 3, 2004, injuring a police officer.

A local legislator said on September 2, 2004, at 9:00 P.M. that 20 male hostages had been executed inside the school. The male hostages had been herded to a different location, away from the children and women, and shot. One man had been executed an hour into the siege.

On September 3, 2004, the terrorists freed 26 young children and their mothers. Gunfire was often heard coming from inside the school. Talks were suspended. Freed hostages said the terrorists had mined the school and suspended 16–18 bombs from the ceiling of the gymnasium, where many of the hostages were herded.

The terrorists used gas masks to ensure that if would-be rescuers flooded the area with knockout gas, as had been done in the 2002 Moscow theater siege, they would not be affected.

On September 4, 2004, around 1:00 P.M., the 52-hour siege ended when troops rushed the school after hearing explosions in the gym. The troops had not planned on rushing the school, but had no choice when the terrorists opened fire on fleeing children. At least 338 hostages, including 156 children; 10 Russian Special Forces rescuers; and 30 terrorists died from gunshot wounds, fire from the explosions, shrapnel, and the collapsing roof of the gymnasium.

More than 1 percent of Beslan's population was killed.

Itar-TASS reported that the attack was financed by Abu Omar as-Seyf, an Arab alleged to represent al Qaeda in Chechnya, and directed by Chechen rebel leader Shamil Basayev. An escaped hostage said she recognized some of the terrorists as having earlier done construction work on the school, leading investigators to suggest that they had hidden their weapons in the school during construction.

A Muslim group claiming loyalty to Ayman al-Zawahiri claimed credit on a website.

On September 5, 2004, the Russian government announced on state television that it had lied to the public about the scale of the hostage crisis. The broadcast made no apology that the government had claimed that only 354 hostages were inside the school. Questions remained about how many terrorists there were (reports varied from 16 to 40); how many terrorists were alive, free, or captured; how many people died; and how many had been captive. Many believed the death toll was higher than the official figure of 338. (On September 6, 2004, the government dropped the number to 334, including 156 children, and said that 1,180 hostages were involved.)

A captured terrorist identified as Nur-Pashi Kulayev was put on Russian state television on September 6, 2004. He was injured and had trouble talking, but said that "we gathered in the forest and the Colonel—it's his nickname—and they said we must seize the school in Beslan." He credited Basayev with giving the orders. He noted that another Chechen commander, Aslan Maskhadov, also gave orders. His group included Arabs, Uzbeks, Chechens, and people of other nationalities. "When we asked the Colonel why we must do it, he said, 'Because we need to start war in the entire territory of the North Caucasus.'" Many of the school terrorists had also taken part in the June raids in Ingushetia that killed 90 people. The *Washington Post* reported that a Western intelligence service indicated that some of the terrorists came from Jordan and Syria.

Authorities detained relatives of Basayev and Maskhadov on the second day of the siege.

Russian authorities said that surveillance tape of the terrorists indicated that they had argued among themselves as to whether to escape or continue the siege. The group was led by four men and took phoned orders from Chechen commander Basayev. The leaders included a Chechen, a Russian, an Ingush, and an Ossetian, and were identified by their code names of Abdullah, Fantomas, The Colonel, and Magas.

- Fantomas was a bodyguard of Basayev.
- Abdullah (aka Vladimir Khodoyev, variant Khodov), had fought alongside Basayev earlier. He had upbraided the other gunmen when they permitted hostages to take a drink of water late in the takeover.
- The Colonel was often in the gym and was believed by the survivors to be a Russian.
- Magas (aka Ali Taziyev), 30, was a former police officer who disappeared on October 10, 1998, while working as a guard for a local official, according to press accounts. He and another police officer were guarding the official's wife in a market when Chechens kidnapped the trio. She was ransomed in late 1999. The other officer's body was found in 2000. Magas joined the terrorists and led an attack in Ingushetia in June. Some authorities believed he had staged the kidnapping and had joined the terrorists earlier. He became head of the Ingush Jamaat, a group allied with the Chechens. He led the June raids in Ingushetia, killing dozens of prosecutors and policemen. Magas is a common name, first heard in the terrorist milieu in the April 2004 assassination attempt against Ingushetian president Murat Zyazikov. Police initially believed he was Magomed Yevloyev. A man by that name was killed in Malgobek, but it was later determined that he was an unrelated murder suspect. Another Magomed Yevloyev was killed in Galashki, but he also was not the right Magas.

All four leaders were killed in the gun battle.

The terrorists videotaped the siege; the tape was shown on Russian television on September 7, 2004, and picked up around the world. Authorities also reported that they had tapped into a walkie-talkie call from a terrorist. President Putin reported, "One asks, 'What's happening? I hear noise,' and the other says, 'It's okay, I'm in the middle of shooting some kids. There's nothing to do.' They were bored, so they shot kids. What kind of freedom fighters are these?" Russian demanded the extradition from the United Kingdom of Zakayev and other Chechen separatists who had been given political asylum.

Security services reported on September 8, 2004, that the terrorist leader shot one of his own men who did not want to take children hostage, then blew up the two women by flipping the electronic control on their detonators. Police also said they had been aided by a local police officer. Authorities said the gym explosion had been an accident when the terrorists were trying to rearrange the explosives. The Kremlin also backtracked on saying that 10 Arabs were involved but continued to claim that a multinational group of extremists was involved. Moscow offered a $10 million reward for the capture or killing of Basayev and Maskhadov. The next day, Chechen rebel websites offered a $20 million bounty for President Putin's capture.

By September 9, 2004, Russian officials had identified six Chechens and four Ingush as involved in the attack squad. Bomb techs defused 127 homemade bombs in the school.

On September 10, 2004, President Putin approved a parliamentary investigation into the attack. He also complained about American and British calls for negotiations with Chechens, suggesting that this was equivalent to calling for negotiations with al Qaeda. Foreign Minister Sergey Lavrov complained that Western countries were giving asylum to Chechen separatists.

On September 16, 2004, a key advisor to President Putin, Aslakhanov, said that the president had been prepared to release 30 Chechens during the siege. Aslakhanov said that he was about to go into the school to talk to the hostage-takers, with whom he had spoken by phone three times, when the explosives went off.

The next day, Basayev, using the alias Abdallakh Shamil, said on Kavkaz-Center, an Islamic website based in Lithuania, that his group was responsible and threatened more attacks on Russian civilians if independence was denied. He said:

> The Kremlin vampire destroyed and wounded one thousand children and adults by giving the order to storm the school for the sake of imperial ambitions. . . . We are sorry about what happened in Beslan. It's simply that the war, which Putin declared on us five years ago, which has destroyed more than forty thousand Chechen children and crippled more than five thousand of them, has gone back to where it started.

The posting said that the terrorists "made a fatal mistake" by allowing a Russian emergency services vehicle onto school grounds to remove bodies of people killed in the initial storming of the building. He claimed that two terrorists who went outside to watch the removal of the bodies were shot by troops. He said that the terrorists had deployed 20 mines, connected together in one circuit. "I personally trained this group in a forest, and I tested this system. Either all bombs would have exploded or not a single one. . . . We suggest that independent experts should check the fragments and types of wounds," implying that Russian bombs had killed the children. The posting claimed that there were 33 hostage-takers, including 2 Arabs. Basayev said that the operation cost 8,000 euros (circa $9,800) plus some weapons stolen from Russian forces. "I don't know bin Laden, don't receive any money from him, but would not mind."

On January 29, 2005, the parliamentary investigating commission said that some law enforcement officers were involved. Two accomplices had been detained, three were being sought, and paperwork was in the process to arrest two more. On May 29, 2007, a Russian court granted amnesty to three police officers who had been charged with negligence for failing to prevent the attack.

On May 17, 2005, the trial began of lone surviving terrorist Kulayev on charges of murder and terrorism in the case. On May 16, 2006, the chief justice of the Supreme Court in North Ossetia ruled that Kulayev had taken part in murder and terrorism. On May 26, 2006, he was sentenced to life in prison.

July 7, 2005
U.K. Subway Bombings

Overview: In the United States, the al Qaeda attack on the homeland is called 9/11; in the United Kingdom, London's emotional equivalent was 7/7 (and the failed copycat attack in late July). London was brought to a standstill with bombings of the subway and bus systems as thousands of Londoners wondered if they would be the next victims.

Incidents: On July 7, 2005, bombs exploded in three train stations and on a nearby double-decker bus, killing at least 49 people and wounding more than 700. (The tally eventually rose to 56 dead.) Several al Qaeda–affiliated groups, including the Abu Hafs al-Masri Brigades, the Group of al Qaeda of Jihad Organization in Europe, and the Secret Organization of al Qaeda in Europe, claimed credit. Each device contained less than 10 pounds of explosives, enough to hide in a backpack. Timing devices apparently were used. Police worked with Spanish officials to determine whether there were links with the 3/11 Madrid train bombings in 2004.

The bombs were apparently to form a cross radiating from King's Cross, but the plan was foiled when one terrorist could not get on a train and had to settle for a bus.

The bombings came a day after London was announced as the host for the 2012 Summer Olympics. They also came during the G-8 summit in Gleaneagles, Scotland, where world leaders held discussions about increasing aid to Africa.

The bombs were nearly simultaneous. First reports indicated that at 8:51 A.M., a bomb placed on the floor of the third carriage of Circle Line subway train 204 carrying seven hundred passengers went off 100 yards from the Liverpool Street Station, killing 7 and wounding 100. The train was arriving from Aldgate Station. Police identified the bomber as Shehzad Tanweer, son of the Pakistani owner of a Leeds fish-and-chips shop, and a good friend of fellow bomber Hasib Hussain. Tanweer was a student of physical education at Leeds Metropolitan University and lived in Leeds' Beeston district. Pakistani authorities said Tanweer visited Pakistan in 2004 and met with Osama Nazir, who was later arrested and charged with a 2002 grenade attack on an Islamabad church in which five people, including two Americans, were killed. Tanweer also spent several days at a madrassa near Lahore that had ties to Lashkar-e-Taiba.

At 8:56 A.M., a device placed on the floor of the first carriage, near the first set of double doors where passengers stand, went off three minutes out of the Russell Square Station en route to King's Cross Station, killing at least 21 people on the Piccadilly Line train 311. More than 900 passengers were on board. The bomber was identified by police as Germaine Lindsay (aka Abdullah Shaheed Jamal), a Jamaica-born British citizen who grew up in a single-parent household in southern England. He converted to Islam at the urging of his mother, who also converted.

At 9:17 A.M., a bomb placed on the floor of the second carriage of Circle Line train 216 leaving Edgware Road Station for Paddington Station exploded, killing seven people. The explosion ripped through a wall and damaged two other trains. The bomber was identified by police as Mohammed Sidique Khan, a teaching assistant at a Leeds public school. He was born in the United Kingdom to Pakistani parents. He was married and the father of an 8-month-old girl. He had recently moved to Dewsbury. He earned a degree in education from Leeds University. He traveled to Karachi, Pakistan, with Tanweer on November 16, 2004, on a Turkish Airlines flight. They had stayed at separate addresses near Lahore. The *Sunday Telegraph* said that Khan, the leader of the team, met in Pakistan in fall 2004 with Mohammed Yasin (alias Ustad Osama), an explosives expert who manufactures suicide jackets for Harkat-e-Jihad.

At 9:47 A.M., a bomb exploded on Bus No. 30 at Tavistock Square, killing 13 people. The bomb had been placed at the rear of the upper deck of the bus, which had been detoured because of the King's Cross/Russell Square bombing. Some theorized that the bomber had intended to hit another train but was prevented from entering a train station when all had closed. Police said Hussain, an unemployed Muslim, then hopped on a bus and was attempting to reset the timer when the bomb went off. The Pakistani lived in Leeds and had completed vocational business studies at Matthew Murray High School. He became more religious two years earlier. He flew to Karachi, Pakistan, on a Saudi Arabian Airlines flight from Riyadh on July 15, 2004.

Killed and injured included citizens from Australia, China, Ghana, Portugal, Poland, and Sierra Leone.

On July 12, 2005, British police and army units raided six houses around Leeds, arresting a relative of one of the four suspected bombers and conducting a controlled detonation at one of the sites. Police said they found quantities of triacetone triperoxide, a highly volatile substance, at one of the houses.

On July 15, 2005, Cairo police arrested Magdy Mahmoud Nashar, a biochemist who had studied at North Carolina State University for a semester in 2000. He allegedly helped rent the terrorists' Leeds town house.

Authorities were searching for a Pakistani man suspected of helping the terrorists who subsequently left the country on July 6, 2005. They were also searching for Mustafa Setmariam Naser, a Syrian–Spanish dual national who organized terrorist camps in Afghanistan and who was believed to be the mastermind behind the 3/11 Madrid train bombing in 2004. Also wanted was Zeeshan Hyder Siddiqui, 25, a Briton trained in bomb-making in an al Qaeda camp who was arrested in Pakistan in May 2005. He claimed to have lived in west London and studied economics at London University.

Police were searching for Haroon Rashid Aswat, who was raised in Batley, United Kingdom, and was an aide to Abu Hamza Masri, the radical Muslim preacher in London. Aswat had traveled to the United States and was involved in a plot to set up a terrorist training camp in Oregon. He had also been in Pakistan, India, and other countries. His cell phone had received 20 calls from several of the London bombers. He comes from the same general area of West Yorkshire as three of the bombers; Khan lived closest to him. Aswat attended schools in Batley and Dewsbury and went to a technical college in Bradford. Zambian police arrested Aswat on July 20, 2005, as he was crossing into the country from Zimbabwe. He was deported to the United Kingdom on August 7, 2005, and arrested on U.S. warrants that he helped plan the terrorist training camp in Oregon. The United States requested his extradition from the United Kingdom.

On July 23, 2005, a 17-year-old male was remanded in custody and charged with an arson attack on the home of Germaine Lindsay, one of the bombers.

On August 24, 2005, Bangkok police arrested Atamnia Yacine, an Algerian, on charges of possessing 180 fake French and Spanish passports and overstaying his visa. Thai police believe he supplied the fake IDs used in the 7/7 attacks.

On September 1, 2005, *Al Jazeera* aired footage by Khan, one of the bombers, who complained of "atrocities" against Muslims. "Until you will stop the bombing, gassing, imprisonment and torture of my people, we will not stop this fight. . . . We are at war, and I am a soldier and now you too will taste the reality of this situation." He expressed admiration of Osama bin Laden. *Al Jazeera* also ran a tape from Ayman al-Zawahiri, al Qaeda's deputy, calling the "glorious raid" an attack that "has moved our battle right to the enemy's doorstep." He said the bombings were "a slap in the face of the arrogant, crusader British rulers" and "a sip from the glass that the Muslims have been drinking from. . . . We have repeated again and again, and here we are warning one more time: All those who took part in the aggression on Iraq, Afghanistan, and Palestine, we will respond in kind." On September 19, 2005, in a video broadcast by *Al Jazeera*, Zawahiri said, "The blessed London attack was one which al Qaeda was honored to launch against the British Crusader's arrogance and against the American Crusader aggression on the Islamic nation for one hundred years." He also questioned the Afghan elections and condemned the United Kingdom's plan to deport Abu Qatada, an Islamic radical cleric.

In August 2005, a man captured north of Qaim, in western Iraq near the Syrian border, had a computer thumb drive that contained planning information for the 7/7 bombings. Police said he was connected to al Qaeda.

On May 11, 2006, two official reports by the Home Office and a parliamentary committee indicated that while two of the suicide bombers probably had contact with al Qaeda operatives during visits to Pakistan, there was no proof that the organization planned or directed the attacks. The reports said they acted on their own, because of "fierce antagonism to perceived injustices by the West against Muslims." The government also said it had failed to follow up leads on bombers Khan and Tanweer.

On June 5, 2006, an official inquiry concluded that flawed emergency planning, jammed cell phone networks, and radio failures hampered emergency responders after the attack.

On July 5, 2006, Peter Clarke, deputy assistant commissioner of Scotland Yard in charge of antiterrorist operations, said that in the previous year, authorities had "disrupted three, and probably four, attack plans in the United Kingdom."

On July 6, 2006, *Al Jazeera* ran a video of Tanweer, who said, "What you have witnessed now is only the beginning of a string of attacks that will continue and become stronger until you pull your forces out of Afghanistan and Iraq and until you stop your financial and military support for America and Israel." The tape included the presence of Adam Gadahn, a native Californian who works with al Qaeda.

During the British commemoration of the first anniversary of the bombing, an audiotape by Zawahiri indicated that Tanweer and Khan were trained in al Qaeda camps. "Shehzad's motivation for going to the bases of Qaeda al-Jihad was the repression which the British are perpetrating in Iraq, Afghanistan, and Palestine."

On March 22, 2007, British police arrested three men "on suspicion of the commission, preparation, or instigation of acts of terrorism" in the attack. Mohammed Shakil, a Gee Gee cab driver, told his office that he was quitting his job to take leave for family reasons; he was due to fly to Pakistan from Manchester Airport, where he was arrested, as was his traveling companion, Shipon Ullah. The third man, Sadeer Saleem, was arrested in his Leeds house. On July 5, 2007, British authorities charged the trio with conspiring with the bombers between November 1, 2004, and June 29, 2005, saying they handled reconnaissance and planning. On August 10, 2007, Shakil, Saleem, and Waheed Ali pleaded not guilty of conspiracy to cause explosions "of a nature likely to endanger life or cause serious injury." On April 28, 2009, a London retrial acquitted Shakil, Saleem, and Ali of aiding the bombers. Ali and Shakil were found guilty of other charges and were sentenced to seven years in prison.

On May 9, 2007, British police arrested three men and Hasina Patel Khan, widow of one of the bombers, on suspicion of commissioning, preparing, or instigating acts of terrorism by assisting the suicide bombers. Three people were picked up in the West Yorkshire region, specifically Dewsbury and Beeston near Leeds; the other in Birmingham, West Midlands. The other detainees were identified as Khalid Khaliq, who lived on the same street as bomber Tanweer; Arshad Patel, Ms. Patel's brother; and Imran Motala.

On January 21, 2009, authorities in Peshawar, Pakistan, arrested Taifi, a Saudi from Taif who was believed involved in the subway bombings.

The case remains open.

July 23, 2005
Sharm el-Sheikh Bombing

Overview: Although the peace treaty between Egypt and Israel had been honored for several decades, terrorists nonetheless never gave up their quest for an end to the Israeli state and a free Palestine. This struggle included attacks within Israel, as well as on its borders. The most noteworthy attack occurred in the mid-2000s, when 88 people were killed in a resort town popular among foreign tourists.

Incident: On July 23, 2005, shortly after 1:00 A.M., two bombs in two small green Isuzu pickups and a third bomb in a suitcase placed in a parking lot exploded in the Egyptian resort town of Sharm el-Sheikh, on the Red Sea, killing at least 88 people and injuring 119. Early reports suggested that there might have been seven explosions. Most of the dead were Egyptians, but seven foreigners died, including a Czech, an Italian, an American, and two Britons. The American, Kristina Miller, 27, from Las Vegas, was celebrating her birthday on a beach vacation with her boyfriend, Kerry Davies, one of the Britons who died. The wounded included nine Italians, five Saudis, seven Britons, a Russian, a Ukrainian, and an Israeli Arab.

The first bomb went off at 1:00 A.M. in the resort's Old Market, bustling with shops and tourist attractions. At least 17 Egyptians were killed.

The second bomb went off a few minutes afterward at the Ghazala Gardens Hotel, a 176-room resort in Naama Bay. The hotel had been the site of several high-level diplomatic meetings. The driver of the car bomb crashed through a barrier along the hotel's driveway, hit two cars, and drove into the hotel's domed entrance near the reception area.

The third bomb exploded in the Moevenpick Hotel's parking lot in Naama Bay.

Observers suggested that the bombings, like with the recent London subway bombings, had the hallmark of al Qaeda and might have been ordered by its leadership.

The Abdullah Azzam Brigades, also known as al Qaeda in Syria and Egypt, said on a website:

> Your brother succeeded in launching a crushing blow on the Crusaders, Zionists, and the infidel Egyptian regime in Sharm el-Sheikh. We reaffirm that this operation was in response to the crimes committed by the forces of international evil, which are spilling the blood of Muslims in Iraq, Afghanistan, Palestine and Chechnya.

The group had claimed credit for the earlier Taba bombings on October 7, 2004, and an April 2005 bombing in Cairo. The previously unknown Holy Warriors of Egypt (Mujahideen of Egypt) sent a fax to the *Associated Press* claiming credit and naming five bombers.

Police were searching for five Pakistanis who were part of a group of nine Pakistanis who arrived in Sharm el-Sheikh from Cairo on July 5, 2005. Police identified them as Mohammed Anwar, 30; Mohammed Aref, 26; Mohammed Akhtar, 30; Musaddeq Hussein, 18; and Rashid Ali, 26. Police ran DNA tests of the remains of an Egyptian and a foreigner suspected of being bombers. They identified the Egyptian as Moussa Badran, a resident of northern Sinai with links to Islamists. By July 26, 2005, authorities had detained 140 people.

A senior police official said that the terrorists intended to bomb the 292-room Iberotel Grand Sharm but were stopped at a checkpoint and set off their bombs in an arcade of shops. Police apparently had a tip on a planned attack against casinos several days before the hotel bombings. On July 27, 2005, police said they were searching for 15 Islamic militants and believed that the hotel attacks were tied to the resort attack in the fall of 2004.

On August 1, 2005, police surrounded Mohammed Saleh Flayfil, 30, a Bedouin wanted for this bombing and the 2004 Taba attacks in a quarry in Mount Ataqaa, 17 miles east of the Cairo–Suez highway. In a gun battle with police, Flayfil and his wife were killed and his daughter, 4, was wounded.

On August 12, 2005, Egyptian security forces separately arrested a man and a woman following a gun battle in which two police officers were wounded during a raid on the suspects' Sinai hideout, 15 miles east of Ismailia.

On September 29, 2005, Egyptian police in the Sinai Peninsula shot to death Khaled Musaid and Tulub Murdi Suleiman in a gun battle in the Mount Halal area, near where fellow Sharm el-Sheik bombing suspect Moussa Badran had been shot earlier that day. The duo was suspected of having organized the bombing.

November 26, 2008
India Mumbai Attacks

Overview: On November 26, 2008, 10 gunmen landed in the Mumbai, India, harbor and terrorized the city for almost three days. The terrorists carried photographs prepared by a U.S. citizen who had scouted the sea route from Pakistan to Mumbai and the sites to be attacked. Some of the terrorists had lived in Mumbai a few months earlier, pretending to be students and getting oriented to the sites. Sites where foreigners congregated were particularly targeted. The gunmen used electronic devices to communicate with each other and to monitor media coverage and police plans. They used Global Positioning System equipment, carried CDs with high-resolution satellite images, and switched SIM cards in multiple cell phones. When the smoke cleared, 195 people had been killed.

Incident: On November 26, 2008, at 9:00 P.M., at least 10 college-aged male terrorists deploying from Karachi, Pakistan, slit the throat of the captain of a fishing trawler named the *Kuber* and killed the four crew members. Upon arriving off the shore of Mumbai, India, they landed using a speedboat and a rubber dinghy, split up into four teams, and hailed taxis to get to their first targets. They attacked 10 public facilities, setting off explosives and firing automatic weapons. In the attacks and ensuing battles with Indian commandos, at least 195 people were killed and 350 people were wounded. At least 22 foreigners were killed, among them 6 Americans, a Briton, an Australian, a German, an Italian, and a Japanese citizen. Dozens of Indian and Western hostages were rescued.

At 9:30 P.M., the terrorists struck their first site, the Leopold Café, before moving on to the Taj, a restaurant frequented by tourists. Seven people were killed.

At 10:00 P.M., two gunmen attacked the Chhatrapati Shivaji Terminus railway station, killing 48 people and wounding many more in a 20-minute attack. Shashank Shinde, 46, was killed when he attempted to tackle the assault rifle-wielding terrorists. The two terrorists then fired at the *Times of India* and the Municipal Corporation of Greater Mumbai buildings. Next they killed three police officers and wounded a fourth for their police vehicle.

At 10:30 P.M., the same two gunmen attacked the Metro movie theater, throwing grenades and firing at passengers and pedestrians, killing 10 and injuring 30. Police intercepted them as they sped toward the Taj Mahal Palace and Tower Hotel, killing one terrorist and arresting Mohammed Ajmal Amir Kasab, 21, a Pakistani.

Meanwhile, at 10:15 P.M., at least two other gunmen attacked the 36-floor Oberoi Trident Hotel, killing 24 people in the initial assault. Terrorist Shadullah phoned Indian television from room 1856 to say:

> We demand the release of all mujahideen put in jails. Then will we release these people. Otherwise, we will destroy this place. . . . You must have seen what's happening here. . . . Release them, and we, the Muslims who live in India, should not be harassed. . . . Things like demolition of Babri Masjid and killings should stop.

At 10:40 A.M., on November 28, 2008, India's National Security Guard killed two gunmen. By midnight of November 28, 2008, police had found 41 bodies and rescued 98 hostages. Among the dead were members of the Synchronicity Foundation, a Virginia-based meditation group.

Also at 10:15 P.M., at least three terrorists attacked the landmark Taj Hotel. The terrorists fired on diners at the Sea Lounge restaurant, aiming at tourists. Its 105-year-old Moorish-style rooftop dome was engulfed in flames and smoke. The terrorists knocked on doors of the 565-room hotel, calling for American and British citizens to come out. Some 250 guests, including Americans, Europeans, and South Koreans, were trapped 4 hours on the rooftop where they fled for safety. The commando rescue operation began at 4:30 A.M. A running gun battle ensued as hostages fled down the stairs and through windows. At 2:30 A.M. on November 28, 2008, after a 60-hour siege, Indian Marine commandos gained control. The commandos killed four terrorists. Four hundred hostages were freed. At least 11 commandos died in the gunfire, including Hemant Karkare, chief of Mumbai's counterterrorism squad. More than 30 hostages were killed, including 10 kitchen staff. One wing of the hotel was gutted.

Between 10:45 and 11:15 P.M., terrorists attacked the Cama and Albless Hospital, where three hospital workers and two police officers died, and the Gokuldas Tejpal Hospital. Two terrorists were captured after they hijacked a police van to escape from the hospital.

At midnight, terrorists bombed the Mazgaon Dockyard.

The next morning on November 27, 2008, at 4:30 A.M., terrorists took hostages at the Chabad Lubavitch Jewish Center in the Nariman House business and residential complex, including eight Israelis and U.S. citizens Rabbi Gavriel N. Holtzberg, 29, and his wife, Rivka, 28. Terrorist Imran Babar phoned an Indian television station during the attack, citing the 2002 riots in Gujarat that killed more than 1,000 people, the 1992 destruction of the centuries-old Babri mosque by Hindu mobs, and India's control over part of Kashmir.

Are you aware of how many people have been killed in Kashmir? Are you aware of how your army has killed Muslims? We die every day. It's better to win one day as a lion than die this way.

Later that day, commandos surrounded the facility. The terrorists killed five hostages, including the rabbi and his wife. On November 28, 2008, at 11:30 A.M., commandos airlifted to the building's roof and dropped smoke bombs. By 7:00 P.M., fighting was over. One commando died.

The northern district's Ramada Hotel and the Vile Parle were also attacked.

At least 15 police officers died in the attacks, including Balasaheb Bhosale, a police official who tried to stop a gunman at a rail station. Sandeep Unnikrishnan died defending Indian civilians. Police later seized the explosives-laden *Kuber*.

On November 30, 2008, government officials said the official casualty numbers were 174 people dead and 239 wounded. Authorities said a third of the victims were Muslims. Indian Muslim leaders refused to permit the nine dead terrorists to be buried in Muslim cemeteries. Home Minister Shivraj Patil resigned.

Police said the nine dead gunmen came from central Punjab Province of Pakistan. They identified them as Abu Ismail, Hafiz Arshad, Babr Imran, Javed, Shoab, Nazih, Nasr, Abdul Rahman, and Fahad Ullah, all between 20 and 28 years old.

Surviving terrorist Kasab admitted membership in Lashkar (renamed Jamaat-ud-Dawa in 2005) and claimed that terrorist group members had trained for a year before the attack at four Lashkar camps near Muzzafrabad, Mansera, Muritke, and Karachi. On February 25, 2009, India charged Kasab with 13 crimes, including murder, "waging war against India," and entering a train station without a ticket. Two unnamed Pakistani Army officials accused of training the gunmen were also charged. Indian citizens Fahim Ansari and Sabauddin were accused of providing maps for the attacks. The charge sheet ran to 11,280 pages, citing more than 2,000 witnesses and naming 37 others alleged to have planned the attacks.

During his trial, Kasab testified that Zaki-ur-Rehman Lakhvi (variant Lakhwi), Pakistani head of the Lashkar-e-Tayyiba, had plotted the attacks. Doctors declared Kasab of adult age when he claimed he was underage and could not be tried as an adult. After pleading guilty and stating he was "ready to die," on December 18, 2009, he recanted his confession, saying he was a mere tourist and was tortured into the confession. The HBO documentary *Terror in Mumbai* reported that Kasab had been sold to the terrorists three months before the attack by his father so that his brothers and sisters could marry. On January 18, 2010, Kasab told the court that four of the gunmen were Indian, despite government claims that all of the terrorists were Pakistanis. On May 3, 2010, a Mumbai court issued a 1,522-page verdict that convicted Kasab of most of the eighty-six counts against him. He and an accomplice gunned down 58 people and wounded 104 others at the train station. The next day, he was sentenced to death. On February 21, 2011, the Mumbai High Court upheld Kasab's death sentence. On November 21, 2012, Kasab was executed by hanging.

Others investigated, sought, charged, or arrested included Tauseef Rehman and Mukhtar Ahmed Sheikh for buying 22 SIM (subscriber identity cards) used by the terrorists; Laskar leaders Lakhvi, Yusuf Muzammil, and Hafiz Sayeed (on June 2, 2009, the Lahore High Court in Pakistan ruled that there was insufficient evidence to hold Sayeed); Jaish-i-Muhammad leader Masood Azhar; Lashkar detainee Zarar Shah (on December 31, 2008, Shah confessed to involvement in planning the attacks, according to Pakistani authorities); and Hamad Ameen Sadiq, shown by a trail of evidence followed by Pakistani Federal Investigation Agency officials to be the "main operator" of the conspiracy. Hafiz Muhammad Saeed, cleric and head of the banned Jamaat-ud Dawa, was placed under house arrest in connection with the case by Pakistan on September 21, 2009. India said Saeed had masterminded the Mumbai siege. On October 12, 2009, a Lahore court dismissed all charges for lack of evidence. On May 25, 2010, Pakistan's Supreme Court confirmed the ruling.

By February 12, 2009, Pakistani interior minister Rehman Malik had admitted that "some part of the conspiracy has taken place in Pakistan." On November 25, 2009, a court in Rawalpindi, Pakistan, charged seven individuals with acts of terrorism, money laundering, supplying funds for terrorism, and providing tools for terrorism. All pleaded not guilty. They all faced the death penalty. They were identified as mastermind Lakhvi, Umar Abjul Wajid, Shahid Jameel Riaz, Jameel Ahmed, Mohammad Younas Anjum, Mazhar Iqbal, and Sadiq. A November 2009 *HBO* documentary reported the terrorists called themselves the Army of the Righteous.

On December 9, 2009, U.S. citizen David Coleman Headley was charged in Chicago with videotaping targets—including the Taj Mahal and Oberoi hotels, the Leopold Café, the Jewish outreach center, and the train station—and briefing the Mumbai attackers. Authorities said he even took boat trips to scout out the town's main harbor, a trip the terrorists later took on the operation. After pleading not guilty, on January 14, 2010, Headley was recharged along with Tahawwur Hussain Rana in a 12-count indictment that included a violent attack on Danish newspaper *Jyllands Posten* along with helping in the Mumbai attack.

On March 18, 2010, Headley pleaded guilty in U.S. District Court in Chicago to charges that he had scouted the targets for the Mumbai attack and planned the Danish newspaper attack. In a plea agreement, Headley agreed to testify against codefendant Rana. The Department of Justice agreed not to seek the death penalty. The United States granted access to Indian, Pakistani, and Danish investigators but not extradition. The plea agreement indicated that he was in contact with an al Qaeda cell in Europe. On January 24, 2013, Headley was sentenced to 35 years in prison.

Epilogue: On April 25, 2011, prosecutors in the U.S. District Court in Chicago charged four Pakistanis—Sajid Mir, Abu Qahafa, Mazhar Iqbal, and Major Iqbal—in a superseding indictment with some combination of aiding and abetting the murder of U.S. citizens in India; conspiracy to murder, maim, and bomb public places; and providing material support to Lashkar-e-Taiba in connection with the Mumbai attack. None were in U.S. custody. Headley claimed that Major Iqbal was a member of Pakistan's Directorate for Inter-Services Intelligence (ISI). Prosecutors said Mir was Headley's handler; Qahafa trained others in combat techniques; and Mazhar Iqbal was a Lashkar commander who passed messages to Headley via defendant Rana.

On May 23, 2011, Headley told the Chicago court in Rana's trial that the ISI recruited him and played a key role in the Mumbai attacks. He told the court that "ISI provided assistance to Lashkar: financial, military, and moral support." He said that ISI Major Iqbal chose the targets—including the Chabad House—route, and safe house, and that Iqbal was involved in the plot to attack *Jyllands-Posten* in Denmark.

The 2010s

The early years of the 2010s included *worst* attacks that were not as spectacular as others on the list, but nonetheless showed the continuing determination of radical Islamists to continue their misinterpretation of the Koran's call for jihad. Of note was the expansion of the al Qaeda franchise to the Horn of Africa, where al-Shabaab initially established a beachhead in the failed state of Somalia, already overrun by seafaring pirates. The group expanded its scope of operations, killing scores of World Cup fans in Kampala, conducting operations in Kenya, and attacking Ethiopian and other African peace keepers. At least one faction of the fissiparous al-Shabaab expressed formal fealty to al Qaeda Central. Meanwhile, Chechen terrorists, many with contacts with the remaining members of al Qaeda Central, continued their depredations on Russian turf. As of this writing, they had not expanded their targeting out of the motherland.

Western responses to terrorists overseas moved from concentration on capturing detainees and holding them for trials, which might not come for years, to conducting unmanned aerial vehicle (drone) operations designed to kill individual terrorists. Two major successes in taking terrorist leaders off the streets entailed the U.S. SEAL Team 6—killing of al Qaeda founder Osama bin Laden in his walled compound in Abbotabad, just outside the Pakistan Armed Forces' equivalent of West Point, and a drone strike that killed American propagandist and al Qaeda in the Arabian Peninsula (AQAP) operational leader Anwar al-Aulaqi, who had been in contact with and inspired numerous individuals who had conducted or tried to conduct operations against U.S. targets.

The death of al-Aulaqi, effectively the minister of propaganda for AQAP, and the loss of bin Laden, the face of the far-flung organization, left gaping holes in al Qaeda's ability to conduct and influence operations. However, their deaths did not end such publications as the online

AQAP magazine *Inspire* nor a host of jihadi and jihobbyist websites, some of which were occasionally hacked and taken offline. *Inspire*, true to its name, inspired several "almosts" for the *50 Worst* list. An Arabic-language tribute to *Inspire*, aimed at Islamist women, appeared in the early years of the decade.

As the decade continued, the United States planned to conduct trials in military courts against several al Qaeda leaders who were responsible for several of the *50 Worst*, including 9/11 and the USS *Cole* attacks.

March 29, 2010
Russia Moscow Subway Bombings

Overview: The Moscow subway is one of the largest in the world, with 7 million riders each day. In a rush-hour attack, two women wearing explosive belts filled with bolts and iron bars boarded and detonated the belts at two different stops along the same line, killing themselves and 40 commuters. The incident shocked the world. One woman was the widow of a terrorist leader, and the other reportedly a young schoolteacher.

Incident: On March 29, 2010, at 7:56 A.M., a female suicide bomber detonated her device on a Moscow subway train at the Lubyanka stop near the Kremlin and Federal Security Service headquarters, killing at least 23 people. Forty-five minutes later, a second female suicide bomber killed at least 12 more people at the Park Kultury station, four stops further on the same train line. Eighty others were wounded in the rush-hour attacks. The explosive belts were packed with bolts and iron bars that served as shrapnel. Chechen rebels were suspected. Police began searching for two suspected female accomplices and released photos of the suicide bombers.

On March 31, 2010, Doku Umarov, who in 2009 had re-formed a suicide battalion, claimed credit. He said the attacks were in retaliation for a raid in February 2010 in which 20 people were killed, charging that authorities used knives to execute innocent forest villagers.

The first bomber was identified by her father, Rasul Magomedov, as his daughter Maryam Sharilova, 28, a schoolteacher in Dagestan. He identified her from a photo of the severed head that had run in the Russian media and that had been sent to him via a friend's cell phone. He said she earned a degree in math and psychology from the Dagestan Pedagogical University in 2005. Upon returning home, she taught computer science at a local school. She was the widow of a terrorist leader who was killed in October 2009.

Investigators announced that the second bomber was Dzhanet Abdullayeva, 17, widow of an Islamist rebel leader. Authorities shared photos of her posing with a handgun and a grenade. She grew up in Khasavyurt,

40 miles from the site of the March 31, 2010, bombing in Dagestan. Her husband, Umulat Magomedov, 30, died in a New Year's Eve shootout with security forces in Khasavyurt. They met via the Internet.

A bus driver said the suicide bombers and a man traveled to Moscow from the North Caucasus with shuttle traders.

Authorities were investigating whether the duo were part of the 30 suicide bombers allegedly recruited by Alexander Tikhomirov before his death. They were to be trained at a madrassa in Turkey.

There is some debate as to whether the women detonated their own belts via cell phone calls or if male counterparts set off the explosives via remote control from a Moscow apartment.

On August 21, 2010, Russian security forces killed Magomed-Ali Vagabov, orchestrator of the suicide bombings, in a raid in Dagestan Province.

July 11, 2010
Uganda World Cup Bombings

Overview: Al-Shabaab considers itself at war with the African Union peace keepers (African Union Mission in Somalia; AMISOM) in Somalia and chose the airing of the World Cup soccer finals to make its point clear that anyone supporting AMISOM is al-Shabaab's enemy. Although an al-Shabaab spokesman claimed the explosive devices were planted, some evidence points to suicide bombers. The Ethiopian Village location may have been chosen because Ethiopia is al-Shabaab's perceived enemy.

Incident: At 10:30 P.M., on July 11, 2010, three bombs at two sites in Kampala, Uganda, killed 74 people and injured another 85 while they watched the World Cup soccer finale on television. The first bomb went off at the Ethiopian Village restaurant. Fifty minutes later, two other bombs exploded at the Kyandondo Rugby Club restaurant. The larger second bomb killed many who were trying to help victims of the initial blast.

The dead included 28 Ugandans, 1 Irish, 1 Indian, 1 American, and 11 Ethiopians and Eritreans. The American was Nate Henn, 25, of Wilmington, Delaware, who worked for the charity Invisible Children. Injuries included broken bones, flesh wounds, temporary blindness, and hearing problems. Five Americans were hospitalized; two were in serious condition. Six injured Americans hailed from the Christ Community United Methodist Church in Selinsgrove, Pennsylvania, and were working with a local congregation as part of an American church mission.

Al-Shabaab claimed credit. Referring to the 6,000 African Union peacekeepers in Somalia as "collaborators," al-Shabaab spokesman Ali Mohamud Rage told a press conference:

> And the best of men have promised and they have delivered. . . . Blessed and exalted among men—(taking) full responsibility. . . . We wage war against the six thousand collaborators; they have received their response. We are

behind the attack because we are at war with them. . . . We had given warning to the Ugandans to refrain from their involvement in our country. We
spoke to the leaders and we spoke to the people and they never listened to
us. May Allah accept these martyrs who carried out the blessed operation
and exploded themselves in the middle of the infidels.

Sheikh Moktar Abu Zubeyr, self-described emir of al-Shabaab in Somalia, posted on an al Qaeda website, "My message to the Ugandan and
Burundian nations is that you will be the target for our retribution to the
massacres perpetrated against the Somali men, women and children in
Mogadishu by your forces." One of the group's commanders, Sheik Yusuf
Sheik Issa, told the *Associated Press* in Mogadishu that "Uganda is one of
our enemies. Whatever makes them cry, makes us happy. May Allah's
anger be upon those who are against us."

During the previous Friday's prayers, al-Shabaab commander Sheikh
Muktar Robow had called for attacks in Uganda and Burundi, which con-
tribute troops to the African Union force in Mogadishu. On July 13, 2010,
al-Shabaab spokesman Yonis said the bombings involved planted explosives, not suicide bombers.

By July 14, 2010, authorities had arrested six people, including four
foreigners, among them two Somalis. Security officials suggested that
the local Muslim extremist group Allied Democratic Forces assisted the
terrorists. Police said they are based in the mountains near the Democratic Republic of the Congo. By July 18, 2010, 20 people were in custody, including citizens of Uganda, Somalia, and Ethiopia. Some were
caught near the borders with Sudan and Rwanda while trying to flee
the country.

On August 11, 2010, Kenyan authorities announced that they had sent
six suspects to Uganda and released a seventh. They included suspected
al-Shabaab members Idris Magondu, a Nairobi driver, and Hussein
Hassan Agade and Mohammed Adan Abdow, both street vendors, Agade
in Nairobi and Abdow in Tawa. Kenyan police said Abdow, a Kenyan of
Somali origin, had made satellite phone calls to al-Shabaab members.

Suspect Salmin Mohammed Khamis, 34, had been released on bail
on August 9, 2010. He was accused of harboring some of the suspects.
He had been acquitted in the 2002 bombing of an Israeli-owned hotel in
Mombasa. In 2003, he confessed to a failed plot to bomb the U.S. Embassy
in Nairobi.

On September 15, 2010, Kampala authorities arrested Omar Awadh
Omar (alias Abu Sahal), a Kenyan and deputy commander of al Qaeda in
the region, and Agade, one of his aides, in connection with the attack. The
Uganda website *New Vision* said the duo were planning a follow-up attack.
Omar was a key logistics and intelligence link to al-Shabaab and deputy of
Fazul Abdullah Mohammed. Authorities said Mohammed was behind the
August 7, 1998, bombings of the U.S. embassies in Tanzania and Kenya.

By October 10, 2010, Ugandan authorities had detained 36 suspects from seven countries—Kenya, Rwanda, Tanzania, Uganda, Somalia, Yemen, and Pakistan. One individual admitted being recruited and trained by al Qaeda. The suspects included businessmen, university students, and leaders of small mosques. Among those detained was al-Amin Kimathi, an activist with the Muslim Human Rights Forum in Nairobi.

Police said suspect Haruna Luyima allegedly was to set off a fourth bomb at a Kampala dance club but changed his mind; he told a press conference in August 2010 that he did not want to hurt innocent people. He claimed he had been recruited into the plot by his elder brother, Isa Luyima. Mohamood Mugisha told police he was given $4,000 by the al-Shabaab plotters to help plan the attacks, rent a house in Uganda, and drive the bombs in from Somalia via Kenya.

The case remains open.

January 16, 2013
Algerian Gas Plant Takeover

Overview: In 2012, a Tuareg rebellion overthrew government authority in northern Mali. Government troops, who had just wrested control of the capital from an ineffective government, were powerless to stop the rebellion, which was soon hijacked by a confederation of Islamist groups, including al Qaeda in the Islamic Maghreb (AQIM). The Islamists quickly instituted an especially harsh interpretation of sharia, amputating appendages and destroying Timbuktu shrines. North African terrorists flocked to northern Mali in hopes of aiding the creation of a regional caliphate. While West African nations indicated willingness to send troops to quell the rebellion, their ability to field a competent military force under UN blessing and Economic Community of West African States control was months away.

When the Islamists began moving south, threatening to take over the rest of Mali, France sent more than 2,000 ground troops and attack aircraft to the country, bombarding Islamist locations. In response, Mokhtar Belmokhtar, who had split with AQIM a few weeks earlier to create his own Islamist terrorist group, conducted the largest terrorist attack in the region in years. Terrorists seized Western hostages to pressure the French to end the incursion. Belmokhtar, whose faction had made millions of dollars since 2003 by kidnapping Westerners and smuggling cigarettes (giving him the nickname Marlboro Man), suddenly received worldwide attention.

The Algerian government, having experienced an exceptionally bloody terrorist campaign in the 1990s, rejected negotiations and went on the offensive, killing and capturing all of the terrorists. Dozens of hostages died during the battle. Later determination that some of the attack squad were involved in the September 11, 2012, attack on the U.S. Consulate in Benghazi, Libya, that killed four American diplomats, including the U.S. ambassador, further heightened concern about growth of this regional AQIM group.

Incident: On January 16, 2013, at 5:00 A.M., at least 32 radical Islamists protesting Algerian support for the French incursion into Mali attacked the country's third largest natural gas pumping station and employee barracks in the south, a remote facility 1,000 miles away from the capital city, killing 2 people and taking at least 573 Algerian and 132 foreign hostages, including 41 Westerners. The facility employs 790 people, including 134 foreigners from 26 countries.

As Algerian security forces escorted Westerners to the Ain Menas Airport, the gunmen, dressed in fatigues and wearing turbans, arrived in three unmarked trucks and attacked the bus. Prime Minister Abdelmalek Sellal later said:

> They wanted to take control of this bus and take the foreign workers directly to northern Mali so they could have hostages, to negotiate with foreign countries. But when they opened fire on the bus, there was a strong response from the gendarmes guarding it.

The gunmen ran off the security forces, seized Algerians and Westerners, and then sent separate teams to take over the gas production facility, an administration building, and the living quarters. An Algerian and a Briton were killed; two security guards, two base guards, and two Westerners were wounded. Many workers hid under beds and on rooftops; several Filipinos who refused to leave their rooms were beaten. Two Europeans were shot in the back, one while fleeing and one in the cafeteria. Many Algerian hostages were permitted to phone home. Algerian women were immediately released.

The terrorists, armed with AK-47s, rounded and tied up the Westerners, placing explosive vests on several. The terrorists announced that Muslims would not be harmed, but the Christians would be killed. They held the remaining Algerians in a separate location, refusing to release them in case the Algerian army killed the hostages and blamed the hostage-takers. The United Kingdom sent a rapid deployment team to Algiers to guard its embassy.

Algerian military forces surrounded the buildings where the hostages were held. Special Forces and the elite Special Intervention Group (GIS) disconnected mobile phone transmitters and scrambled satellite phone connections. Russian-made helicopters ringed the facility.

The gunmen released the Algerians, then made their demands, including an end to "brutal aggression on our people in Mali" and release from prison of their colleagues. The group told a Mauritanian news service it protested "blatant intervention of the French crusader forces in Mali" and said the world was ignoring the Syrian people, who were "groaning under the pressure of the butcher" President Bashar al-Assad. The group complained that Algeria was allowing the French to use its airspace for operations in Mali. An Algerian spokesman said no response was given because Algeria does not negotiate. Leader Belmokhtar said he would trade the Americans for two Islamist terrorists jailed in the United States—Sheikh Omar Abdel-Rahman and Aafia Siddiqui. The terrorists threatened to blow up the plant in the event of a rescue operation.

Late on January 16, 2013, the terrorists attempted to break out of the facility by putting explosives on the hostages and loading them into jeeps to go to Mali. Algerian helicopters fired on the jeeps, killing terrorist on-site leader Mohamed-Lamine Bouchneb. The 11 remaining terrorists moved their hostages into the gas-producing plant that they earlier had tried to set alight. According to Prime Minister Sellal, the dying words of the terrorist leader were "the order for all the foreigners to be killed, so there was a mass execution, many hostages were killed by a bullet to the head." Army snipers then fired on the terrorists.

Belmokhtar released a video on January 17, 2013, saying "We are ready to negotiate with Western countries and the Algerian regime on the condition that they halt aggression and bombing against the Muslim people of Mali . . . and respect their desire to apply sharia on their territory." They hoped to free 100 prisoners jailed in Algeria 15 years earlier. Algerian television broadcast African terrorist leader Abdel-Rahman al-Nigeri saying:

> You see our demands are so easy, so easy if you want to negotiate with us. We want the prisoners you have, the comrades who were arrested and imprisoned fifteen years ago. We want one hundred of them.

He took over the operation after the initial leader was killed. He was later recorded saying, "The Americans that are here, we will kill them. We will slaughter them."

While the terrorists claimed to come from Mali, Algerian authorities said it was a multinational group that included terrorists from Algeria, Tunisia, Canada, Mali, Egypt, Libya, Niger, the Persian Gulf, and Mauritania. They variously called themselves Al-Mulathameen—variant al-Mouwakoune Bi-Dima (Those Who Sign with Blood), Battalion of Blood, the Masked Brigade, and the Brigade of the Masked Ones. AQIM also claimed credit.

The terrorists allowed hostages to talk to France 24 TV, to put more pressure on their government. A British hostage told *Al Jazeera* that the Algerian Army should withdraw to avoid casualties. "We are receiving care and good treatment from the kidnappers. The (Algerian) army did not withdraw and they are firing at the camp. . . . There are around 150 Algerian hostages. We say to everybody that negotiation is a sign of strength and will spare many loss of life." An Irish hostage told *Al Jazeera* that French, American, Japanese, British, Irish, and Norwegian citizens were among the hostages. "The situation is deteriorating. We have contacted the embassies and we call on the Algerian army to withdraw. . . . We are worried because of the continuation of the firing." Japanese media said five workers from Japanese engineering firm JGC Corporation were held.

French catering contractor Alexandre Berceaux barricaded himself in his room for 40 hours. He was freed by Algerian soldiers who also found British citizens hiding on the roof.

BP and Sonatrac, the Algerian national oil company, and Norway's Statoil jointly operate the field. Statoil said 17 of its employees—including 13 Norwegians—were in the area at the time of the attack. Five of them—four Norwegians and a Canadian resident—were safely evacuated to a military camp; two injured individuals received medical treatment.

Some of the Westerners blended in with the Algerians who escaped. Some of the hostages were blindfolded, gagged, and thrown into five jeeps. When a jeep crashed after taking fire from Algerian troops, Stephen McFaul, 36, an electrical engineer from Belfast, Northern Ireland, ran to freedom with explosives strapped around his neck. (McFaul had earlier hidden in a room with a colleague and phoned home.) It is believed that when later military rescuers targeted the jeeps, the other hostages in the jeeps died.

It was initially unclear what happened when the Algerians conducted their three rescue operations with ground troops supported by helicopter gunships. Initial reports form news outlets (Algeria's *Ennahar* TV, *Mauritanian ANI News*, Algeria's APS state media, and *Reuters*) and tallies by countries with citizens held hostage differed as to how many and who were dead, how many and who were feared dead, how many and who had escaped, and how many and who were alive and held hostage. The Algerians did not inform the Americans, British, or Japanese ahead of time when they raided the facility on January 17, 2013. The remaining 20 terrorists, hemmed in on all sides, demanded safe passage with the rest of their hostages. The rescue operation apparently freed the hostages who had been brought to the dorms, but the rest of the facility was still held by the terrorists, who wanted to drive the hostages to other countries.

The Algerian government announced on January 19, 2013, that it had conducted a final rescue mission that ended the siege, during which 23 hostages and 32 terrorists had died. The government said at least 685 Algerian workers and 107 foreigners were freed. During the final assault, 7 hostages and 11 terrorists died. An Algerian security official told local media that the terrorists had turned their guns on the hostages when they failed to destroy the facility, as well as during the final rescue operation. Algerian officials found 21 rifles, six machine guns, two 60-mm mortars, rockets, six 60-mm C5 missiles with launchers, two grenade launchers with eight rockets, Belgian-made antitank mines, and 10 grenades arranged into explosive belts. Operations leader Bouchneb purchased the weapons in Tripoli, Libya.

Government officials found 25 charred bodies at the facility after the final rescue operation. On January 21, 2013, the Algerian government said 38 hostages from 8 countries had died and another 5 hostages were still missing. At least 29 terrorists were killed, including their leader. An Algerian television station said five terrorists had been captured and three were still unaccounted for.

Algerian interrogation of the surviving terrorists and interviews with the freed hostages yielded details on the operation. The Algerian government announced that the terrorists organized the plot in Mali, then entered Algeria via their gathering place in Ghat in southern Libya. The terrorists had inside information about the facility from short-term contract workers for BP who served as drivers, cooks, and guards, providing information about the entrances and exits, the residence complex, the guard systems, and building details. The attackers knew how to shut off production at the site and knew of ongoing labor strife and plans for a strike by catering workers. They told the Algerian hostages, "We know you're oppressed; we've come here so that you can have your rights."

The news media reported that the gas companies had chosen not to deploy armed guards. The workers were no match for the terrorists operating in the dark who brought in mortars, grenade launchers, and 50-caliber machine guns.

The news media reported that several hostages used cell phones to video the siege. They captured executions of hostages, including one via bodybomb. Another showed a terrorist with a car battery between his thighs, two wires in his hands, and wearing an explosive belt, ready to set it off if a rescue was attempted. One video showed the terrorist leader wearing a green military uniform with an explosives belt and carrying a Kalashnikov.

A terrorist spokesman announced on a Mauritanian news site that more attacks within Algeria were coming. The British and American governments publicly vowed to track down the perpetrators. As of late 2013, the search continues.

September 21–24, 2013
Nairobi, Kenya, Westgate Shopping Mall Attack

Overview: By summer 2013, the West and African Union thought it had al-Shabaab on the run. African Union troops overran al-Shabaab's redoubts in Kismaayo and Mogadishu, Somalia's capital. Surviving members faced major schisms. Four senior commanders, including two cofounders, were assassinated in June 2013. Its spiritual guide, Sheikh Hassan Dahir Aweys, fled but was captured and imprisoned in Mogadishu. A very public spat with its prominent American spokesman, Omar Hammami, ended with his assassination by loyalists of Muktar Abdirahman Godane on September 12, 2013. Godane's 2012 swearing of allegiance to al Qaeda's central leadership put it under great pressure to reestablish its credentials as a leader in the jihadi movement. Al-Shabaab's claim to jihadi leadership was tenuous despite the occasional attack beyond Somalia's borders on African Union troop contributors Kenya and Uganda. Bomb-and-run attacks on Kenyan churches and bus stops paled in comparison to a days-long barricade-and-hostage shootout that killed scores of Kenyans and foreigners and hijacked the world's headlines at the same time the UN General Assembly was hosting its annual General Debate by heads of state.

Incident: At noon, on September 21, 2013, a multinational team of more than a dozen al-Shabaab terrorists threw grenades and fired at two entrances to the upscale, 80-shop, 6-year-old Westgate Mall in Nairobi's affluent Westlands district. The terrorist team shot at least one man inside his car and hit two more pedestrians before entering the mall. At least three security officers were hospitalized following the initial attack. The gunmen then seized dozens of hostages, but told Muslims to leave as they were targeting non-Muslims. Some hostages were held for four days until a two-day government rescue operation ended the siege. The terrorists killed at least 62 people and wounded 175 people, including foreigners. Authorities had issued a warning to the expatriate community to avoid the mall after receiving a threat against it. Al-Shabaab said the attack was in revenge for Kenyan participation in the African Union attacks against al-Shabaab in Somalia.

Following the initial attack, police surrounded the mall and conducted an on-and-off gun battle with the terrorists, who still held dozens of hostages. An Army helicopter and two armed vehicles joined police efforts. At least one terrorist died during the initial confrontation. Another was hospitalized under police custody; he later died.

Initial reports said some terrorists wore masks or burkas to hide their identities. Twitter postings from al-Shabaab indicated that all of the terrorists were males, although some reports included the presence of a white English-speaking British woman among the attackers. Police believed she was Samantha Lewthwaite (aka Natalie Faye Webb), 29, known as the "white widow" of suicide bomber Germaine Lindsey, who died in the July 7, 2005, attack on London's transportation system. Kenyan authorities wanted Buckinghamshire-born Lewthwaite for financing al-Shabaab and al Qaeda. Surviving shoppers said she spurred terrorists to more killing, giving orders in English that were translated into Swahili.

Early in the siege, Kenyan president Uhuru Kenyatta vowed, "We shall hunt down the perpetrators wherever they run to. We shall get them, and we shall punish them for this heinous crime." He later added, "They shall not get away with their despicable, beastly acts. Like the cowardly perpetrators now cornered in the building, we will punish the masterminds swiftly and indeed very painfully."

At least 1,000 people escaped from the mall and were allowed to depart after authorities checked for weapons. Some, including several wounded children, were pulled out on shopping carts. Several shoppers reported the smell of tear gas. Some shoppers heard gunfire inside the mall and ran outside, but heard shots there, too, so they ran back inside. Several hid in restrooms and stairwells. At least one woman climbed through an air vent to safety. Uche Kaigwa-Okoye hid with 20 others for five hours in a women's restroom before fleeing. Manish Turohit, 18, who hid in a parking garage for two hours, reported that the gunmen were armed with AK-47s and wore vests with hand grenades attached. Kamal Kaur, a journalist for Radio Africa, said a bullet missed her son, bounced off a wall, and killed a nearby child. The terrorists went from store to store asking questions of the shoppers before shooting and throwing grenades. Three area hospitals treated more than 293 people and reported wounded ranging in age from 2 to 78.

The dead included many Kenyans and at least 18 foreigners. President Kenyatta lost his nephew Mbugua Mwangi and his nephew's fiancée Rosemary Wahito, who were at the mall shopping for wedding rings. Ruhila Adatia-Sood, 31, journalist and popular Kenya media personality, was killed while hosting a children's cooking competition at the mall. She was six months pregnant. Others killed included U.K. businessman Louis Bawa's wife and 8-year-old daughter; Ross Langdon, 33, award-winning London-based Australian architect, and his partner Elif Yavus, 33, malaria specialist who was working for the Bill, Hillary and Chelsea Clinton Foundation and who was about to give birth in two weeks; Canadian diplomat Annemarie Desloges, 29, liaison officer to Canada's High Commission to Kenya, her husband Robert Munk was among those injured; and Kofi Awoonor, 78, Ghanaian poet and professor who had served as ambassador to Brazil, Cuba, and the United Nations, his son was among those injured.

The terrorists said via Twitter posts that they would not negotiate with the government because the group was retaliating "for the lives of innocent Muslims" killed by Kenyan forces leading an African Union offensive against al-Shabaab that began in 2011. At one time or another, the attackers stated:

- "We'll not negotiate with the Kenyan government as long as its forces are invading our country, so reap the bitter fruits of your harvest."
- "When justice is denied, it must be enforced. Kenyans were relatively safe in their cities before they invaded us & killed Muslims #Westgate."
- "The Mujahideen are still strong inside #Westgate Mall and still holding their ground. All praise is due to Allah!"
- "[The operation was] far greater than how the Kenyans perceive it."
- "There are countless number of dead bodies still scattered inside the mall, and the mujahideen are still holding their ground."

- "[The hostages are] still alive looking quite disconcerted but, nevertheless, alive."
- "You [the government] could have avoided all this and lived your lives with relative safety. Remove your forces from our country and peace will come."

Twitter closed down five al-Shabaab accounts, but a sixth popped up. Al-Shabaab spokesman Ali Mohamud Rage later said, "We will make them suffer what we suffer in southern Somalia, we are giving a warning to the Kenyan government and to all those who support it. . . . If not, know that this is just a taste of what we will do . . . you should expect black days."

The government countered that it was in control and simply conducting mopping-up operations against the terrorists.

The terrorist group posted the names of nine attackers, including three Americans, two Somalis, and one each from Canada, Finland, Kenya, and the United Kingdom. Kenyan authorities said the Americans were of Somali extraction, aged 18 or 19. Al-Shabaab's media office later told *Reuters*, "Those who describe the attackers as Americans and British are people who do not know what is going on in Westgate building." Investigators were looking into possible connections of the terrorists with the Somali refugee community in the Eastleigh neighborhood of Nairobi and Somali diaspora in Minneapolis, Minnesota.

Large explosions rocked the mall the second day of the siege. Some shoppers trapped in the mall managed to leave after the initial mass escape. They included Cecile Ndwiga, who hid under a car in the basement parking garage. U.S. law enforcement, military, and civilian personnel and Israeli Special Forces operatives arrived to assist Kenyan colleagues during the crisis. Four mall restaurants were Israeli owned.

Kenya launched what it deemed a "major" rescue operation on September 22, 2013, freeing several hostages—many suffering from dehydration—to the sound of loud explosions and gunfire. Kenya's National Disaster Operation Centre tweeted, "This will end tonight. Our forces will prevail. Kenyans are standing firm against aggression, and we will win." Nine bodies were recovered. On September 23, 2013, four more explosions were heard at the mall during gun battles in which 3 terrorists were killed and 10 arrested; 11 Kenyan soldiers were wounded. Smoke billowed from the mall's main department and grocery store, Nakumatt.

Al-Shabaab spokesman Rage posted an Internet audio file saying that the hostage-takers had been ordered to "take punitive action against the hostages" in the event of a rescue operation. The BBC in Somalia interviewed an Abu Ammar, who claimed credit for organizing the attack.

On September 24, 2013, the government began its final push. An explosion went off at 6:30 A.M., and two more at noon. Three floors of the four-story mall collapsed, trapping people.

At the end of the siege, the government said 61 civilians, 6 members of the security forces, and 5 terrorists—possibly including Lewthwaite—died during the four days. Eleven terrorists were detained. Another 65 people were reported missing. It was unclear whether any terrorists managed to escape by changing clothes and mingling with the fleeing hostages. Police said they were defusing booby traps. Local police identified one of the dead terrorists as Hassan Abdi Dhuhulow, 23, a Norwegian citizen of Somali extraction.

On September 26, 2013, Interpol issued a "Red Notice"—an internationally wanted persons alert—for Lewthwaite (alias Sherafiya). Kenya wanted her on charges of being in possession of explosives and conspiracy to commit a felony in December 2011. As of late 2013, she remained at large.

The *Associated Press* reported that on October 5, 2013, U.S. Navy SEALs conducted an operation in Barawe, southern Somalia, but were unable to locate the suspect in the Westgate case.

On November 4, 2013, Kenyan authorities charged four Somali men—Mohamed Ahmed Abdi, Liban Abdullah Omar, Hussein Hassan Mustafah, and Adan Dheq—and ordered them imprisoned until a court hearing. They pleaded not guilty to charges that included illegally harboring a fugitive.

The *Worst* 51–68

The criteria for inclusion in the *Worst 50* can easily be argued. Some multi-casualty events, such as the late 1970s arson against an Iranian theater that killed 347 people, did not make the list because they are virtually unknown outside the host country. Other campaigns—two series of 100 letter bombs mailed at the same time, but most of which were intercepted; the October 2001 anthrax attacks; the Unabomber bombings; the Hizballah kidnappings of Westerners in Beirut; and similar serial events—were not included because no single event or small group of events were lethal or newsworthy enough in their own right.

These types of events, however, are still worth mention. Some broke new ground in the terrorist repertoire, introducing a new type of attack, an innovation in the use of an old tactic, an uptick in lethality, or the crossing of a heretofore silently agreed upon barrier against attacking a specific class of target.

September 4, 1969
Brazil U.S. Ambassador Burke Elbrick Kidnapping

Overview: The Elbrick kidnapping established for Latin American terrorists a model for getting leverage against the United States and the local government—a low-risk hostage-taking of a prominent American (usually an ambassador, military figure, or corporate executive) to obtain multimillion dollar ransoms; release of scores, if not hundreds, of political prisoners; publication of the group's manifesto to audiences in the millions; and publicity in general for the organization. The kidnapping was comparatively clean, meaning with little bloodshed, and the hostage was treated well throughout his captivity. The safe house–negotiation template, with an exit strategy for the kidnappers as part of their calculus, stood for several years as the standard for Latin American and Western European leftist revolutionary groups.

Incident: On September 4, 1969, Charles Burke Elbrick, U.S. ambassador to Brazil and former deputy assistant secretary of state for European Affairs, was kidnapped from his car on his way to the embassy following lunch at home. Four armed members of the Revolutionary Movement of October 8 (MR-8) and the National Liberation Action blocked the path of his vehicle with their cars on a Rio de Janeiro street. The group left a ransom note demanding the release of 15 unidentified political prisoners who were to be flown to Chile, Mexico, or Algeria and the publication of a three-page manifesto. Elbrick's chauffeur, an embassy employee for four years, was left behind unharmed. Elbrick suffered a scalp-type wound on his right forehead where he was hit by the butt of a .38 caliber revolver. The group warned that if their demands were not carried out within 48 hours, they would be "forced to carry out revolutionary justice" by killing Elbrick. An hour after his capture, he was questioned about the activities, membership, and contacts of the Central Intelligence Agency (CIA) in Brazil by two men who the ambassador believed were outside communists, "unlike the kidnappers themselves who did not claim to be communists."

The Brazilian National Security Council, composed of three military ministers acting during the convalescence of President Arthur da Costa e Silva, met in emergency session on September 4, 1969, and the next day authorized the newspapers to print the manifesto, which claimed that the kidnapping was:

> not an isolated act. It is another one of the innumerable revolutionary acts already carried out: bank holdups, where funds for the revolution are collected, returning what the bankers take from the people and their employees; raids on barracks and police stations, where arms and ammunition are obtained for the struggle to topple the dictatorship; invasions of jails when revolutionaries are freed to return them to the people's struggle; the explosion of buildings that signify oppression; the execution of hangmen and torturers. With the kidnap of the ambassador we want to demonstrate that it is possible to defeat the dictatorship and the exploitation if we arm and organize ourselves. We show up where the enemy least expects us, and we disappear immediately, tearing out the dictatorship, bringing terror and fear to the exploiters, the hope and certainty of victory to the midst of the exploited. Mr. Elbrick represents in our country the interests of imperialism, which, allied to the great bosses, the big ranches and the big national bankers, maintain the regime of oppression and exploitation.

Foreign Minister José de Migalhaes Pinto announced the same day that 15 political prisoners would be released. Mexico and Chile immediately offered political asylum, and two hours later, the names of the prisoners that the terrorists wanted released were placed in a suggestion box at a suburban supermarket. They were Gregorio Bezzera, a leading member of the clandestine communist party, who had been in prison since 1964; Wladimir Palmeira, former president of the Metropolitan Student Union in Rio, arrested in 1968 and sentenced in August to three years imprisonment for leading student demonstrations against the government; Flavio Tavares, a newspaperman charged in 1966 with organizing guerrilla activities and recently arrested on charges of membership in a terrorist group called the Revolutionary Movement of July 26; Ricardo Zarattini, former National Student Union officer, jailed for subversive activities among peasants; Luiz Travassos, former National Student Union president who was also active in the radical movement of the Roman Catholic Church; José Dirccu de Oliveira e Silva, also a former president of the National Student Union; Ricardo Villas Boas de Sarega and Maria Augusta Carneiro, both student leaders arrested on May 1, 1969, for allegedly firing at a policeman who was attempting to prevent them from distributing antigovernment literature; Onofre Pinto, a former air force sergeant, arrested and charged with killing U.S. Army Capt. Charles R. Chandler on October 12, 1968; Ivens Marchetti, a São Paulo architect, also charged with Chandler's murder; José Ibrahim and Rolando Prattes, labor leaders in the São Paulo area; Argonauto Pacheco da Silva, labor leader and former São Paulo legislator; Joao Leonardo da Silva Rocha, a São Paulo lawyer; and Mario Galgardo Zanconato, a former medical student, who said in Mexico City on September 8, 1969, that he had organized eight bank robberies in Minas Gerais to raise funds for the revolutionary movement.

On September 6, 1969, a member of the armed forces who disagreed with the government's capitulation attempted to prevent the prisoners' release. Two hundred navy men surrounded the airport but dispersed when they were ordered back to their barracks. The plane took off late with the 15 for Mexico City, where they were granted political asylum. Thirteen of the group turned up later in Cuba.

Arrests soon followed. Police surrounded the house where Elbrick was being kept (it had been rented in the true name of one of the kidnappers), but allowed the group safe passage in return for his release. One member returned to his parents' home for a change of clothes and was arrested. From him, it was learned that the MR-8 approached guerrilla theorist Carlos Marighella and the National Liberation Action with their plan for the kidnapping.

The Brazilian government had believed that it had previously crippled the terrorist movements. On July 27, 1969, it had arrested 29 MR-8 members, 7 more on August 7, 1969, and several dozen on August 10, 1969. This time a nationwide roundup was initiated, resulting in the arrests of more than 4,000 suspects. The government passed Institutional Act 14, which decreed the death penalty for subversion, the first time capital punishment was allowed in Brazil since 1891. Police powers of the military were also greatly expanded.

The groups sent another manifesto after Elbrick's release in which they argued that they had no personal hostility toward the ambassador, but had taken him as a symbol of "big North American capitalists."

In November 1969, the police announced the death of Marighella.

In December 1969, student Claudio Torres de Silva received a 10-year sentence for his part in the kidnapping, while three others were being held on related charges. In February 1970, the army announced that 18 people had been in on the planning and execution of the kidnapping and that 4 had been apprehended; the others had fled to Cuba.

Members of the attack squad were interviewed in places of safety months after the incident. An MR-8 member in Algiers, Fernando Gabeira, claimed that he had been in on the two-month planning period, during which the group had infiltrated a woman into the military intelligence agency, DOPS, where she collected information about the ambassador's travel habits. Twelve terrorists who had previously engaged in bank robberies used a rented villa on Marques Street, near Elbrick's home, as their headquarters. In late June 1970, Silvia de Araujo Magalhaes gave a similar interview in Algiers. She recounted that Elbrick was held in an apartment on the Barau de Petropolis in the Santa Teresa district. Elbrick had a bathroom with a shower, but the windows were sealed. His cook was Gabeira, a former editor of the *Journel do Brasil*. Elbrick was allowed to write three letters to his wife. The group felt compassion for him, giving him a book by Ho Chi Minh inscribed, "To our first political prisoner, with the expression of our respect for his calm behavior in action."

March 1, 1973
Sudan U.S. Ambassador Cleo Noel Assassination

Overview: The Black September Organization (BSO) of Palestinian terrorists had already established a reputation for being willing to kill hostages during negotiations. Their barricade-and-hostage method established in the 1972 Munich Olympics attack appeared to other terrorists who watched the siege play out to be a success, with the terrorists attacking a symbolic American target, killing prominent Americans, yet getting only a legal wrist-slap and quick freedom. American diplomats, on the other hand, worried about the potential unintended consequences of a declared preemptive no-negotiations policy.

Incident: On March 1, 1973, eight Black Septembrists, driven in a Land Rover with Palestine Liberation Organization (PLO) diplomatic plates, seized the Saudi Arabian Embassy in Khartoum, Sudan. After unsuccessfully bargaining for the release of imprisoned terrorists, they murdered two American members and one Belgian member of the diplomatic corps—U.S. ambassador Cleo A. Noel Jr.; George C. Moore, the departing U.S. chargé (for whom the diplomatic reception was being held); and Guy Eid, the Egyptian-born chargé at the Belgian Embassy.

The attack began at 7:00 P.M., when a Land Rover, driven by Abu Salem, deputy chief of Fatah's Khartoum office, crashed through the embassy's unguarded gate. The terrorists fired machine guns and revolvers while some guests escaped by jumping over the embassy wall. Others hid and fled. Noel sustained an ankle wound from a ricochet, and Eid was shot in the leg. Noel and Moore were bound with ropes, punched, and kicked, according to Japanese chargé d'affaires Shigeru Nomoto. The terrorists also held Sheikh Abdullah el-Malhouk, the Saudi ambassador and party host, his wife, and four children, and Jordanian chargé d'affaires Adli el-Nazir. Later the children were allowed to leave. Some diplomats identified themselves as representatives of Arab or Eastern Bloc states and were also immediately released. The terrorists had hoped to seize the West German ambassador, but he had left earlier in the evening. Also on the group's assassination list was U.K. ambassador Raymond Etherington-Smith, who left the party earlier to greet at the airport British under secretary of state Anthony Kershaw, who was arriving for an official visit.

The group set a 24-hour deadline for their demands for the release of prisoners to be met. They demanded that the United States release Sirhan Sirhan, who had assassinated Senator Robert Kennedy on June 5, 1968; that Israel release all women detained in Israeli jails, including the two surviving hijackers of the Sabena plane hijacking on May 8, 1972, in Austria; that West Germany release imprisoned members of the Baader-Meinhof Gang responsible for an incident on May 11, 1972; and that Jordan release Abu Daoud and the 16 Black Septembrists accompanying him on February 15, 1973, as well as Maj. Rafreh Hindawi, a Jordanian officer who had been sentenced to life imprisonment for plotting against the Amman government. To underlie the group's determination, one of the terrorists appeared on a balcony and tossed a grenade from one hand to another. The group's leader allowed a doctor to enter the embassy to treat Moore's wounds.

On March 2, 1973, Sudanese interior minister Mohammed el Bahir told the terrorists by telephone that Jordan had refused their demands for Daoud, Hindawi, and others. The terrorists then dropped their demand for release of prisoners in Israel "since Sudan cannot contact the Zionist enemy," as well as for those held in West Germany, since they were unable to capture the West German ambassador, but "we insist and reconfirm that we will not leave the embassy or release the hostages or even guarantee their lives except if the Palestinian prisoners held in the prisons of the reactionary regime of Jordan are freed." The group also held firm on their demand for Sirhan's release.

U.S. president Richard Nixon sent Deputy Under Secretary of State William Macomber Jr. to Khartoum to advise the Sudanese on their negotiations. Macomber and his group initially landed at Cairo. The attendant publicity of his visit appeared to please the terrorists, and officials got the impression that the group was willing to fly to Cairo to continue the negotiations. Unfortunately Macomber's flight to Khartoum was unable to take off because of an ongoing sandstorm. In addition, President Nixon refused the demand for the release of Sirhan, claiming that the United States could not give in to political blackmail. He told the nation:

> We cannot do so and we will not do so. Now, as to what can be done to get these people released, Mr. Macomber is on his way there for discussions; the Sudanese Government is working on the problem . . . but we will not pay blackmail.

Many Foreign Service officers later criticized Nixon's statements, claiming that these had deleterious effects upon the negotiations.

Egyptian president Sadat had attempted to defuse the situation by sending an Egyptian plane to Khartoum to pick up the terrorists and their hostages and fly them back to Cairo. At the time the trio was murdered, senior members of Fatah were waiting at Cairo airport. Sadat hoped that the Fatah members would be able to persuade the group to surrender.

Members of Israeli intelligence managed to monitor the ultrahigh-frequency shortwave that the terrorists were using to keep in touch with their leaders at headquarters. At one point, someone at their headquarters in Beirut said, "Remember the blood, Nahr el-Badawi," a Palestinian refugee camp in Lebanon that had been attacked a few days previously by the Israelis. Many took this to mean that the group had been instructed to execute their hostages. (Other reports claim that the message was "Cold River" or "The organization orders, repeat orders, you to carry out Operation Cold Water on number one, two, and three.") At around 9:30 P.M., on March 2, 1973, the group took the trio to the basement and emptied 40 rounds, beginning by firing at their legs after the ambassador and chargés had been allowed to make out their wills and had thanked the Saudi ambassador for the party, saying "I'm very sorry it has turned out this way, but I want you to know it is not your fault." The terrorists phoned the U.S. Embassy, announcing "We have executed the two Americans and the Belgian." The terrorists were informed that they would not be allowed a flight out of the country, and a few hours later, they ended the 60-hour siege by releasing their remaining hostages and surrendering to Sudanese authorities.

BSO soon released a statement in Beirut vowing to continue attacks against "Zionist and American imperialism and their agents in the Arab world." The Khartoum operation was characterized as:

> not at all aimed at bloodshed but had sought the release of our imprisoned heroes . . . as a result of the arrogance and the obstinacy of American

imperialism, represented by Nixon's statements and by the attitude of hire-
ling tools in Jordan, our revolutionaries carried out the death sentences on
three hostages. . . . The United States shared in plotting to slaughter our people, conspiring against our Arab nation and our national struggle. . . . [Moore
was seen as] the plotting brain of the American Central Intelligence Agency
and one of those directly responsible for the September massacres. . . . We
wish to affirm to the world that the Black September militants have never
known fear and will not know it. . . . Its members would not be intimidated
by the hypocritical cries of condemnation or the tears of those whom we
have never seen shed a tear throughout a quarter of a century during which
this people has been subjected to all kinds of torture and persecution. Those
who ostensibly weep today over the execution of three enemies of the Arab
nation, for which the United States has been directly responsible, realize that
thousands of the sons of this people have been atrociously slaughtered and
that thousands of others are suffering all kinds of torture in Jordanian and
Israeli jails. . . . War against Zionist and American imperialism and their
agents in the Arab world will continue. Our rifles will remain brandished
against both the substance and the shadow.

Many observers believed that BSO had intended to kill the diplomats
before initiating the attack to recoup the prestige the organization had lost
in the Bangkok operation on December 28, 1972.

The Sudanese raided the Khartoum office of the PLO and discovered many documents that linked Fatah and the PLO to the operation.
Reporter Christopher Dobson learned that the PLO Khartoum office's
chief, Fawaz Yassin, organized the attack; his deputy, Rizig Abu Gassan, led the team; and the No. 3 man, Karam from Fatah, drove the
Land Rover. Documents seized included instructions for the raiders and
a map of the embassy. Karam later confessed to Fatah complicity, and
Gassan, who had made Fatah broadcasts over Sudanese radio, said at a
magistrate's court preliminary hearing, "We are proud of what we have
done." Yassin was in Libya a few days prior to the attack. He met the
seven BSO members at the airport when they arrived from Beirut and
saw their luggage through customs. They had smuggled in five pistols, eight grenades, and Kalashnikovs. Yassin then flew to Libya a few
hours before the raid and left instructions for the attack and the assassination of Ethiopian emperor Haile Selassie and the West German and
British ambassadors. Colonel Qadhafi refused a request for the return
of Yassin and helped him to a People's Democratic Republic of Yemen
sanctuary. The news media reported that the Black Septembrists had
hoped to fly their American hostages to the United States, where they
would assassinate them.

A Sudanese court of inquiry indicted the eight on five counts, including murder, but released two of them for lack of evidence in October 1973. A Khartoum court convicted them of murder on June 24, 1974,
and sentenced them to life, but Sudanese president Gaafer el-Nimeiry

immediately commuted each sentence to seven years. He also announced that the group would be handed over to the PLO. They were flown to Cairo the next day. It appears that Egypt placed the group at the disposal of the PLO in November 1974.

December 27, 1974
U.S. Ambassador Shelton Party Attack

Overview: The previous year's barricade-and-hostage takeover in Khartoum gave other terrorists a model of how such an operation could yield tremendous publicity. Among the Latin American groups carefully taking notes was the Sandinista National Liberation Front (Frente Sandinista de Liberación Nacional, FSLN), which eventually came to power in Nicaragua and then held on to power during clashes with the U.S.-backed Contras. The FSLN was named after Gen. Agusto Sandino, who had opposed the U.S. occupation of Nicaragua from 1927 to 1933 and who was shot on orders given by the father of the then Nicaraguan president, Anastasio Somoza.

Incident: On December 27, 1974, nine FSLN members invaded the Managua suburban home of the former agricultural minister, Dr. José Castillo, who was hosting a party in honor of the U.S. ambassador Turner B. Shelton. Shelton had already left the party before the initial assault in which three guards and Castillo were killed and two others were injured. Among the 25 hostages were Alejandro Montiel Arguello, Nicaragua's foreign minister; Guillermo Sevilla-Sacasa, Nicaragua's ambassador to the United States; the Nicaraguan ambassador to the United Nations; the mayor of Managua; the local Esso manager; and Chile's ambassador to Nicaragua. The terrorists, wielding submachine guns, threatened to shoot one of their hostages every 12 hours if they were not paid $5 million. They also demanded that the government release 14 political prisoners, fly them with the prisoners to Havana, and broadcast a revolutionary communiqué, which took over an hour to read. After 61 hours of negotiations with the Archbishop of Managua and the Papal Nuncio acting as intermediaries, the government agreed to pay $1 million and release the prisoners, as well as broadcast the statement. The hostages were released at the airport as crowds cheered the terrorists, who flew with the intermediaries and the ambassadors of Spain and Mexico to Havana to ensure their safety. Mauricio Duarte Alvarez, who was suspected of planning the attack, was killed in Jinotepe on January 10, 1975. The government suspended all constitutional guarantees after the attack and created a special antiterrorist unit recruited from members of the U.S.-trained National Guard. The government claimed that the FSLN, which had been established in 1958 by Carlos Fonseca Amador, had received guerrilla training in Cuba and the Soviet Union.

December 23, 1975
CIA Chief of Station/Athens Richard Welch Assassination

Overview: Attacks on U.S. diplomats had become commonplace by the mid-1970s. An even more prized target was Central Intelligence Agency (CIA) officials, particularly chiefs of station. Although CIA officials prided themselves on clandestine tradecraft, a leftist pastime became outing these officers, using techniques suggested by patron states and Philip Agee, a CIA defector. The leftist November 17 Organization, whose members avoided arrest for decades, set the terrorist bar even higher with the assassination of Chief of Station/Athens Richard S. Welch.

Incident: On December 23, 1975, three gunmen assassinated Welch, the Athens CIA chief of station, in Palaion Psyhiko as he and his wife returned home after a Christmas party at the home of U.S. ambassador Jack B. Kubisch. His wife was not injured. Welch's name, along with that of other U.S. Embassy employees, had been published on November 25, 1975, in the *Athens Daily News*, which claimed that his position of special assistant to the ambassador and first secretary at the embassy was a cover for his CIA position. On December 28, 1975, an advertisement was placed in Athens by the Organization of November 17 claiming responsibility. On December 15, 1976, Evanghelos Mallios, who was claimed in reports to be one of the most brutal torturers in the former Greek regime, was assassinated outside his home. Ballistics tests found that the .45 caliber gun was the same one used to kill Welch.

On December 8, 2003, a special Athens tribunal convicted the leader, chief gunman, and 13 other 17 November members for killings and attacks that began with the Welch assassination. The group's leader, French-born Alexandros Giotopoulos, was sentenced on December 17, 2003, to 21 life terms and 25 years. Hit man Dimitris Koufodinas was sentenced to 13 life terms and 25 years.

March 9, 1977
Takeover of Washington, D.C., Buildings

Overview: Terrorist attacks within the United States were a fairly rare occurrence in the 1970s, confined to comparatively simple bombings and the occasional take-me-to-Cuba hijacking. A mix of leftist radicals, right wingers, and other idiosyncratic groups accounted for the bulk of the attacks. The most prominent religious-based attack during this period was the multiple barricade-and-hostage operation conducted by a heretofore little-known African American Muslim sect, which held sieges in three Washington, D.C., locations. The case was also notable for its heavy media coverage, to the dismay of the police. Authorities through the decades have complained about media coverage issues, noting that many terrorist groups seek publicity and that the media plays into their hands.

Incidents: On March 9, 1977, in the first of three coordinated barricade-and-hostage operations, seven Hanafi Muslims took over the B'nai B'rith national headquarters in northwest Washington, D.C. The group was led by the sect's spiritual leader, Khalifa Hamaas Abdul Khaalis, 54, who was born Ernest Timothy McGee. At around 11:00 A.M., the group drove a rental truck to the building and brought in rifles, handguns, machetes, long knives, and a crossbow. One hundred-forty people were initially trapped inside the building, but 35 escaped, were freed during a police sweep of the building, or were released because of illness during negotiations. A total of 105 hostages were released 39 hours later at the end of the siege. While it appeared that the group was hoping to seize the organization's high-ranking officials, most of the B'nai B'rith leaders were attending a luncheon at the Shoreham Americana Hotel in honor of Israeli prime minister Yitzhak Rabin.

The hostages initially were treated roughly—some pistol-whipped—by the Hanafis. Shortly after the takeover, five of the seriously wounded hostages were allowed to leave the building.

Khaalis's manipulation of the media was well orchestrated. Reporters from newspapers and radio stations throughout the United States, as well as from Mexico, France, and Australia, called, but Khaalis would not always speak with them. Despite the heavy press coverage, the phone appeared to be Khaalis's only source of information. However, it appeared that the radios were monitored in another siege location and that operational information was relayed to the B'nai B'rith headquarters, which appeared to be the command center for the three operations.

The second attack occurred at noon, when three Hanafi Muslims took over the Islamic Center at 2551 Massachusetts Avenue, NW, in Washington, D.C. The terrorists were armed with two rifles, a shotgun, a pistol, knives, and machetes and went to the office of the director of the center, Dr. Mohammad Abdul Rauf, who was taken hostage along with 10 others. Among the hostages were five Egyptian Center employees, three Americans, the tour guide, a Bangladeshi, and a Colombian. The Turkish Embassy reported that the caretaker, Davaz Mustapha, and his son were also held. The attackers were masters of dramatic effects. They threatened to kill a Colombian student and held guns to his head; however, they were willing to negotiate for the release of ill hostages. Several hostages later pointed out that an all-news radio station was constantly playing.

The final Hanafi siege began at 2:30 P.M. at the Washington, D.C., City Council offices in the District Building at 14th and E Streets, NW. Two men parked a Diamond taxi outside the 14th Street entrance, left the emergency lights flickering, and went past the unguarded entrance and up to the stairs. One man carried a shotgun, the other a machete. At the top of the five flights of stairs, the gunmen mistakenly turned left, away from the mayor's office they had come to seize. Besides the mayor, it appeared that the attackers were seeking city council member Arrington Dixon, who had sponsored a council-passed resolution favorable to the Nation of Islam (Black Muslims), the Hanafi rival. After firing a shotgun and hitting several people, they moved down the corridor to the offices of council chairman Sterling Tucker and herded their hostages inside. Mayor Washington and other staff members locked themselves in their offices. Washington managed to leave the building under heavy escort at around 6:00 P.M. during the first night of the siege. A shotgun blast killed Maurice Williams, of WHUR radio, and a building guard. One pellet hit city council member Marion S. Barry, Jr., who would later become mayor.

Although many news agencies cooperated with police, the degree of responsibility shown by many varied greatly. WMAL-TV's news director said he felt no need to honor a police request not to broadcast that some city employees had barricaded themselves in the District Building unknown to the raiders. WTOP radio broadcast unconfirmed reports that a group of motorcyclists "who might be Hanafi Muslims" were heading for the Grammercy Hotel. It was later learned that the motorcyclists were official escorts for the diplomats engaged in the negotiations. WTTG aired a 40-second segment of the proscribed *Messenger* film on the first day of the siege. Police complained that interviews with hostages were tying up needed phone lines to the hostage sites and Hanafi headquarters. Press treatment of the incident led U.S. UN ambassador Andrew Young to suggest press curbs for such episodes. Whenever station WMAL broadcast that food had been brought to the B'nai B'rith building, one of the gunmen would appear a short time later to pick it up. This led police to deduce that the raiders were monitoring radio reports.

All of the hostages were released on March 11, 1977, with Khaalis and the three terrorists at the Islamic Center released on their own recognizance. Khaalis's freedom was short-lived, ending in his arrest on March 31, 1977.

The government charged each defendant with 24 counts of armed kidnapping. With the exception of Khaalis, the jury convicted each of eight counts of kidnapping that arose from the episodes in which they participated, acquitting them of the attacks in which they were not present. They were also acquitted of conspiracy. Abdul Muzikir, Abdul Nuh, and Khaalis were convicted of murder in the second degree and assault with intent to kill. On September 6, 1977, Abdul Adam received 44–132 years; Abdul Latif received 36–108 years; Abdul Shaheed received 36–108 years; Abdul Salaam received 40–120 years; Abdul Hamid received 36–108 years; and Abdul Razzaq received 40–120 years. Hamaas Kaalis received 41–123 years for the B'nai Brith attack. Abdul Rahman and Abdul Rahim received 28–84 years, and Abdul Qawee received

24–72 years for the Islamic Center attack. Abdul Nuh received 58 years to life and Abdul Muzikir received 78 years to life for the District Building attack.

September 5, 1977
Hans-Martin Schleyer Kidnapping
and Assassination

Overview: By the mid-1970s, the West German Red Army Faction (RAF), commonly referred to as the Baader-Meinhof Group after its leaders Andreas Baader and Ulrike Meinhof, had become prominent among Western European leftist terrorists. The roots of the RAF and other like-minded leftist violence-prone revolutionaries—such as the Swiss Petra Kraus Group, Italian Red Brigades, French Direct Action, leftist members of the Provisional Irish Republican Army, and British Angry Brigade—could be traced to the leftist riots of 1968 throughout Western Europe and the United States. The groups conducted joint training operations, often with the support and sometimes hosting of various Palestinian leftist terrorists, and reached out to radicals such as Illich Ramirez Sanchez (alias Carlos), who provided his operational services on a freelance basis. The Baader-Meinhof Group specialized in assassinations of major industrialists, government leaders, and military commanders, along with the occasional bombing and bank robbery to keep the coffers filled. The late 1970s saw most of their major leaders in jail, with their release demanded frequently by skyjackers and other hostage-takers. The issue of their incarceration came to a head during the RAF kidnapping of West German industrialist Hanns-Martin Schleyer. German unwillingness to release the group's members led to several of the prominent prisoners taking their own lives, a new wrinkle on the RAF's "propaganda of the deed." Their suicides—characterized by many supporters as actually conducted by prison guards—were followed by a bombing campaign. The RAF went through several other mini-generations and splintering before the last of its prominent members renounced terrorism years later.

Incident: On September 5, 1977, members of the RAF, successors to the Baader-Meinhof Group, kidnapped Schleyer, president of the West German employers' association, the Confederation of Industry; member of the board of directors of Mercedes-Benz; and West Germany's most famous industrialist. Between 10 and 15 terrorists firing submachine guns ambushed his two-car convoy at an intersection in Cologne during rush hour as he was driven to his apartment. The group pushed a baby carriage across a one-way street, halting his Mercedes sedan. The terrorists then fired over 200 rounds, killing two police escorts, a security agent, and a driver. They dragged Schleyer from his limousine into a minibus, which was later found abandoned in a garage under a Cologne high-rise building. The minibus contained a letter with a demand for the release of several West German terrorists.

Various groups made demands, ultimately articulated by the Siegried Hausner Commando Group of the RAF, which called for freedom for 11 terrorists who were to be accompanied on a flight out of the country by Martin Niemoeller, an evangelical theologian. Each prisoner was to be given $43,000 and a flight to his or her choice of country. The government was further instructed to promise not to attempt to obtain extradition. Five of the 11 incarcerated Baader-Meinhof Group terrorists were women. The 11 were Andreas Baader, Gudrun Ensslin, and Jan-Carl Raspe, the most well-known surviving members of the original Baader-Meinhof Group; Karl-Heinz Dellwo, Hanna Elise Krabbe, and Bernd Roesner, who took part in the April 24, 1975, attack on the West German Embassy in Stockholm by the Socialist Patients' Collective; Guenter Sonnenberg and Verena Becker, two suspects in the assassination of prosecutor Siegfried Buback; and Ingrid Schubert, Irmgard Moeller, and Werner Hopper, who were in custody for robbery, suspicion of murder, and attempted murder, respectively.

The Schleyer kidnapping, following closely the assassinations of German attorney general Buback in April 1977 and banker Juergen Ponto in July 1977 and an aborted rocket attack in Karlsruhe, heightened public concern regarding terrorism. Business executives sought increased protection through the legal system, and sales of security services boomed. The government, remaining firm in the face of the kidnappers' threats, refused to release the prisoners and was supported by the public, according to various polls.

The hijacking of a Lufthansa jetliner on October 13, 1977, by terrorists apparently acting in concert with Schleyer's kidnappers greatly increased the pressure on the government to release the prisoners. The successful rescue operation at Mogadishu, Somalia, turned the advantage back to the government but put Schleyer's fate in doubt. Schleyer's well-being was further jeopardized by the suicides in prison of Baader, Raspe, and Ensslin, as well as the self-inflicted wounds of Moeller.

On October 19, 1977, the Siegfried Hausner Command announced that it had killed Schleyer. Ninety minutes after the news of Schleyer's death, the Federal Criminal Office released the names of 16 persons suspected of being involved in the crime. Among them were Susanne Albrecht, Silke Maier-Witt, Adelheid Schulz, Angelika Speitel, Siegrid Sternbeck, and Willy Peter Stoll, who were also on the wanted list in connection with the murder of Ponto, chairman of the Dresdner Bank board of directors. Christian Klar was wanted for the murder of Attorney General Buback. Police believed Brigitte Mohnhaupt accompanied Knut Folkerts, who was arrested in Holland in a shootout with police. Also named were Rolf Heissler, who had been released in exchange for Christian Democratic

Union candidate for mayor of West Berlin Peter Lorenz in March 1975, and Friederike Krabbe, believed to be related to one of the Stockholm terrorists, Hanna Elise Krabbe. Also named were Christoph Wackernagel and Rolf Clemens Wagner, who were wanted for bombing attacks. The Federal Criminal Office stated that Joerg Lang, the former partner of radical lawyer Klaus Croissant; Inge Viett, who escaped from the Berlin women's jail; Elisabeth van Dyck, wanted in connection with arms thefts; and Julianne Plambeck, a noted terrorist, were also suspected of involvement in the kidnapping.

Stefan Wisniewski was arrested in France in May 1978 and extradited to West Germany a year later. On November 5, 1979, he was charged in Karlsruhe with murdering Schleyer and his bodyguards, kidnapping, attempted extortion, coercion, and forging documents.

Rolf Wagner was arrested on November 19, 1979, after a gun battle with Swiss police. He was suspected of being the driver of the van used in the getaway. He was one of the four terrorists arrested in Yugoslavia in May 1978 who were later released in a dispute over extradition of Croatian terrorists.

On April 29, 1991, the prosecution in the Stuttgart higher regional court charged RAF member Maier-Witt of having participated in the 1977 kidnapping and murder of Schleyer. Police said she participated in the attempted mortar attack on the Federal Prosecutor's Office that took place on August 25, 1977; the failed assassination attempt on NATO commander-in-chief Alexander Haig in Belgium on June 25, 1979; and in a bank robbery in Zurich, Switzerland, that took place on November 19, 1979. She was arrested in East Germany in August 1990. She was charged with five murders, several attempted murders, and robbery causing subsequent death. On October 7, 1991, a German court sentenced her to 10 years for her part in the three attacks. She was convicted of helping commit the Schleyer kidnapping and confessed to aiding in the Haig attack and the bank robbery in Zurich.

1978–1995
The Unabomber

Overview: Before the "lone wolf" became the template for homegrown violent extremists in the 2010s, Theodore Kaczynski, popularly known as the Unabomber, established that mass mailing package bombs to government officials was an effective terror technique. His 17-year U.S. private campaign of terror lasted from the 1970s into the 1990s. The Kaczynski case raises the question of how many incidents are needed to constitute a designation of an individual as a terrorist, and what constitutes a terrorist versus a disturbed individual cloaked in political rhetoric. The loner

Kaczynski showed most of the characteristics of classic terrorists of his era, including interest in publicity for his cause and willingness to use violence to influence a wider group than the immediate victims. His attacks presaged the October 2001 anthrax attacks attributed by the Federal Bureau of Investigation (FBI) to scientific researcher Bruce E. Ivins, whose motives remain unclear.

Incidents: On October 7, 1993, the FBI put out a $1 million reward for Kaczynski's arrest. By that time, he was responsible for at least 14 parcel and emplaced bombings. His terrorist resume eventually included

- On May 25, 1978, one person was injured at the University of Illinois at Chicago.
- On May 9, 1979, one person was injured at Northwestern University in Evanston, Illinois.
- On November 15, 1979, a bomb exploded in the cargo hold of American Airlines flight 444 as it flew from Chicago to Washington, D.C. Twelve persons suffered smoke inhalation. The device was designed to explode at high altitude.
- On June 10, 1980, following receipt of a letter saying that he would receive a book he needed, Percy Wood, a former president of United Airlines, received a book-sized package containing a bomb at his Chicago home.
- On October 8, 1981, a bomb was disarmed in a business classroom at the University of Utah in Salt Lake City.
- On April 25, 1982, a pipe bomb attack was directed against Patrick C. Fischer in Nashville, Tennessee.
- On May 5, 1982, one person was injured at Vanderbilt University in Nashville, Tennessee, when a package addressed to a professor exploded.
- On July 2, 1982, a professor of electrical engineering and computer science was injured in a faculty lounge at the University of California at Berkeley.
- On May 8, 1985, police disarmed a bomb mailed to the Boeing Corporation in Auburn, Washington.
- On May 15, 1985, John Hauser, a graduate student at the University of California at Berkeley, saw a black notebook inside a plastic container in the computer lab in which he was working alone. Upon opening the container, the bomb tore off part of his right hand, ending his career as an Air Force fighter pilot.
- On November 15, 1985, a secretary was injured by a package bomb mailed to Professor James V. McConnell at the University of Michigan in Ann Arbor.
- On December 11, 1985, Hugh C. Scrutton, a Sacramento, California, businessman, was killed when he picked up a bomb disguised as a block of wood near an entrance to his computer rental store.
- On February 20, 1987, a bomb was placed in the parking lot behind CAAMS in Salt Lake City, Utah.
- On February 20, 1989, a man was injured by a bomb left behind a computer store in Salt Lake City.

- On June 22, 1993, a letter bomb exploded in the home office of Charles Epstein, a geneticist at the University of California at San Francisco, wounding him in the abdomen, chest, face, and hands. UNABOM had identified himself as FC in two earlier letters, claiming to be part of an anarchist group.

- On June 24, 1993, a package bomb exploded in the office of Yale University computer scientist David Gelernter, famed for developing the Linda computer language that had applications in publishing and animation. He lost use of a hand and his right eye was lacerated.

- On December 10, 1994, a mail bomb killed Thomas Mosser, 50, executive vice president and general manager of Young and Rubicam, Inc. Worldwide, one of the world's largest ad agencies.

- On April 25, 1995, a package bomb mailed to the lobbying offices of the private California Forestry Association in Sacramento, California, killed Gilbert B. Murray, 47, its chief lobbyist for the timber industry. The package was post-marked from Oakland, California, and addressed to a colleague, William Dennison, former president of the association.

On June 27, 1995, UNABOM sent a letter to the *San Francisco Chronicle* in which he threatened to blow up an airliner leaving Los Angeles International Airport in the next six days. The next day, he sent a lengthy manifesto to the *Washington Post, Penthouse,* and *New York Times,* demanding that one of the publications print the screed as a way to halt the killings.

On August 2, 1995, the *Washington Post* and the *New York Times* published excerpts from his manifesto *Industrial Society and Its Future.* On August 3, 1995, *Penthouse* publisher Bob Guccione published a full-page open letter in the *New York Times* to the Unabomber in which he offered "one or more unedited pages in *Penthouse* every single month" if the bomber stopped bombing.

The FBI arrested Kaczynski on April 3, 1996, in a one-room cabin in the hills near Lincoln, Montana. Bomb-making paraphernalia was found in the cabin, as was the typewriter that matched the fonts used in the Unabomber's manifesto. His brother David had contacted the FBI in February 1996 to say that he believed Ted was the Unabomber. Texts he found in his mother's Chicago house when she was going to sell it were similar to the Unabomber's tract. A bomb blew up in his cabin four days after his arrest.

Kaczynski had graduated from Harvard, earned a doctorate from the University of Michigan, and became a math professor at the University of California at Berkeley.

On June 18, 1996, he was indicted for the killings of Gilbert B. Murray in 1995 and Hugh C. Scrutton in 1985, and the injuries of David Gelernter and Charles Epstein in 1993. He was charged with transporting an explosive device with intent to kill or injure and mailing the device. Conviction carried a sentence of death or life in prison. On June 21, 1996, U.S. District Court judge Charles C. Lovell ordered his trial moved from

Helena, Montana, to Sacramento, California. On June 25, 1996, Quin Denvir, Kaczynski's public defender, pleaded not guilty to the charges. On June 28, 1996, Kaczynski was indicted for three more Unabomber attacks, specifically the April 25, 1982, pipe bomb attacks against Patrick C. Fischer in Nashville; the November 1985 pipe bomb attack against James V. McConnell in Ann Arbor, Michigan; and the February 20, 1987, placing of a bomb in the parking lot behind CAAMS in Salt Lake City, Utah. On October 1, 1996, a federal grand jury in New Jersey handed down a three-count indictment against him, charging him in the December 10, 1994, bombing death of Thomas J. Mosser. On December 10, 1996, he pleaded not guilty.

Jury selection began on November 12, 1997. Kaczynski sought to dismiss his lawyers because they planned to introduce the issue of his mental health. On January 20, 1998, prosecutors and defense attorneys agreed that he was mentally competent to stand trial. On January 22, 1998, he pleaded guilty to all 13 federal charges as part of a plea bargain that spared him the death penalty. He was sentenced to serve life in prison without possibility of release. He also admitted that he placed or mailed another 11 bombs for which he was not yet charged. He agreed that he could not appeal any part of the sentence. The judge warned that he would be forced to pay restitution if he received money for his writings, mementos, or interviews. On May 4, 1998, he was sentenced to four life terms plus 30 years in prison and sent to a maximum security cell in Colorado. On October 23, 1999, the Ninth U.S. Circuit Court of Appeals in San Francisco agreed to review his case, finding sufficient evidence to examine his contention that his guilty plea was coerced and that he was inappropriately denied the right to self-representation. However, on February 12, 2001, the court rejected his request for retrial. On August 17, 2001, he lost another appeal for a hearing. On March 18, 2002, in *Kaczynski v. U.S. 01–7251*, the Supreme Court rejected his attempt to withdraw his 1998 guilty plea and obtain a new trial.

On May 19, 2011, the FBI requested a DNA sample as part of its look into whether he was involved in the September 29, 1982, deaths of seven people who took potassium cyanide–laced Tylenol in the Chicago area, where he occasionally stayed at his parents' home. He refused to voluntarily give a sample. The Tylenol poisonings do not fit with his standard modus operandi. As of this writing, the Tylenol case remains officially unresolved.

1985–1986
Lebanon Kidnappings of Westerners

Overview: By 1985, Hizballah (the Party of God) had established itself as a parallel government in Lebanon, providing services that the weakened

Lebanese government was unable to offer, while also conducting a highly publicized series of kidnappings of dozens of Westerners.

Incidents: Sometimes termed the Lebanon Hostage Crisis when considering years 1982–1992, the years 1985 and 1986 saw a significant uptick in Western kidnappings by Hizballah that included journalists, prominent theologians, a university president, and teachers. Negotiations for the hostages' release took months, sometimes years. Among them were Terry Anderson, Rev. Terry Waite, Rev. Lawrence Jenco, Joseph Cicippio, Thomas Sutherland, David Jacobsen, and Frank Reed. The 1985 kidnappings began on January 3 with Eric Wehrli, the Swiss chargé d'affaires. At least six people died in 1985 and 1986, including William F. Buckley, former Central Intelligence Agency (CIA) Chief of Station kidnapped in 1984.

Elements of a frustrated U.S. administration quietly reached out to the Iranian regime, offering to provide arms in exchange for Tehran pressuring its Hizballah protégés to release the hostages. While hostages were eventually freed, the arms-for-hostages plan ultimately led to a fissure between the administration and Congress that took years to heal. Attempts to bring the hostage-takers to justice came in fits and starts. The most prominent of the kidnappers, Imad Fayez Mugniyah, was killed on February 12, 2008, by a car bomb in Syria.

On October 14, 1992, former U.S. hostages Joseph Cicippio and David Jacobsen sued Iran for $600 million in U.S. District Court in Washington, saying it orchestrated their abductions in an effort to recover millions of dollars frozen in the United States. The suit sought damages for kidnapping, physical abuse, false imprisonment, inhumane medical treatment, loss of job opportunities, and pain and suffering. While terrorist victims often won major awards from courts, few were able to collect from state sponsors of terrorist attacks or from the terrorist groups and their aboveground wings.

January 25, 1993
CIA Headquarters Route 123 Entrance Attack

Overview: Although the term "lone wolf" terrorist became popular among U.S. terrorism-watchers only in the late 2000s and early 2010s, the first inkling of a homegrown Islamic terrorist problem surfaced on January 25, 1993, when Pakistani citizen Amal Kasi, 28, opened fire just outside the Central Intelligence Agency (CIA) in Langley, Virginia, killing two CIA employees as they headed in to work one morning.

Kasi's attack was the latest in a string of attempts to target CIA employees, the most successful being the 17 November Group's assassination of Chief of Station/Athens Welch in 1975 and Hizballah's kidnapping on March 16, 1984, and murder on June 3, 1985, of Chief of Station/Beirut Buckley in 1985. The bloodiest attack came two decades later, when an al Qaeda suicide bomber killed seven people at an Agency base in Khost, Afghanistan. The Kasi killings led legislators to look at loopholes in gun laws.

Incident: On the morning of January 25, 1993, Kasi stopped at a red light at the Route 123 entrance to the CIA in Langley, Virginia, got out of his car, and fired a Chinese-made AK-47-type assault rifle into the cars of CIA employees waiting to make the left turn, killing two people and injuring three others. He fired left, then right, then left again, firing at least two shots per victim. The turn signal had just turned green, and some cars flew across the intersection to get out of the way.

The dead were Dr. Lansing C. Bennett, 66, and Frank Darling, 28. The wounded were Nicholas Starr, 60, an intelligence analyst; Calvin Morgan, 61, an engineer; and Stephen E. Williams, 48, an AT&T employee.

Nearby schools, including the Potomac School and the Country Day School, locked doors and monitored radios as rumors spread that the gunman was on the loose in the nearby woods.

Darling's wife, Judy, was with him in the couple's Volkswagen Golf when Kasi shot him. She was treated for shock at a nearby hospital. Three bullet holes were found in the windshield.

Starr managed to drive to the entrance gate to the 258-acre compound before he collapsed. He underwent 12 hours of surgery, having lost 11 pints of blood from the wound to his arm that severed the bone, an artery, and some veins. Fragments from the bullet lodged in his chest and collapsed his left lung. Doctors had to graft a two- to three-inch long piece of artery from his groin area to reconnect the artery in his arm. He since has experienced some impairment in his left arm because one of its three major nerves was severed and another is not working. More than 250 people showed up when the hospital asked for donors of his rare O-negative blood. Another 200 gave blood the next day.

Morgan suffered at least one gunshot wound in the left arm. The bullet traveled up his arm and lodged behind his ear. He was on the operating table for a few hours. His wife, Doris, said he saved himself by diving on the seat of his Cadillac. He was released from Fairfax Hospital after three days.

Williams was treated at Arlington Hospital for a graze wound to his chest and released. A bullet may have been deflected by his rib. He managed to drive his car the 500 feet to the CIA entrance gate to get help.

Police noted that the gunman did not fire at women in the queue.

The gunman drove up and parked his car behind Bennett's Saab in the rightmost of the two left-turn lanes, fourth car in the line for the turn. He walked to the head of the two lines and then calmly walked up to each car, firing his AK-47 with a cold, emotionless expression.

The FBI ran a computer check of fingerprints, but its computer had only the prints of people arrested for felonies. The millions of others in paper files had to be searched manually.

The police bulletin described the gunman as a white male between 20 and 30, weighing 145–165 pounds, having a dark complexion, of medium build and height, and having dark brown or black, medium-length hair.

Hours after the shootings, a man driving a light-brown compact station wagon narrowly missed an Alexandria, Virginia, police officer who was clocking traffic with a radar gun on Slaters Lane, near the George Washington Parkway. The driver reportedly swerved toward the police officer, who leaped out of the way. The car was found abandoned at Potomac Yard.

Among those in the line was former ambassador Gilbert Robinson and freshman senator Bob Smith (R-New Hampshire). Smith told the news media, "He looked in my direction, and then he turned and walked away. He coolly, methodically, with no expression, with no words, he simply walked up to the cars and fired shots point-blank at people. It was a pretty horrible sight."

Agency officials said that they planned a small monument as a memorial to the two men who were killed. The median strip was littered with flowers and flags from CIA employees. In a memorial service attended by thousands of CIA employees, First Lady Hillary Clinton offered the president's condolences.

At 4:00 P.M., eight hours after the shooting, Kasi walked into Crescent Groceries, a few miles away in Herndon, and attempted to purchase a one-way ticket to Pakistan. Pakistani immigrant Mohammad Yousaf, owner of the store where Kasi was a regular customer, called his Arlington store to arrange the purchase. An Arlington store employee then called Super Travel, an Alexandria, Virginia, travel office owned by a Pakistani immigrant. Kasi paid $740 in cash for the ticket and promised to return the following afternoon. Kasi came back at 1:30 P.M. the next day. Yousaf gave him a ride in his Caprice Classic to National Airport.

Ballistics experts determined that the gun was a Chinese SKS gas-operated rifle with 10 rounds. There are several knockoffs of the AK-47, such as the AKM, which carries 30 rounds. *WTOP* radio reported that the 7.62 mm Russian AK shells could also fit a U.S. Ruger. The gunman fired at least 10 rounds, hitting the 5 victims 8 times.

On January 28, 1993, Kasi's Pakistani roommate, Zahed Ahmed Mir, 39, reported Kasi missing to Fairfax police. He said that he last saw him on January 25, 1993.

On January 30, 1993, Kasi called Mir to tell him that he had to leave town in a hurry. He said that someone would come back to get his belongings and that he would never return. Mir believed that it was a long-distance call.

On February 6, 1993, Mir called police and said that he believed Kasi was the killer. Mir's call was among 2,700 tips police received. On

February 8, 1993, Kasi's roommate let police into the apartment, and police found two semiautomatic pistols, a bulletproof vest, and 550 rounds of ammunition in addition to the AK-47-type assault rifle used in the killings. The ammunition, 11 magazines for the assault rifle, and pistols were found in a suitcase.

On February 9, 1993, police announced that ballistics tests demonstrated that Kasi's AK-47 was the weapon used in the shootings. He was charged with capital murder, which carries the death penalty as the maximum sentence; first-degree murder; three counts of malicious wounding; five weapons charges; and federal charges of fleeing prosecution. He apparently had no previous record and had never been in a mental hospital. He apparently was not a member of any radical group, had no affiliation with any terrorist group, and had no affiliation with the CIA.

On February 10, 1993, police announced that a fingerprint found on a shell casing on 123 matched those of Kasi's immigration records.

Kasi was issued a business visa in Karachi, Pakistan, in the name of "Mir Aimal Kansi" on December 4, 1990. His birth date was listed as October 22, 1964.

Kasi had entered the United States on a flight to John F. Kennedy Airport in New York on March 3, 1991 (some records say February 27, 1991). He did not turn in an entry card. Immigration and Naturalization Service (INS) officials did turn up a card for "Kansi." Two weeks after arriving in the United States, Kasi reported that he had lost his passport. He filed an application for asylum (because of political persecution, based on flimsy evidence of fear of the rival Baluchs) with the INS office in Arlington, Virginia, on February 3, 1992. He said that he had not gone through INS inspections and listed relatives named Kansi on the application. He was permitted to stay in the United States while the application was being considered. (U.S. law prohibits deportation of immigrants whose requests are pending.) He was granted a one-year work permit that was due to expire on February 13, 1993. He had not applied to renew the permit.

Kasi was born on October 2, 1964, the son of Abdullah Jan Kasi, a well-known Quetta building contractor who died in 1989. His father founded Pakistan Particle Board in Karachi in the early 1970s. His father's will left 20 million rupees (circa $500,000) for the construction of the Kasi Ward, a medical general ward in Civil Hospital, Quetta. His mother died in 1982. His well-respected Pashtun family includes two brothers and three stepbrothers and also runs the Faran and Novelty Hotels and a dozen shops in Quetta. His father sent him to a prestigious private grammar school, unlike other children of the family. Kasi graduated from Baluchistan University in Quetta with a master's degree in English literature. He inherited $100,000 after his father's death. His family was not a strictly observant Muslim family. His friends said he was "fun-loving" and was not close to any religious group or university student group.

In 1988, he became close to students affiliated with the Pashtun Students Organization (PSO), the student wing of Mahmood Khan Achakzai's Pakhtun-khwa Milli Awami Party. Former PSO leader and former Kasi friend Nasrullah Khan Achakzai told the press, "He was a patient listener of our political ideology which was heavily influenced by the revolution in Afghanistan. Aimal never accepted my offers to work in the front line." Nasrullah, now a lawyer in Quetta's lower courts, said that at the time, the group believed that "the CIA had killed fifteen million innocent people in Afghanistan." He admitted having led the 1989 demonstration against an American professor, during which Kasi fired shots. Kasi frequently carried a weapon and often used threats and intimidation to get higher grades.

In early 1989, a small group of students at the Department of English at Baluchistan University shouted "Death to America" in protesting a presentation by an American professor on T. S. Eliot. Kasi fired shots into the air. The teachers called off the lecture and the American professor left town the next day. Professors and students remembered Kasi as changing from a shy student in 1987 to a short-tempered, angry youth in 1989 who used strong-arm tactics against senior teachers.

On February 12, 1993, the Virginia General Assembly unanimously consented to the introduction of legislation that would require aliens to get a judge's permission before buying or possessing assault rifles. A Fairfax County ordinance had permitted Kasi to buy the rifle without a waiting period, unlike the 72-hour delay required for handgun sales. Moreover, police cannot check immigrants' criminal backgrounds in other countries when they try to buy guns. Police noted that there are a large number of gunsmiths in the county. To compare, there are 500 licensed gun sellers in Fairfax to only 240 service stations.

On February 16, 1993, Islamabad's *The News* reported that Pakistan had asked Iran to join the search for Kasi. Iran had earlier indicated that Kasi was not in the country. The paper suggested that the FBI was exploring whether Kasi was part of the growing number of Afghan war veterans trained in Pakistan who had lately turned their expertise against pro-U.S. governments in the Middle East and Africa.

Foreign media offered suggestions as to Kasi's whereabouts. On February 26, 1993, Islamabad's *The Nation* said that he was staying with Hezb-e Eslami leader Engineer Golboddin Hekmatyar at Jalalabad, Afghanistan. Correspondent Umer Alam wrote that U.S. commandos were unable to find him in Quetta.

On March 9, 1993, Islamabad's *Pakistan Observer* said that Kasi was in India, whose intelligence services had hired him.

In May 1993, the FBI said that Kasi had been spotted a few times in Pakistan, where two FBI agents were searching for him.

On May 15, 1993, Yosseff Bodansky, head of the House Republican Task Force on Terrorism and Unconventional Warfare, claimed in a book that

Kasi was trained by Iranian intelligence, sent to Washington, and "activated" to carry out the killings. He also said the Iranians were behind the World Trade Center bombing.

On June 16, 1993, a team of Pakistani Frontier Corps paramilitary personnel raided some 200 houses of the Kasi tribe in Quetta in an attempt to find the killer. The family informed the officials that Kasi had left for the United States a couple of days earlier. Family members complained that the troops swooped in from ladders perched on top of the houses, sans search warrants. The provincial authorities said that they were not informed before the raid, having been told instead that the militiamen were seeking Chakar Khan Chakarani who was wanted for shooting dead some militiamen in Kashmore District a few months earlier.

On August 23, 1993, the FBI announced a $100,000 reward for information leading to Kasi's arrest. The FBI earlier in August announced that it was withdrawing its agents from Pakistan.

On October 2, 1995, the United States increased the reward for information leading to Kasi's arrest to $2 million. Posters and matchbooks with Kasi's photo were distributed. The *Associated Press* reported that Washington was also offering relocation to the United States for anyone who provided information leading to Kasi's arrest.

Five FBI agents captured Kasi on June 15, 1997, at a hotel near the Pakistan–Afghanistan border. He was led there by bounty hunters seeking the $2 million reward. He had registered two days earlier as Hafiz-ur Rehman in the two-story Hotel Shalimar in Derra Ghazi Khan, in eastern Punjab Province. At 4:00 A.M., a dozen men ran into the hotel, banged on the door to room 213, and then took Kasi into custody.

President William Jefferson Clinton said the arrest showed that the United States "will not relent in the pursuit of terrorists . . . no matter how long it takes, no matter where they hide."

Kasi was flown into Dulles International Airport on June 17, 1997, and turned over to Fairfax County, Virginia, police. He had signed a several-page confession during the flight to the United States. He was arraigned on June 18, 1997, and held in the Fairfax County Adult Detention Center without bond. He was charged with one count of capital murder, one count of first-degree murder, three counts of malicious wounding, and five counts of using a firearm in the commission of a felony.

Pakistani media and lawyers' associations complained that he had been taken away illegally without extradition hearings. At least three lawsuits were filed against the government. The local authorities had several times attempted to organize raids against locations believed to be Kasi's hideouts, but many suspected that his wealthy family, which held important government positions, had been tipped off, letting him escape. On June 24, 1997, 5,000 demonstrators in Quetta called Kasi a hero.

On November 3, 1997, his trial began, with Kasi pleading innocent to capital murder, felony murder, three counts of malicious wounding, and five counts of use of a firearm during a felony. Each count of malicious wounding carried a sentence of 5–20 years; each firearms conviction carried a sentence of 3 years. The prosecutor changed the official spelling of the defendant's name to "Kasi" to reflect the way he signed a statement made to the FBI.

On November 6, 1997, FBI Special Agent Bradley J. Garrett testified regarding Kasi's confession. Kasi chose the AK-47 because it was more accurate than a handgun. He brought 150 rounds of ammunition in case he had to "deal with" responding police officers. He was angry for the U.S. bombing of Iraq and allegedly killing Palestinians. He was also upset with CIA involvement in Muslim countries and wanted to send the United States a message to stop these activities. He chose to attack the CIA rather than the Israeli Embassy in Washington because he thought it would be easier and the CIA employees would not be armed. He aimed for the men's chests.

Kasi was found guilty of all charges on November 10, 1997. The jury needed only four hours to deliberate. The jury recommended a life term plus 78 years and $400,000 in fines for nine of the felonies.

On November 12, 1997, Pakistani terrorists shot to death four American auditors for Union Texas Petroleum in Karachi. Kasi had predicted retaliation for his case by his sympathizers. The Kasi jury was sequestered; panel members said they feared for their safety after their initial verdict of guilty. The Aimal Secret Committee said it would keep killing Americans.

On November 14, 1997, the jury recommended the death penalty. The family said it would appeal. Kasi's death sentence would be appealed automatically to the Virginia Supreme Court.

On January 23, 1998, Judge Brown sentenced Kasi to death for killing Darling, observing "Mr. Kasi planned to shoot innocent people. He shot Frank Darling and returned to blow part of his head off while his wife sat beside him. He planned this killing. His acts were the product of a depraved mind, but not a brain-damaged mind." According to court records, Kasi told the court, "I don't feel proud for it. This is the result of the wrong policy toward Islamic countries. I don't expect any justice or mercy from this country or court." He was also sentenced to life plus 78 years and $400,000 in fines for killing Bennett.

On September 16, 1998, Kasi's attorney, Elwood E. Sanders, Jr. told the Virginia Supreme Court that Kasi's arrest violated a 1935 treaty. Donald R. Curry, senior assistant attorney general, said the treaty did not specifically prohibit the type of arrest the FBI agents made. On November 6, 1998, the Virginia Supreme Court upheld the death sentence.

On February 18, 1999, Kasi told reporters he wanted the International Court of Justice to hear his case because he had not received justice in the United States. He wanted Amnesty International and Pakistan to take up his cause. He claimed to be a political prisoner who "did my

moral duty by attacking CIA." He said he had no regrets about killing the two CIA employees but would have preferred killing the CIA
director.

On June 24, 1999, the U.S. Supreme Court rejected without comment
Kasi's appeal of the Virginia Supreme Court, ruling that Kasi lacked the
legal right to claim that his seizure violated the U.S. Constitution because
he was seized overseas. The U.S. Supreme Court rejected his claim that
his seizure by the FBI in Pakistan violated international treaties, that
his confession was illegally obtained, and that his constitutional rights
against unreasonable seizure were violated.

On August 15, 2002, the U.S. Court of Appeals of the Fourth Circuit rejected Kasi's appeal of his death sentence.

Kasi was executed by lethal injection on November 14, 2002, at 9:00 P.M.
The killer's remains were returned to Pakistan on November 18, 2002.
Some 2,000 Pakistanis at the Quetta airport chanted anti-U.S. slogans.

2001
Anthrax Attacks

Overview: Terrorist-watchers have been puzzled by the paucity of terrorist attacks using unconventional weapons, such as biological, chemical, and radiological material. Aside from the occasional poisoning and
the large-scale attacks by the Aum Shin Rikyo cult in Japan, such attacks
have been the province of individuals with little scientific knowledge and
minimal political motivation. As became evident, such biological weapons
attacks—or inadvertent release—quickly can get out of control, infecting
individuals well beyond the original targets of the perpetrators. The time-
line of victims in the U.S. anthrax crisis, which began in the fall of 2001,
demonstrates how quickly a few spores released in one seemingly confined malicious act sent the spores globetrotting across the United States
and across the seas.

Because the anthrax attacks in the United States followed closely behind the 9/11 attacks, many observers suggested that terrorists had at
long last decided that since the U.S. homeland was now fair game, so, too,
were biological weapons attacks. Many believed that al Qaeda or individuals inspired by the group were behind the release. Opportunistic claims
on behalf of terrorist groups kept this line of inquiry—at least by the press
and the public—open for some time. The case also showed the difficulties
in attributing this type of attack to a perpetrator, with authorities following incorrect leads for years. The FBI ultimately came to believe that the
attack was the work of a single researcher, who possibly was attempting
to demonstrate the vulnerability of the U.S. defense system. The suicide
of the most prominent suspect ended the opportunity to establish his culpability to the satisfaction of an army of conspiracy theorists.

Incidents: The nationwide anthrax crisis began on October 5, 2001, when *Sun* tabloid assistant photo editor Robert Stevens, 63, died of inhalation anthrax in Boca Raton, Florida. Stevens worked for American Media, Inc. (AMI), the headquarters of the *National Enquirer, Globe,* and *Sun* tabloids. He fell unconscious on October 2, 2001, before anyone suspected anthrax. In coming weeks, anthrax-laced letters were sent to other media outlets and Congress and affected mail-handling stations in Washington, D.C.; New Jersey; New York; and Florida.

Health authorities initially believed Stevens might have contracted the anthrax during a hike in North Carolina. Suspicion moved to the mails, however, as others tested positive for anthrax spores. Letters coming from outside the county first go to the West Palm Beach main mail-processing center, which was swept for anthrax spores. Spores were found inside a vacuum cleaner in the Blue Lake sorting facility in Boca Raton. Nearly 100 spores were found in the Boca Raton postal building, which sorts mail for AMI. At AMI, mailroom employee Ernesto Blanco, 73, contracted inhalation anthrax on October 15, 2001; he was released from the hospital in mid-October. Administrative clerk Stephanie Dailey tested positive for exposure, but did not become ill. At least 1,100 people were tested and given Cipro or other antibiotics.

Anthrax was found in a letter sent to Senate Majority Leader Thomas Daschle (D-SD). The letter, postmarked Hamilton Township, New Jersey, on October 9, 2001, went through the Processing and Distribution Center there. It may have come from central New Jersey, possibly West Trenton. Similar letters sent on September 18, 2001, to NBC News anchor Tom Brokaw and to the *New York Post* may also have originated there. They had similar block-lettered handwriting on the envelopes and were dated September 11, 2001. The misspelled *Post* letter read, "Take penacilin now." The Daschle letter asked, "Are you afraid?" All three letters finished, "Death to America. Death to Israel. God is Great." West Trenton letter carrier Teresa Heller, 32, contracted cutaneous anthrax; no one on her route was affected. No spores were found in swipe tests, but more thorough tests, including air samples, were conducted on October 25, 2001. All 24 postal employees were tested and treated with antibiotics.

At the Hamilton Township center, the next step on the letters' journeys, Patrick O'Donnell, 35, contracted cutaneous anthrax on October 19, 2001. Richard Morgano may have contracted cutaneous anthrax. Two suspected inhalation cases were reported. Spores were found in several areas tested, and more than 1,100 people received nasal swabs. All 1,000 postal employees were treated with antibiotics; another 2,500 contractors and busi-nesses that pick up or deliver bulk mail were advised to test and treat employees.

The letters moved on to the Hub and Spoke Program Facility in Carteret, New Jersey. While no mail is sorted there, it is put onto trucks for various destinations, including New York and Washington. About 100 employees were tested and treated with antibiotics.

The New York letters moved on to Morgan Station in Manhattan, the city's largest mail sorting center with 5,500 workers. Anthrax spores were found on four bar code mail-sorting machines on October 25, 2001. Cipro was offered to 7,000 postal workers at Morgan Station and five other Manhattan post offices.

The Brokaw letter moved on to Rockefeller Center Station, where employees were put on Cipro. It arrived at NBC headquarters, where two employees apparently developed cutaneous anthrax. Erin O'Connor, 38, an assistant to NBC News anchor Tom Brokaw, opened the letter. Another probable case was a female desk assistant.

The *New York Post* letter was stopped by the Times Square Station mail facility, where employees were put on Cipro. Editorial assistant Johanna Huden developed cutaneous anthrax on September 22, 2001; a second employee was probably also affected.

Employees were put on Cipro at Ansonia Station, where mail for *ABC News* is handled. Although no letter was found, the 7-month-old son of an ABC freelance producer was diagnosed with cutaneous anthrax on October 15, 2001; the child had visited the Manhattan office on September 28, 2001.

Radio City Station mail employees were also put on Cipro; they process mail for *CBS News* headquarters. Although no letter was found, Claire Fletcher, 27, an assistant to *CBS News* anchor Dan Rather, tested positive for cutaneous anthrax on October 18, 2001.

Anthrax contamination was reported on October 13, 2001, in a letter from Malaysia sent to Microsoft License, Inc., in Reno, Nevada. It had sat unopened for several weeks.

Traces of anthrax were found in the state troopers' office in New York governor George E. Pataki's Manhattan office on October 17, 2001; it may have been tracked in.

Meanwhile, mail going to Washington, D.C., locations went to the Brentwood Sorting Facility in Washington, D.C. Postal workers Thomas L. Morris Jr., 55, and Joseph P. Curseen, 47, died of inhalation anthrax before their symptoms' causes were diagnosed as anthrax. Two others were hospitalized, and some 2,000 workers were tested and treated with antibiotics. At an airmail center near BWI Airport, 150 employees were tested and treated, and 2,000 employees at 36 branch post offices in D.C. were tested and treated.

From Brentwood, mail bound for Capitol Hill went through the Walter Reed Army Institute of Research mailroom and the Capitol Police, a screening facility. A Daschle aide opened an anthrax-laced letter in his sixth floor office in the Hart Senate Office Building on October 15, 2001. Some 22 Congressional staffers and 6 Capitol Police tested positive for exposure; another 2,000 Congressional employees were tested and treated with antibiotics. Spores were found in mail-processing machinery at the Dirksen Senate Office Building on October 20, 2001. Traces were also found in the Ford House Office Building that day and in the Longworth House Office Building on October 26, 2001. Authorities also checked the Southwest Post Office on 45 L Street, SW, where spores were found, and the Congressional Mail Processing Center on P and Half Streets, SW.

On October 19, 2001, a letter sent to the *New York Times* office in Rio de Janeiro and a travel brochure sent to a family in Buenos Aires—both from the United States—tested positive for anthrax. Letters sent to Kenyan addresses were initially reported as testing positive but later negative. There were numerous anthrax hoaxes worldwide, including in the United Kingdom, Peru, Fiji, Germany, Pakistan, France, and the Netherlands.

From October 15 to 20, 2001, more than 130 clinics and doctor's offices that provide abortion services in 15 states on the East Coast, D.C., and the Midwest received letters threatening death by anthrax. The letters said, "Army of God. You've been exposed to anthrax. You're dead." The group is a collection of antiabortion advocates who have bombed clinics and assassinated doctors. Their letters had return addresses from the U.S. Secret Service in Atlanta, Georgia, and the U.S. Marshals Service in Cleveland, Ohio, and contained white or brown powder. They were postmarked from Atlanta, Cleveland, Columbus, Knoxville, Chattanooga, and Washington, D.C. None of them tested positive for anthrax. More than 80 letters threatening anthrax exposure were mailed to clinics between October 1998 and January 2000—all were hoaxes. Some 280 letters were sent during October 2001; another 270 letters went out in the first week of November 2001.

On November 29, 2001, the FBI named Clayton Lee Waagner, 45, an antiabortion militant from Kennerdell, about 60 miles north of Pittsburgh, the primary suspect in sending the hoax letters. He had escaped from the DeWitt County Jail in Clinton, Illinois, in February 2001 while awaiting sentencing on firearms and stolen car charges that could have put him in prison for life. Since his escape, the married father of eight was believed to have committed several bank robberies. He was wanted for bank robbery, unlawful possession of an unregistered bomb device, carjacking, and felony possession of firearms. FBI investigators matched a fingerprint in his family home in Pennsylvania to a fingerprint on one of the mailings. He had also told a fellow antiabortionist that he was responsible for the mailings. He posted a message on an antiabortion website in June 2001 crediting God for his escape and saying that he was a "terrorist to abortionists." He made the FBI's Top Ten Fugitives list in September 2001.

Neal Horsley claimed that Waagner held him hostage in his home in Carrollton, Georgia. Horsley runs the Internet's Nuremberg Files of abortion providers. Waagner traveled more than 100,000 miles, visiting

Washington, the Dakotas, Minnesota, Michigan, Missouri, and the East and South several times.

Waagner was arrested on December 5, 2001, in a Kinko's copy shop in Springdale, Ohio, a Cincinnati suburb, after an employee recognized him from a wanted poster and called the U.S. Marshals Service. Waagner had driven expensive cars, stayed at nice hotels, and bought rounds at bars with his stolen money. He was driving a stolen Mercedes Benz and had $9,000 in his pocket, along with a loaded .40 caliber handgun, and several fake IDs. He had been visiting copy centers to use the stores' computers to read about himself on the Internet. He was initially charged with a firearms violation and later charged in two bank robberies in Harrisburg, Pennsylvania, and Morgantown, West Virginia, and suspected of several others. After an initial arrest in September 1999 in Illinois, he told the court that he had staked out 100 clinics in 19 states.

On September 19, 2002, Waagner was indicted in Philadelphia on charges of mailing anthrax hoax letters to women's clinics around the country. He was also charged with posting a message on an antiabortion website saying he had been following clinic employees home and planned to "kill as many of them as I can." While on the run, he mailed at least 550 letters to women's clinics in 24 states. Scores of clinic workers underwent decontamination procedures. On October 17, 2002, he pleaded not guilty. During his trial on November 22, 2003, Denise Orlowski, of the antiabortion Pregnancy Resource Clinic of North Penn, testified that she opened a hoax letter with white powder on October 15, 2001. An ophthalmologist and psychologist also received the letters, apparently because their names were incorrectly listed in the *Yellow Pages* under "abortion providers." On December 3, 2003, Waagner was found guilty of 51 out of 53 counts, including the most serious charge of threatening to use a weapon of mass destruction. On August 23, 2004, U.S. district judge Anita Brody delayed his sentencing, saying the Supreme Court must first clarify the legality of federal sentencing rules.

Anthrax contamination was reported on October 23, 2001, at the White House mail security center at Bolling Air Force Base. One employee was hospitalized with inhalation anthrax on October 24, 2001, after apparently contracting it at the State Department's mail sorting facility in Sterling, Virginia. Trace amounts of anthrax were found on October 25, 2001, at the Central Intelligence Agency's (CIA's) Materials Inspection Facility in northern Virginia; no one (including the author) tested positive. On October 25 and 26, 2001, positive tests were announced at mailrooms of the Walter Reed Army Medical Center and its research institute. Contamination was announced on October 26, 2001, at the U.S. Supreme Court's off-site mail facility—the court was shut down. The Centers for Disease Control and Prevention (CDC) said that it would check 300 mail distribution centers and 76,000 Washington area postal workers linked to Brentwood.

By November 9, 2001, three Washington area mail workers hospitalized for inhalation anthrax on October 19, 2001, were in improved condition. Leroy Richmond, 57, of Stafford County, was in fair condition. An unidentified worker at Brentwood was in good condition. Winchester resident David Hose, 59, an employee of the State Department's mail facility in Sterling, was listed in fair condition at Winchester (Virginia) Medical Center.

The main post office in Princeton, New Jersey, was shut on October 27, 2001, after a single spore of anthrax was detected in a mail bin.

The news media reported on October 27, 2001, that the FBI and CIA were examining the possibility that domestic right-wing terrorists or domestic supporters of Islamic extremists were behind the anthrax attacks. The press also reported that not all of the anthrax spores were identical; some had been milled and chemically treated so that they would more easily make it to a victim's lungs. The Office of Homeland Security reported that the spores in Florida, New York, and Washington came from the Ames strain, which is commonly used in universities around the world. The strain was first isolated in Ames, Iowa. The *Washington Post* reported on October 25, 2001, that the Daschle letter spores were treated with a chemical additive that could have been developed in the United States, Russia, or Iraq. However, on October 29, 2001, federal officials said that the spores were not mixed with bentonite, a mineral compound used by Iraq's biological weapons program, although silica was evident. Investigators also tested the rental cars of 9/11 hijackers Mohamed Atta and Waleed M. Alshehri; no anthrax was found.

Investigators were troubled by the death of Kathy T. Nguyen, 61, a hospital worker who checked into a hospital on October 28, 2001, and subsequently died on October 31, 2001, from pulmonary anthrax. She may have received a letter that crossed paths with the Daschle letter; otherwise, the reason for her contracting anthrax was unexplained. She worked the late shift in the basement stockroom of the Eye, Ear, and Throat Hospital on Manhattan's East Side. A letter mailed to Art Auto Body at 1207 Whitlock Avenue, around the corner from her Bronx apartment, passed through the same New Jersey sorting machine within seconds of the Leahy letter. It was postmarked October 9, 2001.

Spores were found at a post office in Kansas City, Missouri, in early November 2001.

On November 2, 2001, the Karachi Urdu-language *Daily Jang*, Pakistan's largest daily newspaper, closed the newsroom after white powder received in an envelope by a reporter the previous week tested positive for anthrax. It was the third confirmed case of anthrax being sent to a Karachi business in the previous two weeks. The envelope was hand-delivered to the paper's front counter on October 23, 2001. The envelope was supposed to contain a press release from a social welfare organization. There was no accompanying note. Senior executives at Habib Bank and a Dell Computer distributor also received anthrax'd mail around October 19, 2001.

The Trenton, New Jersey, post office might have been the source of the anthrax letters. The *New York Post* letter of September 18, 2001; the Tom Brokaw letter of the same date; and the October 9, 2001, Daschle letter originated there. Mail going to the Carteret, New Jersey, facility went on to New York, where there were four cutaneous cases and one death of nonpostal employees. In Trenton, a male postal worker contracted cutaneous anthrax on September 26, 2001, as did another on October 14, 2001. A Trenton female postal worker contracted inhalation anthrax on October 14, 2001; another Trenton female postal worker contracted inhalation anthrax on October 15, 2001. There was a suspected case of a male postal worker at the Bellmawr Regional Post Office who might have contracted cutaneous anthrax on October 13, 2001. Yet, another woman contracted cutaneous anthrax on October 17, 2001, in Trenton. Mail trucked from Trenton via Carteret to Brentwood led to several cases of anthrax. A male postal worker contracted inhalation anthrax on October 19, 2001; another male postal worker died on October 21, 2001, as did another male postal worker on October 22, 2001. Yet, another male Brentwood postal worker contracted inhalation anthrax on October 22, 2001, as did a male State Department mail facility worker on October 25, 2001. Contamination of D.C. federal and postal facilities served by Brentwood included the Walter Reed Army Institutes of Research mailroom, a CIA mail facility, a Justice mail facility, a White House remote mail facility, a Supreme Court mail facility, a Veterans Administration hospital mailroom, Southwest Station, Friendship Station, Dulles Finance Station, and Pentagon Station mailrooms. Anthrax spores were found on November 9, 2001, in four more branch post offices in central New Jersey that feed into the Hamilton Township facility, where the three tainted letters were processed. An unnamed 56-year-old woman was hospitalized with inhalation anthrax on October 28, 2001. New Jersey had seven contaminated post offices. A nonpostal worker who works near Trenton, New Jersey, had skin anthrax on October 29, 2001; she was released from the hospital. Another unnamed worker left the hospital after contracting inhalation anthrax on October 30, 2001, at the Hamilton Township mail center. Traces were found on October 29, 2001, at mailrooms of an Agriculture Department agency, a federal building in Southwest where the Department of Health and Human Services and Voice of America have offices, and a nearby building used by the Food and Drug Administration.

Spores were found in the mailroom of the Veterans Administration Medical Center in D.C. on November 3, 2001.

On November 10, 2001, a small amount of anthrax spores was found in the Hart Senate Office Building and the Longworth House Office Building offices of Senators Larry E. Craig (R-Idaho), Dianne Feinstein

(D-California), and Bob Graham (D-Florida) and Representative Elijah E. Cummings (D-Maryland).

Cross-contamination from the Daschle and New York letters led to anthrax discoveries at a central New Jersey sorting facility; to the diplomatic pouch at the U.S. Embassy in Vilnius, Lithuania; to a diplomatic pouch going to the U.S. Embassy in Lima, Peru (the latter arrived on October 31, 2001); and to a diplomatic pouch at the U.S. Consulate in Yekaterinburg, Russia. A suspect letter to the U.S. Consulate in Lahore, Pakistan, turned out to be harmless when tested on November 7, 2001. Pakistan said there were three cases of anthrax contamination before the Lahore letter, including an October 23, 2001, letter to the Karachi newsroom of the Urdu-language *Daily Jang* newspaper.

By November 11, 2001, 32,000 people were on antibiotics and 300 buildings had been checked.

FBI profilers suggested that the anthrax came from a male loner with a scientific background.

Anthrax traces were found at Howard University's main mailroom on November 11, 2001. The *Washington Post* reported that spores had also been found at the offices of at least 11 senators in the Hart Senate Office Building: Senators Max Baucus (D-Montana), Barbara Boxer (D-California), Jon S. Corzine (D-New Jersey), Larry E. Craig (R-Idaho), Russell Feingold (D-Wisconsin), Dianne Feinstein (D-California), Bob Graham (D-Florida), Joseph I. Lieberman (D-Connecticut), Richard G. Lugar (R-Indiana), Barbara A. Mikulski (D-Maryland), and Arlen Specter (R-Pennsylvania). Traces were also found in the Longworth House Office Building offices of Representative Elijah E. Cummings (D-Maryland).

More spores were found on three sorting machines in a State Department mail-processing facility in Sterling, Virginia, on November 13, 2001. The building was closed on October 24, 2001, when an employee there was hospitalized with inhalation anthrax. The victim was released from a Virginia hospital on November 9, 2001. Eight of 55 environmental samples tested positive.

Thirty FBI SWAT team members, some in biohazard suits, raided the homes of three Chester, Pennsylvania, city officials of Pakistani descent. They set up decontamination tents, but did not find any equipment used to grow or process anthrax. Chester health commissioner Irshad Shaikh, 39, shared a home with his brother, Masood Shaikh, who works in the city's lead abatement program. Neighbors said the FBI took away green garbage bags of possessions. A few blocks away, accountant Asif Kazi, 39, lived in a brick row house, which FBI agents swabbed.

On November 13, 2001, the CDC said it would test the blood of Jerry Weisfogel, a New Jersey cardiologist who believed he may have had cutaneous anthrax in early September 2001.

A fourth anthrax letter was found on November 16, 2001, in quarantined mail addressed to Senator Patrick J. Leahy (D-Vermont), who chaired the Senate Judiciary Committee. It had the same Trenton, New Jersey, October 9, 2001, postmark and same handwriting as previous anthrax envelopes. The letter was sent to Fort Detrick, a U.S. Army lab, for more testing. The letter was the only one found in 280 barrels of Congressional mail examined by the FBI. Postal investigators believe that the letter was misrouted through the U.S. State Department mail-handling facility, leading to the infection of a State Department mail handler. On December 6, 2001, investigators reported that the Leahy envelope contained a letter identical to the Daschle letter.

A $1.25 million reward was posted for information leading to a conviction. Information could be sent to 1-800-CRIME-TV.

In mid-November 2001, all three floors of AMI in Florida tested positive for anthrax. Health officials suggested that more than one letter was involved.

On November 19, 2001, the U.S. Bureau of Prisons announced positive anthrax tests at two locations in a mailroom at 320 First Street, NW, Washington, D.C. Meanwhile, the CDC announced it would test a substance found in a letter the Chilean government said came from Switzerland.

On November 20, 2001, the Russell Senate Office Building offices of Senators Edward M. Kennedy and Christopher Dodd reportedly tested positive for anthrax.

On November 21, 2001, Ottilie Lundgren, 94, who was largely housebound in Oxford, Connecticut, died of inhalation anthrax. Medical investigators found no apparent source of her infection. On November 30, 2001, investigators discovered a trace amount of anthrax outside of a letter sent to a home in Seymour, Connecticut, 1.5 miles from Lundgren's home, supporting the theory that she had come into contact with a cross-contaminated letter. The Seymour letter was postmarked in Trenton, New Jersey, on October 9, 2001, and sent to John S. Farkas, 53, an estate liquidator living at 88 Great Hill Road. Trace amounts of anthrax were found at a Wallingford, Connecticut, post office that sorts mail for Oxford.

On November 23, 2001, the CDC said that the letter sent to Antonio Banfi, a pediatrician in Santiago, Chile, on November 13, 2001, had anthrax spores indistinguishable from the Daschle, Leahy, Brokaw, and *New York Post* spores. Banfi received the letter at the Calvo Mackenna Hospital pediatric lab. It was postmarked in Zurich, Switzerland, but had an Orlando, Florida, return address. The envelope contained a small amount of white powder and papers (however, on November 28, 2001, the *Washington Post* said that the envelope did not contain powder). It was the first confirmed case of anthrax mailed overseas; earlier reports of anthrax in Kenya and the Bahamas were incorrect. However, on November 28, 2001, CDC said that the anthrax in the letter did not match the Ames strain pathogens in the 18 anthrax cases in the United States. The letter was a solicitation for the purchase of a medical book or journal from an Orlando, Florida, publisher.

Anthrax was found in a bin of mail delivered to the Federal Reserve Board's Washington headquarters on December 6, 2001, and in a diplomatic pouch at the U.S. Embassy in Vienna, Austria, on December 13, 2001. A powder-filled envelope that was opened on December 17, 2001, in the office of Deputy Secretary of State Richard Armitage was a hoax; it had been sent from a Texas prison on October 29, 2001.

In mid-December 2001, the government offered anthrax vaccine to 3,000 people. The CDC and local medical services gave conflicting advice regarding whether to take the vaccine or another 40 days of antibiotics; the science was catching up to the new experiences with anthrax. Few postal workers took the vaccine; numerous congressional staffers did.

Genetic fingerprinting suggested that the Capitol Hill anthrax originated from a sample at the U.S. Army Medical Research Institute of Infectious Diseases at Fort Detrick, Maryland, which had sent Ames strain samples to four other labs in the United States and United Kingdom. Investigators attempted to determine whether an individual who had been fired from a lab and made threats was responsible. Authorities also examined whether the attacker wanted to make money from cleanup and medical responses.

Tests conducted and analyzed December 23–28, 2001, found residual anthrax spores on a mail-sorting machine at the Morgan Processing and Distribution Center in New York. It had tested positive, then negative, in October 2001.

A third attempt began on December 28, 2001, to clean out the Hart building. The second effort was suspended on December 17, 2001. This time the plan was to fill the ventilation system with chlorine dioxide gas.

On January 22, 2002, the Hart Senate Office Building finally reopened after several tests found no remaining traces of anthrax spores. The building cleanup cost $20 million.

On January 31, 2002, traces of anthrax were found at the Federal Communications Commission mail-processing center at 9300 East Hampton Drive in Prince George's County, Maryland.

On February 20, 2002, Ernesto Blanco, 74, was back at work in the mailroom of AMI in Boca Raton, Florida, after surviving a case of inhalation anthrax that had killed his coworker.

A Vanderbilt University and New York University Medical School mathematical model released on May 13, 2002, indicated that anthrax contaminated at least 5,000 letters in the eastern United States.

On September 15, 2002, FBI investigators suggested that the anthrax at AMI was spread by more than two dozen photocopy machines in the three-story, 68,000 square foot building. Spores went from the first-floor mailroom, on to reams of copy paper stored there, and into the air by fans inside the machines loaded with the copy paper. Anthrax was found on the keyboard in photo editor Stevens's office; he died in October 2001 of anthrax, the first of five fatalities nationwide.

On May 10, 2003, the FBI announced that it had discovered in Maryland's Frederick Municipal Forest's ice-covered ponds what may have been the method the individual used to put the anthrax into envelopes without becoming infected. Divers found a submerged airtight chamber. The *Washington Post* reported that investigators found a clear box with holes that could accommodate gloves and vials wrapped in plastic. The FBI began draining one of the spring-fed ponds on June 9, 2003, to find further evidence. On July 31, 2003, the FBI announced that no anthrax had been found.

On September 24, 2003, Maureen Stevens, widow of Robert Stevens, the *Sun* tabloid editor who died of anthrax, sued the government for $50 million, saying that lax security at the Army Medical Research Institute of Infectious Diseases at Fort Detrick, Maryland, was responsible. The U.S. government settled on the case on November 28, 2011, for $2.5 million in a filing in U.S. District Court in West Palm Beach, Florida. It did not admit liability or negligence.

On August 5, 2004, federal agents searched the home of Dr. Kenneth M. Berry, 48, in Wellsville, New York, a small town on the Pennsylvania border south of Buffalo. Agents also searched a home in Lavellette on the New Jersey beaches. Berry had worked for five years as an emergency room physician in Wellsville before he resigned in October 2001. He claimed to be the former president of an organization of emergency physicians. In 1997, he founded the nonprofit PREEMPT Medical Counter Terrorism group. PREEMPT teaches medical and defense professionals how to respond to a biological terrorist attack. It may be that a patent application for a chemical and biological surveillance system made Berry a person of interest. He applied for the patent on September 28, 2001, the same day the first anthrax letters were postmarked in Trenton, New Jersey. On August 18, 2004, the University of Pittsburgh Medical Center announced that his employment would end on November 8, 2004, and he would be on leave until then. On November 6, 2004, he pleaded guilty to assaulting his wife and daughter and was sentenced to a 2-year probation and a $1,000 fine.

On November 24, 2004, Chief Judge Claude M. Hilton in Alexandria, Virginia, dismissed Steven J. Hatfill's lawsuit against the *New York Times* Company and columnist Nicholas D. Kristof. Hatfill had been identified by Attorney General John D. Ashcroft as a "person of interest" in the anthrax investigation. Hatfill, 50, was a former scientist at Fort Detrick in Frederick, Maryland, who had studied biological warfare agents. In January 2007, Judge Hilton threw out Hatfill's defamation lawsuit, which had been reinstated by the U.S. Court of Appeals for the Fourth Circuit in 2005. On June 27, 2008, the U.S. Department of Justice settled Hatfill's lawsuit against the government for $5.85 million. The government did not admit wrongdoing. On July 18, 2008, the U.S. Court of Appeals for the Fourth Circuit dismissed Hatfill's libel lawsuit against the *New York Times*.

On February 22, 2007, the Boca Raton offices that were closed in the anthrax attack reopened. The building had been sold in 2003 by AMI for $40,000 to developer David Rustine.

On July 29, 2008, biodefense scientist Bruce E. Ivins, who had worked at the Army lab at Fort Detrick, committed suicide after learning that he was going to be indicted by federal prosecutors in the case. They had intended to offer a plea bargain of life in prison. He had two patents that were used by Vax Gen, Inc., to create anthrax vaccines after the 2001 attacks. Colleagues also suggested that he had mental problems. A final determination of his motivation(s) could not be made.

February 27, 2002
India Sabarmati Express Train Firebombing

Overview: A large Muslim mob firebombed a coach on the Sabarmati Express, a bullet train that makes a two-day trip from Ahmedabad to Darbhanga, India, as it passed through Godhra. Fifty-nine Hindu pilgrims were killed. Different investigations have concluded that the incident was an accident and a preplanned conspiracy. What is certain is that rioting spread through the state and nationwide deaths reached 1,000.

Incident: On February 27, 2002, a Muslim mob threw firebombs and acid at the Sabarmati Express train as it was pulling away from a rail station in the Muslim neighborhood of Godhra in western India, killing 59 people and injuring another 43. Those killed included 25 women and 15 children. The Vishwa Hindu Parishad (World Hindu Council) activists on the train were shouting provocative slogans while the train was in the rail station. They were returning from Ayodhya, where they wanted to construct a temple where the 16th-century Babri Mosque was destroyed in 1992 by a Hindu mob. Many Hindus believe the site was the birthplace of Lord Ram, a Hindu god.

India sent troops to Gujarat after two days of rioting that killed nearly 300 people. Some 1,200 people were arrested statewide. Police killed 17 rioters after receiving a shoot-on-sight order. At least 27 Muslims were burned alive in their homes in Ahmadabad.

The attacks continued into March 2, 2002, when a mob of 500 Hindus torched a Muslim residence in Sardarpura, killing another 29 Muslims and seriously burning 20 others. The nationwide death toll passed 350.

By mid-March 2002, the nationwide death toll passed 700. The toll ultimately reached 1,000.

On March 17, 2002, Gujarat police announced the arrest of a Muslim man who was the prime suspect in the attack.

On February 19, 2003, Indian authorities charged 131 suspects in the arson attack; 65 of them were in custody, including a man accused of organizing the attack, Maulvi Husain Haji Ibrahim Umarji, a Muslim cleric from Godhra. The suspects were charged under the Prevention of Terrorism Act; no Hindus have been charged under the act.

On February 22, 2011, a Gujarat court convicted 31 Muslims on charges of murder and criminal conspiracy, but acquitted 63 defendants, including Umarji, 70, who was believed to be a key conspirator. On March 1, 2011, the court sentenced 11 to death and 20 to life in prison.

March 2, 2004
Baghdad and Karbala Mosques Attack

Overview: The U.S./Coalition ousting of Iraqi ruler Saddam Hussein was met by a host of terrorist factions that arose from the remnants of the Ba'ath Party, the defeated Iraqi military, various Sunni and Shia groups, and foreign terrorists who rushed to the scene, eager to attack the West on Arab soil. Thousands of attacks were conducted against Coalition forces, civilians, and clerics of the wrong faith. Car bombings killing dozens were not uncommon. The Baghdad and Karbala attacks were somewhat more deadly, but otherwise typical of the seemingly unending violence against civilian targets during the occupation.

Incident: On March 2, 2004, terrorists conducted six attacks against Shi'ite worshippers in Baghdad and Karbala, Iraq, a Shi'ite holy city, killing at least 143 people and injuring more than 400 others. The attacks involved planted explosives and possibly mortars. No one claimed credit, although Sunnis were blamed. At least three suicide bombers were involved in the attacks against the gold-domed Imam Kadhim Mausoleum shrine and other areas. The president of the Iraqi Governing Council the next day said the death toll was 271; the U.S.-led Coalition said it was 181 dead and 573 injured.

The commander of the U.S. Central Command, General John Abizaid, U.S. Army, blamed Abu Musab al-Zarqawi, a Jordanian with ties to al Qaeda, who led al Qaeda in Iraq, which had used various cover names.

Fourteen Iraqis were taken into custody late in the day near Baqubah, 30 miles northeast of Baghdad. One suspect led a cell of Wahhabi Muslims. Forces south of Baghdad detained a man wearing a police uniform and carrying fake police identification. He said he was part of the terror network that launched the attacks. He had planned to blow up two police stations. The detainee said the terrorists were mercenaries who were paid $2,000–$4,000 per job, depending upon the number of deaths. The next day, military officials said 15 people, including 5 Persian speakers, had been detained in Karbala.

Zarqawi was killed in a coalition airstrike on June 7, 2006. The U.S. State Department's Rewards for Justice Program had offered $25 million for his apprehension.

October 7, 2004
Sinai Hilton Taba Hotel Suicide Bombings

Overview: A coordinated attack on the Taba Hilton Hotel and two nearby resort campsites often used by vacationing Israelis signaled the possible entrance of al Qaeda to the Sinai Peninsula. Adding incongruity to the devastating attacks was that the hotel is often used for Middle East peace negotiations.

Incident: On October 7, 2004, at 9:45 P.M., a Peugeot SUV loaded with 440 pounds of explosives crashed into Egypt's five-star Taba Hilton, killing at least 32 people, injuring more than 100, and ripping the front off the 11-story hotel, which had housed vacationers from Israel, Russia, and Egypt. Among the dead were 3 receptionists, a secretary, a tourist policeman, the hotel security officer, the rental car man, 6 or 7 Egyptians, 2 Italians, 16 Israelis, and a Russian. The body of a woman was found in a bathtub that had fallen from the eighth floor to the ground. Israel's Deputy Defense Minister Zeev Boim said the powerful bombing appeared to be the work of al Qaeda, observing "It's not the kind of attack that we know comes from Palestinian terror organizations." Two American employees of the U.S. Embassy in Israel were among the scores of wounded. All the vacationers fled, many to Israel, only 300 yards away. Although 150 people were unaccounted for, Israeli officials believed that many had crossed the border into Israel.

Meanwhile, a 440-pound car bomb exploded at 10:00 P.M. at the resort of Ras Shytan (variant Ras al-Sultan), 30 miles south of Taba, killing 5 people and injuring another 38. A suicide bomber drove a taxi near the dining room of the Moon Island Resort, killing two Egyptians—the hotel's assistant chef and a buffet manager. A third Egyptian and two Israelis later died of their wounds. Some witnesses claimed a missile had been fired at the hotel. Later reports said that it was a timer-detonated jeep. Among the injured was Mohammed Ramadan, 24, a chef on duty, who suffered deep wounds to his head and arms. He said he heard a second car bomb go off outside the gates of Mobarak, the camp next door. A security guard had stopped the driver, who ran off and abandoned the car. No one was harmed in the blast, which went off via a timer.

Another 440-pound car bomb went off at the resort of Nuweiba, 40 miles south of Taba.

The next day, the United States issued a travel advisory for the next three months for the northeastern Sinai Peninsula. The State Department said Americans did not appear to have been targeted.

On October 10, 2004, Egyptian police reported that a Bedouin tribesman confessed to selling the explosives that might have been used in the bombings. The Bedouin said he was told by the purchasers that the

The Worst 51–68 219

explosives would be used in the Palestinian territories. Police were also investigating the possible involvement of Palestinian terrorists.

On October 25, 2004, Egyptian police announced the arrests of five people involved in planning the bombings. They said Ayad Said Salah, the Palestinian leader of the attacks, died accidentally in the blasts. He had lived in el-Arish, in the northern Sinai near the Gaza border. Also dead was Egyptian terrorist Suleiman Ahmed Saleh Flayfil at the hotel. Two other Egyptians still at large were identified as Mohamed Ahmed Saleh Flayfil (Suleiman's brother) and Hammad Gaman Gomah. Officials said that the three cars used in the bombings had been stolen. The explosives were pulled from artillery shells and other battlefield materials found across the Sinai from battles in World War II, 1967, and 1973. The timers came from washing machine parts.

Three Egyptian citizens identified as Younes Mohammed Mahmoud, Osama al-Nakhlawi, and Mohammed Jaez Sabbah were sentenced to death in November 2006 for the bombing.

July 11, 2006
India Mumbai Train Bombings

Overview: Train bombings by various Kashmiri separatists, Maoists, Islamic insurgents, and others became fairly common methods of attacks in the 1990s and 2000s in India. India and Pakistan often traded charges of assisting terrorists operating across their borders. The Mumbai train bombings continued a tradition begun by Italian right-wing terrorists and Spain-based al Qaeda terrorists. This particular incident was especially bloody, leaving more than 1,000 dead or wounded at the scene.

Incident: On July 11, 2006, during a monsoon rain, terrorists set off eight bombs between 6:00 and 6:30 P.M. in first class rail cars at the Mahim railway station in Mumbai, India, killing 207 people and wounding more than 800. Police detained 350 people for questioning. A man claiming membership in al Qaeda told a Kashmiri news service that the group had set up a branch in Kashmir and praised the attacks.

India's prime minister said that the terrorists had assistance from inside Pakistan. Authorities believed the terrorists were members of the Pakistani-based Lashkar-e-Taiba Islamic insurgents or perhaps smaller homegrown groups, including the Students Islamic Movement of India. Lashkar spokesman Abdullah Ghaznavi denied involvement.

On July 13, 2006, the Anti-Terrorism Squad released photos of suspects Sayyad Zabiuddin and Zulfeqar Fayyaz. Police said that they had been on the run since May 2006, when police in western India arrested three Muslim insurgents and confiscated arms, ammunition, and plastic explosives. A man known as Rahil was a third person being sought.

On July 14, 2006, police in Nepal arrested two Pakistanis in connection with the 2001 seizure of plastic explosives in Katmandu. Police were looking into the detainees' connection to the Mumbai bombings.

Police said on July 17, 2006, that the military explosive RDX, ammonium nitrate, and fuel oil were used in the bombs.

On July 20, 2006, police arrested a trio in connection with the bombing, saying the suspects had links with terrorists in Nepal and Bangladesh, and unspecified links to Pakistan. Khaleel Aziz Sheikh and Kamal Ahmed Ansari were picked up in Bihar State, while Mumtaz Ahmed Chowduhury was detained in Mumbai. None were charged. A fourth suspect, Tanvir Ahmed Ansari, 32, a practitioner of traditional Muslim medicine, was picked up on July 24, 2006. He allegedly contacted Muslim militants during a 2001 visit to Bahrain and learned to make bombs during a 2004 visit to Pakistan. Another two Indian Muslims, one a chemical engineer, were arrested on July 26, 2006; police believe they provided logistical support and trained in Pakistan. The same day, the Indian Army in Kashmir said it was questioning two soldiers for links to Lashkar.

Senior Indian police officials claimed that six of the eight suspects had trained in Pakistan in arms and explosives, and that one detainee said he had been trained by a member of Lashkar. Among the detainees were Faisal Shaikh, 30, a Lashkar leader in Mumbai; his younger brother, Muzamil, 23, a software engineer who had recently tried to get a job with Oracle, the U.S. software firm; Zameer Shaikh, 31, a key maker in Mumbai; Sohail Shaikh, 30, from Pune; and Tanvir Ansari. On July 31, 2006, police arrested two more people, including a journalist.

On September 30, 2006, Mumbai police commissioner A. N. Roy said his investigation had determined that Pakistan's Director for Inter-Services Intelligence (ISI) was behind the bombing, a charge Pakistan rejected. He claimed ISI planned the attacks in March 2006 and trained the bombers in Bahawalpur, Pakistan, citing evidence provided by the bombers under truth serum. Roy said, "The terror plot was ISI-sponsored and executed by Lashkar-e-Taiba operatives with help from the Students Islamic Movement of India." As of the interview, 15 people, including 11 Pakistanis, had been arrested in the case. Three Indians remained at large; a Pakistani was killed in the bombings. Roy said the bombs were packed into pressure cookers. Some of the Pakistanis went across the India–Pakistan border; others went through Nepal and Bangladesh. They were housed by cooperative Indians in Mumbai apartments. Police found the terrorists when they tracked a caller from Mumbai to the Nepalese border. They arrested a suspect who led them to others.

On November 30, 2006, Indian police filed charges against 28 members of Lashkar-e-Taiba and the Students Islamic Movement of India. Thirteen were in custody. They could face the death penalty.

The case remains under investigation.

September 20, 2008
Islamabad Marriott Hotel Bombing

Overview: Islamabad is Pakistan's Washington, D.C., and this distinguished Marriott Hotel is conveniently located near government buildings and embassies. The nighttime explosion caused a natural gas line to burst into flames and engulf most of the building. It left a 6 feet wide and 20 feet deep crater near the hotel. Amazingly, the hotel was rebuilt and reopened by the end of the year. Although several theories about individual and group perpetrators were investigated, no consensus or proof was established.

Incident: On September 20, 2008, a suicide dump truck bomb carrying a ton of explosives went off at Islamabad's Marriott Hotel, killing at least 60 and injuring 266. Some observers said the death toll could reach 100. At least 21 foreigners, including the Czech Republic's ambassador, were among the casualties. Several guards who had examined the truck were killed. Two Department of Defense employees were dead, a contractor was missing, and three State Department officers were hurt. Pakistani authorities said the attackers had targeted the official residence of Prime Minister Yousaf Raza Gilani, a block away from the hotel. Authorities blamed terrorists from South Waziristan, saying Baitullah Mehsud, leader of the Tehrik-e-Taliban, was the chief suspect. By October 24, 2008, police had arrested four men in Punjab who were suspected of "indirect involvement" in the bombing. The government blamed Lashkar-i-Jhangvi for assisting the attackers. The detainees were acquitted for lack of evidence.

On January 1, 2009, the BBC reported that an air strike killed al Qaeda's Pakistan operations chief Usama al-Kini, whom U.S. officials said was behind the hotel bombing and the 1998 embassy attacks in Kenya and Tanzania.

December 30, 2009
Afghanistan Bombing of CIA Khost Base

Overview: An individual claiming to have intelligence on al Qaeda's leadership was brought onto the Central Intelligence Agency (CIA) base in Khost Province, Afghanistan, by his Jordanian handler. The individual instead blew himself up while trying to take as many Americans with him as he could. Some used this incident to question U.S. security and the wisdom of training Afghan forces in preparation for U.S. troop withdrawal. Some questioned whether this was an act of terrorism or an act of war. CIA director Leon E. Panetta recentered the discourse when he said, "Their devotion to duty is the foundation of our country. . . . Our resolve is unbroken, our energy undiminished and our dedication to each other and to our nation unshakable."

Incident: On December 30, 2009, Jordanian Humam Khalil Abu-Mulal al-Balawi, a Taliban terrorist posing as an agent willing to provide details to the CIA and Jordanian intelligence regarding the al Qaeda leadership, set off an explosives belt under his clothes, killing seven CIA officers and a Jordanian and wounding eight people, including six Americans, at Forward Operating Base Chapman in Khost Province. The murdered Americans were identified as Khost base chief Jennifer Lynne Matthews, 45, of Fredericksburg; Daren James LaBonte, 35, of Alexandria; Scott Michael Roberson, 39; Harold E. Brown Jr., 37; Elizabeth Hanson, 30; and security contractors Jeremy Jason Wise, 35, and Dane Clark Paresi, 46. The Jordanian was identified as Sharif Ali bin Zeid, a captain in the Jordanian Dairat al-Mukhabarat al-Ammah (General Intelligence Department), who was running the supposed agent. Arghawan, the Afghan external security chief, was also killed. Al Qaeda later took credit for the attack. On January 7, 2010, Mustafa Abu Yazid, al Qaeda's commander of operations in Afghanistan and its No. 3 leader, took credit for the attack as revenge for the deaths of Baitullah Mehsud, leader of the Taliban in Pakistan, and al Qaeda operatives Saleh al-Somali and Abdullah al-Libi.

The White House website on December 31, 2009, carried President Barack Obama's message to the CIA workforce, in which he said:

I write to mark a sad occasion in the history of the CIA and our country. Yesterday, seven Americans in Afghanistan gave their lives in service to their country. Michelle and I have their families, friends, and colleagues in our thoughts and prayers. These brave Americans were part of a long line of patriots who have made great sacrifices for their fellow citizens, and for our way of life. The United States would not be able to maintain the freedom and security that we cherish without decades of service from the dedicated men and women of the CIA. You have helped us understand the world as it is, and taken great risks to protect our country. You have served in the shadows, and your sacrifices have sometimes been unknown to your fellow citizens, your friends, and even your families. In recent years, the CIA has been tested as never before. Since our country was attacked on September 11, 2001, you have served on the front lines in directly confronting the dangers of the 21st century. Because of your service, plots have been disrupted, American lives have been saved, and our Allies and partners have been more secure. Your triumphs and even your names may be unknown to your fellow Americans, but your service is deeply appreciated. Indeed, I know firsthand the excellent quality of your work because I rely on it every day. The men and women who gave their lives in Afghanistan did their duty with courage, honor and excellence, and we must draw strength from the example of their sacrifice. They will take their place on the Memorial Wall at Langley alongside so many other heroes who gave their lives on behalf of their country. And they will live on in the hearts of those who loved them, and in the freedom that they gave their lives to defend. May God bless the memory of those we lost, and may God bless the United States of America.

CIA.gov posted CIA director Panetta's statement that:

those who fell yesterday were far from home and close to the enemy, doing the hard work that must be done to protect our country from terrorism. We owe them our deepest gratitude, and we pledge to them and their families that we will never cease fighting for the cause to which they dedicated their lives—a safer America. Families have been our Agency's first priority. Before sharing this information with anyone else, we wanted to be in contact with each of them. This is the most difficult news to bear under any circumstances, but that it comes during the holidays makes it even harder. In coming days and weeks, we will comfort their loved ones as a family. They are in our thoughts and prayers—now and always. . . . Yesterday's tragedy reminds us that the men and women of the CIA put their lives at risk every day to protect this nation. Throughout our history, the reality is that those who make a real difference often face real danger.

The website also said that "Director Panetta credited U.S. military doctors and nurses with saving the lives of those wounded in the attack. In honor and memory of the dead, he requested that the flags at CIA Headquarters be flown at half-staff."

On January 2, 2010, the bomber's video-will appeared on the Internet. He said:

The Jordanian and the American intelligence services offered me millions of dollars to work with them and to spy on mujahideen [holy warriors] here, but hamd'allah [thanks be to God] I came to the mujahideen and I told them everything. We arranged together this attack. What we strive for cannot be exchanged for all the wealth in the world. This attack will be the first of the revenge operations against the Americans. . . . We say that we will never forget the blood of our Emir Beitullah Mehsud, God's mercy on him. To retaliate for his death in the United States and outside the United States will remain an obligation on all emigrants who were harbored by Beitullah Mehsud. . . . God's combatant never exposes his religion to blackmail and never renounces it, even if he is offered the sun in one hand and the moon in the other.

He had posted on September 2009 on an al Qaeda website, "If [a Muslim] dies in the cause of Allah, he will grant his words glory that will be permanent marks on the path to guide to jihad, with permission from Allah. If love of jihad enters a man's heart, it will not leave him even if he wants to do so. What he sees of luxurious palaces will remind him of positions of the martyrs in the higher heaven."

In a memorial ceremony at CIA Headquarters, President Obama called the dead "American patriots who loved their country and gave their lives to defend it. . . . There are no words that can ease the ache in your hearts. But to their colleagues and all who served with them—those here today, those still recovering, those watching around the world, I say: Let their sacrifice be a summons. To carry on their work. To complete this mission. To win this war and to keep our country safe." The director of the CIA, Panetta, added, "They are the heart and soul of this great country. Their devotion to duty is the foundation of our country. . . . We will carry this fight to the enemy. . . . Our resolve is unbroken, our energy undiminished and our dedication to each other and to our nation unshakable." The White House issued the following press release:

> February 5, 2010
> President Obama and CIA Director Panetta Speak at CIA Memorial Service
>
> The Central Intelligence Agency today held a memorial service at its head-quarters for the seven Americans killed in eastern Afghanistan on December 30th. Family members and more than a thousand Agency officers gathered in attendance, along with guests including President Obama and senior officials from the Intelligence Community, the White House, and the Pentagon, as well as members of Congress.

President Obama spoke of the country's gratitude to the families. "Everything you instilled in them—the virtues of service and decency and duty—were on display that December day. That is what you gave them. That is what you gave to America. And our nation will be forever in your debt." He told CIA officers that their "seven heroes" were at the vanguard of a mission vital to national security. "Let their sacrifice be a summons. To carry on their work. To complete this mission. To win this war, and to keep our country safe."

CIA director Panetta paid tribute to the talent and accomplishments of the fallen, telling their loved ones that CIA officers "simply cannot do these jobs-we can't do these jobs-without the love and support of our families." He called the seven "genuine patriots" who "lived up to our highest principles," and pledged that CIA would strive to be worthy of them. Panetta added, "As they worked to protect lives, they sacrificed their own. For this, we honor them-now and always. . . . We will carry this fight to the enemy. Our resolve is unbroken, our energy undiminished, and our dedication to each other and to our nation, unshakable."

President Obama gave the following remarks at the memorial for the CIA officers at CIA Headquarters in Langley, Virginia:

> America's intelligence agencies are a community, and the CIA is a family. That is how we gather here today. I speak as a grateful Commander-in-Chief who relies on you. There are members of Congress here who support you. Leaders—Leon Panetta, Steve Kappes—who guide you. And most of all, family, friends and colleagues who love you and grieve with you.
>
> For more than sixty years, the security of our nation has demanded that the work of this agency remain largely unknown. But today, our gratitude as citizens demands that we speak of seven American patriots who loved their country and gave their lives to defend it: [Names redacted.]

They came from different corners of our country—men and women—and each walked their own path to that rugged base in the mountains. Some had come to this work after a lifetime of protecting others—in law enforcement, in the military; one was just a few years out of college.

Some had devoted years, decades, even, to unraveling the dark web of terrorists that threatened us; others, like so many of you, joined these ranks when 9/11 called a new generation to service. Some had spent years on dangerous tours around the globe; others had just arrived in harm's way.

But there, at the remote outpost, they were bound by a common spirit. They heard their country's call and answered it. They served in the shadows and took pride in it. They were doing their job and they loved it. They saw the danger and accepted it. They knew that the price of freedom is high and, in an awful instant, they paid that price.

There are no words that can ease the ache in your hearts. But to their colleagues and all who served with them—those here today, those still recovering, those watching around the world—I say: Let their sacrifice be a summons. To carry on their work. To complete this mission. To win this war, and to keep our country safe.

To their parents—it is against the natural order of life for parents to lay their children to rest. Yet these weeks of solemn tribute have revealed for all to see—that you raised remarkable sons and daughters. Everything you instilled in them—the virtues of service and decency and duty—were on display that December day. That is what you gave them. That is what you gave to America. And our nation will be forever in your debt.

To the spouses—your husbands and wives raised their hand and took an oath to protect and defend the country that they loved. They fulfilled that oath with their life. But they also took your hand and made a vow to you. And that bond of love endures, from this world to the next. Amidst grief that is sometimes unbearable, may you find some comfort in our vow to you—that this agency, and this country, will stand with you and support you always.

And to the beautiful children—I know that this must be so hard and confusing, but please always remember this. It wasn't always easy for your mom or dad to leave home. But they went to another country to defend our country. And they gave their lives to protect yours. And as you grow, the best way to keep their memory alive and the highest tribute you can pay to them is to live as they lived, with honor and dignity and integrity.

They served in secrecy, but today every American can see their legacy. For the record of their service—and of this generation of intelligence professionals—is written all around us. It's written in the extremists who no longer threaten our country—because you eliminated them. It's written in the attacks that never occurred—because you thwarted them. And it's written in the Americans, across this country and around the world, who are alive today—because you saved them.

And should anyone here ever wonder whether your fellow citizens truly appreciate that service, you need only remember the extraordinary tributes of recent weeks: the thousands of Americans who have sat down at their computers and posted messages to seven heroes they never knew; in the outpouring of generosity to the memorial foundation that will help support these proud families.

And along a funeral procession in Massachusetts, in the freezing cold, mile after mile, friends and total strangers paying their respects, small children holding signs saying, "Thank You." And a woman holding up a large American flag because, she said simply, "He died for me and my family."

As a nation, we pledge to be there for you and your families. We need you more than ever. In an ever-changing world where new dangers emerge suddenly, we need you to be one step ahead of nimble adversaries. In this information age, we need you to sift through vast universes of data to find intelligence that can be acted upon swiftly. And in an era of technology and unmanned systems, we still need men and women like these seven—professionals of skill and talent and courage who are willing to make the ultimate sacrifice to protect our nation.

Because of them, because of you, a child born in America today is welcomed into a country that is proud and confident, strong and hopeful—just as Molly Roberson welcomed her daughter Piper this week, both of whom join us today. Piper will never know her dad, Scott. But thanks to Molly, she will know what her father stood for—a man who served his country, who did his duty, and who gave his life to keep her safe.

And on some distant day, years from now, when she is grown, if Piper—or any of these children—seeks to understand for themselves, they'll need only come here—to Langley, through these doors, and stand before that proud Memorial Wall that honors the fallen.

And perhaps they'll run their fingers over the stars that recall their parent's service. Perhaps they'll walk over to that Book of Honor, turn the pages, and see their parent's names. And at that moment of quiet reflection, they will see what we all know today—that our nation is blessed to have men and women such as these. That we are humbled by their service, that we give thanks for every day that you keep us safe.

May God bless these seven patriots, may he watch over their families. And may God bless the United States of America.

On March 8, 2010, an air strike in Miram Shah, North Waziristan, Pakistan killed a dozen people, including Hussein al-Yemeni, a senior al Qaeda bomb expert and trainer believed to have been behind the Khost attack.

On August 20, 2010, federal authorities charged Pakistani Taliban leader Hakimullah Mehsud with the Khost attack. The charges, unsealed on September 1, 2010, included conspiracy to murder a U.S. national while outside the United States and conspiracy to use a weapon of mass destruction against a U.S. national while outside the United States.

On October 19, 2010, CIA's Office of Public Affairs released the director of CIA Panetta's statement on the Khost attack to employees, entitled *Lessons from Khost*:

Last December, our Agency family lost seven courageous and talented colleagues in a terrorist attack at Forward Operating Base Chapman in Khost,

Afghanistan. These dedicated men and women were assigned to CIA's top priority—disrupting and dismantling al-Qa'ida and its militant allies. That work carries, by its very nature, significant risk. CIA is conducting the most aggressive counterterrorism operations in our history, a mission we are pursuing with a level of determination worthy of our fallen heroes. We will sustain that momentum and, whenever possible, intensify our pursuit. We will continue to fight for a safer America.

Earlier this year, I directed that a task force of seasoned Agency professionals conduct a review of the Khost attack. The purpose was to examine what happened, what lessons were learned, and what steps should be taken to prevent such incidents in the future. In addition, I asked Ambassador Thomas Pickering and Charlie Allen, a highly accomplished former Agency officer, to conduct an independent study of the Khost attack and to review the work of the task force. They concurred with its findings. One of CIA's greatest strengths is our ability to learn from experience, refine our methods, and adapt to the shifting tactics of America's enemies.

The review is now complete, and I would like to thank those who participated. They did our Agency a great service. It was, to be sure, a difficult task—especially since key insights perished with those we lost. Perfect visibility into all that contributed to the attack is therefore impossible. But based on an exhaustive examination of the available information, we have a firm understanding of what our Agency could have done better. In keeping with past practice, we will provide the Khost report to the Office of Inspector General.

In highly sensitive, complex counterterrorism operations, our officers must often deal with dangerous people in situations involving a high degree of ambiguity and risk. The task force noted that the Khost assailant fit the description of someone who could offer us access to some of our most vicious enemies. He had already provided information that was independently verified. The decision to meet him at the Khost base—with the objective of gaining additional intelligence on high priority terrorist targets—was the product of consultations between Headquarters and the field. He had confirmed access within extremist circles, making a covert relationship with him—if he was acting in good faith—potentially very productive. But he had not rejected his terrorist roots. He was, in fact, a brutal murderer.

Mitigating the risk inherent in intelligence operations, especially the most sensitive ones, is essential to success. In this case, the task force determined that the Khost assailant was not fully vetted and that sufficient security precautions were not taken. These missteps occurred because of shortcomings across several Agency components in areas including communications, documentation, and management oversight. Coupled with a powerful drive to disrupt al-Qa'ida, these factors contributed to the tragedy at Khost. Each played an important role; none was more important than the others. Based on the findings of the task force and the independent review, responsibility cannot be assigned to any particular individual or group. Rather, it was the intense determination to accomplish the mission that influenced the judgments that were made.

There are no guarantees in the dangerous work of counterterrorism, but the task force identified six key areas that deserve greater focus as we carry out that vital mission. We will:

- Enforce greater discipline in communications, ensuring that key guidance, operational facts, and judgments are conveyed and clearly flagged in formal channels.
- Strengthen our attention to counterintelligence concerns while maintaining a wartime footing.
- Apply the skills and experience of senior officers more effectively in sensitive cases.
- Require greater standardization of security procedures.
- More carefully manage information sharing with other intelligence services.
- Maintain our high operational tempo against terrorist targets, even as we make adjustments to how we conduct our essential mission.

I have approved 23 specific actions recommended by the task force, some of which I ordered implemented months ago. They provide for organizational and resource changes, communications improvements, tightened security procedures, more focused training, and reinforced counterintelligence practices. These include:

- Establishing a War Zone Board made up of senior officers from several components and chaired by the Director of the National Clandestine Service. It will conduct a baseline review of our staffing, training, security, and resources in the most dangerous areas where we operate.
- Assembling a select surge cadre of veteran officers who will lend their expertise to our most critical counterterrorism operations.
- Creating an NCS Deputy within the Counterterrorism Center, who will report to the Director of the Counterterrorism Center and ensure a more integrated effort across Agency offices.
- Conducting a thorough review of our security measures and applying even more rigorous standards at all our facilities.
- Expanding our training effort for both managers and officers on hostile environments and counterintelligence challenges.
- Creating an integrated counterintelligence vetting cell within our Counterterrorism Center that focuses on high-risk/high-gain assets, evaluates potential threats, assesses "lessons learned," and applies the latest technology and best practices to counterterrorism operations.
- Designating a senior officer to ensure that all the recommendations are indeed implemented.

We've now taken a hard look at what happened and what needed to be done after the tragedy at Khost. While we cannot eliminate all of the risks involved in fighting a war, we can and will do a better job of protecting our officers. Drawing on the work of the task force and its insights, it's time to move forward. Nothing in the report can relieve the pain of losing our seven fallen colleagues. By putting their lives on the line to pursue our nation's terrorist enemies, they taught us what bravery is all about. It is that legacy that we will always remember in our hearts.

October 31, 2010
Iraq Our Lady of Salvation Church Takeover

Overview: Terrorist attacks following the coalition incursion into Iraq in 2003 became commonplace, with some months logging hundreds of incidents by numerous terrorist groups, bitter-enders, and other insurgents. While most of the attacks were against coalition forces and civilians who happened to be in the wrong place, by the end of the first decade of the new millennium, some attacks against the minority Christian population began to worry government officials and others regarding a potential trend of confessional violence.

Incident: One especially grievous attack was the October 31, 2010, takeover of Baghdad's Our Lady of Salvation Church (Sayidat al-Nejat). In the late afternoon, terrorists parked their Dodge SUV in the back of the church and threw several bags over the compound wall. Guards at the neighboring Baghdad Stock Market in the Karada neighborhood engaged in a gun battle with terrorists, during which two guards died and four were injured. The terrorists set off their truck bomb, then set off explosives at the rear door of the church. They ran inside and took 120 hostages.

The terrorists phoned two employees of al-Baghdadiya television to demand the release of female prisoners in Egypt and Iraqi prisoners in Iraq. The Iraqi-owned, Egypt-based station later broadcast the demand. The Iraqi government later shut down the station. The Islamic State of Iraq (another name for al Qaeda in Iraq) posted on a website:

> The Mujahideens raided a filthy nest of the nests of polytheism, which has been long taken by the Christians of Iraq as a headquarters for a war against the religion of Islam and they were able by the grace of God and His glory to capture those were gathered in and to take full control of all its entrances.

Following a four-hour siege, the Golden Force antiterrorist unit stormed the Assyrian rite Catholic church. A terrorist threw a grenade into a room where the congregants were assembled. Thirteen hostages escaped.

During the gun battle, two terrorists set off their explosives belts containing ball bearings. Thirty hostages and seven security officers died. Forty-one hostages and 15 rescuers were wounded. Police arrested eight suspects. They found three Yemeni and two Egyptian passports, possibly belonging to the suicide bombers.

The Islamic State of Iraq reiterated its demand following the conclusion of the incident. On November 3, 2010, the group announced the passage of its deadline for Egypt's Copts to release women who had converted to Islam. It warned that it would attack Christians anywhere. "We will open upon them the doors of destruction and rivers of blood."

By the end of November 2010, Iraqi authorities had arrested a dozen al Qaeda in Iraq suspects, including its Baghdad leader, Huthaifa al-Batawi, in connection with the case.

Ishtar Television reported that three individuals were sentenced to death and a fourth to 20 years in prison on August 2, 2011. An Iraqi appeals court upheld the death sentences and the three were executed on February 2, 2012.

July 22, 2011
Oslo Shooting and Bombing Spree

Overview: Although the West had seen numerous would-be "lone wolf" Islamic terrorists, inspired by the calls to jihad of Osama bin Laden, Anwar al-Aulaqi, and others, the most successful lone wolf terrorist of the early part of the millennium was a right-wing racist Norwegian who set off a massive car bomb and conducted a major shooting spree before being apprehended. The actions of Anders Behring Breivik, 32, resurrected the issue of what constitutes a terrorist attack versus the actions of a deranged psychopath cloaked in a political veneer. The answer raises questions about the legal status and ultimate resolution in the courts, prisons, and psychiatric facilities of such individuals.

Incident: On July 22, 2011, Breivik set off a car bomb at 3:26 P.M. near the 17-story building that houses the prime minister's office in Oslo, starting a fire at the neighboring Oil Ministry in Oslo. Eight people died and 30 were injured.

Two hours later, wearing a police uniform, Breivik arrived at a Youth Labor Party political conference on Utoya Island, 25 miles to the northwest. He told the students to bunch together, then opened fire, killing at least 68 people and injuring another 66. At least 60 victims were teens. He shot several of them in the water, as they were trying to swim away from the island. It took a police patrol 25 minutes to respond to emergency calls. An emergency team from Oslo had to borrow motorboats from local residents, getting to the island an hour after the first call. The patrol found Breivik within two minutes. He surrendered without a fight and apparently had no plans for a getaway. Police seized his Glock pistol and automatic weapon.

Breivik quickly told police that he was responsible, deeming the attacks "atrocious but necessary." He faced 21 years in prison. He claimed he acted alone and pleaded not guilty.

Police noted that he had shown right-wing tendencies in his Internet postings. His lawyer, Geir Lippestad, said his fundamentalist Christian client was insane. Breivik had joined an anti-immigrant party. He opposed Islam, multiculturalism, and "cultural Marxists." Authorities noted his recent purchase of tons of fertilizer, a possible bomb component. He had written a 1,500-page English-language manifesto, entitled *2083: A European Declaration of Independence*, which called for a civil war. It also explained how he made the Oslo bomb. The document was illustrated with symbols of Knights Templar. The screed was reminiscent of Unabomber Ted Kaczynski's manifesto, which it quoted. Breivik also videotaped himself wearing quasi-military uniforms.

On August 24 2012, Oslo District Court found him sane and guilty, and sentenced him to 21 years of preventive detention, which could be renewed and keep him imprisoned for life.

Unsuccessful Attempts

Several attacks were foiled, or did not reach the level of destruction, death, or political and economic consequences initially planned by their perpetrators. If the terrorists had been successful, their incidents would have been included in the *50 Worst*.

Many of the plots involved innovative tactics designed to circumvent security procedures, such as bombs in airplane passengers' underwear, shoes, and carry-on drinks; computer printer toner cartridges hidden in airline cargo; simple binary chemical agents; and multiple simultaneous bombings of aircraft pre- and postdating 9/11. They also involved attacks on high-profile targets, both persons and facilities. Terrorists dreamed of attacks on the Pope, the White House, U.S. Capitol, Central Intelligence Agency (CIA) Headquarters, Times Square, the Space Needle, and other major monuments. Of particular concern to authorities was that many of the plots were attributed to "lone wolves"—individuals perhaps inspired by larger terrorist organizations but acting on their own.

May 13, 1981
Attempted Papal Assassination

On May 13, 1981, in Vatican City, Mehmet Ali Agca, 24, an escaped rightist Turkish terrorist, fired five shots from a Browning 9-mm pistol at Pope John Paul II as the pontiff was being driven in Saint Peter's Square in front of 10,000 worshippers. The attacker hit the Pope three times and wounded two tourists: Ann Odre, 58, of Buffalo, New York, and Rose Hall, 21, of Jamaica. Agca was charged on May 14, 1981, with the attempted assassination of the Pope, who recovered from his wounds. The terrorist had previously threatened the Pope during his visit to Turkey in November 1979. He claimed he wanted to assassinate the "king of England," but gave up that plan when he discovered that the king is a woman. He also planned to murder UN secretary general Kurt Waldheim and Simone Veil, president of the European Parliament. He claimed friendship with George Habash, but the Popular Front for the Liberation of Palestine denied any contact with him. He was also affiliated with the Gray Wolves, a rightist organization associated with the Nationalist Action Party.

Agca had escaped from Turkey after being imprisoned for the murder of prominent journalist Abdi Ipekci.

On July 19, 1981, Turkey asked for Agca's extradition. On July 22, 1981, after a three-day trial and a one-day hunger strike, Agca was sentenced to life imprisonment in Rome.

Suspicion that the Communist Bloc was behind the assassination attempt roiled Western press and intelligence observers for years. According to the Italian press, the publicity-conscious Agca soon began to talk about his suspected sources of support and tied Bulgarian intelligence to the case. On December 8, 1982, Italian newspapers claimed that Agca had confessed that Bulgarian intelligence had ordered him to kill the Pope. He claimed that he escaped into Bulgaria with the help of Oral Celik, a Turkish terrorist with ties to the Bulgarians. In Sofia, he was aided by another Turk, Bekir Celenk, whom Italian police have linked to arms and drug smuggling. Celenk introduced Agca to Sergei Ivanov Antonov, a Rome station chief for Balkan Airlines; Teodorov Ayvazov, a cashier for the Bulgarian Embassy in Rome; and Jelio Kolev Vassiliev, former secretary to Bulgaria's military attaché in Rome. Celenk and the Bulgarians allegedly offered Agca DM 3 million ($1.25 million) to kill the Pope. Agca was captured with a paper bearing the phone numbers of the Bulgarian embassy and consulate, Balkan Airlines, and Ayvazov's residence.

On March 29, 1986, having heard from over 100 witnesses, Judge Severino Santiapichi announced that the Rome jury of two judges and six lay jurors acquitted the three Bulgarians of charges of plotting to assassinate the Pope because of insufficient evidence.

During the "Trial of the Century," which began on May 27, 1985, Agca often strained his credibility by contradicting his testimony, admitting lying, and at the start of proceedings, announcing that he was Jesus Christ. Agca claimed that the Soviet Komitet Gosudarstvennoy Bezopasnosti (KGB; Committee for State Security) was involved in the assassination attempt. Agca, already serving a life sentence for firing the shots, was sentenced to a year in prison for illegal possession of the automatic pistol. He was extradited to Turkey in 2000 after serving nearly 20 years in Italy. On January 18, 2010, Turkey released Agca from Sincan's prison after he served time for the Ipekci murder.

January 1995
Bojinka Planned Bombing of 10 U.S.-Bound Planes

On April 13, 1995, U.S. prosecutors indicted Ramzi Yousef with the bombing of an airliner on December 11, 1994, that killed Japanese passenger

Haruki Ikegami and injured 10 people, and of planning to bomb other U.S. airliners in the Bojinka plot. The bombing charge carried the death penalty. He was believed to have boarded the plane in Manila, placed a bomb under a seat in a life-vest holder, and then deplaned at Cebu before it left for Tokyo. He was sentenced on January 8, 1998, to life plus 240 years for the World Trade Center bombing of February 26, 1993. He had also plotted with Wali Khan to bomb a dozen U.S. airliners over the Pacific in the Bojinka plot and to assassinate Pope John Paul II and U.S. president Bill Clinton in Manila. Authorities believed the Manila bombing was a test run for the attacks on the dozen planes. He also planned to crash a hijacked plane into the Langley Virginia, headquarters of the Central Intelligence Agency (CIA). Authorities said he had developed the plan with his relative, Khalid Sheikh Mohammed, who would go on to become the key planner of the 9/11 attacks. Mohammed also claimed credit for numerous other al Qaeda attacks. He was placed on the Federal Bureau of Investigation's (FBI's) Ten Most Wanted List on April 21, 1993, and captured on February 7, 1995, in Pakistan. As of late 2013, he was awaiting trial in Guantanamo Bay military prison.

December 15, 1999
Planned Millennium
Bombing of Space Needle and Airport

Ahmed Ressam, an Algerian attempting to enter Port Angeles, Washington, was arrested on December 15, 1999, by Washington State Police and customs officials as he arrived by ferry from Canada. He was transporting two 22-ounce bottles of nitroglycerin, more than 100 pounds of urea, and homemade timers in his rental car. The detonating device consisted of circuit boards linked to a Casio watch and a 9-volt battery, similar to one used early by Osama bin Laden associates. He was earlier arrested and jailed for 15 months for arms trafficking with terrorists. He and his associates in Canada were members of Algeria's Armed Islamic Group and were believed to be working for Osama bin Laden. In March 1998, he had attended an al Qaeda camp in Afghanistan.

Ressam attempted to flee after Customs Inspector Diana M. Dean asked him to step out of his Chrysler 300, the last car off the ferry. Inspector Carmon Clem removed the trunk floor board and discovered suspicious packages. Senior Inspector Mark Johnson patted down Ressam for weapons and felt something in a jacket pocket. Ressam slipped out of his jacket and started running. He was chased down six blocks away from the ferry customs port. He was carrying a false Canadian passport and driver's license with two different names. Witnesses said they saw a possible accomplice walk off the Coho Ferry as Ressam was being arrested.

On December 22, 1999, Ressam was charged in a Seattle federal court with knowingly transporting explosives across the Canadian border, having false identification papers, and making false statement to U.S. Customs Service officials.

A spokesman for the Montreal police said that Ressam lived for a time with Karim Said Atmani, who was extradited by Canada to France on charges that he participated in the 1995 Paris subway bombing that killed 4 and injured 86. Montreal police announced that they had arrested 11 men, mostly Algerians, during the past four months for thefts during the previous two years of 5,000 items, such as computers, cell phones, passports, and credit cards. Some were believed to be aiding Islamic radicals.

French officials said Ressam was linked to Fateh Kamel, an Algerian veteran of the Afghan war, who was tied to the 1996 bombers in Paris who left one bystander and several Islamic radicals dead.

Canadian Mounties raided Ressam's apartment house in Montreal's East End, where they found a .357 Magnum pistol and instructions for making bombs.

On December 28, 1999, Seattle mayor Paul Schell announced the cancellation of Seattle's millennium party at the Space Needle because of fears of a terrorist attack. Authorities believed Ressam had planned to bomb the facility.

Ressam was convicted on April 7, 2001, in the New Year's Day 2000 bomb plot and sentenced in June 2001 to 130 years in prison. The jury found him guilty on nine criminal counts, including terrorism and assorted charges involving transporting explosives, smuggling, and using false passports. The same day, he was convicted in absentia by a Paris court for belonging to a terrorist group of Islamic militants; he was sentenced to five years. On July 3, 2001, he told a federal jury in U.S. District Court in Manhattan that his group planned to set off a huge bomb at the Los Angeles International Airport.

December 22, 2001
The Shoe Bomber

Richard Colvin Reid, 28, a drifter who boarded American Airlines flight 63 in Paris on December 22, 2001, attempted to set off explosives hidden in his shoes with a match. He boarded without any luggage or additional ID, traveled alone, and had a one-way ticket—all tip-offs that should trigger suspicions. He lit a match and when confronted by a flight attendant, put it in his mouth. After she alerted the pilot by intercom and returned, he tried to set alight the inner tongue of his sneaker, which had been drilled out and had protruding wires. She tried to stop him, but Reid threw her against the bulkhead. He bit a second flight attendant on the thumb. The crew and several passengers overpowered him; several passengers suffered minor injuries. Two French doctors on board used the plane's medical kit to sedate him three times; other passengers tied him to his window seat in row 29. The pilot diverted the flight to Boston's Logan International Airport, escorted by two U.S. Air Force F15 fighter jets. The crew questioned Reid, who claimed his father is Jamaican and his mother British and that he was traveling to the Caribbean to visit family members. Some media outlets reported that he was a Muslim convert. The FBI took the man into custody for "interference with a flight crew," a felony. On December 24, 2001, he was formally charged in court in Boston with interference with flight crews by assault or intimidation.

Tests on the shoes indicated a substance consistent with C-4. The ignition devices were later "disrupted" and the shoes were detonated in an open field. The FBI said there were two "functional improvised explosive devices" inside the sneakers.

French police said that the suspect was born in Sri Lanka and named Tariq Raja (alias Abdel Rahim). Other reports said he may have had dual citizenship. French media reported that he had tried to board the same flight on December 21, 2001, but was stopped by police unsure of his passport.

Following the incident, some airports began random inspections of passenger footwear. It soon became a standard requirement that passengers remove their shoes when going through a Transportation Security Administration (TSA) inspection in the United States.

Reid and al Qaeda suspect Zacarias Moussaoui attended the primarily black Brixton Mosque in London, although worshipers could not establish that the two attended together. Some al Qaeda detainees in Afghanistan said they recognized Reid from photos that appeared in the media.

At an initial hearing on December 28, 2001, FBI witness Margaret Cronin said that the bomb could have blown a hole in the plane's fuselage, leading to explosive decompression of the cabin. Because Reid was in a window seat, the blast could also have ignited the fuel tanks.

On October 4, 2002, after initially asking that references to al Qaeda training be dropped in the indictment in return for a guilty plea, he pleaded guilty to all eight charges, including attempting to blow up the airliner. On January 30, 2003, he was sentenced to life in prison. He was placed in a special isolation unit of the Supermax prison in Florence, Colorado.

2003
Mubtakkar Chemical
Weapons Attack on NYC Subway

U.S. journalists have reported that al Qaeda deputy Ayman al-Zawahiri in 2003 called off a planned chemical weapons attack via mubtakker against the New York City subway system, saying that the group had something even more impressive planned. The mubtakker is a very simple binary chemical device that generates lethal hydrogen cyanide gas.

August 10, 2006
Planned Liquid Bombings of U.K.-to-U.S. Planes

British authorities broke up an apparent al Qaeda plot to use liquid explosives and common electronic devices as detonators to destroy at least 10 planes flying from the United Kingdom to the United States. Among the affected airlines were American, United, Continental, and British Airways. British police detained 41 people in the investigation. One worked at Heathrow Airport. Seven other people, including two Britons, were held in Pakistan as "facilitators" of the plot after their arrest in Lahore and Karachi. Two Britons had been arrested in Pakistan a week earlier. Pakistan claimed that the conspiracy was centered in Afghanistan.

Logistical and financial support came from Karachi and Lahore. At least 17 of the suspects in U.K. custody had family ties to Pakistan, where several had traveled in recent months.

British and U.S. authorities quickly tightened airport security measures, banning a host of common items from carry-on baggage, including all liquids, toothpaste, contact lens solutions, and suntan lotion. Authorities feared that some of the plotters remained at large and could still detonate such explosives.

On August 11, 2006, U.K. authorities identified 19 suspects. Pakistan said there were "indications of Afghanistan-based al Qaeda connection" and that it had detained a "key person," British national Rashid Rauf, on August 9, 2006. The Bank of England froze the accounts of the 19 men aged 17–35. They had Muslim names, many of them common to Pakistan, although Pakistani officials said they were U.K.-born. At least 14 were from London.

Reports differed as to how the bombs would be constructed. Some said that they would be assembled on the planes, with a peroxide-based solution and simple carry-on items such as a disposable flash camera or a music player. Others said that the explosive was a red gel that would be hidden in bottles of red Gatorade. If the would-be terrorist was asked to drink the Gatorade, he could do so while still hiding the gel.

British authorities found a martyrdom tape made by one of the detainees.

Pakistani intelligence said that a local charity had diverted money from earthquake relief operations to the planned attacks. Some $10 million had been raised, but less than half was used for earthquake relief. Other sources said that the investigation centered around Jamaat-ud-Dawa, a Pakistani charity front for Lashkar-e-Taiba.

On October 24, 2006, Mark Mershon, head of the FBI's New York field office, said investigators believed that the terrorists planned to blow up the nonstop flights over U.S. cities, not the Atlantic, to maximize casualties and economic impact. One of the plotters also planned to attack nuclear power plants, gas pipelines, oil refineries, tunnels, electric grids, Internet service providers, London's financial district, and Heathrow Airport's control tower.

On September 8, 2008, the jury of the Woolwich Crown Court convicted Abdullah Ahmed Ali, Assad Sarwar, and Tanvir Hussein of "conspiracy to murder persons unknown." On September 14, 2009, Justice Richard Henriques sentenced Ali, Sarwar, and Hussein to life in prison with a possibility of parole, and Umar Islam to 22 years.

December 25, 2009
The Underwear Bomber

Umar Farouk Abdulmutallab, a 23-year-old Nigerian, tried to light pentaerythritol tetranitrate (PETN), a powdery plastic explosive, taped to his legs and hidden in his underwear to take down Northwest Airlines flight 253, an Airbus 330 that originated in Amsterdam that was about to land in Detroit. A faulty detonator stymied the explosion and he sustained second and third degree burns on his thighs. He claimed that an al Qaeda bomb maker in Yemen had trained him and provided the device. He said he was inspired by al Qaeda in the Arabian Peninsula operational chief Anwar al-Aulaqi, an American who was killed in an airstrike. On February 16, 2012, the U.S. District Court in Detroit sentenced Abdulmutallab to life in prison without possibility of parole.

May 1, 2010
Would-Be Bombing of Times Square

Two street vendors noticed smoke pouring out of a 1993 Nissan Pathfinder SUV parked on 45th Street and Broadway near 7th Avenue in Times Square in New York City. A small explosion went off. Police found the SUV contained three propane tanks, two filled 5-gallon gas containers, two alarm clocks with batteries, 152 consumer-grade M-88 fireworks containing black powder, and 100 pounds of fertilizer in plastic bags. Police also found keys to the apartment and getaway car of Faisal Shahzad, a naturalized U.S. citizen from Pabbi, Pakistan, who was living in Connecticut.

The Pakistani Taliban released a video to claim credit for the attack, saying it was in retaliation for the deaths of two al Qaeda in Iraq leaders and of Pakistani Taliban leader Baitullah Mehsud, the 2007 Pakistani Army storming of the Red Mosque in Islamabad, drone strikes, and treatment of a female detainee.

On May 3, 2010, police arrested Shahzad, who had just taken his seat on Emirates Airlines flight 202 from New York's John F. Kennedy International Airport to Dubai.

Shahzad told authorities that he was trained in bomb making in Waziristan, Pakistan, by the Pakistani Taliban. He said he had considered attacking Grand Central Terminal, Rockefeller Center, the World Financial Center, and Sikorsky, Inc. He said he would have set off a second bomb two weeks after the Times Square bomb, and would have continued a campaign of attacks until he was killed or captured.

On September 8, 2010, Pakistan charged Shahid Hussain, Shoaib Mughal, and Humbal Akhtar—close friends of Shahzad—with criminal conspiracy to commit terrorism by setting up meetings with Pakistani Taliban leaders, facilitating his training, and sending him $13,000.

Shahzad enthusiastically pleaded guilty to terrorism charges. On October 5, 2010, he was sentenced to life in prison.

October 29, 2010
Printer Toner Cartridge Bombs on Planes

Authorities found two Yemen-origin pentaerythritol trinitrate (PETN) package bombs addressed to Chicago synagogues on cargo planes in Dubai and the United Kingdom. The UPS and FedEx parcels were addressed to Diego Deza, who was a Grand Inquisitor during the Spanish Inquisition, and Reynald Krak, who was a French Knight of the Second Crusade who killed Muslim pilgrims. Kurdish warrior Saladin beheaded him at the Battle of Hattin in 1187.

Al Qaeda in the Arabian Peninsula (AQAP) bomb maker Ibrahim Hassan al-Asiri was believed to be behind the operation. He was believed to have built the underwear bomber's outfit and to have hidden a PETN-based bomb in the body cavity of his brother, Abdullah, who became a suicide bomber who wounded Saudi prince Mohammed bin Nayef in August 2009.

The November 20, 2010, edition of *Inspire*, AQAP's online magazine, explained how it had conducted the Operation Hemorrhage attacks, which cost only $4,200. The group argued for small-scale attacks, rather than the 9/11 spectaculars of al Qaeda Central, observing "This supposedly 'foiled plot' will without a doubt cost America and other Western countries billions of dollars in new security measures."

February 17, 2012
Would-Be Suicide Bomber at U.S. Capitol

Amine el-Khalifi, a Moroccan illegally in the United States, was arrested a few blocks from the U.S. Capitol, wearing what an undercover agent had told him was a suicide vest. He was charged with attempting to use a weapon of mass destruction against federal property. He faced life in prison. On June 22, 2012, he pleaded guilty in federal court in the Eastern District of Virginia to one count of attempted use of a weapon of mass destruction against U.S. property. On September 14, 2012, he was sentenced to 30 years in prison as part of the plea agreement.

Bibliography

INCIDENT DESCRIPTIONS

Incident descriptions and biographies of perpetrators and their support apparatus are drawn from more detailed treatments found in the following books and articles. Readers looking for listings of the dead and wounded or court details are directed to these volumes (listed chronologically). In turn, each volume lists sources used for the entries in those books. Of particular use were accounts by the *Associated Press, United Press International, Reuter, Foreign Broadcast Information Service, ABC FM Radio News, NPR, ABC, NBC, CBS Evening News, Al Jazeera,* the *Detroit Free Press, New Haven Register, New York Times, Washington Post, Washington Star, Washington Times, Los Angeles Times, Chicago Tribune,* the *Economist,* and *US News and World Report,* along with the annual terrorism chronologies put out by the U.S. Central Intelligence Agency, U.S. Department of State, and National Counter Terrorism Center and chronologies made available by the RAND Corporation, Oklahoma City's Memorial Institute for the Prevention of Terrorism, and the University of Maryland's START program. The original sources for the books are on deposit with the U.S. Department of Justice. The Further Reading section offers books and articles that provide additional details on these events.

Mickolus, Edward F. *Annotated Bibliography on International and Transnational Terrorism.* Available in *Legal and Other Aspects of Terrorism* Course Handbook Series, No. 310. New York: Practicing Law Institute, 1979.

Mickolus, Edward F. *The Literature of Terrorism: A Selectively Annotated Bibliography.* Westport, CT: Greenwood, 1980.

Mickolus, Edward F. *International Terrorism: Attributes of Terrorist Events, 1968–1977, ITERATE 2 Data Codebook*. Ann Arbor, MI: Inter-University Consortium for Political and Social Research, 1982.

Mickolus, Edward F. *ITERATE: International Terrorism: Attributes of Terrorist Events, Data Codebook*. Ann Arbor, MI: Inter-University Consortium for Political and Social Research, 1976.

Mickolus, Edward F. *Terrorism, 1988–1991: A Chronology of Events and a Selectively Annotated Bibliography*. Westport, CT: Greenwood, 1993.

Mickolus, Edward F. *Terrorism, 2005–2007: A Chronology*. Westport, CT: Praeger, 2008.

Mickolus, Edward F. *Terrorism, 2008–2012: A Worldwide Chronology*. Jefferson, NC: McFarland, 2014.

Mickolus, Edward F. *The Terrorist List: The Middle East*. 2 vols. Santa Barbara, CA: Praeger, 2009.

Mickolus, Edward F. *Transnational Terrorism: A Chronology of Events, 1968–1979*. Westport, CT: Greenwood, 1980.

Mickolus, Edward F., with Peter Flemming. *Terrorism, 1980–1987: A Selectively Annotated Bibliography*. Westport, CT: Greenwood, 1988.

Mickolus, Edward F., with Susan L. Simmons. *Terrorism, 1992–1995: A Chronology of Events and a Selectively Annotated Bibliography*. Westport, CT: Greenwood, 1997.

Mickolus, Edward F., with Susan L. Simmons. *Terrorism, 1996–2001: A Chronology*. 2 vols. Westport, CT: Greenwood, 2002.

Mickolus, Edward F., and Susan L. Simmons. *Terrorism, 2002–2004: A Chronology*. 3 vols. Westport, CT: Praeger, 2006.

Mickolus, Edward F., and Susan L. Simmons. *The Terrorist List: Asia, Pacific, and Sub-Saharan Africa*. Santa Barbara, CA: Praeger, 2011.

Mickolus, Edward F., and Susan L. Simmons. *The Terrorist List: Eastern Europe*. Santa Barbara, CA: Praeger, 2011.

Mickolus, Edward F., and Susan L. Simmons. *The Terrorist List: North America*. Santa Barbara, CA: Praeger, 2011.

Mickolus, Edward F., and Susan L. Simmons. *The Terrorist List: South America*. Santa Barbara, CA: Praeger, 2011.

Mickolus, Edward F., and Susan L. Simmons. *The Terrorist List: Western Europe*. Santa Barbara, CA: Praeger, 2011.

Mickolus, Edward F., Todd Sandler, and Jean Murdock. *International Terrorism in the 1980s: A Chronology, Volume 1: 1980–1983*. Ames, IA: Iowa State UP, 1988.

Mickolus, Edward F., Todd Sandler, and Jean Murdock. *International Terrorism in the 1980s: A Chronology, Volume 2: 1984–1987*. Ames, IA: Iowa State UP, 1989.

FURTHER READING ON EVENTS AND TERRORISTS MENTIONED IN *THE 50 WORST* AS WELL AS METHODOLOGIES FOR THE STUDY OF TERRORISM

Abrahms, Max. "Why Terrorism Does Not Work." *International Security* 31, no. 2 (2006): 42–78.

Ackerman, Gary A. "Reid, Richard (1973–)." In *Encyclopedia of World Terrorism, 1996–2002*, edited by Frank Shanty and Raymond Picquet, 206–7. Armonk, NY: M. E. Sharpe, 2003.

Anderson, Sean, and Stephen Sloan. *Historical Dictionary of Terrorism*, 2nd ed. Lanham, MD: Scarecrow, 2002.

Anonymous. *Through Our Enemies' Eyes: Osama bin Laden, Radical Islam, and the Future of America*. Washington, DC: Brassey's, 2002.

"The Arab Communist Organisation" IV-42, 350 *Fiches du Monde Arabe*, August 6, 1975.

Arey, James A. *The Sky Pirates*. New York: Scribner's, 1972.

Arnold, Ron. *Ecoterror: The Violent Agenda to Save Nature: The World of the Unabomber*. Bellevue, WA: Free Enterprise, 1997.

At Ground Zero: 25 Stories from Young Reporters Who Were There. New York: Thunder's Mouth, 2002.

Atkins, Stephen E. *Encyclopedia of Modern American Extremists and Extremist Groups*. Westport, CT: Greenwood, 2002.

Atkins, Stephen E. *Encyclopedia of Modern Worldwide Extremists and Extremist Groups*. Westport, CT: Greenwood, 2004.

Atkins, Stephen E. *The 9/11 Encyclopedia*, 2 vols. Westport, CT: Praeger Security International, 2008.

Avdan, Nazli. "Controlling Access to Territory Economic Independence, Transnational Terrorism, and Visa Politics." *Journal of Conflict Resolution*, 2013.

Baer, Robert. *See No Evil: The True Story of a Ground Soldier in the CIA's War on Terrorism*. New York: Crown, 2002.

Barrett, Jon. *Hero of Flight 93*. Hartford, CT: Advocate, 2002.

Baumann, Carol Edler. *The Diplomatic Kidnappings: A Revolutionary Tactic of Urban Terrorism*. The Hague: Nijhoff, 1973.

Bell, J. Bowyer. *The IRA, 1968–2000: Analysis of a Secret Army*. Portland, OR: Frank Cass, 2000.

Benjamin, Daniel, and Stephen Simon. *The Age of Sacred Terror*. New York: Random House, 2002.

Beresford, David. *Ten Men Dead: The Story of the Irish Hunger Strike*. London: Grafton, 1987.

Bergen, Peter. *Holy War, Inc.: Inside the Secret World of Osama bin Laden*. New York: Free Press, 2001.

Bergen, Peter. *Manhunt: The Ten-Year Search for bin Laden from 9/11 to Abbottabad*. New York: Broadway Books, 2013.

Bergen, Peter, and Katherine Tiedemann. "The Almanac of Al Qaeda: FP's Definitive Guide to What's Left of the Terrorist Group." *Foreign Policy* 179 (May/June 2010): 68–71.

Berko, Anat, and Daniel Pipes. *The Smarter Bomb: Women and Children as Suicide Bombers*. New York: Rowman and Littlefield, 2012.

Bermudez, Joseph S. *Terrorism: The North Korean Connection*. New York: Crane Russak, 1990.

Bloom, Mia. *Dying to Kill: The Allure of Suicide Terror*. New York: Columbia University Press, 2007.

Bocca, Giorgio. *Il Terrorising Italiano 1970–1980*. Milan, Italy: Biblioteca Univesale Rizzoli, 1981.

Bodansky, Yossef. *Bin Laden: The Man Who Declared War on America*. New York: Random House, 2011.

Bohn, Michael K. *The Achille Lauro Hijacking: Lessons in the Politics and Prejudice of Terrorism*. Washington, DC: Brassey's, 2004.

Bourret, J.C. *Wiee in Franzoeisches Sonder kommando die in Nov. 1979 Besetzte Moskee in Mekka Befreite.* Paris: France Empire, 1981.

Bowden, Tom. "The IRA and the Changing Tactics of Terrorism." *Political Quarterly* 47, no. 4 (1976): 425–38.

Brackett, D.W. *Holy Terror: Armageddon in Tokyo.* New York: Weatherhill, 1996.

Brackett, D.W., and John F. Quin. "The Aum Cult." In *Changing Trends in Terrorism,* Annual Convention of the Association of Former Intelligence Officers, Washington, DC, October 25, 1996.

Brandon, Henry. "Jordan: The Forgotten Crisis (1): Were We Masterful." *Foreign Policy* 10 (Spring 1973): 158–70.

Burger, Ethan S., and Serguei Cheloukhine. *Counterterrorism in Areas of Political Unrest: The Case of Russia's Northern Caucasus.* New York: Springer, 2013.

Cameron, Gavin. "A Multi-track Microproliferation: Lessons from Aum Shinrikyo and al Qaida." *Studies in Conflict and Terrorism* 22, no. 4 (1999): 277–309.

Catanzaro, Raimondo, ed. *The Red Brigades and Left-Wing Terrorism in Italy.* London: Pinter, 1991.

Chalk, Peter, ed. *Encyclopedia of Terrorism,* 2 vols. Santa Barbara, CA: ABC-Clio, 2013.

Christopher, Warren, ed. *American Hostages in Iran: The Conduct of a Crisis.* New Haven, CT: Yale, 1985.

"Chronology of Hijackings of US Registered Aircraft and Current Legal Status of Hijackers, as of January 1, 1976." Washington, DC: Federal Aviation Administration, Civil Aviation Security Service, 1976–1977.

"Chronology of Unlawful Interference with Civil Aviation." Montreal: International Civil Aviation Organization, 1969–1976.

Ciarrapico, Giuseppe. *Libro Biancosul Terrorismo Tedesco da Schleyer a Mogadiscio.* Rome: Ciarrapico, 1978.

Clarke, Richard A. *Against All Enemies: Inside the White House's War on Terror: What Really Happened.* New York: Free Press, 2004.

Coll, Steve. *The Bin Ladens: An Arabian Family in the American Century.* New York: Penguin, 2008.

Coll, Steve. *Ghost Wars: The Secret History of the CIA, Afghanistan, and Bin Laden, from the Soviet Invasion to September 11, 2001.* New York: Penguin, 2004.

Coogan, Tim Pat. *The Troubles: Ireland's Ordeal 1966–1996 and the Search for Peace.* New York: Rinehart, 1996.

Cooley, John K. *Green March, Black September: The Story of the Palestinian Arabs.* London: Frank Cass, 1973.

Cox, Matthew, and Tom Foster. *Their Darkest Day; the Tragedy of Pan Am 103 and Its Legacy of Hope.* New York: Grove Weidenfeld, 1992.

Creed, Patrick, and Rick Newman. *Firefight: Inside the Battle to Save the Pentagon on 9/11.* New York: Ballantine, 2008.

Cruikshank, Paul, ed. *Al Qaeda,* 5 vols. New York: Routledge, 2012.

Cunningham, Karla. "Terror's 'Invisible Women.'" Op-ed. *Los Angeles Times,* April 19, 2012, http://articles.latimes.com/2012/apr/04/opinion/la-oe-cunningham-women-jihadists-20120404.

Davis, Brian L. *Qaddafi, Terrorism, and the Origins of the US Attack on Libya.* New York: Praeger, 1990.

Dobson, Christopher. *Black September: Its Short, Violent History.* New York: Macmillan, 1974.

Dobson, Christopher, and Ronald Payne. *The Carlos Complex*. New York: Putnam's, 1977.

Dolnik, Adam, and Keith M. Fitzgerald. *Negotiating Hostage Crises with the New Terrorists*. Praeger Security International Series. Westport, CT: Praeger, 2007.

Dolnik, Adam, and Richard Pilch. "The Moscow Theater Hostage Crisis: The Perpetrators, Their Tactics, and the Russian Response." *International Negotiations* 8 (2003): 577–611.

Drake, Richard. *The Aldo Moro Murder Case*. Cambridge, MA: Harvard University Press, 1995.

Dunlop, John B. *The 2002 Dubrovka and 2004 Beslan Hostage Crises: A Critique of Russian Counter-Terrorism*. Soviet and Post-Soviet Politics and Society, Vol. 26. Stuttgart, Germany: ibidem-Verlag, 2006.

Dwyer, Jim, David Kocieniewski, Deidre Murphy, and Peg Tyre. *Two Seconds under the World: Terror Comes to America—The Conspiracy behind the World Trade Center Bombing*. New York: Crown, 1994.

Eadie, Pauline E. "Legislating for Terrorism: The Philippines' Human Security Act 2007." Law Special Edition. *Journal of Terrorism Research* 2, no. 3 (2011): 24–33.

Emerson, Steven, and Brian Duffy. *The Fall of Pan Am 103: Inside the Lockerbie Investigation*. New York: Putnam, 1990.

Evans, Martin, and John Phillips. *Algeria: Anger of the Dispossessed*. New Haven, CT: Yale University Press, 2008.

Fair, Christine, and Don Rassler. *The Fighters of Lashkar-e-Taiba: Recruitment, Training, Deployment and Death*. West Point, NY: Combating Terrorism Center, US Military Academy, 2013.

Faligot, Roger. *Nous Avons Tue Mountbatten! L'IRA Parle*. Paris, France: J. Picollec, 1981.

Farrell, William R. *Blood and Rage: The Story of the Japanese Red Army*. New York: Macmillan, 1990.

Fink, Mithcell, and Lois Mathias. *Never Forget: An Oral History of September 11, 2001*. New York: Regan Books, 2002.

Fishkoff, Sue. "Documentary Recalls the Horrors of Ma'alot School Massacre." *Jewish Telegraphic Agency*, May 5, 2011. http://www.jta.org/2011/05/05/arts-entertainment/documentary-recalls-the-horrors-of-maalot-school-massacre.

Flemming, Peter A. "International Terrorism in Western Europe." Annual Convention of the International Studies Association/Midwest, Indianapolis, IN, November 1986.

Flemming, Peter A., Edward Mickolus, and Todd Sandler. "Research Note: Using the ITERATE and DOTS Databases." *Journal of Strategic Security* 1, no. 1 (2008): 57–75.

Freeman, Michael, David Tucker, and Steffen Merten. "Pathways to Terror: Finding Patterns Prior to an Attack." *Journal of Policing, Intelligence and Counter Terrorism* 5, no. 1 (2010): 75–85.

Gaibulloev, Khusrav, and Todd Sandler. "Determinants of the Demise of Terrorist Organizations." *Southern Economic Journal* 79, no. 4 (2013): 774–92.

Gehman, Harold W. "Lost Patrol: The Attack on the *Cole*." *US Naval Institute Proceedings* 127, no. 4 (April 2001): 34–37.

Gelernter, David. *Drawing Life: Surviving the Unabomber*. New York: Free Press, 1997.

Groussard, Serge. *The Blood of Israel: The Massacre of the Israeli Athletes, the Olympics, 1972*. New York: Morrow, 1975.

Gunaratna, Rohan. *Inside al Qaeda: Global Network of Terror*. New York: Columbia University Press, 2002.

Gunaratna, Rohan. "Lebanon." "Imad Mugniyah (1962)." "Ahmed Saeed Omar Sheikh (1973–)." "Ramzi Ahmed Yousef (1968–)." "Abu Zubaydah (1971–)." In *Encyclopedia of World Terrorism, 1996–2002*, edited by Frank Shanty and Raymond Picquet. Armonk, NY: M. E. Sharpe, 2003.

Guterman, Kineret. "The Dynamics of Stereotyping: Is a New Image of the Terrorist Evolving in American Popular Culture?" *Terrorism and Political Violence* 25, no. 4 (2013): 640–52.

Hamilton, John. *Terror in the Heartland: The Oklahoma City Bombing*. Edina, MN: Abdo, 1996.

Hansen, StigJarle. *Al-Shabaab in Somalia: The History and Ideology of a Militant Islamist Group, 2005/2012*. New York: Columbia University Press, 2013.

Heikal, Mohamed. *Autumn of Fury: The Assassination of Sadat*. New York: Random House, 1983.

Hewitt, Christopher. "Patterns of Terrorism in the USA, 1955–1999: An Historical Perspective on Terrorism-Related Fatalities, 1955–98." *Terrorism and Political Violence* 12, no. 1 (2000): 1–14.

Heyman, Edward, and Edward Mickolus. "Imitation by Terrorists: Quantitative Approaches to the Study of Diffusion Patterns in Transnational Terrorism." In *Behavioral and Quantitative Perspectives on Terrorism*, edited by Yonah Alexander and John M. Gleason, 175–228. New York: Pergamon, 1981.

Heyman, Edward, and Edward Mickolus. "Observations on 'Why Violence Spreads'" *International Studies Quarterly* 24, no. 2 (1980): 299–305.

"Hijackings by Japan's Red Army." *Japan Quarterly* (January–March 1978): 8, 11.

Hockenos, Paul. "The Ghosts of Munich 1972 and the Birth of the Modern Olympics." *The Nation*, July 27, 2012, http://www.thenation.com/article/169122/ghosts-munich-1972-and-birth-modern-olympics.

Hoffman, Bruce. "The Cuban Anti-Castro Terrorist Movement." *Terrorism Violence Insurgency Journal* 5, no. 1 (1984): 15–21, 29.

Hoffman, Bruce. *Recent Trends and Future Prospects of Iranian-Sponsored International Terrorism*. Report R-3783-USDP. Santa Monica, CA: RAND, March 1990.

"Incidents of Terrorism and Hijackings in the US 1980–1983." *Terrorism Violence Insurgency Journal* 5, no. 1 (1984): 30–39.

Jenkins, Brian Michael. "International Terrorism: A New Mode of Conflict." California Arms Control and Foreign Policy Seminar Research Paper 48. Los Angeles: Crescent Publications, January 1975.

Jenkins, Brian Michael. "International Terrorism: A New Mode of Conflict." In *International Terrorism and World Security*, edited by David Carlton and Carlo Schaerf, 13–49. London: Croom Helm, 1975.

Jenkins, Brian Michael, and Janera Johnson. "International Terrorism: A Chronology, 1968–1974." Report R-1597-DOS/ARPA. Santa Monica: RAND, March 1975.

Jenkins, Brian Michael, and Janera Johnson. "International Terrorism: A Chronology, 1974 Supplement." Report R-1909-1-ARPA. Santa Monica: RAND, February 1976.

Jiwa, Salim. *The Death of Air India Flight 182*. London: Star Book, 1987.

Jonas, George. *Vengeance: The True Story of an Israeli Counter-Terrorist Team*. New York: Simon and Schuster, 1984.

Jones, Seth G. *Hunting in the Shadows: The Pursuit of Al Qa'ida since 9/11*. New York: Norton, 2012.

Jureidini, Paul A., and William E. Hazen. *The Palestinian Movement in Politics*. Lexington, MA: Heath, 1976.

Kaplan, David E. "Aum Supreme Truth." In *Toxic Terror: Assessing Terrorist Use of Chemical and Biological Weapons*, edited by Jonathan B. Tucker. Cambridge, MA: MIT Press, 2000.

Kaplan, David E., and Andrew Marshall. *The Cult at the End of the World*. New York: Crown, 1996.

Katz, R. *Day of Wrath: The Ordeal of Aldo Moro: The Kidnapping, the Execution, the Aftermath*. Garden City: Doubleday, 1980.

Kern, Soeren. "Spain Faces Difficulties in Judging Islamic Terrorists." *Grupo de Estudios Estratégicos*, October 23, 2007, http://www.gees.org/articulos/spain_faces_difficulties_in_judging_islamic_terrorists_4749.

Kessler, Ronald. *The CIA at War: Inside the Secret Campaign against Terror*. New York: St. Martin's, 2003.

Kimmage, Daniel. "Al-Qaeda Central and the Internet: Counterterrorism Strategy Initiative Policy Paper. Executive Summary." *Foreign Policy* (May/June 2010), http://www.foreignpolicy.com/articles/2010/04/26/al_qaeda_central_and_the_internet.

Koch, Peter, and Kai Hermann. *Assault at Mogadishu*. London: Corgi, 1977.

Kohl, James, and John Litt. *Urban Guerrilla Warfare in Latin America*. Cambridge, MA: MIT Press, 1974.

Kuriyama, Yoshihiro. "Terrorism at Tel Aviv Airport and a 'New Left' Group in Japan." *Asian Survey* 13 (March 1973): 336–46.

Lahoud, Nelly, Stuart Caudill, Liam Collins, Gabriel Koehler-Derrick, Don Rassler, and Muhammad al-'Ubardi. *Letters from Abbottabad: Bin Ladin Sidelined?* West Point, NY: Harmony Program, The Combating Terrorism Center, 2012.

Large, David Clay. "Massacre in Munich: The Olympic Terror Attacks of 1972 in Historical Perspective." *Historically Speaking* 10, no. 2 (2009): 2–5.

Levitt, Matthew. *Hezbollah: The Global Footprint of Lebanon's Party of God*. Washington, DC: Georgetown University Press, 2013.

Lewis, Bernard. "License to Kill: Usama bin Ladin's Declaration of Jihad." *Foreign Affairs* 77, no. 6 (November/December 1998): 14–19.

Lifton, Robert Jay. *Destroying the World to Save It: Aum Shinrikyo, Apocalyptic Violence, and the New Global Terrorism*. New York: Metropolitan, 1999.

Lippold, Kirk. *Front Burner: Al Qaeda's Attack on the USS Cole*. New York: Public Affairs, 2012.

Mahoney, Inez. "Diverging Frames: A Comparison of Indonesian and Australian Press Portrayals of Terrorism and Islamic Groups in Indonesia." *International Communication Gazette* 72, no. 8 (2010): 739–58.

Melman, Yossi. *The Master Terrorist: The True Story behind Abu Nidal*. New York: Adama, 1986.

Metraux, Daniel A. "Religious Terrorism in Japan: The Fatal Appeal of Aum Shinrikyo." *Asian Survey* 35, no. 12 (December 1996): 1140–54.

Michael, George. *Lone Wolf Terror and the Rise of Leaderless Resistance*. Nashville: Vanderbilt University Press, 2012.

Michel, Lou, and Dan Herbeck. *American Terrorist: Timothy McVeigh and the Oklahoma City Bombing*. New York: Reagan, 2001.

Mickolus, Edward F. "Chronology of Major Terrorist Events, 1996–2002." In *Encyclopedia of World Terrorism*, edited by Frank Shanty and Raymond Picquet, 577–97. Santa Barbara, CA: M. E. Sharpe, 2003.

Mickolus, Edward F. "Chronology of Transnational Terrorist Attacks upon American Business People, 1968–1976." In *Political Terrorism and Business: The Threat and Response*, edited by Yonah Alexander and Robert A. Kilmarx, 297–318. New York: Praeger, 1979.

Mickolus, Edward F. "Comment: Terrorists, Governments, and Numbers; Counting Things Versus Things That Count." *Journal of Conflict Resolution* 31, no. 1 (1987): 54–62.

Mickolus, Edward F. "Deadly Logic: Will Hostile Computer Code Become the Terrorism of the 1990s?" Paper prepared for Seminar on Countering Terrorism, sponsored by Terrorist Activities Subcommittee of the American Society for Industrial Security, Washington DC, June 13, 1990.

Mickolus, Edward F. "Disorder in the New World Order? The Future of Terrorism." *National Forum: The Phi Kappa Phi Journal* (Fall 1992): 33–4. Reprinted in *Global Agenda*, edited by Charles Kegley and Eugene Wittkopf. Boston: McGraw Hill, 1994.

Mickolus, Edward F. "An Events Data Base for Studying Transnational Terrorism." *Quantitative Approaches to Political Intelligence: The CIA Experience*, edited by Richards J. Heuer, 127–63. Boulder, CO: Westview, 1978.

Mickolus, Edward F. "How Do We Know We're Winning the War against Terrorists? Issues in Measurement." *Studies in Conflict and Terrorism* 25, no. 3 (2002): 151–60.

Mickolus, Edward F. "International Terrorism in 1979." Paper presented to the Annual Convention of the Academy of Criminal Justice Sciences, Oklahoma City, OK, March 1980.

Mickolus, Edward F. "International Terrorism: Review and Projection." Address to the Conference on Terrorism and the American Corporation, sponsored by Probe International, Inc., New York City, September 14–15, 1976; updated for Los Angeles, January 11–12, 1977; and Chicago, September 26–27, 1977.

Mickolus, Edward F. "Multilateral Legal Efforts to Combat Terrorism: Diagnosis and Prognosis." *Ohio Northern University Law Review* 6, no. 1 (1979): 13–51.

Mickolus, Edward F. "Negotiating for Hostages: A Policy Dilemma." *Orbis* 19, no. 4 (1976): 1309–25. Reprinted in *Contemporary Terrorism: Selected Readings*, edited by John D. Elliott and Lesley Gibson, 207–21. Gaithersburg, MD: International Association of Chiefs of Police, 1978.

Mickolus, Edward F. "Project ITERATE: Quantitative Studies of Transnational Terrorism." Paper presented to the Annual Convention of the Northeast Political Science Association, Jug End, South Egremont, MA, November 11–13, 1976. Reprinted by the U.S. Department of State, INR/XR as FAR 26105-N.

Mickolus, Edward F. "Reflections on the Study of Terrorism." Paper presented to the Panel on Violence and Terror of the Conference on Complexity: A Challenge to the Adaptive Capacity of American Society, 1776–1976, sponsored by the Society for General Systems Research, Loyola College Conference Center, Columbia, MD, March 24–26, 1977.

Mickolus, Edward F. "September 11, 2001 Attacks." In *Encyclopedia of World Terrorism*, edited by Frank Shanty and Raymond Picquet, 19–28. Santa Barbara: M. E. Sharpe, 2003.

Mickolus, Edward F. "Statistical Approaches to the Study of Terrorism." In *Terrorism: Interdisciplinary Perspectives*, edited by Seymour Maxwell Finger and Yonah Alexander, 209–69. New York: John Jay, 1977.

Mickolus, Edward F. "Studying Terrorist Incidents: Issues in Conceptualization and Data Acquisition." Paper presented to the Annual Convention of the International Studies Association, Los Angeles, CA, March 1980.

Mickolus, Edward F. "Tracking the Growth and Prevalence of Terrorism." In *Managing Terrorism: Strategies for the Corporate Executive*, edited by George S. Roukis and Patrick J. Montana, 3–22. Westport, CT: Greenwood, 1983.

Mickolus, Edward F. "Transnational Terrorism." In *The Politics of Terrorism*, edited by Michael Stohl, 147–90. New York: Marcel Dekker, 1979.

Mickolus, Edward F. "Trends in Transnational Terrorism." In *Terrorism in the Contemporary World*, edited by Marius Livingston, 44–73. Westport, CT: Greenwood, 1978.

Mickolus, Edward F. "What Constitutes State Support to Terrorists ?" *Journal of Terrorism and Political Violence* 3, no. 1 (1989): 287–93. Reprinted in *Violence and Terrorism 91/92*, edited by Bernard Schechterman and Martin Slann. 2nd ed., 38–40. Sluice Dock, CT: Dushkin, 1991.

Mickolus, Edward, and Edward Heyman. "ITERATE: Monitoring Transnational Terrorism." In *Behavioral and Quantitative Perspectives on Terrorism*, edited by Yonah Alexander and John M. Gleason, 153–74. New York: Pergamon, 1981.

Mickolus, Edward, Edward S. Heyman, and James Schlotter. "Responding to Terrorism: Basic and Applied Research." In *Responding to the Terrorist Threat: Security and Crisis Management*, edited by Stephen Sloan and Richard Schultz, 174–89. New York: Pergamon, 1980.

Milbank, David L., with Edward Mickolus. *International and Transnational Terrorism: Diagnosis and Prognosis*. Washington, DC: U.S. Document Expediting Project, Library of Congress, April 1976.

Moghadan, Assaf. "How Al Qaeda Innovates." *Security Studies* 22, no. 3 (2013): 466–97.

Moss, David. "The Kidnapping and Murder of Aldo Moro." *European Journal of Sociology—Great Britain* 22, no. 2 (1981): 265–95.

Mudd, Philip. *Takedown: Inside the Hunt for Al Qaeda*. Philadelphia: University of Pennsylvania Press, 2013.

Nacos, Brigitte L. "Revisiting the Contagion Hypothesis: Terrorism, News Coverage, and Copycat Attacks." *Perspectives on Terrorism* 3, no. 3 (2009): 3–12.

National Commission on Terrorist Attacks. *The 9/11 Commission Report: Final Report of the National Commission on Terrorist Attacks Upon the United States*. New York: Norton, 2004.

Nzes, Fredrick. *Terrorist Attacks in Kenya Reveal Domestic Radicalization*. West Point, NY: The Combating Terrorism Center, 2012.

O'Hern, Steven. *Iran's Revolutionary Guard: The Threat That Grows While America Sleeps*. Washington, DC: Potomac, 2012.

Olmeda, José A. "A Reversal of Fortune: Blame Games and Framing Contests After the 3/11 Terrorist Attacks in Madrid." In *Governing after Crisis: The Politics of Investigation, Accountability and Learning*, edited by Arjen Boin, Allan McConnell, and Paul Hart, Chapter 3, 62–84. Cambridge: Cambridge University Press, 2008.

Pedahzur, Ami. *The Israeli Secret Services and the Struggle against Terrorism (Columbia Studies in Terrorism and Irregular Warfare)*. New York: Columbia University Press, 2009.

Pillar, Paul. *Terrorism and American Foreign Policy*. Washington, DC: Brookings Institution, 2001.

Randal, Jonathan. *Osama: The Making of a Terrorist*. New York: Knopf, 2004.

Ranstrop, Magnus. *Hizballah in Lebanon: The Politics of the Western Hostage Crisis*. New York: Macmillan, 1996.

Ranstrop, Magnus. "Interpreting the Broader Context and Meaning of bin Laden's Fatwa." *Studies in Conflict and Terrorism* 21, no. 5 (September/October 1998): 321–30.

Reader, Ian. *A Poisonous Cocktail? Aum Shinrikyo's Path to Violence*. Copenhagen, Denmark: Nordic Institute of Asian Studies, 1996.

Reeve, Simon. *The New Jackals: Ramzi Yousef, Osama bin Laden and the Future of Terrorism*. Boston: Northeastern University Press, 1999.

Reeve, Simon. *One Day in September: The Full Story of the 1972 Munich Olympics Massacre and the Israeli Revenge Operation, Wrath of God*. New York: Arcade, 2000.

Ressa, Maria A. *Seeds of Terror: An Eyewitness Account of al Qaeda's Newest Center of Operations in Southeast Asia*. New York: Free Press, 2003.

Riedel, Bruce. *The Search for al Qaeda: Its Leadership, Ideology and Future*. Washington, DC: Brookings Institution, 2008.

Robinson, Eugene. "Exiles." *Washington Post Magazine* (July 18, 2004): 22–4, 33–7.

Sageman, Marc. *Leaderless Jihad: Terror Networks in the 21st Century*. Philadelphia: University of Pennsylvania Press, 2007.

Scott, Charles W. *Pieces of the Game: The Human Drama of Americans Held Hostage in Iran*. Atlanta: Peachtree, 1984.

Seale, Patrick. *Abu Nidal: A Gun for Hire*. New York: Random House, 1992.

Shanty, Frank, and Raymond Picquet, eds. *Encyclopedia of World Terrorism, 1996–2002*. Armonk, NY: M. E. Sharpe, 2003.

Siler, Michael. "Kenya and Tanzania." In *Encyclopedia of World Terrorism, 1996–2002*, edited by Frank Shanty and Raymond Picquet, 416–20. Armonk, NY: M. E. Sharpe, 2003.

Smith, Colin. *Carlos: Portrait of a Terrorist*. London: Sphere, 1976.

Snow, Peter, and David Phillips. *The Arab Hijack War*. New York: Ballantine, 1970.

Sobel, Lester A., ed. *Political Terrorism*. New York: Facts on File, 1975.

Steinhoff, Patricia. "Portrait of a Terrorist: An Interview with Kozo Okamoto." *Asia Survey* 16 (September 1976): 830–45.

Stevenson, William. *90 Minutes at Entebbe*. New York: Bantam, 1976.

Stohl, Michael. "Don't Confuse Me with the Facts: Knowledge Claims and Terrorism." *Critical Studies on Terrorism* 5, no. 1 (2012): 31–49.

"Subject: Japanese Red Army." Washington, DC: Embassy of Japan, n. d.

Thompson, John. "Ressam, Ahmed (1967)." In *Encyclopedia of World Terrorism, 1996–2002*, edited by Frank Shanty and Raymond Picquet, 208–9. Armonk. NY: M. E. Sharpe, 2003.

Tinnin, David B., with Dag Christensen. *The Hit Team*. Boston: Little, Brown, 1976.

Travalio, Gregory M. "Terrorism, International Law, and the Use of Military Force." *Wisconsin International Law Journal* 18, no. 1 (2000): 145–91.

Tu, Anthony T. *Chemical Terrorism: Horrors in Tokyo Subway and Matsumoto City*. Fort Collins, CO: Alaken, 2002.

United Kingdom. House of Commons. *Report of the Official Account of the Bombings in London on 7th July 2005*. London: The Stationery Office, May 11, 2006.

United States. Department of State. Cabinet Committee to Combat Terrorism Working Group. *Chronology of Attacks upon Non-Official American Citizens, 1971–1975*. Washington, DC: GPO, January 20, 1976.

United States. Department of State. Cabinet Committee to Combat Terrorism Working Group. *Chronology of Hijackings 1968 through 1975*. Washington, DC: GPO, 1976.

United States. Department of State. *Chronology of Significant Terrorist Incidents Involving US Diplomatic/Official Personnel, 1963–1975*. Washington, DC: GPO, January 20, 1976.

United States. Department of State. *Country Reports on Terrorism, 2012*. Washington, DC: GPO, May 2013.

United States. House of Representatives. 90th Congress, 2nd session. Committee on Foreign Affairs. Subcommittee on Inter-American Affairs. "Hijackings of Planes to Cuba and Frustrated Attempts to Hijack." In Appendix A. *Air Piracy in the Caribbean Area*, 9–11. Report. Washington, DC: GPO, December 10, 1968.

Yun, Minwoo. "Hostage Taking and Kidnapping in Terrorism: Predicting the Fate of a Hostage." *Professional Issues in Criminal Justice* 2, no. 1 (2007): 23–40.

Country Index

Name and Group Index

About the Authors

EDWARD F. MICKOLUS wrote the first doctoral dissertation on international terrorism while earning a PhD from Yale University. He then served in analytical, operational, management, and staff positions in the Central Intelligence Agency (CIA) for over 30 years, where he was CIA's first full-time analyst on international terrorism; analyzed African political, economic, social, military, and leadership issues; wrote political-psychological assessments of world leaders; and managed collection, counter intelligence, and covert action programs against terrorists, drug traffickers, weapons proliferators, and hostile espionage services. He founded Vinyard Software, Inc., whose products include the ITERATE (International Terrorism: Attributes of Terrorist Events) text and numeric datasets and DOTS (Data on Terrorist Suspects). Clients include 150 universities in 21 countries. He is also a senior instructor in creativity, analytical techniques, briefing, collaboration, and integration for several federal intelligence and law enforcement agencies. His 24 books include a series of multivolume chronologies and annotated bibliographies on international terrorism, *The Secret Book of CIA Humor*, *Coaching Winning Model United Nations Teams*, 17 book chapters, 100 articles and reviews in refereed scholarly journals and newspapers and presentations to professional societies, and 14 humorous publications. His journal articles cover such fields as international law, international organizations, African politics, psychology, sociology, education, automotive history, humor, creativity, collaboration, and computer software. Books in preparation include *The Counterintelligence Chronology*, *Stories from Langley: A Glimpse Inside the CIA*, *First Tour* (first of a series of espionage novels), *Two Spies Walk Into a Bar: More Espionage Humor*, *Wit and Wisdom of Fortune Cookies*, *That's Not Quite All, Folks: Movie Easter Eggs*, *The Creativity Calendar*, *The Ties That Blind*, *Prez/ex-Prez* (a novel), and *His Words: Jesus's Biblical Quotations*.

SUSAN L. SIMMONS, MA, is an independent editor, writer, and writing consultant who specializes in coaching writers and editing books, journal articles, and dissertations in the fields of international relations, psychology, art history, education, biography, music, religion, and medicine. She also works with novelists, poets, and popular nonfiction writers. She is the coauthor with Edward Mickolus of *Terrorism, 1992–1995*; *1996–2001*; *2002–2004*; and *The Terrorist List* (5 vols.).